Athenian Ostracism and its Original Purpose

Athenian Ostracism and its Original Purpose

A Prisoner's Dilemma

MAREK WĘCOWSKI

Translated by
LIDIA OŻAROWSKA

OXFORD
UNIVERSITY PRESS

Great Clarendon Street, Oxford, OX2 6DP,
United Kingdom

Oxford University Press is a department of the University of Oxford.
It furthers the University's objective of excellence in research, scholarship,
and education by publishing worldwide. Oxford is a registered trade mark of
Oxford University Press in the UK and in certain other countries

© Marek Węcowski 2022

The moral rights of the author have been asserted

First Edition published in 2022

Impression: 1

All rights reserved. No part of this publication may be reproduced, stored in
a retrieval system, or transmitted, in any form or by any means, without the
prior permission in writing of Oxford University Press, or as expressly permitted
by law, by licence or under terms agreed with the appropriate reprographics
rights organization. Enquiries concerning reproduction outside the scope of the
above should be sent to the Rights Department, Oxford University Press, at the
address above

You must not circulate this work in any other form
and you must impose this same condition on any acquirer

Published in the United States of America by Oxford University Press
198 Madison Avenue, New York, NY 10016, United States of America

British Library Cataloguing in Publication Data

Data available

Library of Congress Control Number: 2022941404

ISBN 978-0-19-884820-2

DOI: 10.1093/oso/9780198848202.001.0001

Printed and bound in the UK by
TJ Books Limited

Links to third party websites are provided by Oxford in good faith and
for information only. Oxford disclaims any responsibility for the materials
contained in any third party website referenced in this work.

In grateful memory of Pierre Lévêque and Pierre Vidal-Naquet

Preface and Acknowledgments

The reader of this book may notice that it dedicates relatively little space to the well-known tools of Athenian ostracism: the ostraka, or ceramic sherds, on which the Athenians scratched names of unpopular, or perhaps too popular, politicians. This is because the idea of this book originates in the conviction that previous explanations of the mechanisms and genesis of the Athenian ostracism are not sufficient and that there are still many questions about ostracism to which no satisfactory answers, or indeed answers of any sort, have been provided. This standstill seems natural, given that scholars of Athenian democracy had long been awaiting, with ever-increasing appetite, a full scholarly publication of the largest collection of the Athenian ostraka: the sherds from the Kerameikos. They were published in 2018.[1] However, the decision not to focus particularly on ostraka was not motivated by the insufficient availability of this material thus far, but by what in my opinion is a deeper reason behind the said impasse. From the beginning of research on ostracism in the fourth century BC until the present day, scholars have invariably concentrated on the day when the Athenians voted, using ostraka, on exiling one of their politicians. Thus, scholarship has consistently neglected other aspects and stages of what was actually a long-term procedure which could lead to ostracising a preeminent citizen of Athens every year.[2]

It seemed to me that it would be worth proposing a new research questionnaire and asking a set of new, or relatively new, questions. One of them, fundamental in my opinion but hardly ever clearly formulated in scholarship hitherto,[3] I shall present to the reader at the start with an idea of the situation which a contemporary student of ostracism has to face. How can we explain the fact that in the several decades during which this institution functioned in Athens, our sources inform us about merely a

---

[1] By Stefan Brenne: *Kerameikos 20.1–2*. The reasons why this monumental and extremely painstaking work (originally launched in 1968) took so long are briefly presented in *Kerameikos 20.1*, pp. xvii–xviii.
[2] Before the explosive increase in the number of excavated ostraka in the 60s of the previous century, there had been a few departures from this rule, such as, notably, Carcopino (1935) esp. 53–72.
[3] With the sole exception of Forsdyke (2005) 145. But see below, n. 14 and esp. p. 38.

dozen or so cases of an actual exile of an Athenian politician? And what are the implications of this for our interpretation of ostracism in general?

In this book, apart from the attempt to offer new answers to basic questions about each particular element of the procedure of ostracism as well as about the history of the institution (in the second chapter of the first part), on the one hand, I present a detailed analysis of the 'pre-history' of Athenian ostracism (in the first chapter of this work), while using, on the other hand, an interpretative model derived from classical game theory: the 'prisoner's dilemma' (in the last chapter).

While presenting my interpretation of Athenian ostracism as a mechanism enforcing compromise within the Athenian political élite (for instance, in a paper delivered at the Humboldt University of Berlin in November 2008 and at the conference of the American Philological Association in January 2010), I have often faced the crucial objection that such a reconstruction of its primary aims over-optimistically presupposes a very high level of long-term rational calculation on the part of this institution's creators, of the later Athenian politicians, as well as of the Athenian people in general. This is where the theory of 'the evolution of cooperation', formulated by the political scientist and mathematician Robert Axelrod based on the 'iterated prisoner's dilemma', comes to the fore.[4]

An excellent analogy to the Athenian political life is provided by the situation in which two (or more) 'players' repeatedly make simultaneous decisions, extremely hazardous and fateful, on cooperation or escalation of conflict. They are guided by their previous experience of interaction and feelings such as gratitude, trust, hatred, or desire for vengeance. In the context of Axelrod's theory, we can better understand in which situations and on what conditions even the most conflicted 'players' may decide to cooperate, and that making such decisions does not have to be enforced by some external authority or by their own profound and long-term calculation. In short, such decisions may be quite intuitive. In this work, I shall try to demonstrate that by introducing ostracism in Athens, the architect of Athenian democracy Cleisthenes deliberately put the Athenian élites in a situation which we would describe today as 'iterated prisoner's dilemma'.

---

[4] Herman (2006) remarkably develops this idea by applying it to the 'morality and behaviour in democratic Athens' in general. Meanwhile, he does not apply Axelrod's theory to ostracism (but see a brief comment in Herman (2006) 403). Cf. also Simonton (2017) esp. 62–68, applying the 'iterated prisoner's dilemma', within a broader perspective of the 'collective action problem', to classical Greek oligarchy, which is much closer to my current subject.

PREFACE AND ACKNOWLEDGMENTS   ix

Paradoxically, applying the theory of 'the evolution of cooperation' conveniently fits in with the radically brilliant idea of John K. Davies presented in his essay 'Democracy without theory' (2003). '[T]he product of deep and long-standing unease about the ways of approaching the phenomenon of emergence, consolidation, and spread of Greek democracy', his paper claims that the Athenian democracy was 'little more than a bogged-up set of responses to particular situations and crises' and that it was based on 'the perceived need to *prevent* this or that unpleasant or undesirable development or practice from continuing or from gaining a foothold'.[5] Ultimately, this is how I interpret the idea of introducing, and giving a specific procedural shape to, the Athenian ostracism.

*

It took a long time for my book to be ready. In the meantime, I benefited from the help and support of many scholars, and above all, from critical discussions with them. Being aware of the problematic nature of the ideas presented here, I must immediately add emphatically that none of them can be held responsible for my mistakes, deficiencies, and omissions. As always, I owe more than I can express to Benedetto Bravo and to many discussions with Adam Ziółkowski, Krystyna Stebnicka, Aleksander Wolicki, and conversations and exchanges with Kostas Apostolakis, Judy Barringer, Jan Bremmer, Mirko Canevaro, Adam Gendźwiłł, Edward Harris, Sergei Karpyuk, Michael Lurie, Kathleen Lynch, Christian Mann, Michał Mydłowski, Łukasz Niesiołowski-Spanò', Cameron Pearson, Irene Polinskaya, Adrian Robu, and Lina van 't Wout. While publicly presenting different parts of this work on several occasions, I received many helpful comments and suggestions from my audiences. I seize this opportunity to thank my hosts: Lucia Athanassaki, Krystyna Bartol, Sabina Crippa, Jerzy Danielewicz, Herbert Heftner, Moritz Hinsch, Vera Hofmann, Maurizio Giangiulio, Colin King, Michael Lurie, Jan Meister, and Gunnar Seelentag. Serendipitously, from the very beginning of my work on ostracism, I could

---

[5] I quote here, respectively, Davies (2003) 320 and 323. Cf. already Forrest (1966) 202–203. In my opinion, this perspective does not preclude interpreting the development of the Athenian democracy in rational terms based on the 'systematic interrelations' (cf. Murray (1990) esp. 10–11) between separate 'responses to particular situations and crises' in Athens. '[I]f we can detect an increasing degree of coherence in a society through its reforms, and if the principles governing the social system become clearer through change, then we may say that the society itself displays a high degree of rationality, not merely in the sense of internal coherence, but also in the sense of a self-conscious recognition of the reasons for change and the consequences of institutional reform.' (Murray (1990) 8–9; incidentally, in his paper, O. Murray is mainly concerned with the fourth-century democracy.)

discuss my ideas with my friends from the European Network for the Study of Ancient Greek History. I am profoundly thankful to Josine Blok, Kostas Buraselis, Gunnel Ekroth, Lin Foxhall, Hans Joachim Gehrke, Maurizio Giangiulio, André Lardinois, Nino Luraghi, Irad Malkin, Christian Mann, Oswyn Murray, Christel Müller, Thomas Heine Nielsen, Vinciane Pirenne-Delforge, François de Polignac, Kurt A. Raaflaub, Robert Rollinger and Rosalind Thomas. I am particularly grateful to John K. Davies, Kathleen Lynch, Marcin Matera, Radosław Miśkiewicz, Irene Polinskaya and Aleksander Wolicki for their comments on various parts of this book and to the anonymous reviewers and referees of this book for the Foundation for Polish Science and for the Oxford University Press, as well as to James Sickinger, who shared with me his yet unpublished work discussing the most recent finds of the American School of Classical Studies in the Athenian Agora, and to Laura Gawlinski for her suggestions regarding recent excavations in the Agora. The American School of Classical Studies: Agora Excavations has agreed for the use of several illustrations in its possession (Fig. 1.1, 3.1, 3.2, 3.3, 3.5) and Ms. Sylvie Dumont helped me immensely in the process. The copyright of one illustration (Fig. 3.5) is provided by Hellenic Ministry of Culture and Sports/Organization of Cultural Resources Development (H.O.C.R.E.D.). I also thank Dominika Grzesik for sharing with me her forthcoming book on honorific culture in Delphi in the Hellenistic and Roman periods (now Grzesik (2021)).

Last but not least, my special thanks go to Herbert Heftner and Vera Hofmann, and the organisers of the unforgettable *Ostrakismos-Workshop: Der hellenistische und römische Ostrakismosdiskurs—Überlieferung, Wandel und zeitgenössische Intentionen* (Institut für Alte Geschichte, Universität Wien, November 23–24, 2018), an unparalleled occasion to exchange ideas on Athenian ostracism and its tradition. We are still waiting impatiently for the publication of the second volume of the *Ostrakismos-Testimonien* by the remarkable Viennese team, gathering and commenting on ostracism testimonies of the post-classical times.

This work was made possible by the financial support received from the National Science Centre (research project 2012/05/B/HS3/03755) and the tenure of the scholarship awarded by the Polish-American Fulbright Commission (Fulbright Senior Research Award, Princeton University). During this time, I also benefited from the hospitality of the Department of Classics of Princeton University, École Française d'Athènes, British School at Athens, the Netherlands Institute at Athens, Dr Joanna Clark in Princeton and Dr Paweł Piskorski in Pomiechówek. I am also very grateful for the long-term financial support of my research to the Institute of History, University of Warsaw, particularly to the Institute's new incarnation, The Faculty of History, for funding the copyrights of the illustration provided by the Ashmolean Museum in Oxford (Fig. 3.4).

This is a substantially modified and updated version of the earlier Polish edition of my book. This translation has been co-funded by the Foundation for Polish Science. I am most grateful to Lidia Ożarowska for her remarkable work and human indulgence. (Incidentally, in sections 1.2.2, 3.4., and the most part of my 'Epilogue and Conclusions', I am the sole person responsible for the translation.) I wish to thank Benjamin Isaac for the permission to use here, rewritten as 1.2.2, my paper from *Scripta Classica Israelica* 37 (2018).

Finally, and most importantly, this book would not have come to be without the patience and constant support of my Family. JmM, thank you.

A Postscript: Regrettably, it was too late for me to accommodate in my argument an important study by Martina Zerbinati, *L'ostracismo ateniese: un'istituzione politica emblematica del nuovo assetto democratico di V secolo a.C.* Ph.D. diss., Università degli Studi del Piemonte Orientale, 2018/2019.

Contents

List of Illustrations xvii
List of Abbreviations xix

Introduction 1

PART I: KEY ISSUES IN THE STUDY OF ATHENIAN OSTRACISM

1. Ostracism before Ostracism? 17
   1.1 Was there Ostracism beyond Athens in the Archaic Period? 17
      1.1.1 Traces of *Ostrakophoriai* in the Greek World 18
      1.1.2 Ostracism and the 'Politics of Expulsion' in Archaic and Classical Greece 37
   1.2 Ostracism before Ostracism in Archaic Athens? 40
      1.2.1 Archaic Ostraka from the Athenian Agora and the Ostracism of Classical Times 40
      1.2.2 Vaticanus Graecus 1144 and the Mirage of the So-called 'Bouleutic Ostracism' 45
      1.2.3 Ostracism and the Scapegoat Ritual 59
   1.3 Conclusions: The Invention of Democratic Athens 63

2. Towards a Reconstruction of Ostracism in Athens: The Facts 66
   2.1 Cleisthenes or the 'Generation of *Marathonomachoi*'? Dating the Law about Ostracism 67
      2.1.1 Ps.-Aristotle, Harpocration, and Androtion's *Atthis* 67
      2.1.2 Cleisthenes, the Inventor of Ostracism? 77
   2.2 Athenian Ostracisms of 508/507 BC–ca. 416 BC 78
      2.2.1 The Extant Athenian Ostraka and the Study of the History of Ostracism 78
      2.2.2 The List of Athenian Ostracisms in *Athenaion Politeia* and its Possible Sources 86
      2.2.3 Ostracisms Attested in Literary Sources and Disputable Ostracisms 99
      2.2.4 The End of Athenian *Ostrakophoriai* 'around 416 BC' 113
      2.2.5 The Issue of Possible *Ostrakophoriai* Unattested in Literary Sources 115

xiv CONTENTS

3. Towards a Reconstruction of Ostracism in Athens:
   The Procedures   120
   3.1 The Question of the Availability of the Law about
       Ostracism in Fourth-century Athens   121
   3.2 The Procedure and Chronology of Ostracism   124
       3.2.1 Between *Epicheirotonia* and *Ostrakophoria*   124
       3.2.2 The Topography of Ostracism   134
       3.2.3 The Pan Painter and the Day of *Ostrakophoria*   146
       3.2.4 Interim Conclusions: *Ostrakophoria* and the Agora   155
       3.2.5 The Conundrum of the 'Quorum' of Ostracism and the
             Issue of Ineffective *Ostrakophoriai*   158
       3.2.6 The Hypothetical 'Quorum' of the *Epicheirotonia* of
             Ostracism in the Fifth Century BC   172
   3.3 The Issue of the Potential Evolution of Ostracism in Athens
       in the Fifth Century BC   177
       3.3.1 The Puzzle of the Geography of Exile in the Law
             about Ostracism   177
       3.3.2 The Duration of Exile from Athens in the Law
             about Ostracism   181
   3.4 Conclusions: A Reconstructed Procedure of Athenian
       Ostracism   185

PART II: TOWARDS AN INTERPRETATION
OF THE ORIGINAL AIMS OF ATHENIAN
OSTRACISM

4. The Historical Context of the Cleisthenian Law about
   Ostracism   189
   4.1 Cleisthenes' Reforms or 'Athenian Revolution'?   189
   4.2 The Law about Ostracism within the System of
       Cleisthenes' Reforms   195

5. The Prisoner's Dilemma—Ostracism and Competition
   among Athenian Political Élites   197
   5.1 The 'Theory of Cooperation' as a Possible Explanatory
       Model   197
   5.2 The Mechanism and the Primary Aim of the Law about
       Ostracism—A Reconstruction Attempt   205
       5.2.1 Ostracism—Against Tyranny or Aristocratic *Stasis*?
             Prevention or Punishment?   211
       5.2.2 The Athenian 'Prisoner's Dilemma', or Ostracism and
             Athenian Political Life   216

5.2.3 Athenian Ostracism and the 'Theory of Cooperation'
I: A Historical Approach   232
5.2.4 Athenian Ostracism and the 'Theory of Cooperation'
II: A Theoretical Approach   236

Epilogue and Conclusions: The Decline and Fall of Athenian
Ostracism   240
    From Pericles to Hyperbolus, or What Went Wrong in
    'ca. 416 BC'?   240
    A Fourth-century Consensus?   248
    General Conclusions: The Logic and Original Goals of Athenian
    Ostracism   250

Bibliography   255
Index Locorum   275
General Index   285

List of Illustrations

1.1 Drawing of the so-called ostrakon of Pisistratus. Fragment of a Geometric lid. Agora Image: 2012.57.1399 (86-40) (Agora Object: P 3629). Courtesy of The American School of Classical Studies at Athens: Agora Excavations.   41

3.1 General plan of the Agora showing distribution of ostraka. Agora Image: 2002.01.2660 (Agora Drawing: PD 2660 (DA 3941); artists: R. C. Anderson, J. Travlos, W. B. Dinsmoor, Jr.). Courtesy of The American School of Classical Studies at Athens: Agora Excavations.   136

3.2 The so-called 'Perischoinisma' in the Athenian Agora, Panathenaic Way, East Trench. Agora Image: 2013.18.0029 (photographer: Craig Mauzy). Courtesy of The American School of Classical Studies at Athens: Agora Excavations.   138

3.3 Model of the Athenian Agora *c.* 400 BC, by P. Demetriades and K. Papoulias, Athens, Agora Museum; Agora Image: 2004.02.0083 (LCT-6) (photographer: Craig Mauzy). Courtesy of The American School of Classical Studies at Athens: Agora Excavations.   142

3.4 Attic red-figure *kylix* of the Pan Painter (*c.* 470–460 BC; H. 8.5 cm, 26 cm in diameter), Oxford, Ashmolean Museum, 1911.617 (= The Beazley Archive, no. 206398). Image © Ashmolean Museum, University of Oxford.   148

3.5 North-Slope ostraka of the 'Themistocles Deposit', after *Agora 25*, Pl. 4. Courtesy of Ephorate of Antiquities of Athens-Ancient Agora/American School of Classical Studies Archive. Image © Hellenic Ministry of Culture and Sports/Organization of Cultural Resources Development (H.O.C.R.E.D.).   151

List of Abbreviations

The abbreviations used in this book are based on the convention used in *L'Année philologique* (for journal titles), and in *The Oxford Classical Dictionary* and *Liddell–Scott–Jones Greek Lexicon* (for ancient authors and their works). The list below contains only abbreviations not included there.

Adler	*Suidae lexicon, edidit Ada Adler* (Stuttgart, 1967–1971) [1928–1938]
Agora 3	R. E. Wycherley, *The Athenian Agora. Results of Excavations Conducted by the American School of Classical Studies at Athens*, vol. 3: *Literary and Epigraphical Testimonia* (Princeton, 1957)
Agora 14	H. Thompson, R. E. Wycherley, *The Athenian Agora. Results of Excavations Conducted by the American School of Classical Studies at Athens*, vol. 14: *The Agora of Athens: The History, Shape and Uses of an Ancient City Center* (Princeton, 1972)
Agora 19	G. V. Lalonde, M. K. Langdon, M. B. Walbank, *The Athenian Agora. Results of Excavations Conducted by the American School of Classical Studies at Athens*, vol. 19: *Inscriptions: Horoi, Poletai Records, Leases of Public Lands* (Princeton, 1991)
Agora 25	M. L. Lang, *The Athenian Agora. Results of Excavations Conducted by the American School of Classical Studies at Athens*, vol. 25: *The Ostraka* (Princeton, 1990)
AIO	Attic Inscriptions Online: <https://www.atticinscriptions.com>
Albini	*Andocide, De pace. Introduzione e commento a cura di Umberto Albini* (Firenze, 1964)
AO	Acropolis Ostraka
A.P.	*The Constitution of the Athenians* (ΑΘΗΝΑΙΩΝ ΠΟΛΙΤΕΙΑ) by Ps.-Aristotle.
APF	J. K. Davies, *Athenian Propertied Families 600–300 BC* (Oxford, 1971)

LIST OF ABBREVIATIONS

Aristoteles 10.1	Aristoteles. Werke in deutscher Übersetzung, vol. 10.1: Staat der Athener. Übersetzt und erläutert von Mortimer Chambers (Berlin, 1990)
ARV²	J. D. Beazley, Attic Red-Figure Vase-Painters, 2nd edn, vols. 1–3 (Oxford, 1963)
BE	Bulletin épigraphique
Beazley Archive	University of Oxford, Classical Art Research Centre, The Beazley Archive: <http://www.beazley.ox.ac.uk/index.htm>
Bekker	Anecdota Graeca Immanuelis Bekkeri, vols. 1–3 (Berolini, 1814–1821)
BNJ	Brill's New Jacoby: <http://www.brillonline.nl>
CAH	The Cambridge Ancient History (Cambridge, 1923–)
CEG	Carmina epigraphica Graeca saeculorum VIII–V a. Chr. n. (vol. 1); ... saeculi IV a. Chr. n. (vol. 2), ed. P. A. Hansen (Berlin, 1983–1989)
Chambers	Aristoteles, ΑΘΗΝΑΙΩΝ ΠΟΛΙΤΕΙΑ. Edidit Mortimer Chambers, accedunt tabulae (Leipzig, 1986)
Chantraine	P. Chantraine, Dictionaire étymologique de la langue grecque. Histoire des mots (nouvelle édition avec suppl.) (Paris, 1999)
Conomis	Dinarchi Orationes cum fragmentis, edidit Nicos C. Conomis (Leipzig, 1975)
Costa	Filocoro di Atene, vol. 1: Testimonianze e frammenti dell'"Atthis". A cura di Virgilio Costa (Roma, 2007)
CVA	Corpus vasorum antiquorum
DAA	Dedications from the Athenian Akropolis. A Catalogue of the inscriptions of the sixth and fifth centuries BC. Ed. with the collaboration of L. H. Jeffery by Antony E. Raubitschek (Cambridge, 1949)
DELG	= Chantraine
Diels–Schubart	Didymos. Kommentar zu Demosthenes (Papyrus 9780) nebst Wörterbuch zu Demosthenes' Aristocratea (Papyrus 5008), bearbeitet von H. Diels und W. Schubart (Berlin, 1904)
Dilts	Heraclidis Lembi Excerpta Politiarum, ed. and tr. Mervin R. Dilts (Durham, N.C., 1971)
Dindorf	Harpocrationis Lexicon in decem oratores Atticos ex recensione Gulielmi Dindorfii, vols. 1–2 (Oxonii, 1853)
E.M.	Etymologicon Magnum seu verius Lexicon saepissime vocabulorum origines indagans ex pluribus lexicis scholiastis et grammaticis anonymi cuiusdam opera

LIST OF ABBREVIATIONS   xxi

	concinnatum. Ad codd. mss. recensuit et notis variorum instruxit Thomas Gaisdorf (Amsterdam, 1962) [1848]
FCG	*Fragmenta Comicorum Graecorum, collegit et disposuit Augustus Meineke*, vols. 1–6 (Berolini, 1839–1857)
FGrHist	*Die Fragmente der griechischen Historiker*, ed. F. Jacoby (Leiden, 1923–1958; repr. 1954–1969)
FHG	*Fragmenta Historicorum Graecorum*, vols. 1–5, ed. C. Müller, Th. Müller, and V. Langlois (Parisiis, 1841–1873)
Fornara	*Translated Documents of Greece and Rome*, vol. 1: *Archaic Times to the End of the Peloponnesian War*, edited and translated by Charles W. Fornara (Baltimore–London, 1977)
Fortenbaugh	*Theophrastus of Eresus. Sources for his Life, Writings, Thought and Influence. Edited and translated by William W. Fortenbaugh et al.*, vols. 1–2 (Leiden–New York–Köln, 1992)
FVS[6]	*Die Fragmente der Vorsokratiker*, 6 Aufl., vols. 1–3, ed. H. Diels, W. Kranz (Berlin, 1952–1959)
Gaisdorf	= E.M.
GGM	*Geographi Graeci minores. E codicibus recognovit, prolegomenis, annotatione, indicibus instruxit, tabulis aeri incises illustravit Carolus Müllerus*, vol. 1–2 (Parisiis, 1882)
Harding	*Androtion and the 'Atthis'. The Fragments Translated with Introduction and Commentary by Ph. Harding* (Oxford, 1994)
IG I[2]	*Inscriptiones Graecae I: Inscriptiones Atticae Euclidis anno (403/2) anteriores*, 2nd edn., ed. F. Hiller von Gaertringen (Berlin, 1924)
IG I[3]	*Inscriptiones Graecae I: Inscriptiones Atticae Euclidis anno anteriores*, 3rd edn., ed. D. M. Lewis, L. H. Jeffery, E. Erxleben, K. Hallof (Berlin, 1981–1998)
IG XII,5	*Inscriptiones Graecae XII,5: Inscriptiones Cycladum*, ed. F. Hiller von Gaertringen (Berlin, 1903–1909)
IvO	*Die Inschriften von Olympia. Bearbeitet von Wilhelm Dittenberger und Karl Purgold* (Berlin, 1896)
K–A [vel PCG]	*Poetae comici Graeci*, ed. R. Kassel, C. Austin (Berlin, 1986–)
Kaibel–Wilamowitz[3]	*Aristotelis ΠΟΛΙΤΕΙΑ ΑΘΗΝΑΙΩΝ. Tertium ediderunt G. Kaibel et U. de Wilamowitz-Moellendorff* (Berolini, 1889)

LIST OF ABBREVIATIONS

Kenyon	Aristotle on the Athenian Constitution, translated with introduction and notes by F. G. Kenyon (London, 1912)
Kerameikos 20.1-2	S. Brenne, Kerameikos. Ergebnisse der Ausgrabungen (Deutsches Arachäologisches Institut), vol. 20.1-2: Die Ostraka vom Kerameikos (Berlin, 2018)
Latte-Hansen	Hesychii Alexandrini Lexicon, recensuit et emendavit Kurt Latte, vols. 1-2: A-O (Hauniae, 1953-1966); vol. 3: Π-Σ, editionem post Kurt Latte continuans recensuit et emendavit Peter Allan Hansen (Berlin-New York, 2005)
LexGrMin	Lexica Graeca Minora, selegit K. Latte, disposuit et praefatus est H. Erbse (Hildesheim, 1965)
Lex. Segueriana	Lexica Segueriana, in: Bekker
LGPN	The Lexicon of Greek Personal Names (Oxford, 1987-)
LSAG²	The Local Scripts of Archaic Greece, ed. L. H. Jeffery (Oxford, 1961); 2nd edn, with a Supplement by A. W. Johnston (Oxford, 1990)
LSJ⁹	H. G. Liddell and R. Scott, rev. H. S. Jones and R. McKenzie, A Greek-English Lexicon. A New Edition, with a Supplement, 9th edn (Oxford, 1968)
ML	A Selection of Greek Historical Inscriptions. To the End of the Fifth Century BC, revised edn, ed. R. Meiggs and D. Lewis (Oxford, 1988)
Marcotte	Les Géographes grecs, vol. 1: Introduction générale. Pseudo-Scymnos, Circuit de la terre. Texte établi et traduit par Didier Marcotte (Paris, 2002)
Müller-Kiessling	Theodori Metochitae Miscellanea philosophica et historica. Graece. Textum e codice Cizensi descripsit, lectionisque varietatem ex aliquot aliis codicibus enotatam adiecit M. Christianus Godofredus Müller, ... editio auctoris morte praeventa, cui praefatus est M. Theophilus Kiessling (Lipsiae, 1821)
Nomima	H. Van Effenterre and F. Ruzé, Nomima. Recueil d'inscriptions politiques et juridiques de l'archaïsme grec, vols. 1-2 (Rome, 1994-1995)
PA	Prosopographia Attica. Edidit Johannes Kirchner, vols. 1-2 (Berolini, 1901-1903)
Pindar, Snell-Maehler	Pindarus, pars I, 7th edn: Epinicia. Post B. Snell edidit H. Maehler (Leipzig, 1984); pars II: Fragmenta, Indices. Edidit H. Maehler (Leipzig, 1989)
Rabe	Scholia in Lucianum. Edidit Hugo Rabe (Lipsiae, 1906)
Rhodes	P. J. Rhodes, A Commentary on the Aristotelian 'Athenaion Politeia', 2nd edn (Oxford, 1992)

LIST OF ABBREVIATIONS xxiii

Sandys	*Aristotle's Constitution of Athens. A revised text with an introduction, critical and explanatory notes, testimonia and indices.* By John Edwin Sandys (London–New York, 1893)
sch	scholia/scholion
Schepers	*Alkiphron. Epistulae.* Edidit M. A. Schepers (Leipzig, 1905)
Schoene	A. Schoene, *Eusebii Chronicorum Libri Duo, edidit...*, vol. 2 (Dublin–Zürich, 1967) [1875]
SEG	*Supplementum Epigraphicum Graecum*, vols. 1–11, ed. J. E. Hondius (Leiden, 1923–1954); vols. 12–25, ed. A. G. Woodhead (Leiden, 1955–1971); vols. 26–41, ed. H. W. Pleket and R. S. Stroud (Amsterdam, 1979–1994); vols. 42–44, ed. H. W. Pleket, R. S. Stroud and J. H. M. Strubbe (Amsterdam, 1995–1997); vols. 45–49, ed. H. W. Pleket, R. S. Stroud, A. Chaniotis and J. H. M. Strubbe (Amsterdam, 1998–2002); vol. 50, eds. A. Chaniotis, R. S. Stroud, and J. H. M. Strubbe (Amsterdam 2003); vols. 51–, ed. A. Chaniotis, T. Corsten, R. S. Stroud, and R. A. Tynbout (Amsterdam, 2005–)
Siewert	P. Siewert, *Ostrakismos-Testimonien I. Die Zeugnisse antiker Autoren, der Inschriften und Ostraka über das athenische Scherbengericht aus vorhellenistischer Zeit (487–322 v. Chr.)* hrsg. von... (Stuttgart, 2002)
Syll.³	*Sylloge inscriptionum Graecarum a Guilelmo Dittenbergero condita et aucta, nunc tertium edita*, vols. 1–4 (Lipsiae, 1921–1924)
Szegedy-Maszak	A. Szegedy-Maszak, *The 'Nomoi' of Theophrastus* (New York, 1981)
ThesCRA	*Thesaurus Cultus et Rituum Antiquorum* (Basel–Los Angeles, 2004–)
Timaeus Sophista	ΤΙΜΑΙΟΥ ΣΟΦΙΣΤΟΥ ΛΕΞΙΚΟΝ ΠΕΡΙ ΤΩΝ ΠΑΡΑ ΠΛΑΤΩΝΙ ΛΕΞΕΩΝ. *Timaei Sophistae Lexicon Vocum Platonicarum, ex codice ms. Sangermanensi nunc primum edidit atque animadversionibus illustravit David Ruhnkenius. Editio tertia, multis partibus locupletior* (Londini, 1824)
Westerink	*Olympiodori in Platonis Gorgiam commentaria*, edidit Leendert Gerrit Westerink (Leipzig, 1970)
Wimmer	*Theophrasti Eresii Opera, quae supersut, omnia Graeca recensuit, Latine interpretatus est, indices rerum et verborum absolutissimos adjecit Fredericus Wimmer...* (Parisiis, 1866)

Introduction

Ostracism made a glittering career in modern culture. In colloquial speech as well as in the specialist language of many disciplines, 'ostracism' is understood as a variably described state of being rejected, excluded, and ignored by the community.[1] Studying the case of Athenian ostracism can also tempt one into going beyond the strictly scholarly outlook.

Indeed, ever since the times of this institution's functioning, the ultimate aim of at least some interpretations of ostracism has been answering the question about its rationality.[2] The rationality of a law allowing to sentence each year, without trial or any possibility of defence, an eminent and accomplished citizen to ten-year exile, often based on unsupported allegations, which we hear so much about in ancient sources, may appear questionable. Athenian democracy has been, from time to time, a point of reference for political debates in our world for around 200 years now. It is not surprising, therefore, that nowadays, when basic principles of liberal democracy are questioned not only by its 'external enemies' but also by some politicians, intellectuals, and certain electoral groups in a democratic process, Athenian democracy is again becoming the subject of interpretations (at times original and ingenious) combining sensitivity to the 'dark sides' of both the ancient and modern democracies.[3] The question about the rationality of ostracism—perhaps the most emblematic institution of ancient

---

[1] See, e.g., studies collected in Forgas, Kruglanski, Williams (2011), esp. chapter 3: K. D. Williams, E. D. Wesselmann, 'The Link Between Ostracism and Aggression', pp. 37–51.

[2] For insightful remarks about the notions of rationality as applied to the Greek *polis*, see the classical paper by Murray (1990). At this juncture, I use the term 'rationality' in its non-specific or pedestrian sense, but cf. above, Preface, n. 5.

[3] See, e.g., Samons (2004). Cf. in general Roberts (1994a). At the end of the eighteenth and in the nineteenth century, at the time of the emergence of the systems which evolved into liberal democracies of the present day, some political thinkers and practitioners acknowledged the achievements and appreciated some values of Athenian democracy, while criticising anarchy and mob rule, and majoritarian tyranny over enlightened minorities in ancient direct democracy as they perceived it. The foundations of new systems were laid in a way which would disallow direct influence of the 'people' or 'mob' on the highest level of the decision-making process. See also Rhodes (2003) esp. 27–69, Giangiulio (2015) 13–21; Cartledge (2016); Blok (2017) 38–40. Cf. Vidal-Naquet (1990) 211–235 and Vidal-Naquet (2000) 198–218 (with Hartog (2018) 164–178).

Athens in the perspective of contemporary mass culture[4]—is essentially the question about the very possibility of the existence of a rational people in a democratic state, the question about the possibility of a compromise and lasting cooperation between the *dēmos* and its élites. While studying this ancient institution, we cannot avoid, and least of all in our times, questions of this sort, no matter how anachronistic they may sometimes seem.

I would like to add here that the discussion on Athenian democracy and its connection to modern democracies may soon be entirely reformulated. It would be a natural result of the ideological and institutional crisis of liberal democracies, which has manifested itself in the Brexit referendum, in the presidential victory and the following presidential term of Donald Trump, Jr in the United States, and in the radical political shift in Central and Eastern Europe, among other momentous events in recent history (and more to come, no doubt). For one thing, the possibility of an institutional and ideological dismantling of our model of democracy—based as it is on the necessity of a compromise between opposing ideologies in the democratic process—through the intransigent use of the existent democratic institutions, brings us closer than ever to the Athenian democracy, constantly threatened by its internal enemies, questioning the very idea of democracy.[5]

*

In late sixteenth-century Venice, Paolo Paruta (1540–1598) systematically pondered the question 'whether the ostracism employed by the Athenians was a just thing and useful for the preservation of a Republic' ('Discorso XV' in Book One, pp. 328–350). Ultimately, his well-balanced answer reads as follows (tr. M.W.):[6]

> Therefore, one can conclude that the idea of the Athenians regarding their ostracism is not to be praised or followed as a matter of fact, but it should be commended and imitated as to its intention, namely, by assuring that ambition or vileness of the few does not threaten the tranquillity of the many and does not disturb and unhinge the State in its entirety.

---

[4] Starting with the shaping of children's historical sensitivity from an early age, as in the case of the French animated series *Once Upon a Time... Man* (*Il était une fois... l'homme*), with one episode dedicated to Athenian democracy.
[5] Cf. Węcowski (2009) 509–518. Interestingly, back then as well as today these attacks (even though at times coming nowadays from both the ends of the political spectrum) occasionally refer to the idea of return to the 'ancestral constitution', a mythical time of unity and prosperity of the *polis*, yet 'untainted' by the alleged 'degeneracies' of the more recent times.
[6] Paruta (1599) 350. Cf. Roberts (1994a) Kindle ed. 128–129.

Almost half a century later, Thomas Hobbes published his Latin treatise *De Cive* (*On the Citizen*, 1642). In its English translation of 1651 (the year of the publication of his *Leviathan*), in Chapter X ('A comparison between three kinds of government, according to their severall inconveniences') we read that

[...] the Athenians inflicted a punishment of ten yeares banishment on those that were powerfull, meerly because of their powers, without the guilt of any other crime; and those who by liberall gifts did seek the favour of the common people, were put to death at Rome, as men ambitious of a Kingdome. In this Democraty and Monarchy were eaven [...].[7]

Favouring himself monarchic autocracy, more suitable for a State as he reckoned, Hobbes has laid the foundations of our modern judgements on Athenian ostracism. Later on, ostracism played a certain role in the Anglo-American tradition—although with varying intensity—in current political debates, permeating to the studies on antiquity and vice versa. John Adams, the second U.S. president, explicitly criticised the Athenians for their ostracism:

[...] [I]nstead of thinking to balance effectually their 'orders,' they established ostracism, to prevent any man from becoming too popular. A check indeed, but a very injudicious one; for it only banished their best men. History nowhere furnished so frank a confession of the people themselves of their own infirmities and unfitness for managing the executive branch of government, or an unbalanced share of the legislature, as this institution. The language of it is, 'We know ourselves so well, that we dare not trust our own confidence and affections, our own admiration and gratitude for the greatest talents and sublimest virtues. We know our heads will be turned, if we suffer such characters to live among us, and we shall always make them kings.' What more melancholy spectacle can be conceived even in imagination, than that inconstancy which erects statues to a patriot or a hero one year, banishes him the next, and the third erects fresh statues to his memory?[8]

---

[7] Hobbes (1651) X, 7.
[8] Adams (1851) 490 (in his erudite 'Defence of the Constitutions of Government of the United States of America, against the attack of M. Turgot, in his letter to Dr. Price, 22 March 1778', vol. 1, chap. vii: 'Ancient Democratical Republics' 2: 'Athens'). Partly quoted by Roberts (1994b) 90; cf. also Roberts (1994a) Kindle ed. 182–184.

Another example may be found in the writings of George Grote, once a politically active 'philosophical radical' and author of a brilliant interpretation of ostracism[9] (undoubtedly one of the most interesting ever written). He saw it fit to defend in his work the rationality and morality of Athenian democracy, in his times widely accused of 'envy, injustice and persecution of its most accomplished people' (Grote (1907) vol. 3, 378), precisely because of the functioning of ostracism in this *polis*.

True, before the late nineteenth century, modern assessments of Athenian democracy were to a large extent coloured by anachronistic historical analogies and in particular by the focus on 'great men' and their relationship with the 'masses'.[10] Still, the two radically opposing judgements can also be found in current scholarship. In the view of some, ostracism will appear to be an effective, although somewhat unusual (even for Greek law), means of defending democracy against its internal enemies, an indispensable tool for protecting the power of *dēmos*. In the worst case, it can turn out to be a political ritual, 'an annual re-enactment of a revolution act', which laid the foundations of democracy and thus led to the overthrow of the tyrannical autocracy. However, in Athens this ritual, fortunately, never degenerated into an organised terror aimed at the 'enemies of the people'.[11] On the other hand, this institution can be regarded as an almost obsessive, and counter-effective at the least, means of institutional oppression of the 'élites' by the 'masses', or even as a result of a peculiar persecution complex of the *dēmos*.[12] The roots of such thinking reach back to ancient times. This discrepancy inspires consideration of the true, original aim of this institution.

*

In the second part of this work, we shall see that the seemingly most important corpus of sources contemporary to Athenian ostracism, namely the ostraka used on the day of voting with potsherds (*ostrakophoria*)[13] or prepared for that day, offer us a varied assortment of gossip and allegations directed at more and less important Athenian politicians. Meanwhile, they

---

[9] Grote (1907) v. 3, 368–380 (the twelve volumes of his *History of Greece* were originally published in 1846–1856). Cf. also below, pp. 214–215. For Grote's views on democracy, and their political and intellectual context, see, e.g., Cartledge (2016) 301–304.
[10] This was largely due to the impact of Plutarch's *Lives* on modern thought. See Roberts (1994a) Kindle ed. esp. 110–117.
[11] See Ober (2007) 98–99. Cf. also Forsdyke (2005), e.g., 145 and *passim*, and Kosmin (2015). Cf. below, pp. 191–193.
[12] Cf., e.g., the authors cited by Forsdyke (2005) 144 with n. 2. The earliest testimonies of this sort of thinking can be found in Plut. *Arist.* 7,2; cf. also *Them.* 22,4–5.
[13] On the terminology of ostracism, see briefly Pollux, 8.19.

are not particularly informative for our interpretation of the aims of ostracism—except for testifying to the high level of political agitation surrounding this institution and illustrating the 'black propaganda' of the time. In most recent studies, in turn, these same allegations often become a point of departure for attempts at answering the question about the aims of this institution. Therefore, it does not surprise that such attempts often come to the disappointing conclusion that it is impossible to establish one dominating motive for ostracism. As a result, they at best highlight a general connection between the governing principle of this institution and the democratic ideal of citizen equality, as almost any outstanding deed or accomplishment of the aristocratic leaders of the *polis* could incite envy, resulting in *ostrakophoria*.[14]

It should be emphasised that an approach of this sort may be linked with dating the introduction of ostracism to the 480s BC (see below, 2.1), which dissociates this procedure from the intentions of the creator of this institution and Athens' reformer, Cleisthenes, and attributes the design of the mechanisms of ostracism to the motives of a self-aware Athenian *dēmos*. As we shall see, this dating is impossible. Therefore, in my work I shall, more traditionally, pose questions regarding the potential plans and calculations of the lawgiver. Let us begin, however, with a short discussion of the views the ancients held in this matter.

Walter Scheidel closes his recent overview of ancient pre-Hellenistic testimonies on ostracism with a conclusion that all of them regard this institution in factual terms rather than through the prism of intentions behind this institution, which may indicate that the original aim of

---

[14] I am summarising here the line of thought of one of the most important experts in the field, Peter Siewert, 'Der ursprüngliche Zweck des Ostrakismos (Versuch einer historischen Auswertung)', in Siewert, pp. 504–509; cf. Siewert (1991). Interestingly, he highlights that his view on the connection between the ideal of democratic equality with ostracism (perceptible only later, in Aristotle, and perhaps implied in Demosthenes) is not shared by his collaborators and co-authors of the volume—Siewert, p. 509 n. 14; cf. also below, where I cite the views of Walter Scheidel. Recently, Forsdyke (2005) has offered a thorough and highly original interpretation of ostracism which seems to me at the same time too general and too specific. On the one hand, she understands ostracism as a symbolic expression of popular power and as a collective ritual, which is very broad and somewhat teleological. On the other hand, Forsdyke interprets the establishment of ostracism primarily as a demotic response to political conflict between élite leaders regarding the power to impose exile, which seems slightly reductionist. A more general methodological objection to Fordyke's analyses is that they seem largely based on a monolithic dichotomy between 'élites' and 'non-élites'. On this issue, see below, p. 13 and my comments on the work of Christian Mann, p. 207.

ostracism was not clear in Athens at the end of the fifth century at the latest.[15] It is difficult to disagree with this statement.

Our oldest source is merely an allusion to ostracising Megakles in 486 BC in Pindar's *Pythian* 7 (ll. 18–21, tr. William H. Race): 'O Megakles, | belonging to your family and forbears. | I rejoice greatly at your recent success, but this grieves me | that envy (*phthonos*) requites your noble deeds.'[16] A similar outlook was presented, most likely already at the beginning of the Peloponnesian War,[17] by Herodotus (VIII 79, 1 = Siewert, T 6):[18] immediately after mentioning that the *dēmos* ostracised Aristides, he adds emphatically in one breath that, having got to know his character (*tropos*), he considers him 'the most noble (*aristos*) and most just (*dikaiōtatos*) man in Athens'. The polemic nature of the writer's statement about the decision to ostracise Aristides is beyond doubt here. There only remains the question of whether, in the light of this single remark on ostracism by Herodotus, we can presume a critical attitude of the historian towards this institution, or on the contrary, Herodotus accentuates his surprise at the fact that in the past even people of this sort went into exile.[19]

To Athenian comedy writers of the second half of the fifth and beginning of the fourth century BC, Cratinus and Aristophanes, ostracism seems to be simply an element of the political reality of a slightly distant past,[20] or of their own times,[21] or an imaginable political eventuality at present.[22]

It is only in the important fragment from Plato Comicus (fr. 203 K–A = Siewert, T 12) that we find an unambiguously negative judgement of a

---

[15] W. Scheidel, 'Aussagen der Testimonien über der Institution des Ostrakismos', in Siewert, pp. 483–494.
[16] Siewert, T (?) 2. The allusion was identified by Wilamowitz–Moellendorff (1893) v. 2, 326–328.
[17] I refer to the fundamental literature on dating the 'publication' of Herodotus' work in Węcowski (2016) 18–19, with n. 9.
[18] Further in my work, while citing particular testimonies by their numbers in the monumental collection by Siewert, I automatically refer to useful commentaries included there.
[19] It is worth remembering that Herodotus had most probably written this before ostracism was disgraced by the exile of Hyperbolus, whereafter the Athenians, in the unanimous opinion of later ancient writers, ceased to see the point in ostracising their fellow citizens. See below, 2.2.4 and 'Epilogue and Conclusions'.
[20] Ar. *Eq*. 819 = Siewert, T 8, on Themistocles; sch. vet. Ar. *Vespae* 947A = Siewert T (?) 10, on Thucydides, son of Melesias. Cf. also Andocides I [*On Mysteries*] 107 (= Siewert, T 17, of 400/399 BC), mentioning a recalling of the ostracised exiles right before the war with Xerxes.
[21] See, perhaps, allusions to the ostracism of Hyperbolus of ca. 416 BC: Ar. fr. 661 K–A; Adespota, fr. 363 K–A.
[22] Cratinus, fr. 73 K–A = Siewert, T 7, on Pericles, cf. below, pp. 120–121; Ar. *Eq*. 855–857 = Siewert T 9, on Cleon, cf. below; perhaps also Plato Comicus, fr. 168 K–A = Siewert T (?) 11, on the *ostrakinda* game, cf. below, pp. 210–211.

particular *ostrakophoria* which resulted in the exile of Hyperbolus. The poet states clearly that this politician, while deserving exile because of his character (*tropoi*), did not, due to his low social status, deserve ostracism, which 'was invented not for people of this sort' ([...] οὐ γὰρ τοιούτων οὕνεκ' ὄστραχ' ηὑρέθη). Thucydides speaks in a similar vein when writing about Hyperbolus' death (VIII 73, 3 = Siewert, T 16, tr. Martin Hammond):[23] 'a worthless fellow who had been ostracised, not out of fear of his power or position, but because he was a pest and a disgrace to the city' ([...] μοχθηρὸν ἄνθρωπον, ὠστρακισμένον οὐ διὰ δυνάμεως καὶ ἀξιώματος φόβον, ἀλλὰ διὰ πονηρίαν καὶ αἰσχύνην τῆς πόλεως).

Here end testimonies dating to the times when Athenian ostracism was still in use. In the fourth century, there appear many interpretations of ostracism as an institution, which will be continued in later tradition, up until the Byzantine times, in various ways.[24] Particularly problematic is a fourth-century rhetorical exercise which was included in Andocides' corpus as a speech [IV] *Against Alcibiades*,[25] where, apart from several allusions to the ostracisms of the fifth century, we find general criticism of this institution from the (fictitious) point of view of an aristocrat in peril of exile. On the one hand, the conventional character of the speech compels us to factor in that the orator intentionally presents only a one-sided perspective, which he could himself easily counter, as part of an alternative rhetorical exercise, with a positive image of ostracism. On the other hand, the author of this speech may be copying motifs known to him from fifth-century literature unavailable to us, assuming that they will prove persuasive, interesting, or novel to the reader.[26]

Pseudo-Andocides (§ 5) ascribes to the lawgiver the intention to discard a 'troublesome citizen' (*ponēros politēs*) from the *polis*, even though it actually removes for 10 years 'the best one' (*ton beltiston*).[27] The orator, conventionally addressing the Assembly, obviously cannot refer to the already mentioned motif of 'envy' or 'ingratitude' of the people, as will Plato (*Gorg.* 516 D = Siewert, T 25), but he seems to be blaming the ill-conceived law of

---

[23] Thucydides I 135,3 (Siewert, T 15) is simply a short mention of the ostracism of Themistocles.
[24] See also below, on the references to ostracism in Plato and orators of the fourth century, pp. 96–98. Cf. also below (1.2.2), on the Roman and Byzantine tradition of ostracism.
[25] Siewert, T 18–21.
[26] Among the references to historical ostracisms, the speech shows some signs of erudite effort, a quest for information which is not widely available. See below, pp. 96–98.
[27] Cf. also further, § 40, on the example for 'good citizens' which may be gained from the orator's exile.

ostracism on the 'lawgiver' (§ 3: *ton thenta ton nomon*), most probably Cleisthenes.²⁸ The earliest testimony of a deeper, even though not necessarily more correct, thought on the intention of the lawgiver introducing ostracism can be found in a fragment by the Atthidographer Androtion (*FGrHist* 324 F 6):

Concerning this man [that is Hipparchos, son of Charmos – M. W.] Androtion says in Book Two [of his *Atthis*] that he was a relative of Pisistratus the tyrant and was the first to be ostracised, since the law about *ostrakismos* had first been established at that time [sic!] on account of suspicion (*hypopsia*) of Pisistratus and his circle because, being a popular leader (*dēmagōgos*) and general (*stratēgos*), he had become a tyrant.   (tr. N.F. Jones, *BNJ*; adjusted by L.O.)

I shall deal with the interpretation of this corrupted text further in my work. Here I would only like to point out the appearance of the motif of 'suspicion' towards the Athenians of their connections with the tyrants and the implied diagnosis that originally, ostracism was meant to prevent the return of tyranny to Athens.

The most important stage in shaping the tradition of considerations on the reasoning behind the ostracism law were Aristotle's studies in *Politics*, followed by the works of his disciples, such as the so-called Ps.-Aristotle, the author of the *Constitution of the Athenians* (further *A.P.*),²⁹ one of the 158 treatises (*politeiai*) created under the supervision of the Stagirite, or Theophrastus of Eresos, whose work *On Laws* discussed ostracism in juxtaposition with other forms of exile and became a point of departure for the entire later tradition regarding ostracism in the ancient and Byzantine times.³⁰ Regardless of the evolution of Aristotle's thought in this matter, which we can trace in his *Politics*, it can be said in most general terms that he considered ostracism as a protective means against excessive 'outgrowth'

---

²⁸ However, see below for arguments presented by the opponents of this view, pp. 77–78.
²⁹ I am taking a stand here against Aristotle's authorship of this work, which not only deviates to some extent from the Stagirite's thought but also seems considerably weaker intellectually than his other works. See Rhodes, pp. 51–63, with references. The roots of this discussion are in the pioneering work by Friedrich Cauer (1891). Cf. Weil (1960); *Aristoteles 10.1*, 75–82; Bertelli (1997). See also Keaney (1970b), Ducat (1992); Lintott (1992); Meister (1997). More specifically for the relationship between *A.P.* and Aristotle's *Politics* as regards ostracism, see W. Scheidel, H. Taeuber, and W. Scheidel, in Siewert, pp. 447–448 and 472–474, respectively.
³⁰ See esp. Raubitschek (1958) and below, pp. 121–122. The presence of considerations on ostracism in Theophrastus, although very limited in extent, was claimed already by Bloch (1940)

(*hyperochē*) of the individual in the *polis*.³¹ Naturally, this was of particular importance in a democratic system, where citizen equality is the crucial ideal.³² Thus, to Aristotle, ostracism seemed to be a preventive measure against tyranny. This fundamental thought was followed by the author of *A.P.* (22.1; 3-4; 6), who ascribed to Cleisthenes the intention to impede the return of tyranny (see above on Androtion); this was to be accomplished through removing from Athens first the people connected with the Pisistratid tyranny and then all those who seemed 'too significant' (22.6: [...] καὶ τῶν ἄλλων εἴ τις δοκοίη μείζων εἶναι μεθίσταντο).

As we can see, the ancient tradition—as well as modern thinkers—was divided into those who ascribed to the people 'envy' or 'ingratitude' towards wealthy Athenians and thus regarded ostracism as a counterproductive (to put it mildly) institution and those who emphasised (as had Aristotle) its rationality in a democratic *polis*, without denying the possibility of its degeneration into a weapon in faction struggle.³³ And although it is indisputable that there existed a general conviction that ostracism was always directed at the noble and the mighty,³⁴ in the second half of the fifth and in the fourth century BC, more detailed information on the intentions of the lawgiver was unavailable to the people—even though at the beginning of the fourth century an inquisitive scholar in Athens could most probably get hold of at least fragments of Cleisthenes' law on ostracism.³⁵

Between the last decade of the sixth century, when Cleisthenes introduced the institution of ostracism, and the last quarter of the fifth century BC, when *ostrakophoria* was used in Athens for the last time, Athenian politics utterly changed. The chances that the Athenians still understood the initial sense of ostracism properly can be a priori considered as slight. At the same time, at least four reasons make me doubt the idea of the principally anti-tyrannical cutting edge of Cleisthenes' law. First of all, as we shall see, the first exile through the procedure of ostracism did not occur until 20 years after its introduction, which was a source of due concern to ancient and modern

---

355–376, cf. Theophrastus fr. 18(b) Szegedy-Maszak, with commentary. Cf. also Connor and Keaney (1969) (with Keaney (1993)). On Plutarch's views in this matter, see, e.g., Plut. *Arist.* 7, 1; *Per.* 4, 3; 9, 5, and esp. *Arist.* 7, 5–6.

³¹ See *Pol.* III 1284 a 17–37; 1284 b 15–30; 1288 a 24–26; V 1305 b 15–21; 1308 b 10–19 (= Siewert, T 24–38). Herbert Heftner discusses briefly the evolution of Aristotle's thought on ostracism (Siewert, pp. 444–446).

³² Cf. also generally D.S. XI 55, 2–3; 86,5; 87, 1–2.

³³ Cf. Aristotle, *Pol.* 1284 b 20–22 (= Siewert, T 35).

³⁴ See above for ancient comments on the exile of Hyperbolus, pp. 6–7.

³⁵ See below, 3.1.

scholars alike. We can obviously imagine that Cleisthenes and his supporters for some reason failed to use this tool earlier on effectively. Still, this supposition would raise the question of why such an inefficient law remained in force throughout this entire period and even several decades afterwards. Secondly, as pointed out by Sara Forsdyke, 'the mildness of the penalty of ostracism' is yet another argument against its original antityrannical intent.[36] Thirdly, special laws against tyranny had existed in Athens already since the time of Solon,[37] so doubling them with a new and clearly unproductive one seems rather odd. Fourthly, and perhaps most importantly, it was observed long ago that in the case of a vote *en masse* of the Athenian *dēmos* on the day of *ostrakophoria*, a populist truly perilous to the state would have little chance of being exiled. Such a fate would most probably befall somebody less popular, and the individual jeopardising citizen equality would further reinforce his own position, potentially increasing his tyrannical tendencies.[38]

In this work, I shall attempt to answer the question about the primary aim of ostracism, following a thorough study of what can be established regarding the history of this institution (historical cases of ostracism) and its procedure (the functioning, or mechanism, of ostracism).

*

In the last decades, scholarship on Athenian ostracism has had a breakthrough, or even several breakthroughs, connected with the avalanche-speed increase of the amount of our sources, particularly through the spectacular discoveries on the Athenian Kerameikos, which multiplied the number of ostraka used in Athenian ostracism known to us. Unfortunately, only the ostraka from the American excavations in the Agora have been granted a timely scholarly publication (*Agora 25*).[39] The final edition of the ostraka from Kerameikos saw the light of day only recently, in 2018 (*Kerameikos 20*). In the meantime, scholars working on them, particularly their ultimate editor Stefan Brenne, had begun publishing studies based on this new massive bulk of inscriptions, which allowed them to initiate truly modern prosopographic, social, and political analyses of this material (esp. Brenne (2001)). However, there is no doubt that comprehensive work on the

---

[36] Forsdyke (2005) 153–154. And the same goes for the idea of ostracism 'as a weapon against traitors' (Forsdyke (2005) 154–155).
[37] See esp. Ostwald (1955).
[38] See, e.g., Mann (2007) 62, with earlier scholarship in his n. 3.
[39] In the last decades around 275 new ostraka were found in Athens, out of which over 150 come from the Agora. Cf. Sickinger (2017a) and (2017b).

Kerameikos ostraka will flourish in the future, following the long-awaited publication by S. Brenne.

On the other hand, in the last decades, a series of unexpected but spectacular discoveries have been made in various parts of the Greek world which testify to the functioning of some forms of ostracism in many political communities—from the northern coast of the Black Sea, through the Peloponnese and Cyrenaica, as far as southern Italy and Sicily. These discoveries enable us to view the Athenian case in a broader historical context and can potentially contribute to a complete alteration of our conception of this institution's origins.[40]

Historical research on ostracism has long been focusing on establishing the historicity and chronology of particular *ostrakophoriai*, on reconstructing the exile geography of the victims of ostracism, as well as on studying the role of particular ostracisms in the political life of Athens at various points in the fifth century.[41] At the same time, philologists have worked arduously on our most important literary texts to learn about the whole procedure, concentrating primarily on testimonies regarding the details of Athenian *ostrakophoriai*. Ostracism has traditionally also been an important element in the studies on ancient law. This historical-philological-legal domain has only recently been enriched with methods and tools of anthropology and sociology. However, despite a considerable change of the research perspective, what has remained unaltered is the pre-eminence of interest in the

---

[40] It is instructive here to compare our current scholarly position with that of Thomsen (1972) p. 13, 50 years ago, who could still faithfully follow Valeton (1887) (with Valeton (1888)) in claiming that 'ostracism in all likelihood originated in Athens and spread from this state to the other city-states in question [*sc.* Argos, Miletus, and Megara – M.W.]. [...] [E]ven if it must be stressed that absolute certainty is out of the question [...]'.

[41] Paradoxically, so far very few monographs have been written on Athenian ostracism and its genesis. The founding work of modern studies on ostracism (i.e., following, on the one hand, the publication of *A.P.* in 1891 and, on the other, the discovery of the first more substantial deposits of ostraka by A. Brueckner in 1910 and T. L. Shear in 1932) is the second edition of Carcopino (1935) (much less so Calderini (1945), with major works of earlier scholarship conveniently discussed in Carcopino (1935) 1–3). Vanderpool (1972) and Thomsen (1972) are still very important (on the latter, cf. Bicknell (1974)). Recently, a robust Russian synthesis has been published by Surikov (2006). Ostracism is a central theme of Forsdyke (2005). Cf. also Kagan (1961); Karavites (1974); Rosivach (1987); Mattingly (1991); Marr, Worswick (1994); Dreher (2000). Of key significance today is the lavishly commented edition of all the pre-Hellenistic testimonies concerning ostracism, including a commented list of ostraka, edited by Peter Siewert in 2002 (another volume of this collaborative work, gathering testimonies from post-classical times, is forthcoming; cf. its review by Kinzl (2006)). Bibliography including earlier works on ostracism can be found, for instance, in Martin (1989); Rausch (1994); Bleicken (1995) 524–526 and in two more recent and exhaustive overviews of the *Ostrakismos-Forschung* in Siewert, 25–32 and in Surikov (2006) 85–123. Rhodes (2015) writes engagingly on the most recent paths of research on Athenian democracy.

Athenian ostraka and the day of voting with ceramic sherds on the Athenian Agora. It can be said without the slightest exaggeration that to the majority of scholars, ostracism equals *ostrakophoria* and that the successive changes and breakthroughs in its study, and the study of its 'tools', the ostraka, are meant, in the unanimous opinion of scholarship today, to bring us closer to a better understanding of ostracism, including its original aims.

In my work, I shall attempt a comprehensive (philological, historical, and archaeological) interpretation of ostracism, including the iconographic material and topographical analysis of this Athenian institution. However, the most important novelty will be the endeavour to break with the tradition, which focused, in my view excessively, on ostraka and *ostrakophoriai*. I aim to study the entirety of the procedure of ostracism, where *ostrakophoria* was only the last chord. Admittedly, it was the most spectacular and therefore the most memorable stage, but taking place only at the point, as I shall try to show, when all the other mechanisms have already been employed. In this context, I also intend to offer more thorough considerations on how we can use the epigraphic material left to us by the Athenians and what limitations should impose on us a more cautious use of it than that practised in the study of ostracism to date.

Finally, to explain the primary aims and the functioning of ostracism as intended by Cleisthenes, I shall include in my work elements of the 'cooperation theory', arising from the study of the mechanism of 'the prisoner's dilemma' in the mathematical game theory. As we shall see, such a simulation, or probabilistic approximation, may facilitate the understanding of the conceivable mechanisms operating in Athenian political life, which to some extent revolved each year around the question of whether or not the Athenian people will decide this time to trigger the procedure of ostracism, ruthless for its élites.

*

One word of warning, or even a disclaimer, is in order here. When discussing Athenian ostracism and its original goals, I will not delve deeper into two big, nay classic, historical questions often associated with the history of this institution. My general conclusions, however, may have some bearing on them both. These are two interconnected problems, one of which is more general and the other more specific.

Did Athenian democracy truly start with Cleisthenes? In other words, does the political system established by his reforms fully deserve to be called 'democracy'? This widespread idea has been questioned in more recent scholarship and for good reasons. Thus, the path is open to interpret democracy in Athens in terms of a long process signposted by consecutive pivotal historical changes, such as the reforms of Ephialtes in 462/461 BC.[42] In this context, simply put, I will not try to answer the question of whether ostracism, ingeniously designed by Cleisthenes, was a democratic institution properly speaking. For me, suffice it to say that it was a momentous novelty of a profound historical impact on Athenian politics henceforward.

The second, and in fact subordinate, big historical question is the classical problem of 'mass and élite in democratic Athens', to use the title of the pathbreaking book by Josiah Ober (1989).[43] This problem actually belongs not only to ancient history but more broadly also to the field of political sociology. But the reasons for which I will not dwell on the issue of 'mass and élite' in democratic Athens are more specific. On the one hand, when studying Athenian ostracism, I try to suspend for the time being any reasoning based on a monolithic, political and/or social or socio-economic dichotomy of 'mass' and 'élite' in Athenian democracy.[44] Instead, I will focus on the phenomenon of political agency, or political leadership, and not on Athenian élites as such. At this point, it should additionally be stressed that I am far from making assumptions usual of elitist political theorists. I take as natural the existence of those functionally acting as leaders of a given community, and as such building circles of support, or followers, around them, without assuming that groups of such individuals are predestined to monopolise political power in a democracy. The latter was simply not the case in the fifth-century Athenian democracy. Therefore, such terms as 'élite' and 'élites' are used here only in a very general and non-specific sense.

On the other hand, I can also dispense with discussing the more general issue of 'masses and élites' because, as far as ostracism is concerned,

---

[42] See esp. Raaflaub (1995); (1998a); (1998b) and (2007) 144–150; for a broad overview of 'the transformations of Athens in the fifth century', see Raaflaub (1998c); cf. Forsdyke (2005) esp. 133–134, with further bibliography; Giangiulio (2015) 40–45. For important methodological caveats, see Raaflaub (1998a) 31–37.

[43] Incidentally, Ober's 'mass and élite model', as they call it, elaborated for the fourth-century Athenian law courts (but applicable, according to Ober, also to the Assembly, the Council, the Areopagus, the theatre, and other public fora), was recently reassessed and modified by Carugati and Weingast (2018). See below, p. 250.

[44] See below (pp. 206–208), my comments on Mann (2007) and my 'General Conclusions'. My decision here is also based on the preliminary results of an ongoing project on archaic and early classical Greek élites which I coordinate at the University of Warsaw (NCN grant no. 2016/21/B/HS3/03096) in collaboration with Xenia Charalambidou, Katarzyna Kostecka, Cameron Pearson, and Roman Żuchowicz. Regrettably, in my reasoning I could not systematically take into account a very interesting new perspective on 'aristocracy' developed in a recent book by Meister (2020). His work reached me when my own book had already been completed.

I subscribe to John K. Davies' concept of 'democracy without theory' (see above), so I study the origins of this institution as a practical political expedient, however far-sighted and sophisticated, and not as a result, or element, of any 'democratic ideology'. Accordingly, I will not discuss ostracism as a potential theme of ideological debates regarding the relationship between 'mass and élite' in Athenian democracy—not because such debates did not take place, but because in my view, they have no bearing on the problem of the original goals of ostracism.

PART I
KEY ISSUES IN THE STUDY OF ATHENIAN OSTRACISM

1
Ostracism before Ostracism?

1.1 Was there Ostracism beyond Athens in the Archaic Period?

An essential issue in the study of the genesis of Athenian ostracism is the question regarding its relative chronology in the Panhellenic context. In other words, whether it is possible to find traces of this or similar institutions outside Athens in the period preceding its introduction by the Athenians. In the case of a positive answer, the primary function of ostracism in Athens would naturally need to be interpreted quite differently than if the answer was negative.

It seems that nowadays increasingly popular among scholars is the conviction that Athenian ostracism was only one of the examples of

> a more generalized Greek practice of using written ballots – whether leaves or potsherds – as a means of determining a penalty (removal from public office or exile). Ostracism-like procedures such as petalism at Syracuse may be local versions of the general Greek practice, and are not necessarily direct imitations of Athenian ostracism.[1]

In what follows, I shall question the validity of this view, proving the chronological priority of ostracism in Athens in relation to all the analogous practices known to us to date in the Greek world. I shall also gather evidence—even if only circumstantial—supporting the thesis of a historical connection and a fairly close imitation of the Athenian model in several different Greek *poleis* in classical times. Of course, such conclusions do not preclude the existence of 'a more generalized Greek practice of using written ballots—whether leaves or potsherds' as the ultimate source of the Athenian use of ostraka for ostracism. Meanwhile, the assumption of an allegedly

---

[1] Forsdyke (2005) 285. In general, see Forsdyke (2005) 285–288 and Surikov (2000) and (2006) esp. 443–471. Cf. also Siewert, T 18, comm. on Ps.-Andoc. *Alc.* 6, by Brigitta Eder and Herbert Heftner, in Siewert, pp. 296–299. See also below, 1.1.2.

inseparable link between such material tools and the institution is deeply rooted in our scholarly practice of focusing on the *ostrakophoria* when studying ostracism.

1.1.1 Traces of *Ostrakophoriai* in the Greek World

In the speech *Against Alcibiades*, the anonymous orator conventionally called Ps.-Andocides states[2] that the Athenians are the only ones among the Greeks to know the institution of ostracism, adding, 'and no other *polis* is willing to follow us [in that respect]' (Ps.-Andoc. *Alc.* 6). This claim, however, should be attributed to the rhetorical exaggeration and the general argumentative strategy of the text. Aristotle remarks in his *Politics* (1302b 17–19) that, due to a natural fear of one-man rule (*monarchia* or *dynasteia*), 'in some places ostracism is used, as for instance in Argos and Athens' (ἐνιαχοῦ εἰώθασιν ὀστρακίζειν, οἷον ἐν Ἄργει καὶ Ἀθήνησιν).[3] An analogical thought, formulated in a similarly polemic way, questioning the exceptionality of Athenian ostracism, can be found in a scholion to Aristophanes' *Knights* (SchVet 855B), which most probably arises from Theophrastus' reflection in *On Laws*:[4] 'Not only the Athenians used ostracism, but also the Argives, the Milesians and the Megarians.'

For one of the *poleis* to which the institution of ostracism was attributed in antiquity, we have solely a literary testimony at our disposal today, but in other cases such information gradually finds confirmation in archaeological data. Moreover, the series of sensational discoveries of the last three decades proved the existence of ostracism in communities for which we do not have any literary tradition on the topic at all.

Let us begin with the *poleis* for which we have only literary texts, in the majority deriving most probably not from local tradition, but from a common source, namely the peripatetic school—from both Aristotle and his disciple Theophrastus, as well as the collaborative 'research project' of 158

---

[2] Eder and Heftner (Siewert, T 18), in their commentary to this passage of Ps.-Andocides (Siewert, pp. 298–299), in order to explain this false statement, are inclined to assume the lack of knowledge about ostracisms outside Athens among the Athenian audience of Ps.-Andocides, or perhaps even in the author himself. This seems to me too pedantic an approach to a text which, according to all probability, was a 'pseudo-epigraphic' rhetorical exercise, and not an actually delivered speech. See above, p. 7 and below, pp. 96–98.
[3] Cf. also Arist. *Pol.* 1284a 18.
[4] For this scholion, see the most recent and detailed reconstruction by Heftner (2018). See below, pp. 158–160.

politeiai, inspired and written partly to cater to Aristotle's needs. The Milesian ostracism mentioned in the scholion to *Knights* is not evidenced in any other source,[5] as far as I know; however, we shall return to it for a moment when discussing the case of Tauric Chersonesos.[6] It is worth mentioning here that Reinhold Merkelbach suggested, based on a testimony by Heraclitus (*FVS*[6] 22 B 121), that a law similar to Athenian ostracism must have also functioned in Ephesus.[7] However, it seems to me that it does not suffice to prove the existence of this institution in Ephesus, even though at first sight the philosopher's vague mention of Hermodoros' exile by fellow citizens (most probably jealous of his personal virtues) resembles some anecdotes about Athenian ostracism.

Very complex in turn is the case of Argos. Neither the relations of this *polis* with Athens in late archaic and classical times nor the intricate issue of democracy in archaic Argos can be discussed here.[8] However, crucial for my considerations is the discovery of an ostrakon with the name Alkandros (in the nominative) during the excavations on the agora of Argos in 1985. Both the shape of this sherd and its inscription (*SEG* XXXVI [1986] 340) strongly resemble the Athenian ostraka; therefore, the excavators very cautiously posed the question of whether this discovery can be regarded as confirming the literary mentions about the functioning of ostracism in Argos.[9] An isolated ostrakon does not allow for any definitive conclusions, but the hypothesis seems very probable. As the French excavators point out, the first Athenian ostrakon, published in 1870, remained isolated for almost 20 years, and the world had to wait until 1910 for the first deposits of ostraka.[10] Let us remember that 100 years later, we have ca. 11000 objects of this kind, and their number will certainly be increasing.

---

[5] Nawotka (1999) 150–151, 177 convincingly argues that in this *polis* ostracism must have belonged to the times following the transformation of Miletus' political system under Athenian influence around the middle of the fifth century BC.
[6] See below, pp. 24–31.
[7] Merkelbach (1969) 202. As far as I know, the first scholar to reach this conclusion, was Bernays (1869) 84–85. See also Bürchner (1905) 2789, who places the hypothetical ostracism of Hermodoros in the context of the (hypothetical) changes of political systems in the *poleis* of Asia Minor freed from the Persian rule by Cimon (D.S. XI 60, 1–2). According to Bürchner, the Ephesian ostracism would be an element of the new, 'purely democratic' order in this *polis*. Lene Rubinstein (in Hansen, Nielsen (2004) no. 844, pp. 1071–1072) speaks about the possible political system changes in Ephesus at that time much more cautiously and does not link Hermodoros' exile with ostracism. Rubinstein is following here the analysis by Gehrke (1985) 58—rightly, I believe.
[8] For an overview see Robinson (1997) 82–88.
[9] Pariente, Piérart, Thalmann, Aupert, Croissant (1986) 764–765, with pl. 1.
[10] Pariente, Piérart, Thalmann, Aupert, Croissant (1986) 765.

In Argos, where the modern city has quite thoroughly destroyed the remnants of the ancient city, no such explosion of discoveries connected with ostracism can be expected, but the ostrakon mentioned above appears to be very significant. What is essential for my argument here is principally its dating. The pot bearing the Argive graffito was most probably made in the first quarter of the fifth century BC, but the inscription is, according to its excavators, more or less a quarter of a century later. If this object was to be regarded as material evidence for the functioning of ostracism in Argos, it would indicate that the procedure was in operation before the mid-fifth century BC. Naturally, we cannot completely exclude the existence of this institution in archaic Argos, but this hypothesis seems to be only as valid as the historical connection between the only dated trace of ostracism and the period of its functioning in Argos.

The beginning of the early classical democracy in Argos is usually placed between the mysterious period of turbulent socio-political changes brought about by the catastrophic defeat of Argos by the Spartans at Sepeia in 494 BC,[11] when 6,000 Argives are reported to have died,[12] and the year 463 BC, the probable date of the staging of Aeschylus' *Suppliants* in Athens, whose plot seems to assume the functioning of democracy in Argos.[13] It is testified to indirectly also by the alliance made by this *polis* with Athens in 462 BC (Thuc. I 102,4). Another play by Aeschylus, the *Eumenides*, seems to be alluding to it in several places.[14] Nevertheless, we cannot establish when ostracism began to be applied in Argos. We are forced to rely on guesswork in this matter. If scholars rightly interpret our chaotic, and for the most part mutually contradictory, accounts of the events in Argos after the battle of Sepeia as a confused echo of revolutionary reform (consisting in including in the citizen body a large number of non-citizens of various status, but primarily dependent rural people),[15] then Cleisthenic inspirations of this reform cannot be ruled out. However, our sources clearly state that it was a

---

[11] The scholarly discussion on the nature of the upheaval which took place in Argos then, after the battle of Sepeia, is briefly recounted by Robinson (1997) 84–88. Cf. Gehrke (1985) 24–26, 361–363.
[12] Hdt. VII 148, 2; cf. Pausanias III 4,10.
[13] See esp. the famous l. 604: δήμου κρατοῦσα χείρ – 'people's sovereign vote (lit. "hand")' (tr. A.H. Sommerstein), with ll. 621–622, 517–518, as well as ll. 601, 698–700 (cf. already Ehrenberg (1950) 516–524), 739, 942–943, where the character of the final decisions taken in the Assembly voting is clearly visible. Cf. Sommerstein (2019) 29–31 (with references) and *ad loc*. Recently, see the excellent succinct discussion by Giangiulio (2015) 47–48.
[14] See, among others, Wörrle (1964) 122–123. Cf. also Dover (1957) 235–236; more moderately Costa (1962) 31–34. See also the still inspiring interpretation by Meier (1980) 144–246.
[15] According to Gehrke (1985) 25; Robinson (1997) 87–88.

temporary situation, and that the 'slaves' prevailing in Argos for a short time lost their position when the sons of those who died at Sepeia reached adulthood. Therefore, the sources of state stability in classical Argos should be sought rather in the 70s of the fifth century BC, when the Argives managed to ultimately subjugate Mycenae and Tiryns in Argolis,[16] thus opening the way for a redistribution of land among citizens, and in consequence for a reorganisation of the citizen body according to new principles. Nevertheless, the political institution of Argos most probably evolved gradually, taking its peculiar form. According to Marcel Piérart, in the light of the epigraphic material known today, the actual beginning of a democratic system should be dated precisely to the years 470–460 BC.[17] Thus, if we were to attempt to determine approximately the time of the emergence of ostracism in Argos, this period would roughly correspond with the dating of the ostrakon discussed above to the second quarter of the fifth century BC. It should, however, be noted that at this point in our analysis we cannot exclude the existence of earlier local traditions, whence the Argive ostracism would arise, even though the radical character of the socio-political changes which took place in Argos in the two first quarters of the fifth century makes such an eventuality much less probable. If, in turn, we tentatively accepted this approximate dating of the appearance of ostracism, it would be necessary to conclude that in this matter the citizens of Argos could have been following the Athenian paradigm.[18]

Another *polis* mentioned in the scholion to Aristophanes' *Knights*, Megara, has a similarly intricate, little-known past in the archaic and early classical times and a tumultuous history of relations with the neighbouring Athens. Unable to discuss details here, I shall only mention that ancient sources firmly claim that a 'radical democracy' (see below) functioned in Megara at some point in the archaic period.[19]

---

[16] See Wolicki (2018) 45–61 for thorough general discussions of the military–diplomatic aspect of the situation on the Peloponnese at that time, accompanying an important discussion of the treaty between Sparta and Tegea.

[17] Piérart (2000) 307–308; cf. also Giangiulio (2015) 30–31. Gehrke (1985) 25 dates the actual beginning of democracy in Argos to the time between 490 and 488 BC. On the institutions of Argos: Piérart (2000) 301–306. For a general view see Wörrle (1964) 122–132.

[18] Wörrle (1964) 126 claims that the relationship between the democratic institutions in Athens and Argos cannot be established.

[19] See esp. Plut. *Mor.* 295D and 304E–F; cf. Arist. *Pol.* 1302b 27–31 (cf. Okin (1985) 14). The straightforward scholarly use of the highly conventional poetry of Theognis for more or less detailed reconstructions of the archaic history of Megara should not be trusted (I hope to deal with this problem in the future; cf. the excellent study by Lane Fox (2000)). See also Gehrke (1985) 106, with references; Robinson (1997) 114–117.

In 1984 on one of the two acropoleis of Megara, Caria, a small black-glazed cup of local production was discovered, dated (on the sole basis of its shape) to the end of the fifth, or the beginning or even the first quarter of the fourth century BC. The vessel is inscribed with a name in the nominative and a patronymic in the genitive: Ἡράκλειτος Παγχάρεος (SEG XXXVII [1987] 371).[20] It should not worry us that we are dealing here not with an ostrakon but with a complete small vase.[21] Similarly to the ostrakon from Argos, the graffito directed at Herakleitos son of Panchares has so far been an isolated one. Still, if we consider that the form of the inscription is identical with many Athenian examples, the literary account of ostracism in Megara makes the connection between the vessel and a local *ostrakophoria* very probable.

As far as outlining the most general framework of the functioning of ostracism in Megara is concerned, we are in a slightly better situation than in the case of Argos. Our random knowledge of Megara's history in archaic times is based on a series of information snippets, which we owe mainly to Aristotle and Plutarch, who refer to more or less striking actions of Megarian 'radical democracy'.[22] It seems significant that neither of them associates the institution of ostracism with this stage of the *polis*' history.[23] In these circumstances, it can be safely assumed that it functioned in Megara in classical times. Although Charalambos Kritzas regards the vessel discussed above as evidence that the Megarians introduced the Athenian institution of ostracism either around the year 460 BC (the date of the alliance with Athens) or in the years 427–424 BC (a short period of democratic rule),[24] the only thing important to me here is that the inscription seems to be generally suggesting the possibility of the functioning of ostracism in Megara, beginning at some point around the middle of the fifth century BC.

---

[20] Kritzas (1987) 62–65.
[21] The ascription of the vessel from Megara to ostracism seems natural due to, among other reasons, the form of the inscription. Graffiti with names of owners are of course found on vases relatively often, but in such a case we would expect an ownership formula with the name in the genitive (often with a verb in the first person to express the possession of this item). A votive function of such a humble vessel is in turn rather improbable. The analogy of form with ostracism inscriptions seems to be decisive here.
[22] A concise overview of sources for the study of archaic Megara can be found in Okin (1985). Cf. recently Robu (2014).
[23] Cf. e.g., Figueira (1985) esp. 297–298.
[24] Kritzas (1987) 65–67, 70–71. However, he does not exclude a later historical context for our inscription (pp. 67–70). Taking into consideration the dating of the ostrakon discussed here to (approximately) the end of the fifth century BC, and on the other hand the political history of Megara in classical times, which was full of dramatic breakthroughs, it seems most probable that ostracism was introduced in this *polis* at the latest possible point close to the inscription's dating, namely in the years 427–424 BC.

It is worth adding that, unfortunately, as in the case of Argos, in the area of ancient Megara, highly eroded throughout centuries, we should not expect abundant future finds which would confirm the existence of ostracism in this *polis*.²⁵

From the hypothetical testimonies of ostracism in mainland Greece and in relative proximity to Athens, let us move on to more remote regions of the 'small Greek world', beginning our presentation of material with Africa and the Black Sea basin. The next place where ostracism functioned seems to be, quite surprisingly, Cyrene.²⁶ In 1994 Lidiano Bacchielli published nine ostraka found the year before in an open stratigraphic context near an altar dating to the mid-fifth century BC. The ostraka were in the layer of material that had served to raise the level of the Cyrenaic agora in Hellenistic times. Six ostraka bear the name of Praxidas son of Zenis, and their discovery enabled a better identification of three further 'ostraka of Praxidas' found earlier (altogether nos. 1–9 in Bacchielli's list). The remaining ostraka of the new series bear inscriptions of Philon son of Lysis (no. 10) and two other preserved in a worse state and reconstructed only partially: [Ἀ]ρίστιπ[πος] | [Δ]αμο[—] (no. 11) and Πειθαγό[ρας] | Εὔκ (no. 12). Palaeographic considerations seem to support dating these inscriptions to the second half of the fifth century BC. However, since we learn from Thucydides (VII 50) that Cyrene militarily supported the expedition of the Spartan commander Gylippos in 413 BC, Bacchielli dates the functioning of the democratic (as he emphasises) institution of ostracism to the times of the struggle between oligarchs and democrats in Cyrene, which we hear about from Diodorus (XIV 34, 4–6; cf. Arist. *Pol.* 1319b 15–23), and thus to the years 413–401 BC. As in the previous cases, I am not sure about all of the arguments in the detailed historical interpretation of the (hypothetical) ostracism in Cyrene.²⁷ However, what is sufficient for me is to conclude that its possible traces are not earlier than the second half of the fifth century BC.

---

²⁵ Another object worth attention comes from Megalopolis in Arcadia, where a triangular terracotta tablet has been found with the name Ξενοπείθης Λ[εον]ίδαυ, dated to the end of the fourth or the beginning of the third century BC. Due to the lack of literary evidence for ostracism in Megalopolis, the form of the object (an intentionally made tablet, and not a random potsherd) as well as the chronology of the find, which is 100 years later than the last instance of application of ostracism in Athens, Ulla Kreilinger interprets this object as a 'tool' used in some lottery procedure, a 'ticket' to a local theatre, or a tablet identifying a member of the Assembly. See Kreilinger (1995) [1997] 383–385.

²⁶ See Bacchielli (1994). Cf. SEG XLIV nos. 1, 2, 3, 4, respectively.

²⁷ Surikov (2000) 109 claims that ostracism was introduced in Cyrene after 440 BC, following the fall of the last monarch, Arcesilaus III, most probably without any connection to Athenian ostracism.

The most problematic but also the most interesting is the case of Tauric Chersonesos.[28] For a long time, scholars were convinced that this colony was established by the citizens of Heraclea Pontica (with the participation of the Delians) in the last quarter of the fifth century BC, but the excavations of the last three decades, including the discovery in the north-eastern part of the city of an archaic cult space (most probably dedicated to Apollo) dated to the end of the sixth century BC,[29] proved that it must have happened 100 years earlier.[30]

These findings may have considerable bearing on the reconstruction of the history of ostracism in the Greek world because so far as many as 45 ostraka, some of them closely resembling the Athenian ones, are known to us from Tauric Chersonesos.[31] The inscriptions on most of them give us

---

[28] Hansen, Nielsen (2004) no. 695 (chapter by Alexandru Avram, John Hind, and Gocha Tsetskhladze).

[29] Giugni (2004) 39. Cf. Avram (2009) 212, with bibliography listed there, in n. 25.

[30] An additional argument supporting this thesis has been proposed by Vinogradov, Zolotarev (1999) 120–125 on the basis of a passage in Ps.-Skymnos (828–834 and 822–827 *GGM* = fr. 12 Marcotte), who mentions a joint colonisation venture of the Heracleans and the Delians, as well as a remark in Thucydides (IV 104, 1–2) about the ritual purification of Delos by Pisistratus, which both the scholars date between 529/528 and 528/527 BC. According to Vinogradov and Zolotarev, the participation of the Delian 'fugitives' makes it possible to date the *ktisis* of Chersonesos to the time directly following this event, which means exactly to the year 528/527 BC. This line of thought is criticised by Bravo (2000) 98–99, n. 66, pointing out the insecurity of the dating of the Delian purification and, most importantly, the fact that in Thucydides' account there is no mention of expulsion of the island's inhabitants. Pisistratus' order was only to remove graves from the area visible from the sanctuary of Apollo. However, Bravo accepts the general dating of Tauric Chersonesos's establishment to the last decades of the sixth century BC. Another important element of Vinogradov and Zolotarev's hypothesis is the participation in the *ktisis* of Chersonesos of a group of Milesians (regarded by Strabo as the initial colonists of Heraclea Pontica; see below, n. 43), which would explain a certain number of Ionian names on the ostraka from Chersonesos discussed below. Avram (2009) 216 ascribes the Ionian element of the onomastics in Chersonesos to a hypothetical participation in the enterprise not of Milesians but of a group of citizens of Sinope (one of the Ionian names on the ostraka nos. 18–21, Kretines son of Mys, could belong to a descendant of Kretines mentioned by Ps.-Skymnos [l. 949–950 *GGM* = fr. 27.8-9 Marcotte] as the founder of Sinope).

[31] See Vinogradov, Zolotarev (1990) 103–109; Vinogradov (1997) 412–419 (partial catalogues of ostraka in two only slightly different versions of the same article) and Vinogradov, Zolotarev (1999), where their more comprehensive edition is announced, which was prevented by the untimely death of Jurij G. Vinogradov. Cf. Dubois in *BE* (2000), no. 487. See also *SEG* XXXIV (1984) 751; *SEG* XXXVII (1987) 654 (where ostraka are still interpreted as 'ballots' for magistrate voting; thus initially Vinogradov (1997) 406, and in the earlier version of the article Vinogradov, Zolotarev (1990) 94–95, questioning the original interpretation of these ostraka as 'tools' of ostracism by Solomonik (1976) 123–124, who dates this material to the fourth century BC; Robu (2014) 98–99 considers with hesitation the possibility that they were 'ballots' for magistrate voting or some court procedures; *SEG* XL (1990) 612. The most up-to-date list of ostraka of the ostracism in Chersonesos is provided, as far as I know, by Giugni (2004) 44–64, whose comprehensive catalogue is much more convenient to use than the partial (and organised according to the dialects of the names occurring on the ostraka) catalogues in the successive

(often only restored) names in the nominative or names in the nominative with a patronymic in the genitive, but several ostraka show similarities with the Athenian ones going much beyond the simple presence of a personal name with a patronymic.³² The most symptomatic is the case of ostrakon no. 34 in Erica Giugni's catalogue, mentioning a person identified as Αἴσχρων Διονυσίο Ἐχεδαμίδος. Taking into consideration the (relative) frequency of the occurrence of the 'candidate's' *demotikon* on Athenian ostraka, the editors believe that we are witnessing a similar practice here; in Chersonesos it would be referring to the division of the citizen body into the so-called *hekatostyes* ('hundreds'), which in Heraclea Pontica coexisted with the traditional Doric *phylai*.³³ The inscription on ostrakon no. 32 has only the ending of the name -αγό]ρης preserved, which was accompanied, as on some of the Athenian ostraka,³⁴ with a short imperative ἴτ[ω, 'let him go'. On a fragmentarily preserved ostrakon no. 15 the name is lost to us, but we have instead a sequence of letters that can perhaps be reconstructed as the vulgar κ]αταπ[ύγōν ('faggot'),³⁵ which we also find on the offensive Athenian ostrakon directed at Themistocles (*Kerameikos* 20.2, 7262 = O 7490; cf. Siewert T 1/150). On ostrakon no. 33, in turn, there is the following inscription: Κοτυτί]ωμ πόρνας | ἔραται τας | νέας, which says (most probably in Doric dialect) no more and no less than, 'Kotytion has a young [new?] harlot'.³⁶ A 'vote' of this sort in an *ostrakophoria* procedure resembles the famous

---

publications by Vinogradov and Zolotarev. The numbering of ostraka used below will be following Erica Giugni. This catalogue, however, includes only 40 objects; about the remaining five ostraka I have no knowledge apart from the fact that they exist.

³² For two fragmentary graffiti (ostraka nos. 30 and 31), if we accept their restoration by Vinogradov, Zolotarev (1999) 118–119 ([ὁ δεῖνα φυγὰ]ς ἀλλὰ χαίρ[ετε]), an indirect, 'retrospective' connection with *ostrakophoria* has been suggested by Giugni (2004) 58, wherein the citizens of Chersonesos would be able to express their contentment or approval of their previous decision. However, it seems more likely that both of these graffiti were simply particularly sophisticated 'votes' in the *ostrakophoria* procedure (the reconstructed formula must have been preceded by a name of the 'candidate', clearly indicating the decision of the voter), which took the form of a peculiar 'spell' to ensure the desired result of the voting.

³³ Cf. Aeneas Tacticus, *Poliorc.* 11,10a. For general information about this *polis* see Hansen, Nielsen (2004) no. 715 and Robu (2014) 293–310. Comprehensively on *hekatostyes* see Robu (2014) 339–360.

³⁴ See below, p. 219 n. 59.

³⁵ This term occurs also in comedy: Ar. *Ach.* 79 and *Vesp.* 687 (see also Pollux, 6.126). On the vulgar word reconstructed here see Dover (1989) 141–144 and Robson (2013) Index, s.v. *katapygōn, kinaidos*, and 'wide-arsed'. However, it should be noted that the editors of *SEG* XL (1990) 612.14 regard this reconstruction as too hazardous and confine themselves to reading there only [–]ατα Π(or O).

³⁶ *SEG* XXXVII (1987) 661. The first editor of the ostrakon, Solomonik (1987) 125–129, interpreted this inscription as a private letter.

Athenian ostrakon (*Kerameikos* 20.2, 3773 = O 2514; Siewert T 1/106) with the inscription, 'Megakles son of Hippocrates, adulterer (*moichos*)'.[37] Having said all that, one should not press such analogies too far, since they all seem fully natural in purely human, or behavioural terms, without even postulating a close connection between the Athenian and the Chersonesian institutions.

Still, the ostraka from Tauric Chersonesos constitute the most extensive corpus of *ostrakophoria* 'tools' next to the Athenian one. Therefore, one can dismiss the fact that no ancient source mentions the functioning of ostracism in this *polis*.[38]

Nevertheless, the ostraka of Chersonesian *ostrakophoriai* present a serious problem because their chronology turns out to be highly disputable (see below, however). They certainly belong to a very long period whose chronological framework cannot be properly established. This is primarily due to the fact that the material of most of the Chersonesian ostraka comes from modest black-glossed vessels and amphorae sherds dated by analogy with these very vessels.[39] In other words, we are dealing with ceramics that cannot be precisely dated. This situation is aggravated by the fact that what is at stake in the discussion on the placement of these ostraka on a timeline is the credibility of the hypothesis about the early establishment of Tauric Chersonesos as a *polis* (see above). Jurij Vinogradov and Michail Zolotarev opt for a very early dating of our ostraka, spanning the entire fifth century BC, beginning with the first decades (500–480 BC), when a considerable number of these objects would have been produced, which serves well their dating of Chersonesos beginnings. Meanwhile, Siergiej Ju. Saprykin dates the ostraka to the first half of the fifth century. Without a detailed discussion of the epigraphic material, he ascribes them to an earlier 'Ionian settlement', which the colonists from Heraclea Pontica would later annihilate.

---

[37] On the above similarities with the Athenian ostraka see already Vinogradov, Zolotarev (1999) 118–119.

[38] Curiously, Aristotle does not write about this either, in spite of referring several times to *staseis* in Heraclea Pontica, the *metropolis* of Chersonesos, in his *Politics*: Arist. *Pol.* 1304b 31–34; 1305b 5–13; 34–37; 1306a 33–1306b 2. See also below.

[39] Irene Polinskaya suggests to me *per litteras* (8 Nov. 2021) 'that body sherds of undecorated black-glossed vessels range widely in date, from the 6th to the 3rd centuries BCE, and that small body sherds of amphorae are also hard to date because the shape (of the whole vessel) is unknown and the fabric (typically used for provenance) is not always possible to determine with certainty'.

John Hind, in turn, unconvincingly excludes their connection with ostracism altogether,[40] placing them as late as the end of the fifth and in the fourth century BC.[41] Both Saprykin and Hind, of course, support the thesis about a late foundation of Chersonesos as a *polis* (with an earlier functioning of a small *emporion* on its spot).[42] Incidentally, let us point out that although the efforts of Vinogradov and Zolotarev to date our ostraka as early as possible are not always convincing (see below), the fact that these ostraka constitute a coherent 'corpus' and were produced during several decades of the fifth century BC suffices for the thesis of a late foundation of Chersonesos to be dismissed. This excludes not only the possibility of a radical demographic and/or political shift, which would have to accompany the destruction of the (hypothetical) Ionian *emporion* by invaders from the Doric Heraclea in the last quarter of the fifth century BC, but also of any peaceful change of this community's status from *emporion* to *polis*.

When asking the question about the dating and genesis of the Chersonesian ostracism, we have to take into consideration the (doubtful) connections of this *polis* with Miletus, the alleged *metropolis* of Heraclea Pontica, which was, in turn, the *metropolis* of Tauric Chersonesos.[43] The scholion to Aristophanes' *Knights* quoted at the beginning of this section

---

[40] See Saprykin (1991) 230–233 and (very similar in form) Saprykin (1998) 232 and *passim*; similarly Zedgenidze (1993); Hind (1998) 143, with n. 57 (it should be highlighted that the author relates the scholarly discussion on the dating of our ostraka in a very unclear and chaotic way: '[...] the series of 26 ostraka of the early 5th century BC is now believed to be more likely to be [sic!] a group of private graffiti on pots also of the late 5th and 4th centuries'). Avram (2009) 213, surprisingly, returns to the earlier hypothesis that the ostraka discussed here were 'ballots' rather than 'tools' of ostracism (see above, n. 31), supporting the thesis about the original status of the sixth-century Chersonesos as an *emporion* (common to Sinope and Heraclea Pontica), which would become a *polis* only after 424 BC (the expedition of Lamachos and the Athenians against Heraclea/Sinope) as a result of colonisation by the Heracleans and the Boeotians (from Delion?). For Avram agrees with Hind (1998) 145, who feels it necessary to correct the 'Delians' in Ps.-Skymnos, ll. 824 and 827 GGM (= fr. 12 Marcotte) to 'citizens of Delion' in Boeotia (see testimonies about this 'town', *polichnion*, in Hansen, Nielsen (2004) 433).

[41] Solomonik (1976) 121–124 dated the ostraka in question to the fourth and the beginning of the third century BC.

[42] The hypothesis of the initial status as an *emporion* is based on the earliest literary mention of this community by Ps.-Scylax (GGM, 68), who refers to the Tauric Chersonesos in this manner. His *Periplous* was written in the times of Alexander the Great, but it is believed that the information on the Black Sea coast reaches back to earlier times, most probably around 500 BC. However, Benedetto Bravo pointed out to me the general imprecision of this work with regard to political systems. The term *emporion* may simply indicate the existence of a commercial port there, where ships could dock during a sea journey.

[43] According to an isolated mention in Strabo, XII 3, 4 (C. 542) (following Theopompus? Cf. FGrHist 115 F 388); the commentary on this fragment by William S. Morison in the BNJ edition is, unfortunately, very cursory: Morison (2014), the initial *metropolis* was Miletus. See, however, the recent discussion on the issue of *ktisis* of Heraclea Pontica in the article by Avram (2009)

mentions the existence, otherwise unattested, of ostracism in Miletus. If we leave aside the isolated remark by Strabo (see above, n. 43), the colonists of Heraclea around 560–550 BC were Boeotians and Megarians;[44] additionally, the ostrakon analysed above has been found in Megara (also mentioned in our scholion), perhaps coming from a local *ostrakophoria*. Therefore, if we dated, following Vinogradov and Zolotarev, the earliest ostraka from Chersonesos to the turn of the fifth century, that is almost contemporarily with Cleisthenes' reforms and nearly a generation before the first attested *ostrakophoria* in Athens,[45] we would have to exclude Athenian inspirations of the Chersonesian ostracism and seek its origins in the Ionian Miletus or the Dorian Megara.[46] Alternatively, we would have to propose a more general hypothesis that in archaic Greece, there existed rituals that constituted a common source of ostracisms and similar institutions attested in various parts of the Greek world.[47] These hypotheses, however, share a logical flaw: they assume that a long-term independent evolution in regions as remote from each other as Attica and Crimea led to the functioning in both these places and at the same time of institutions and procedures whose archaeological testimonies (the ostraka from Athens and Tauric Chersonesos) are very much alike. This seems to me to be hardly probable in principle, even though it cannot be excluded.[48]

On the other hand, it should be noted that, due to the impossibility of precisely dating the ceramic sherds with inscriptions discussed here,[49] Vinogradov and Zolotarev base their dating of the earliest (according to them) ostraka from Chersonesos on rather weak palaeographic arguments,

---

210–211. In his view, this is Strabo's mistake, who confused his notes on Sinope with 'jottings' on Heraclea, and the Ionian toponyms on the *chora* of this *polis* pointed out by scholars come from the time of pre-colonial exploration of this region by the citizens of Sinope.

[44] Testimonies may be found in Bravo (2009) 183. Bravo (2009) esp. 224–225 argues that Apollodoros, in his *Chronicle*, which was used by Ps.-Skymnos, dated the *ktisis* of Heraclea to 554/553 or 553/552 BC.

[45] For discussion see below, 2.1.

[46] Surikov (2000) 108–109 emphasises that ostracisms are strikingly well-represented in Doric regions: Argos, Megara, Cyrene, and Tauric Chersonesos. On ostracism in Miletus, most probably introduced following the Athenian paradigm, see above, n. 5.

[47] On such hypotheses see below, 1.1.2, 1.2.2, and 1.2.3.

[48] The similarities in 'substance' between the content of Athenian and Chersonesian ostraka could, on the one hand, be regarded as trivial, but on the other hand, it could be assumed that the Athenian paradigm had an impact on the ostracism in Tauric Chersonesos at a later point, in the fifth century.

[49] Archaeological problems with such an early dating of these vessel sherds, and particularly the inconsistencies in the dating method applied by Vinogradov and Zolotarev in establishing the chronology of these ostraka, have been briefly discussed by Zedgenidze (1993).

claiming that the three-bar sigma[50] and the letter *chi* in the form of a cross, which occur in Tauric Chersonesos, allow us, by analogy with the letterforms known from Megara of around 500–475 BC, to date some of the Chersonesian inscriptions to 500–480 BC. However, as Siergiej R. Tokhtasyev has demonstrated,[51] these two scholars entirely omitted in their considerations two later Megarian inscriptions (dated to 480–470 and 475–450 BC, respectively), which bear even closer similarity to the Chersonesian ones. It cannot be excluded, therefore, that the letterforms which Vinogradov and Zolotarev regarded as symptomatic for the beginning of the fifth century were present in Megara Nisaia (and in the area remaining under the influence of its script) until the end of that century, that is until the time when the Megarians adopted the Ionian script. Tokhtasyev also emphasises that the idea of using the three-bar sigma as a 'dating' letter must arouse doubts in itself because this letter began to be used in Megara most probably under the influence of the Attic script. Hence, he argues that the earliest Chersonesian ostraka cannot be earlier than 480–450 BC.[52]

Therefore, if following Tokhtasyev, we regarded Vinogradov and Zolotarev's dating of the earliest ostraka as going too far back,[53] we could assume that the Chersonesian ostracism was inspired by the Athenian model, which would better explain the close similarities between the ostraka from Chersonesos and Athens. Dating the historical moment of this

---

[50] For the conclusions of the famous debate regarding 'the three-bar sigma criterion' in Attic epigraphy (conveniently summarised, with relevant bibliography, in Polinskaya (2009), 234 with n. 11-13), see in general Rhodes (2008) and Papazarkadas (2009).

[51] Tokhtasyev (2007). It should be highlighted here that this scholar regards as absolutely unjustified the attempts, so crucial to Vinogradov and Zolotarev's theory, to make historical inferences from the dialectal forms of names found on the ostraka in question (e.g., Vinogradov, Zolotarev (1999) 129–131). Similarly, L. Dubois, *BE* (1991), no. 420. As Dubois and Tokhtasyev emphasise, only four out of all the names on the 45 Chersonesian ostraka have clearly Doric features, and only three display indisputably Ionian features. The remaining names are dialectally ambiguous. Drawing conclusions regarding the successive stages of Tauric Chersonesos colonisation from such feeble data appears very hazardous indeed.

[52] Tokhtasyev (2007) 116–124. Two later inscriptions referred to by the scholar are a funerary epigram of Pollis from Megara (*SEG* XLV [1995] 421) of around 480–470 BC and (most probably) a Megarian inscription from Olympia (*LSAG*² p. 442: 'Bronze arm-band dedicated to Demeter Ktonia') of around 475–450 BC.

[53] Marcin Matera, specialising in the ceramics of this region, is inclined to date (*per litteras*) the entire corpus of amphorae on whose sherds the graffiti of Chersonesian ostracism were scratched to the time between the end of the first half of the fifth century and the end of that century, and the material from the north-eastern part of the city, where the ceramics published by Vinogradov and Zolotarev comes from, to the second and third quarter of the fifth century BC. Moreover, Matera pointed out to me that the Attic black-glossed vessels in this area (which carry the majority of the graffiti connected with ostracism) were treated as objects of considerable value, mended and used for a long time: 'Given that, the secondary use of fragments of these vessels could have taken place long after their production.'

borrowing to the times shortly after the first Athenian *ostrakophoria* is not an issue here. Having applied *ostrakophoria* for the first time in 488/487 BC, the Athenians kept resorting to it annually for five consecutive years (with only one year's gap), which must have made a remarkable impression on the Greek world. In any case, thanks to the testimony in Pindar's *Pythian* VII (ll. 18–21) of 486 BC, we know that the poet was able to use in his work already the second *ostrakophoria*, the exile of Megakles son of Hippocrates from Athens, as a fact commonly known to his Panhellenic audience.[54]

However, even if the hypothesis about the Athenian inspirations for Chersonesian ostracism is accepted, the exceptionality of this case is undeniable. Although, as we remember, several *poleis* rendered only isolated ostraka (for instance, Argos and Megara), based on which it is difficult to formulate any firm historical conclusions, it seems that in places where our knowledge is slightly more detailed or the historical framework of the possible ostracisms more defined (see above on Cyrene and below on Thurii and Sicilian Naxos) we are dealing with exceptional and ephemeral phenomena.[55] The case of Chersonesos is distinct not only, and not even principally, due to the number of ostraka found there so far and their similarity to the Athenian ones, but rather due to their wide chronological distribution. It seems that they were used from a certain point in the second quarter of the fifth century until the end of that century. It testifies to the frequency and persistence of ostracism in Tauric Chersonesos and—what is more—it roughly corresponds to the period of the use of *ostrakophoriai* in Athens.

If we were tempted to diagnose this striking phenomenon, the following hypothesis seems worthwhile. Let us assume that Tauric Chersonesos was established in the last quarter of the sixth century BC in the process of colonisation by a group from among the *dēmos* of Heraclea Pontica, fleeing from aristocrats returning from exile, and perhaps managed by leaders whom Aristotle calls 'demagogues' (comp. Arist. *Pol.* 1304b 31–34).[56] If so, this experience of turbulent *stasis* in Heraclea might have induced the citizens of the new *polis* to seek a lasting means of preventing problems that the colonists were escaping. Such an opportunity arose in the second generation of Chersonesos' history, when information about the first Athenian ostracisms began circulating in the Greek world. It should be

---

[54] See also commentary to Siewert, T 2 (= Siewert, pp. 167–170). Cf. above, p. 6.
[55] See also my preliminary conclusions at the end of this section.
[56] Cf. Vinogradov, Zolotarev (1999) 125–128.

noted that the political revolutions in Heraclea summarised by Aristotle were taking place in the rhythm of exile and return of strong groups of notable citizens (*gnōrimoi*) removed from the *polis* by the *dēmos* and its leaders. The use of ostracism in Chersonesos would be intended to prevent such incidents.[57]

Let us move now to the western regions of the Greek world.[58] A chronologically most recent series of archaeological discoveries fortuitous for the scholars of ostracism happened during the excavation campaign of 2009 in Thurii, and an intriguing find was published by Emanuele Greco almost immediately.[59] The object found was an ostrakon firmly dated— both by palaeographic features and thanks to its clear archaeological context—to the last decades of the fifth century BC.[60] On this sherd was inscribed in three lines a name in the nominative with the patronym in the genitive: Χάρων| Ἀγάθω|νος. Thurii, as a (formally speaking, Panhellenic) colony of Athens, fits perfectly as a follower of Athenian ostracism, and the tumultuous history of this *polis* might have induced its citizens to reach for the Athenian paradigm when facing successive internal struggles or disputes.[61] Neither can it be excluded that the *polis*, founded according to a plan and with the participation of distinguished intellectuals of the time, from the very beginning had the Athenian mechanism of ostracism 'inbuilt'. In Greco's view, the most probable historical context of *ostrakophoria* in Thurii is, nevertheless, the short period when the pro-Athenian faction prevailed in this *polis* in 415–413 BC, before the final defeat of the Athenians in Sicily.[62] Slightly more cautiously, it can be stated that the only evident caesura in the chronology of the (hypothetical) ostracism in Thurii

---

[57] A bit similarly Vinogradov, Zolotarev (1999) 125–128, who, nevertheless, date the beginning of ostracism in Chersonesos to the time immediately after the foundation of this *polis*. The presentation of Chersonesian ostraka and the general historical considerations based on them are repeated by Vinogradov in an article published only posthumously: Vinogradov (2001). Cf. also below (1.1.2) on Sara Forsdyke's 'politics of expulsion'.

[58] Solomonik (1976) 123, n. 13 cites L.D. Dmitrov's statement (*Нариси стародавньої історії Української РСР*, Kiev 1957, p. 274, *non vidi*) that ostraka with citizen names, indicating the functioning of ostracism, have been found also in Tyras; she emphasises, however, that she has been unable to trace this material.

[59] Greco (2010).   [60] Greco (2010) 98–100.

[61] The dramatic history of Thurii is succinctly summarised, with accompanying most recent bibliography, by Greco (2010) 100–101 and Giangiulio (2015) 115–128. See also Berger (1989) 310–312. Ehrenberg (1948) 166–169 makes interesting observations on the Periclean system of the democratic Thurii, and on its relationship with the Athenian paradigm.

[62] Greco (2010) 101.

is the date (once vividly discussed in scholarship) of the establishment of this settlement in 444/443 BC.[63]

Sicilian Naxos has been the site of another unexpected discovery. In 2001, during excavations in the naval arsenal (*neōrion* or *neōria*) of this *polis*, four ostraka from the fifth century BC were found. The broader archaeological context of this find is the second and last stage of the extension works in the *neōria* of Naxos, carried out between 460 and 403 BC, the year when the city and its walls were destroyed by Dionysius I. Interestingly, the four ostraka from Naxos, following the classic formula of Athenian ostracism (name in the nominative and the patronym in the genitive), bring us the names of only two figures. Two ostraka mention Dexiles son of Anthos (nos. 1 and 2), and the inscriptions on the other two bear the name of Hegestratos son of Telesarchos (nos. 2 and 3). The archaeological context and the lettering of ostrakon no. 1 allow us to date it more precisely, to the times soon after the year 430 BC, and Maria Costanza Lentini, who has been directing excavations there for many years, proposed a very compelling hypothesis that all the four ostraka may come from the same *ostrakophoria*.[64]

The most famous institution close to Athenian ostracism is probably *petalismos* from the nearby Syracuse. Our primary source here is Diodorus (XI 86,4–87,6),[65] who gives an account of its introduction in reaction to the unrest connected with a certain Tyndarides and his followers, seeking tyrannical power. Diodorus dates this situation to 454/453 BC,[66] but the remark about the 'frequently' (*pleonakis*) recurring events of this sort makes his chronology a bit fluid there.

To curb the aspirations of potential tyrants in the future, the Syracusan *dēmos*, following the Athenians, resorted to introducing a law similar to the Athenian law of ostracism (86,5). Unlike in Athens, where the name of the person suspected of tyrannical inclinations was written on ostraka, the Syracusans wrote the name of 'the most powerful citizen' on an olive tree

---

[63] After the *stasis*, which resulted in the former inhabitants, the Sybarites, losing their hitherto dominating position. Hansen, Nielsen (2004) no. 74 (chapter by Tobias Fischer-Hansen, Thomas H. Nielsen, and Carmine Ampolo; *ibidem*, p. 306: on the political changes in Thurii). Cf. also the classic article by Ehrenberg (1948).

[64] Schirripa, Lentini, Cordano (2012) 134–146, with phot. 9–12 (part of the article by Lentini).

[65] Cf. Hesychius, *Lex.* Π 2044 ed. Latte–Hansen, *s.v. pet[t]alismos* and Π 2041, *s.v. petal[l]a*. See also Hommel (1938).

[66] Briefly on the historical context of these events Giangiulio (2015) 80–89; Berger (1989) 304–305, and before him Hüttl (1929) 65–71.

leaf (*petalon*),⁶⁷ and the citizen indicated by the (simple) majority of such leaves went into five-year-long exile (87,1).⁶⁸ In Syracuse, this institution was called *petalismos* (87,2 *ad fin.*). Unlike in Athens, where the law of ostracism remained in force 'for a long time', it was quickly (*tachy*) repealed (87,3). The subsequent part of Diodorus' account seems to be his moralising and 'psychologising' interpretation of the effects of the functioning of 'petalism'. After 'the most powerful men' were exiled, the most distinguished citizens, potentially able to serve the *polis* best (which most probably means members of the Syracusan élite), in fear of this law, avoided public activity and devoted themselves to private matters, thus falling into idleness. Meanwhile, 'the most worthless people' (*hoi ponērotatoi*) and the most insolent among citizens were holding public offices, inciting the multitude (*ta plēthē*) to unrest and disorder (87,4). For this reason, *staseis* broke out again and the *polis* was in constant trouble. The worst role was played by numerous demagogues and sycophants, now prevailing in Syracuse, while the Syracusan youth enthusiastically dedicated themselves to rhetorical skills practice. The regard for harmony and justice among citizens disappeared entirely (87,5). That is why the Syracusans rescinded the law of 'petalism', having used it for only a short time (*oligon chronon*) (87,6).

I have summarised Diodorus' account so extensively because some of its details, going beyond the rhetorical *topoi*, will be useful in further considerations. Here I shall highlight only two elements. First, the connection between the functioning of *petalismos* in Syracuse and the activity of demagogues and sycophants as well as the flourishing of the art of rhetoric, which seems to testify to the existence there (analogically to Athens) of a two-stage procedure, in which the option of petalism was first discussed at the Assembly, and the voting with olive leaves occurred only at a later stage.⁶⁹ Secondly, the obvious implication of Diodorus' account, namely

---

⁶⁷ Federica Cordano has recently tried to undermine this consistent ancient tradition, suggesting that the Syracusans might have used lead 'leaves' (this meaning of the word *petalon* is well attested in magical texts of later times) in this procedure. See Schirripa, Lentini, Cordano (2012) 148–149 (with n. 88), where Cordano supports her interpretation with the authority of Pierre Chantraine, admitting at the same time that *DELG*, s.v. *petannymi* relates the etymology of the term *petalismos* to a word meaning 'leaf'. Cordano's interpretation does not seem convincing to me; first, because an important feature of voting of this kind in the entire Greek world where we find traces of *ostrakophoria* was the use of objects which are widely available and of improvised character. Secondly, the analogy with the Athenian *ekphyllophoria* (see below, 1.2.2) seems to be decisive here, even if we do not allow for any historical connection between the two institutions.
⁶⁸ For the Athenian case, see below, 3.3.2.
⁶⁹ A slightly similar view was expressed already by Hüttl (1929) 69.

that in Syracuse, where this law remained in force only for a short time,[70] *petalismos* was used very intensively. As I have already mentioned, Diodorus' chronology is not clear here, but it can be inferred that petalism was resorted to at least once each year, which means that the *dēmos* voted for the carrying out of this procedure every time.[71] Despite the analogies with Athens and the Athenian source of inspiration for the *petalismos* law, stressed by Diodorus, it is precisely here—as we shall see further in this chapter—where the most significant difference between this practice and the Athenian ostracism lies.[72] In most general terms, in Syracuse, a law similar to and (hypothetically) inspired by the Athenian one brought about results quite the opposite to the intended, stimulating *stasis* and political instability instead of preventing them, due to the dissimilarities in political circumstances, but above all to the habitude of the *dēmos* and—crucially—of its leaders being different than in Athens. More specifically, if Diodorus is to be trusted, the result of this institution's functioning was not only the exile of the leaders of the local aristocracy but also an 'internal emigration' of its considerable part. In other words, the Syracusan 'ostracism' immediately slipped out of the local political and social élite's control. Maurizio Giangiulio has recently observed that while in Athens ostracism was considered by the entire citizen body as a proper political mechanism, in Syracuse, torn by political and social divisions, it must have been from the very beginning only a tool of *stasis*, an instrument of political struggle against the 'enemies of the people'.[73]

Drawing tentative conclusions from Diodorus' account to be used in my considerations, I should point out three issues. First, as in several previous cases, but unlike in the case of Tauric Chersonesos, the time of imitating the Athenian ostracism law does not reach back further than mid-fifth century BC. Secondly, as in many previous cases (but not in Chersonesos), it was a short-lived experiment, and we know thanks to Diodorus that it was

---

[70] Pace, e.g., Mitchell (2016) 86, who seems to ascribe to *petalismos* Hermocrates' summary banishment 'by the people', in 411 or 410 BC, alongside other Syracusan *stratēgoi* (Xen. I 1,27; cf. Thuc. VIII 85,3). For the hypothetical context of this banishment, see Beloch (1931) 246, who associates it with a Syracusan 'Verbannungsdekret'.

[71] If in turn we understand the 'short time' as a period of only one or at most two or three years, we could conclude that petalism was practised with frequency greater than annual. This, however, does not seem very likely. Hüttl (1929) 68/69, n. 15 claims that in his account Diodorus 'blended' the multi-annual history of *petalismos* in Syracuse, ascribing it incorrectly to a single year.

[72] It should also be noted that the duration of the exile is shorter than in Athens; cf. below, 3.3.2.

[73] Giangiulio (2015) 86.

unsuccessful.⁷⁴ Thirdly, if the Athenian sources of *petalismos* are accepted as a proven fact,⁷⁵ a hypothesis may be posited that in their decision to realise the quite exotic idea to use olive leaves,⁷⁶ the Syracusan lawgivers were inspired simultaneously by two (slightly similar at any rate) procedures in Athenian democracy, namely ostracism and the so-called *ekphyllophoria*, or the exclusion of a council member from among the Council of Five Hundred through voting precisely with olive leaves, also in a two-stage procedure.⁷⁷

Based on the cases of Syracuse, Taras and Thurii, Shlomo Berger has concluded that the Western Greek democracies of the fifth century were inspired by the Athenian model, which they, however, adapted in the next phase (often changing considerably) to the local conditions and particular needs of each *polis*.⁷⁸ Syracusan *petalismos* seems to confirm this observation. Unfortunately, we know nothing about the history of ostracism in Thurii or Naxos, apart from what can be inferred through analysis from the few *ostraka* discussed above.

*

In most general terms, Aristotle's words about the use of ostracism 'in some places' in the Greek world, which until recently scholars have been reluctant to believe, turn out to be true. We have already found out about six *poleis* so

---

⁷⁴ It is tempting to add here that it did not discourage, as it appears, other (including neighbouring) followers of ostracism. In Thurii ostracism was introduced 10 years after the Syracusan *petalismos* at the earliest (and possibly even 40 years later), and in Sicilian Naxos around a generation after the Syracusan experiment at the latest.

⁷⁵ Some connection between *petalismos* in Syracuse and ostracism was postulated already by Wilamowitz (as quoted by the editor of *IG* XII,5 595 A, F. Hiller von Gaertringen). Another possibility would be to regard this peculiar fact as a trace of some local idiosyncrasy, a continuation of some earlier Syracusan customs. However, we know nothing about any such thing, and I suppose that local Sicilian historians of the classical times would not miss the opportunity to record such information, which Diodorus' sources and the historian himself would certainly cite. It should be noted that Diodorus was so deeply convinced of the connection between *petalismos* and ostracism in Athens that, when writing about the latter, he reflexively ascribed to the Athenian institution the exile duration of the Syracusan one (D.S. XI 55,2).

⁷⁶ Berger (1989) 305, who accepts the Athenian sources of inspiration for this Syracusan institution, regards the application of such 'tools' in Syracuse as an argument supporting the thesis of a ritual character of *petalismos*, which would be performed annually, at the occasion of the festival of Zeus Eleutherios. However, we do not have any information about it in the available sources. Although Diodorus (XI 72,2) extensively relates the decision of the Syracusan Assembly to institute an annual festival of this deity (with impressive hecatombs) and to erect a colossal statue of Zeus, he does it in connection with the introduction of democracy after the abolition of Thrasybulus' tyranny, an event preceding the introduction of *petalismos* in Syracuse by 10 years.

⁷⁷ On this procedure see further, 1.2.2. Giugni (2004) 19 also sees some connection between *petalismos* and *ekphyllophoria*.

⁷⁸ Berger (1989) esp. 312–314.

far for which ostracism is archaeologically attested. Two out of which (more about this in a moment) bear far-reaching analogies to the material context of this institution in Athens.

Some scholars have been induced to regard Athenian ostracism as only one of many possible examples of an older practice, widely spread throughout archaic Greece, first by Vinogradov and Zolotarev's very early dating of the earliest ostraka from Tauric Chersonesos, and secondly by certain general comparative considerations, which I shall critique in sections 1.2.1 and 1.2.3. Here I shall only emphasise that the revision of the early dating of the Chersonesian material removes the most important and most substantial argument for the existence of a (hypothetical) Panhellenic practice of using ostraka to 'indict' or rather to 'indicate' a citizen of the *polis* in a quasi-judicial political procedure.

Apart from the cases of Argos and Tauric Chersonesos, none of the communities analysed above shows archaeological traces of the existence of ostracism before the middle, or even the last two decades, of the fifth century BC. This encourages the assumption a priori that all these local variants originate in the Athenian paradigm, well-known all over the Greek world.[79] I have already discussed above the exceptional case of Tauric Chersonesos, concluding that the hypothesis of the Athenian inspirations of ostracism there—at least equally probable as the opposite thesis—better explains the close similarity between the Chersonesian and the Athenian ostraka. This seems to be supported by the analogical material context of the sherds found in various parts of the Greek world. It should be remembered that the exceptional abundance of ostraka found in the Agora, the Kerameikos and on the slopes of the Acropolis in Athens, as well as the specific content of particular larger deposits, are partly the result of the way of 'disposing' of the votes cast during *ostrakophoria*.[80] In places where a slightly larger number of ostraka have been found, namely Cyrene and Tauric Chersonesos, the used and counted objects were most probably deposited similarly to Athens. This may explain the occurrence in our material of pairs of ostraka with the same 'candidate' name (as many as six of such pairs among 40 objects in Chersonesos) or even a significant prevalence of one name of a potential victim of ostracism (as in Cyrene).

---

[79] Naturally, this phenomenon should be regarded in the wider context of the emergence and evolution of democracy outside Athens. See esp. Schuller (1995); Robinson (1997) and (2011); see also Brock (2009) and Giangiulio (2015) *passim*. Cf. Węcowski (2009) 519–523.

[80] See below, 2.2.1, on the epigraphic sources for the study of ostracism.

Apart from inferences based on the relative chronology of all ostracisms, an argument supporting the Athenian origin of the local variants in the Greek world is the identical—even though, admittedly, very rudimentary— general formula of the *ostrakophoria* inscriptions in Athens and beyond; this is additionally enhanced by more detailed content analogies between the Athenian and the Chersonesian ostraka. The case of the Syracusan *petalismos*, an institution similar to ostracism, functioning around the mid-fifth century BC, also seems to be better understood with the assumption of the Athenian sources of its inspiration, which are stressed by Diodorus.

1.1.2 Ostracism and the 'Politics of Expulsion' in Archaic and Classical Greece

In her remarkable book entitled *Exile, Ostracism and Democracy. The Politics of Expulsion in Ancient Greece*,[81] Sara Forsdyke wrote that the quite common surprise which the Athenian practice of ostracism arouses in modern times, including in modern scholarship, proves that we still do not understand its meaning correctly. The ancients (even though their views on this institution and on the democracy using it differ) often saw it as an efficient political tool and a rational solution (but see above, p. 9). That is why Forsdyke decided to investigate the immediate political and ideological context of ostracism, by which she rightly (albeit perhaps too narrowly) understood the practice, the legislation, and the conceptions the Greeks had regarding exile.

In the archaic and classical times, up until the famous decree by Alexander the Great, exiles constituted one of the most pressing social and political problems of the Greek world. The general pattern was that power struggles in *poleis* often resulted in the exile of the leaders of the losing faction or even larger political groups, sometimes accompanied by their entire families.[82] Such expulsions often involved property confiscations, and return was usually possible only by force of arms; the exiles changed places with their persecutors, thus propelling the wheel of political and personal vengeance, destabilising the life of a particular community and its neighbours. The exiles often found support in the nearby *poleis*, whence they

---

[81] Forsdyke (2005); see already Forsdyke (2000). More recently, cf. Gray (2015) esp. 110–157.
[82] For *staseis* in individual *poleis* in classical times see the classic work by Gehrke (1985) esp. 11–199. For the late classical period, but reaching far back, cf. in general Gray (2015).

attempted to reclaim their position in their own city. From a certain point of view, it can be argued that many vital aspects in the history of archaic Greece—from various episodes of Greek colonisation to some political transformations and features of legislation in many *poleis*—resulted directly from the problem discussed here. In general, Forsdyke's 'study of intra-élite politics of exile [...] does not simply confirm that intra-elite competition was a catalyst to the institutional development of the early polis but, more important, shows how fragile these early state structures were in the face of violent competition between small groups of elites.'[83]

When juxtaposed with this practice and 'ideology' of exile in archaic and classical Greece, the case of Athenian ostracism must appear as exceptional. The reduction of the number of potential victims to one person a year, the precisely specified duration of exile (10 years) and the decreed orderly and peaceful procedure of the outcast's return, with no threat of material consequences throughout all this time (they have all their property left behind in the city at their disposal)—all these are strikingly mild and regulated solutions, introducing to the practice (and 'ideology') of the Athenian political life an otherwise unknown quality, at the same time ensuring internal tranquillity and stability in the *polis*, unattainable elsewhere.

Forsdyke interprets the introduction of ostracism in Athens as an act in which the *dēmos* intercepted from the Athenian élites full control over the 'politics of expulsion'—control both in practical terms (measured by the pragmatism of people's decisions regarding exile) and symbolically, as the Athenian *dēmos* will henceforth have the monopoly on the exclusion of citizens from the community. The rarity of use of ostracism by the Athenians will additionally create an image of kindness and temperance of the *dēmos*.

I should immediately make it clear that my principal doubt concerns the dichotomic picture of the interplay between 'élites' and 'the non-élites' and, as a result, the implied full self-awareness and complete 'sovereignty' of the *dēmos* within the Athenian *polis* already at the turn of the fifth century BC.[84] As it will become clear later in my argument, I am equally critical of the overall interpretation of the institution of ostracism at its late-archaic beginnings in symbolical terms in general and in terms of symbolical power of the people in Athens particularly. In brief, on the one hand, I believe that the process of

---

[83] Forsdyke (2005) 279. Cf. Simonton (2017) 99–100, for a criticism of Forsdyke's general idea of the 'politics of exile'.
[84] Forsdyke follows here Josiah Ober; cf. Ober (2007). Cf. below, pp. 90–95.

achieving full 'sovereignty' by the *dēmos* within a *polis* and the associated symbolic control over the *polis* was not yet as advanced in the last decade of the sixth and the first two decades of the fifth century BC as Forsdyke's conception assumes. On the other hand, and more generally, I think that symbolic and ritual interpretations of Athenian political institutions, illuminating as they may be for their particular aspects and practices, tend to offer a rather one-sided view of Athenian democracy.

However, I shall discuss this issue further in my work. Here I would only like to emphasise that the idea of considering the genesis and the original aim of ostracism in the context of the practice and 'ideology' of exile in archaic Greece seems valid to me. Consequently, I can use Forsdyke's observations on the 'politics of expulsion' to formulate tentative conclusions from my overview of traces of *ostrakophoriai* outside Athens.

The first remark is most general. In the light of the 'politics of expulsion', ostracism seems to be a legal–political solution meeting the needs of many Greek political entities at various stages in their history. The idea to imitate the Athenian institution when this 'model' became available seems understandable or perhaps even natural in some cases. From this point of view, one could venture the statement that scholars studying ostracism outside Athens so far might have been too hasty to assume the necessity of a connection between the local variants with the times of democracy in a given *polis*, operating there in the Athenian or similar form. We can easily imagine the introduction of ostracism in a *polis* dominated by politically active aristocratic élites or at least not (or not yet) dominated by the masses of the *dēmos*. Such must have been, at least to some extent and until a certain point, the case of Athens. Secondly, therefore, remaining at the general level, it is particularly in Athens of the end of the sixth and the beginning of the fifth century BC that ostracism might have not necessarily appeared as a radically, so to say, 'people-oriented' institution. In practice, the conditions on which the members of Athenian élites went into exile were much more favourable to individuals and their social circles than the alternative solutions in similar historical circumstances.

Thirdly, moving on to a more specific level, when we take into consideration the more or less hypothetical historical context of individual ostracisms outside Athens (wherever such context is available for consideration), we seem to be able to tentatively propose the following interpretation of the circumstances of the introduction of ostracism (or *petalismos*), modelled on the Athenian one, in some Greek *poleis*. It would emerge in a situation of crisis, in reaction to *stasis* or a threat of dangerous ambitions of groups or individuals, bringing hope for a peaceful, political, and time-limited solution to the crisis and constituting an alternative to violent and irreversible means, which make a future reconciliation of the opposing parties problematic. In short, we would then be dealing with a procedure analogical to the appointment of an internal or external conciliator, who is to settle down the situation in a conflicted *polis*. It should be noted that the application of such solutions is attested in the history of Cyrene in the times preceding the evidenced functioning of ostracism.[85] Another distinctive aspect of this peculiar 'remedy' for an internal crisis in a *polis* would be limiting its use to individuals, excluding action directed at groups of citizens, whole communities or even particular families, thus reducing the scale and impact of the conflict.

1.2 Ostracism before Ostracism in Archaic Athens?

Scholars studying the origins of ostracism have several good reasons to ask themselves about the possible Athenian prototypes of this institution. The existence of an archaic 'ostracism before ostracism' in Athens could put that of the times of Athenian democracy, and particularly its primary aims and functions within the newly emerging political system, in a completely new light.

1.2.1 Archaic Ostraka from the Athenian Agora and the Ostracism of Classical Times

In the excavation season of 1934 in the central part of the Athenian Agora, an ostrakon was found, which still excites scholars' imagination. On a fragment of a large vessel from Geometric times, a graffito with Pisistratus' name has been recognised: Πισίσ<τ>ρατος (inv. P 3629; see Fig. 1.1).[86] This inscription was engraved on a vase, very old already at that point, and most probably found coincidentally. According to Lilian H. Jeffery, the inscription should be dated to the sixth or even the seventh century BC. Given the prosopographic information available for Athens, two people known to us

---

[85] For the arbitration in Cyrene by Demonax of Mantinea, see Herodotus, IV 161,1–2.
[86] See Vanderpool (1949) 405–408. This ostrakon was mentioned for the first time in the excavation report: Shear (1935) 179.

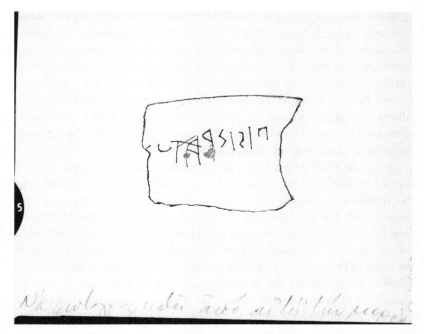

Fig. 1.1 Drawing of the so-called ostrakon of Pisistratus. Fragment of a Geometric lid. Agora Image: 2012.57.1399 (86-40) (Agora Object: P 3629). Courtesy of The American School of Classical Studies at Athens: Agora Excavations.

by the name of Pisistratus seem to be our options: the Athenian tyrant of the sixth century and the Athenian archon of 669/668 BC.[87] Regardless of its exact dating, the ostrakon—bearing a striking resemblance to the sherds used during the fifth-century *ostrakophoriai*[88] and found precisely on the site where they were held—was inevitably interpreted as potential evidence for 'ostracism before ostracism'.[89]

---

[87] *LSAG*²: 70. The third possibility, the grandson of the tyrant Pisistratus the Younger, archon of the end of the sixth century BC, should be discarded straight away on the basis of palaeographic criteria.

[88] Cf. below, 2.2.1. Unlike possessive or votive inscriptions on pottery, this class of inscriptions gives personal names in the nominative and, most importantly, it is clear that we are dealing with reused ostraka and not with fragments of previously inscribed vessels, because their writing conforms to the shape and size of the sherd. I owe this point to Kathleen Lynch (*per litteras*, August 30, 2021).

[89] Recently, see, e.g., Schmitz (2014) 61–62.

In a brilliant article of 1994, Claude Mossé and Annie Schnapp Gourbeillon refer to the remark by Jean-Pierre Vernant, who, in his analysis of *Oedipus Rex*, connected this ambivalent character—a 'divine king' and a scapegoat (*pharmakos*) of the *polis* at the same time—with the institution of Athenian ostracism.[90] Formulating their conclusions very cautiously, the two scholars posited that in the times before Cleisthenes, there could have existed in Athens a ritual practice consisting in subjecting most accomplished citizens of the *polis* to a kind of 'ordalium'.[91] It is from this custom that the Athenian ostracism of classical times would emerge.[92]

Even though we do not have any evidence of this, the existence of such a ritual in archaic Athens cannot be excluded, naturally.[93] Nonetheless, the ostrakon mentioned above does not constitute any proof in this matter. First, many different interpretations are possible here. Margherita Guarducci asked herself whether it could have happened that during one of the ostracisms of the classical times some Athenian wrote on the ostrakon the name of Pisistratus as a tyrant par excellence.[94] As we remember, such a solution is implausible for palaeographic reasons, but it points out the abundance of potential explanations for the circumstances in which this inscription was made. Eugene Vanderpool hesitantly suggested that this ostrakon should be taken as a trace of voting in the Areopagus on exiling the tyrant Pisistratus.[95] An additional argument for him was another find from the Agora (inv. P 10159; on a large amphora sherd of the seventh century, discovered among sherds of proto-Attic vessels), bearing the name of Aristion. A character of this name is mentioned in *A.P.* (14.1) as the collaborator of the future tyrant who suggested granting armed bodyguards to Pisistratus. Such a person would naturally be exiled from Athens alongside the tyrant.[96] Already before, Alfred Brueckner had proposed a political

---

[90] Mossé, Schnapp Gourbeillon (1994) 48–50. For more on the possible connections between the scapegoat ritual and ostracism, see below, 1.2.3.

[91] Mossé and Schnapp Gourbeillon refer in this context also to Solon, who is traditionally credited with a 10-year-long voluntary exile (*A.P.* 11.1) and to the quasi-ritual return from exile of the tyrant Pisistratus (Hdt. I 60; *A.P.* 14.4).

[92] The ritual aspects of the classical ostracism would be a good testimony of that. However, see below, 1.2.3.

[93] The small number of archaic ostraka of (potentially) 'political' character does not in itself constitute an argument opposing this thesis. It suffices to mention here the single ostraka from Argos and Megara, where, thanks to non-epigraphic testimonies, we are entitled to believe in the functioning of ostracism.

[94] Guarducci (1941–1943) 123.

[95] See also below (1.2.2) on hypotheses considering the alleged 'bouleutic' stage in the evolution of Athenian ostracism.

[96] See Vanderpool (1949) 406–408 (no. IIb), with Pl. 60.

OSTRACISM BEFORE OSTRACISM? 43

interpretation of two sixth-century ostraka found on the Acropolis with the word δημώλης inscribed,[97] which he understood as referring to 'one who lost membership in his *dēmos*',[98] and in consequence as concerning people such as, for instance, bearers of the 'Cylonian miasma'. Therefore, Brueckner regarded the ostraka as a trace of an institution foreshadowing Cleisthenes' ostracism, and perhaps also an indication of the Areopagus' activity in this respect already before the time of Solon.[99]

To assess the validity of the above 'political' interpretations of the several archaic Athenian ostraka, let us point out first that Vanderpool's hypothesis becomes probable only on the condition that we accept the very insecure identification of Aristion as the tyrant Pisistratus' associate.[100] Secondly, it should be emphasised that the placement of the graffiti on both the Acropolis ostraka excludes the possibility of this word being accompanied by a name or names. This, in turn, means that accepting their 'political' interpretation, we would have to consider them as an argument for the existence of a completely different way of voting, and perhaps also, more generally, of entirely different use of ostraka in some Athenian political–judicial procedure of the archaic times. Although it cannot be excluded that at this time in Athens decisions of this sort were made by two institutions (for instance, the Areopagus and Solon's Council of the Four Hundred) or that in one of them two different types of voting were carried out with the use of ostraka, it seems to me that at this stage of analysis, hypotheses should not be multiplied unnecessarily.[101]

Since more ostraka of similar dating and analogical in form have been found in Athens,[102] Vanderpool recognised the possibility that other Athenian ostraka, equally enigmatic in character and coincident in dating, were produced by people practising their writing skills or by bored

[97] Brueckner (1915) 22–24. The two inscriptions were published by Graef, Langlotz (1933) no. 1316 with Pl. 92 (= *IG* I² 913: δεμόλεϵ[ς]) and 1317 (= *IG* I² 913 in the commentary: δεμόλες). Let us note on the margin that no. 1316 (of around 550 BC) was inscribed on a sherd of a large vessel from Geometric times, as was the ostrakon with Pisistratus' name.
[98] Brueckner (1915) 24 (and following him *LSJ*, *s.v.* δημώλης). Cf. Schmitz (2014) 61–62.
[99] Similarly, Carcopino (1935) 82, n. 1.
[100] Comparatively, unlike for its cognate name Aristōn (203 results), an *LGPN* II search for Aristiōn does not yield very numerous results (79 in total). Still, the odds are very much against this identification.
[101] Develin (1977) 12–16, who cautiously proposes a nonetheless very detailed picture of Athenian 'ostracism before ostracism' in archaic times (based on the testimony of codex Vaticanus Graecus 1144, which he interprets in the light of a hypothetical special law against tyranny executed by the Council of the Four Hundred; see below, 1.2.2), completely ignores the existence of the Acropolis ostraka mentioned above.
[102] With the name in the nominative, but usually without the patronymic.

Athenians scratching their own or their friends' or lovers' names in their free time.[103] Special attention is due here to another ostrakon from this 'group', found in an archaeological context indicating early sixth century BC. On this ostrakon, a female name is inscribed: Deimeneia (inv. P 4794).[104] I deem it evident that a political interpretation of this inscription is not viable. It cannot be entirely excluded that (according to Vanderpool's suggestion) we are dealing here with the name of the beloved scratched by a lover, but I believe the probability of this is slight. It should be highlighted that formally, this ostrakon is no different than the other ones discussed by the scholar, including the 'Pisistratus ostrakon'. This observation, in turn, brings us to the fundamental methodological problem weighing on this discussion.

Vanderpool, Jeffery, Guarducci, and within the broader framework of their theory also Mossé and Schnapp Gourbeillon, presume a connection between the 'Pisistratus ostrakon' and some (or a very particular) political or judicial institution because similar ostraka found on the same site were used in a political context 200 or 100 years later (depending on the dating of the Pisistratus in our inscription). It is precisely this assumption that I find unsubstantiated. It is, of course, conceivable that there existed a direct historical link between the ostraka of archaic Athens and those used in *ostrakophoriai* of the classical times. However, it is more probable that in the seventh or sixth century BC ostraka with names in the nominative were applied in other (perhaps even diverse) circumstances unknown to us. As we remember, the specifically political use of ostraka in the *ostrakophoria* procedure is unparalleled in the Greek world before classical times, when various Greek *poleis* begin, as I have been trying to demonstrate, to follow the Athenian model (see above, 1.1.1). In this context, historical probability prevents us from making an easy association between the 'Pisistratus ostrakon' (and other of this kind) and ostracism functioning in Athens in the fifth century BC. In any case, the current state of our knowledge does not allow us to responsibly use this material in the study of the beginnings of Athenian ostracism.

Additionally, the advocates of the thesis about the existence of 'ostracism before ostracism' in Athens should be particularly concerned about the absolute lack of information about an 'ostracism' (or about an attempt at it) of Pisistratus in our tradition. At the minimum, it testifies to the fact that

---

[103] Vanderpool (1949) 407–408. His entire argumentation is adopted by Jeffery in *LSAG²*: 70.
[104] Vanderpool (1949) 406 (no. IIc), with il. 10. See already Shear (1935) 179, Pl. 6 (bottom left).

Herodotus, our main source of information on archaic Athens, while mentioning the successive exiles of the tyrant from Athens, believed that ostracism there did not reach as far back as the times before Cleisthenes.[105] Naturally, writing in the second half of the fifth century BC, Herodotus could have been mistaken, but in the light of his silence, the speculations of modern scholars and the historical models conceived by them dwindle in their persuasive power.

1.2.2 Vaticanus Graecus 1144 and the Mirage of the So-called 'Bouleutic Ostracism'

In the *Proceedings of the Philological Faculty of the [Polish] Academy of Learning* of 1894, Leon Sternbach (1864–1940) published the *editio princeps* of the concluding part of a fifteenth-century (or perhaps a fourteenth-century) Byzantine manuscript known as *Vaticanus Graecus* 1144 (foll. 215^v–225^v), an interesting but bizarre collection of excerpts (apophthegms, gnomae, and pieces of historical material).[106] Excerpt 213 has only reached the wider scholarly world, and the students of the Athenian democracy in particular, almost 80 years later when reprinted and interpreted in 1972 by John J. Keaney and Antony E. Raubitschek.[107] Ever since, *Vaticanus Graecus* 1144 no. 213 has occupied a very special place in the scholarly debates surrounding the law of ostracism in Athens, and it seems that in recent decades some scholars tend to take it, however cautiously and not without hesitation, as somehow trustworthy and hence pointing to the existence of a law or custom predating the attested law of ostracism. Accordingly, the notion of the so-called 'bouleutic ostracism' has become increasingly popular. On this theory, the Athenian ostracism was originally voted by the Boulē and only later transferred to the Athenian people at large.[108] Meanwhile, the majority approach is to abstain from judging the

---

[105] Develin (1985a) 8–9, with n. 5, mentions this problem cursorily.
[106] Sternbach (1894a) 192.
[107] Keaney, Raubitschek (1972). Sternbach's edition of other pieces of historical material from the same manuscript, devoted inter alia to Alexander the Great, entered scholarly debates right away as they were published in a widely circulating Viennese journal: Sternbach (1894b).
[108] Thus, e.g., Develin (1977) (this scholar later rescinded his support to this theory in Develin (1985a) and (1985b)); Bicknell (1974) 817–819; McCargar (1976a) 248–252; Longo (1980); Lehmann (1981); Doenges (1996); Forsdyke (2005) 283–284 (cf. Schmitz (2014) 56 and Hall (1989)). Cf. Costa, p. 230.

trustworthiness of this late Byzantine account.[109] Very rarely, it is discarded altogether, but without giving any reason.[110] The thrill of the account of the Vatican excerpt is obvious. If true, its historical implications would be far-reaching. As Antony Raubitschek put it,

> [it] resolves at once the questions whether the law was instituted after the expulsion of Hippias or after the victory of Marathon, and whether or not Cleisthenes was its author. Evidently, the law was introduced (in the boule?) by Cleisthenes in the short period between the end of tyranny and his own exile, and it was administered by the Boulē of Four Hundred. Its provisions were the same as those of the later law, except that a simple majority of the four hundred councillors determined the victim. After Cleisthenes returned and had his constitution enacted, nothing was said or done about the law of ostracism till the treason of Marathon raised the specter of tyranny again, and all of our more detailed accounts of ostracism describe the working of the law as it was renewed immediately after Marathon.... It is also clear that the boule of the Four Hundred existed until it was replaced by that of the Five Hundred, and that Herodotus (V, 72,2) speaks of its activities at that very time.[111]

Furthermore, if one is willing to go one step further, one could even end up interpreting a more general historical and cultural context of ostracism, delving into its archaic 'prehistory', so to say.[112]

In what follows, I will discuss these scholarly theories, but to show that excerpt no. 213 regarding ostracism is a worthless mix of the pieces of information we otherwise know (save for one detail) from other Roman and Byzantine sources. It was conceived in late Byzantine scholarship by misinterpreting, ingeniously manipulating, or conflating well-known elements of ancient lexicographical traditions. If I am right in what follows, the phantom of the 'bouleutic ostracism' should be laid to rest.

---

[109] Thus, e.g., Stein-Hölkeskamp (1989) 194; Bleicken (1995) 525; Siewert, p. 31.
[110] See esp. Rhodes, p. 268 (with an addendum, p. 774) and M. Chambers in *Aristoteles 10.1*, p. 240, who posits a misunderstanding between ostracism and the *ekphyllophoria* in this account. And rightly so, as we shall see.
[111] Keaney, Raubitschek (1972) 90. Cf. also Longo (1980).
[112] Thus, e.g., Develin (1977) and Mossé, Schnapp Gourbeillon (1994).

OSTRACISM BEFORE OSTRACISM? 47

Let us take a closer look at the text itself (fol. 222^rv):

(1) Κλεισθένης τὸν ἐξοστρακισμοῦ νόμον ἐς Ἀθήνας εἰσήνεγκεν.
(2) ἦν δὲ τοιοῦτος·
(3) τὴν βουλὴν τινῶν ἡμέραιν (βουλήν τινῶν ἡμερῶν Sternbach) σκεψαμένων (σκεψαμένην Sternbach)
(4) ἐπιγράφειν ἔθος <ἦν suppl. Sternbach> εἰς ὄστρακα
(5) ὅντινα δέοι τῶν πολιτῶν φυγαδευθῆναι
(6) καὶ ταῦτα ῥίπτειν εἰς τὸ τοῦ βουλευτηρίου περίφραγμα.
(7) ὅτῳ δὲ ἂν ὑπὲρ διακόσια γένηται τὰ ὄστρακα
(8) φεύγειν ἔτη δέκα,
(9) τὰ ἐκείνου (ἑαυτοῦ Sternbach) καρπούμενον.
(10) ὕστερον δὲ τὸν δῆμον (τῷ δήμῳ Sternbach τοῦ δήμου Develin) ἔδοξε νομοθετῆσαι
(11) ὑπὲρ ἑξακισχίλια γίνεσθαι τὰ ὄστρακα τοῦ φυγαδευθῆναι μέλλοντος.

(1) It was Cleisthenes who introduced the law of ostracism to Athens. (2) The law was as follows: (3) During certain days of deliberation [or perhaps: 'after certain days of deliberation'—M.W.], the Council (4) had the habit of writing down on a potsherd (5) [the name of] the one among the citizens whom it was necessary to exile (6) and to throw [the ostraka] into the enclosure of the Bouleuterion. (7) The one who received more than two hundred ostraka, (8) had to go to exile for 10 years, (9) with the right of using his own property [in Attica]. (10) Later, the *dēmos* decided to introduce a law[113] (11) that the ostraka of the one to be exiled should be more than 6000.

Regrettably, we cannot establish the historical value of this text based on external criteria. On the one hand, scholarly attempts at identifying the ultimate ancient source of this account in its present form are not likely to succeed.[114] On the other hand, its relative authority among our extant ancient sources is again difficult to establish. While it is true that *Vaticanus Graecus* 1144 no. 213 is isolated and unparalleled in the current state of our evidence,

---

[113] Develin (1977) 13, wanted to emend τὸν δῆμον into τοῦ δήμου, and translated it as follows: 'it was decided to establish a law that the ostraka of the *dēmos* [stressed] should amount to 6000 if a man was to go into exile', while admitting it would be 'a compressed statement'.
[114] Cf. next footnote.

it must be admitted that the rich mainstream account on the Athenian ostracism, headed by *A.P.* 43.5 and fragment 30 of Philochorus (in F. Jacoby's *FGrHist*), may also represent a single line of tradition.[115] Another way to validate the authority of the excerpt's account would be to find some corroborative pieces of historical information in it. But here again we find ourselves in the realm of inconclusiveness. Two possible elements stand out, it is true, as being likely to be reliable. First, the idea of fencing off some spot in the Athenian Agora in the process, the *periphragma* of our excerpt, is paralleled (without the mention of the Bouleuterion involved, though) in other accounts of the *ostrakophoria*, or the vote using ostraka.[116] Secondly, the phrase τὰ ἐκείνου (or ἑαυτοῦ) καρπούμενον, recurring in several sources,[117] most probably belonged to the original text of the law of ostracism.[118] Both elements, however, can only prove some relationship between the Byzantine account and the aforementioned 'mainstream tradition' of ostracism and do not bespeak any degree of originality, let alone independent authority, of this account. What is left to the supporters of the 'bouleutic ostracism' are general historical considerations based on the alleged coherence of the excerpt.[119] One detail is particularly important here, namely the very idea of ostracising a citizen by the Boulē combined with the fact that the 'mainstream tradition' mentions the role of the Boulē (and that of the archons) in supervising the vote of *ostrakophoria*.[120] As such, this piece of information may suggest that the fifth-century practice was based on an earlier and 'bouleutic' procedure of ostracism. However, it is fair to observe with many scholars that the *bouleutai* were the only possible choice for the supervision of the vote since the voters, we are told, approached the area using 10 entrances, one for each *phylē*.[121] Only the elected representatives of the Athenian tribes could be used to check the identity of their fellow citizens and thus to prevent potential impostors from voting. Besides that, nothing suggests any historical link between the Boulē and ostracism as attested for the fifth century. Quite the contrary, the

---

[115] See esp. Raubitschek (1958) (cf. already Bloch (1940) 355–376), for Theophrastus as the ultimate source of this tradition. Develin (1977) 11 would prefer to see the Atthidographer Androtion in this role. In general, see below, pp. 158–160.
[116] Cf. in particular Philochorus, *FGrHist* 328 F 30, with Costa, pp. 227–228, for parallel accounts. For the topography of ostracism, see below, 3.2.2.
[117] See also below, p. 122.   [118] Cf. Longo (1980) 263.
[119] Thus, e.g., J. J. Keaney, in Keaney, Raubitschek (1972) 90.
[120] Cf. esp. Philochorus, *FGrHist* 328 F 30. See below, pp. 165–166, 185.
[121] See, e.g., Raubitschek (1956).

automatically conducted preliminary vote in the Assembly whether to hold ostracism (A.P. 43.5), with no probouleumatic procedures involved, is not suggestive of possible 'bouleutic' precedents of ostracism.[122]

Next comes the problem of the alleged logic or coherence of the excerpt. In 1985, Robert Develin withdrew from his earlier attempts at defending not so much the authority of the *Vaticanus Graecus* 1144 (or that of its source) but some pieces of information included in it. In his second paper on the issue, in the face of the chaotic nature of the excerpt itself, Develin made a strong methodological point when he asked how its writer really worked: 'Was he here copying directly from a source? Or was he working from notes? Or was he relying on memory?'. And, since the text as we have it is obviously in need of emending, 'are these emendations made in order to reconstruct the writer's source or to correct his grammar? Consideration of this may provide a clue as to the writer's dependability.'[123]

Develin pointed out several cases of the writer's 'sloppiness' such as the necessity of emending σκεψαμένων into Sternbach's σκεψαμένην, the unmentioned subject of the Boulē's 'examination', but also the strange *genetivus temporis* τινῶν ἡμερῶν, which can either mean 'after some days [of examination]', as scholars usually translate it, or literally 'during certain days [of examination]'. The latter would indicate a specific time of the year, but the writer of the excerpt is extremely careless and vague in all this. Next, he argued, the phrase ὕστερον δὲ τὸν δῆμον ἔδοξε νομοθετῆσαι of the manuscript resists emendation and it is not necessary to change it with Sternberg into more meaningful τῷ δήμῳ or into τοῦ δήμου (with Develin 1977) ἔδοξε. Be that as it may, a good constitutional source could not have omitted the crucial fact that the vote of ostracism would be executed by the *dēmos* itself since the introduction of the requirement of six thousand ostraka. As it stands now, the excerpt only says that the *dēmos* decided to change the number of ostraka required to expel a citizen from Athens. At best, the writer is drastically abbreviating his source, but, as Develin concludes,

> we seem at least to be in the presence of an inattentive mind. My impression is that that the writer was working from memory or at the most from notes on a matter that had already been distorted by Byzantine times. The point is that if he has been so slack in his expression, we can hardly have confidence in the content. It can be argued that this does not necessarily

---

[122] As emphasised by Develin (1985a) 13.   [123] All quotations from Develin (1985a) 14.

follow, but this is just one more consideration in the case against a text which has very little chance of inserting another stage into the history of ostracism.[124]

I, for one, could not agree more.

*

Let me stress that the reason why the negative arguments against the idea of the 'bouleutic ostracism' have failed to persuade many scholars is that one would need to explain the provenance of the extravagant Byzantine version, even if it was abbreviated and distorted by the writer of the excerpt, to put this account to rest with a clear conscience. Unless proven otherwise, we do read of the vote of ostracism in the Boulē in *Vaticanus Graecus* 1144 no. 213 after all.

At this juncture, it may prove instructive to take a look at two more Byzantine accounts of ostracism, one roughly contemporary with our manuscript and one predating it by several generations. Let me begin with the first one.

In the fourteenth-century *Miscellanea* (pp. 608–609 ed. Müller–Kiessling) by Theodoros Metochites († 1332), an interesting collection of excerpts and variegated material stemming from classical sources in political and constitutional issues (essays nos. 94–109), we read the story of the ostracism of Aristides as an example of the perversity of the Athenian *dēmos*. In general, the author rather faithfully follows Plutarch's account from the *Life of Aristides*,[125] except for one curious mistake: for the *ostrakophoria*, the Athenians gather from all quarters in the ... Bouleuterion (p. 609 Müller–Kiessling: ὡς ἤθροιστο μὲν ὁ δῆμος παντόθεν εἰς τὸ βουλευτήριον). This unparalleled and topographically absurd idea is, however, naturally integrated into an account that otherwise follows the 'mainstream tradition' on ostracism. The author, no doubt relying on his memory, misconstrued the procedure and confused ostracism with another piece of information regarding an issue similar enough to the *ostrakophoria* to be imperceptibly blended into his account about ostracism.

Another late Byzantine account of ostracism is even more confusing. We owe it to John Tzetzes († ca 1180) and his poetic *Chiliades* in accentual verse

---

[124] Develin (1985a) 15.
[125] On this writer and his 'personal encyclopaedism', but also on Plutarch's role in his work, see recently Featherstone (2011). Raubitschek (1958) 101–102, quotes Metochites account, but abstains from commenting on the idiosyncrasies of this version.

(13. 441–486 Kiessling, story no. 489). Once again, the narrative follows Plutarch's *Life of Aristides*, including the famous anecdote about the illiterate Athenian willing to expel Aristides, but this time we are facing a maddening stream of associations and pieces of quasi-erudite information. Among other things, we learn that the Athenians did not exile anyone right away, but waited for a specific day (l. 445: ἡμέραν ὡρισμένην) when they listened to a thousand accusers against the one they were about to banish and then they wrote down his name on ostraka and threw them in the gymnasium of Kynosarges (l. 449).[126]

> Thus, if the specified day a thousand shells were found, | Without any sympathy the person was exiled. | If the shells were less than that, though, | He could stay in his homeland, achieving forgiveness. | Because of the shells ostracism stands for banishment, | The same as to which Aristides the Just was submitted. (ll. 452–457; tr. N. Giallousis)

This account provides us with several unparalleled nonsenses about ostracism (such as the mention of Kynosarges) but contains some elements matching both the version found in Metochites and especially that of the Vatican excerpt: (1) the idea of throwing ostraka into some specific enclosure (not the Bouleuterion, though); (2) the notion of a specific day to do it; (3) the idea of a time-lag between some preliminary indication of the guilty one and the actual day of voting; (4) a time-lag devoted to some form of deliberation on the guilt (although this is very unclear in *Vat. Gr.* 1144); (5) a precise number of ostraka required to exile the suspect, but very different from that of the 'mainstream tradition' (not six thousand, but two hundred, as in the Vatican excerpt, or one thousand, as in the *Chiliades*).

In Tzetzes, it all gets utterly confused, but he might have been following, recalling it from his memory, a source underlying the account of *Vaticanus Graecus* 1144 no. 213 as well, since the correspondences between the two are striking indeed. In the remaining part of story no. 489 in the *Chiliades*, we may find a key to identify not the source itself, but at least the class of evidence Tzetzes might have followed.

The anecdote about the illiterate Athenian keen on exiling Aristides ends with the line stating that 'thus exile (*exoria*) was named ostracising'

---

[126] On this strange idea, see below, p. 56 n. 143.

(l. 476).¹²⁷ Immediately afterwards, we read 'but we also call it *ekphyllophorēsis*', i.e., the sentence passed by leaves (l. 477).¹²⁸ However,

> In places where potsherds were hard to find | They used leaves in the place of potsherds | And did everything else just as I said, | But they dropped them not in Kynosarges, | But in a place where the leaves could be hidden and kept dry. | So, whether we use the word ostracism or *ekphyllophorēsis* for exile (*exoria*) | We mean the very same thing. | But there were people that were banished in autumn time | Because of the trees leaves and the blowing of the winds. (ll. 478–486; tr. N. Giallousis, adapted)

For Tzetzes, then, ostracism and *ekphyllophorēsis* is one and the same thing, a type of banishment in Athens, and the difference between them is most probably that of the availability of the 'instruments' of the vote in a given place and at a given time of the year. This last idea looks rather ingenious and might well have been a novel concept of the writer. Original or not, he combined here, relying again solely on his memory, ostracism and the Athenian institution of *ekphyllophoria* or *ekphyllophorēsis*, the 'leafing-out' of the Boulē.¹²⁹

As regards the excerpt from *Vaticanus Graecus* 1144, scholars have long envisioned the possibility that this excerpt confused ostracism with *ekphyllophoria* but discounted it as a 'desperate'¹³⁰ or at least 'not very convincing'¹³¹ hypothesis. If anything, students of ostracism allowed for the idea of some historical link between *ekphyllophoria* and 'bouleutic ostracism' in Athens.¹³²

---

¹²⁷ Cf. also Eustathius, 1161.34–35.
¹²⁸ For institutions where voting procedures involved tree-leaves, see, e.g., *IG* XII,5 595 A, l. 11–15 (Ceos, 3rd cent. BC–early 2nd cent. BC) and *petalismos* in Syracuse (above, pp. 32–35).
¹²⁹ To eliminate one of its members as guilty of some wrongdoings, the Council first voted using tree-leaves. Then, more regular voting pebbles were used (sch Aeschin. 1 (*In Tim.*) 111 = 242a–b Dilts). We hear of this institution from Aeschin. 1 (*In Tim.*) 110–112, from references to a lost speech by Deinarchos (*Against Polyeuktos*, the testimonia collected as no. II in N. Conomis' Teubner (pp. 74–76)). Cf. also Antiphon, VI [*On the choreutes*] 49. Harpocration, s.v. *ekphyllophorēsai* (109.1 Dindorf); *Suda*, s.v. *ekphyllophorēsai kai ekphyllophoria* (721 Adler) is a corrupted version of the tradition, on which see below; *Lex. Segueriana* (ed. Bekker I.248.7), s.v. *ekphyllophorēsai*; *E.M.* (325.9 Gaisdorf), s.v. *ekphyllophorēsai kai ekphyllophoriai*. See also Pollux, 8.19–20. Cf. Busolt, Swoboda (1926) 1023–1024 and Rhodes (1972) 144–146. *Ekphyllophoreō* (*ekphyllizō* being unattested) sounds rather archaic (I owe this point to J. Danielewicz).
¹³⁰ Thus Keaney, Raubitschek (1972) 90. Cf. also Longo (1980) 259 n. 6.
¹³¹ Develin (1977) 12–13. Develin (1985a) 12 is not so sure any more that the *ekphyllophoria* can be eliminated as a possible source of confusion.
¹³² See, e.g., Hall (1989) 96–99.

OSTRACISM BEFORE OSTRACISM? 53

Indeed, there is a strong analogy between one of the strange passages of the Vatican excerptum (l. 3: τὴν βουλήν τινῶν ἡμερῶν σκεψαμένην), on the one hand, and a passage of the entry *ekphyllophorēsis* (or *ekphyllophorēsai kai ekphyllophoria*) in the Byzantine lexicographic tradition: 'the Boulē used to look into his [i.e., of the potential wrongdoer from among its members— M.W.] case' (ἐσκόπει ἡ βουλὴ περὶ αὐτοῦ). This is what we find in the *Suda* (E 722 Adler), in the *Etymologicum Magnum* (325.9 Gaisdorf), and in the *Lexica Segueriana* (ed. Bekker, *Anecdota Graeca* I, 248.7).[133] In his reassessment of the historical value of *Vaticanus Graecus* 1144 no. 213, R. Develin observed that 'in the Suda (E 722 Adler) reasons given and terminology used are such that a mistake or two along the way could have led to a wrong ascription to ostracism' in the Vatican excerpt.[134]

Actually, there is more to be said about the Byzantine lexicographic tradition of the *ekphyllophoria* (and *ekphyllophorēsis*). In the *Suda* entry (s.v. *ekphyllophorēsai kai ekphyllophoria*, E 722 Adler), we read that:

> If ever any of the citizens appeared to be a wrongdoer and [thus] unworthy of belonging to the Council of the 500, the council used to look into his case, [*sc.* to determine] whether he ought to be a councillor no longer but expelled from the synod altogether.
> (tr. D. Whitehead for the Suda On Line: http://www.stoa.org/sol/)

In other representatives of the same tradition (*Lexica Segueriana*, s.v. *ekphyllophorēsai*, ed. Bekker I, 248.7 and *Etymologicum Magnum*, s.v. *ekphyllophorēsai kai ekphyllophoriai*, 325.9 ed. Gaisdorf) we find the same curious mistake, as they mention 'any of the citizens' (τις τῶν πολιτῶν) instead of 'any of the members of the Boulē' as the subject of the Council's scrutiny. In his edition of the *Etymologicum Magnum*, Thomas Gaisdorf naturally suggests the necessary correction into τις τῶν βουλευτῶν in his apparatus (*quod praeferendum videtur*), following the authority of the much shorter entry *ekphyllophorēsai* in Harpocration (109.1 Dindorf).[135] The

---

[133] This is the most extensive lexicographical entry on the issue, preserved in an eleventh-century codex (now called Parisinus Coislinianus 345 and 347) combining several short treatises on Greek syntax and five anonymous works dubbed *Lexica Segueriana*, after the original owner of the codex (Pierre Ségurier, 1588–1672) or *Lexica Bekkeriana*, after their editor Imanuel Bekker. Our entry belongs to *Lexeis rhetorikai*, most probably stemming from a lexicon to Attic orators. Cf. Sandys (1921) 416.
[134] Develin (1985) 12.
[135] As observed by W. Dindorf (Oxford, 1853, *ad loc.*), *Hanc gl.[ossam] omisit Suidas, alia substituta copiosiore.*

emendation looks no doubt indispensable to suit the *ekphyllophoria* procedure, but the Byzantine tradition is consistent in keeping the nonsensical phrase 'any of the citizens' instead of 'members of the Council'. It is true that Byzantine lexicographers never directly and literally confuse ostracism with *ekphyllophoria*, and they only connect the two because both institutions used other 'instruments' of the vote than the regular *psēphoi* (see below, p. 57).[136] However, I think there is no other solution but to assume that the lexicographic entries studied above stemmed from an earlier confusion between the procedure of ostracism regarding all the citizens of Athens and that of *ekphyllophoria* concerning only the members of the Council of Five Hundred. Indeed, if we compare the lexicographic version (εἴ ποτέ τις τῶν πολιτῶν ἀδικεῖν ἐδόκει καὶ ἀνάξιος εἶναι τοῦ συνεδρίου τῶν φ', ἐσκόπει ἡ βουλὴ περὶ αὐτοῦ, εἰ χρὴ αὐτὸν μηκέτι βουλεύειν, ἀλλ' ἐλαθῆναι καὶ τοῦ συνεδρίου) with the text of our Vatican excerpt (τὴν βουλὴν τινῶν ἡμερῶν σκεψαμένην... ὅντινα δέοι τῶν πολιτῶν φυγαδευθῆναι κτλ.) it looks rather obvious, first, that the latter version is based, however confusedly, on Byzantine traditions about *ekphyllophoria* and/or, secondly, that the lexicographers and the writer of *Vaticanus Graecus* 1144 no. 312 fell victim to an earlier conflation of the information about ostracism with that about *ekphyllophoria*.

Now, the tenth-century *Suda*, the eleventh-century manuscript of the *Lexica Segueriana*, and the twelfth-century *Etymologicum Magnum* share the same meaningful mistake, but the 'cross-fertilisation', so to speak, between the material regarding *ekphyllophoria* and that on the Athenian ostracism is also attested in the fourteenth-century *Miscellanea* by Theodoros Metochites (the enclosure of the Bouleuterion as the voting booth) and, in a massive and imaginative combination of the two, in the *Chiliades* by John Tzetzes in the second half of the twelfth-century. I think there can be no doubt at this point that we are entitled to add to this list the account about ostracism in the fifteenth- or fourteenth-century *Vaticanus Graecus* 1144, roughly contemporary with Metochites' work or slightly postdating it. Thus, our sole witness to the existence of the phase of the 'bouleutic ostracism' in Athens proves worthless.

In the following, I would like to speculate on the possible mechanisms of the appearance of this particular vision of the history of ostracism in the Vatican excerpt.

---

[136] *Suda*, E 722 Adler; *Lex. Segueriana* ed. Bekker I, 248.11–14; *E.M.* 325.15 Gaisdorf.

OSTRACISM BEFORE OSTRACISM? 55

*

As already mentioned, Harpocration's lexicon in the later second century still offers an 'uncontaminated' entry on *ekphyllophorēsai* (109.1 Dindorf):[137]

εἰ ἐδόκει τις τῶν βουλευτῶν ἀδικεῖν, διεψηφίζετο ἡ βουλὴ περὶ αὐτοῦ εἰ χρὴ αὐτὸν μηκέτι βουλεύειν. ἀντὶ δὲ ψήφων φύλλοις ἐχρῶντο, δι' ὧν ἕκαστος ἐπεσημαίνετο τὴν αὐτοῦ γνώμην κτλ.

If any of the *bouleutai* appeared to be a wrongdoer, the Council voted on his case, whether he ought to stop to perform the function of a councillor. Instead of voting-pebbles they used leaves, on which each councillor would indicate his own opinion [...].

In this entry, there is still no trace of comparing *ekphyllophoria* with ostracism based on their original voting 'instruments', just a brief mention of voting-pebbles. Accordingly, those subject to the Council's scrutiny are logically the members of the Boulē and not the Athenian citizens at large.

Now, based on the (now epitomised) *Onomasticon* by Pollux of Naucratis, a contemporary of Harpocration in the latter part of the second century, we may perhaps tentatively suggest the hypothetical ultimate source of the Byzantine 'cross-fertilisation' of the material about ostracism and *ekphyllophoria*.

In Pollux 8.18–20, a much more extended treatment of *ekphyllophoria* than that of Harpocration can be found. As John K. Davies kindly suggested to me *per litteras*, the sequence of ideas underlying the (epitomised) Pollux here 'reflects a sophisticated selection process that has occurred at some point'. The author's regular style is abandoned in paragraph 17 to present various types of *skeuē dikastika* and then to offer antiquarian reasoning regarding three administrative procedures used to penalise an individual in Athens, namely the *diapsēphisis*, the *ekphyllophoria*, and ostracism. In other words, three *ad hominem* public procedures must have been clearly distinguished here, which bespeaks a solid original treatment of some important aspects of Athenian law.[138] In this context, we find a detailed account of the Athenian *ekphyllophoria*, mentioning the procedure of 'leafing-out' as

---

[137] On some problems with using Harpocration, cf. e.g. Kinzl (1991a).
[138] Cf. also Maffi (2007) esp. 30–31.

executed both by the *dikastai kata dēmous*[139] and in the Athenian Boulē. Here, the terminology regarding the technicalities of voting yields to that of exile and the remark that the Boulē used leaves instead of voting pebbles. Next, the writer switches to the terminology of ostracism and then to a brief account about ostracism, which obviously originated in the 'mainstream tradition' of ostracism, best preserved in fragment 30 of Philochorus of Athens. Here, the *Onomasticon* tells us only about the need to build an enclosure encompassing some part of the Athenian Agora and about the requirement of six thousand ostraka to effectively exile a citizen from Athens.[140]

Of course, this is a drastically abbreviated account, by the epitomator of Pollux, of *diapsēphisis, ekphyllophoria*, and ostracism. The original and more detailed treatment of the three issues would be a perfect candidate, I would argue, for the ultimate source of the Byzantine conflation of the traditions regarding ostracism with those about *ekphyllophoria*. It is worth noticing that of the five elements uniting the accounts of *Vaticanus Graecus* 1144, of Theodoros Metochites, and John Tzetzes (see above), only two, the idea of some enclosure used as a voting booth and the number of ostraka required, are found in Pollux. The epitomator skipped one particularly important element which was no doubt present in earlier Byzantine sources,[141] namely the precise time of the year when *ostrakophoria* was held in Athens (see below, pp. 124–131), which must have given rise to the three other elements of the Byzantine accounts, including the idea of a time-lag for deliberation before the actual vote of ostraka.[142]

If the pieces of information regarding *ekphyllophoria* and ostracism closely neighboured one another in a fuller version of what we read now as Pollux's 8.18–20,[143] one crucial analogy would strike any reader of such a text, namely the fact that both the institutions must have been described

---

[139] Cf. esp. A.P. 16.5; 26.3; 48.5; 53.1, as commented by Rhodes, *ad loc.* Cf. also Dem. XXIV (*In Tim.*) 122.

[140] Cf. Philochorus, *FGrHist* 328 F 30, with Costa, pp. 228–232. For the issue of the 'quorum' of the Athenian ostracism, see below, pp. 158–177.

[141] Note that a passage from Pollux's account on ostracism is present in a marginal note to the sixth-century Neoplatonist commentary on Plato's *Gorgias* by Olympiodorus (33.3.2, p. 171.25 Westerink).

[142] What is missing in Pollux, among other things, is also the paraphrase of the law of ostracism. As observed above, p. 48, one element of the text of this law is adduced by the Vatican excerpt.

[143] One additional argument in favour of this hypothesis may be Tzetzes' strange idea of throwing the ostraka into the Kynosarges (*Chiliades*, 8.448–459, 465, and 481). Raubitschek (1958) 87 brilliantly observed that this mistake might have resulted from confusing

similarly in that they both were organised in a two-stage procedure, involving a preliminary vote and the final vote after some period of time left for consideration. This fact might have been the ultimate source of confusion resulting in one of the 'meaningful errors' studied above.[144] From this point of view, one can even say that conflation of the two institutions could have been natural in the late lexicographical tradition, when Byzantine scholars realised, among other things, the fundamental similarity between the procedures and between the exotic 'instruments of vote' in both cases.

Only when positing an early Byzantine erudite tradition of the kind postulated above can one try to explain the actual form of the account about ostracism we find in *Vaticanus Graecus* 1144 no. 312, or to put it otherwise, to understand the mechanism of 'conflation' we encounter in the Vatican version.

When faced with the (hypothetical) corrupt, or better confused tradition, which merged some elements of the material on *ostrakophoria* with that on *ekphyllophoria* (most probably by abbreviating accounts on both subjects), Byzantine lexicographers could, of course, rely on alternative sources of information, so they could easily dissociate ostracism from *ekphyllophoria* in their own works. However, as we have seen, some significant errors were still left in their lexical entries, which proves the existence of their shared and corrupt source(s). This fact is best explained, I think, if we assume that, in principle, the lexicographers simply cut their source-material to come up with what they considered the corrected and reasonable version of the evidence they had at their disposal for *ekphyllophoria*. Meanwhile, Theodoros Metochites let one element of the conflated tradition creep into his account of *ostrakophoria*. He just relied on his memory and instinctively 'enriched' his otherwise Plutarchean narrative by a memorable detail, the Bouleuterion as the venue of the vote of ostraka.

Tzetzes, using most probably the same source-material as Theodoros (i.e., Plutarch's *Life of Aristides* combined with our hypothetical early Byzantine

---

ekphyllophoria with the procedure of separating citizens from those illegally inscribed as citizens, or *nothoi* (cf. Tzetzes, *Chiliades*, 8.449–450 with Pollux, 8.18, where this procedure is only briefly touched upon), who were ordered to the Kynosarges (cf. *Suda*, s.v. *eis Kynosarges* [EI 290 Adler]). In a similar vein, the compressed *Suda* entry *ekphyllophorein* (E 721 Adler) might have originated in the same source, too. Cf. also the technical language of sch Aeschin. 1 (*In Tim.*) 111 = 242a–b Dilts.

[144] εἴ ποτέ τις τῶν πολιτῶν ἀδικεῖν ἐδόκει καὶ ἀνάξιος εἶναι τοῦ συνεδρίου τῶν φ', ἐσκόπει ἡ βουλὴ περὶ αὐτοῦ, εἰ χρὴ αὐτὸν μηκέτι βουλεύειν, ἀλλ' ἐλαθῆναι καὶ τοῦ συνεδρίου, in the case of the lexicographical entries on *ekphyllophoria*, and τὴν βουλὴν τινῶν ἡμερῶν σκεψαμένην... ὅντινα δέοι τῶν πολιτῶν φυγαδευθῆναι κτλ., in the Vatican excerpt.

source stemming from Pollux) and relying on his memory as well, provided his readers with his own blend of earlier and already confused traditions adding his ingenious speculations and witty ideas to this mixture. The important point is that what Tzetzes did, among other things, was trying to reconcile the confused data and amusingly explain the relationship between *ostrakophoria* and *ekphyllophoria* by linking the difference between them with the problem of availability of ostraka and of leaves in different places and different seasons of the year. We can think of a similar principle behind the account of ostracism as given by the excerpt of *Vaticanus Graecus* 1144.

As established beyond any reasonable doubt by Robert Develin (see above), the writer of the excerpt was sloppy and inattentive, so the intellectual effort I postulate here ought to be ascribed to his immediate source, which must have worked on similar data to that of the lexicographers, John Tzetzes and Theodoros Metochites. At this juncture, it is important to bear in mind that this immediate source of our excerpt was surely not a lexicographer, but most probably a serious writer who tried to come up with a reasonable narrative of ostracism, just as Tzetzes did in a much less serious context.

Based on the already 'contaminated' tradition, which confused ostracism with the institution of *ekphyllophoria*, the Byzantine scholar conceived a coherent and meaningful account (to be later confusingly copied by the writer of Vat. Gr. 1144). Its fundamental premise, just like in the case of John Tzetzes, was the idea that *ekphyllophoria* (or *ekphyllophorēsis*) was tantamount to ostracism as just another name for the Athenian form of exile (*exoria* in Tzetzes, *apheinai* in Pollux). When confronted with what seemed to him a corrupt view of the relationship between the two, the resolute Byzantine erudite made an ambitious decision to seamlessly integrate the two aspects of the pre-existing tradition by arranging them in diachronic order and thus conceiving a meaningful account of the historical development of ostracism. On the one hand, he was aware of the high requirement of six thousand ostraka cast by the *dēmos* at large and, on the other hand, of the vote in the much narrower circle of the Council of Five Hundred. Consequently, it was only natural for him to ascribe the less known and less spectacular practice of 'leafing out' to an earlier 'phase' of what he considered ostracism. The only 'fact' our scholar needed to invent, or better introduce, was the substitution of the rule of two hundred votes against the exiled citizen by six thousand votes by the decision of the *dēmos* made 'later' (*hysteron*). This temporal adverb, only vaguely suggesting a chronological relationship between the two 'stages' of ostracism, was the most straightforward and rather elegant solution to all the problems encountered by our Byzantine scholar.

As a result, an original but entirely baseless account of the 'evolution' of ostracism was born, ripe for some twentieth-century students of this institution to be seduced by its unexpected novelty.

1.2.3 Ostracism and the Scapegoat Ritual

Having discarded three groups of sources used by the supporters of the historicity of 'ostracism before ostracism' (traces of *ostrakophoriai* in the Greek world allegedly predating ostracism in Athens, the so-called Athenian 'political' ostraka of the archaic times, and the purported evidence of Athenian 'bouleutic', i.e., pre-democratic ostracism), we are left with one more argument to consider. As I have already mentioned, some scholars see a clear connection with the scapegoat ritual in the logic of Athenian ostracism of historical times.[145] This idea is sometimes transferred further onto the analysis of the genesis and 'prehistory' of this Athenian institution.[146] I shall consider hypotheses of this kind at the end of this chapter, leading to more general conclusions regarding the potential existence of 'ostracism before ostracism' in Athens and beyond (1.3).

A local variant of the scapegoat ritual is well-attested for Athens in sources describing the Ionian festival of Thargelia.[147] However, our sources do not associate this festival or its ritual with ostracism by any means. David Mirhady is right, then, to challenge the general link between ostracism and the scapegoat ritual, increasingly popular in scholarship. Apart from

---

[145] Louis Gernet was the first to reach this conclusion, followed by Jean-Pierre Vernant, in Vernant, Vidal-Naquet (1973) 124–126 (with nn. 115 and 120, where the scholar refers to a lecture delivered by Gernet in February 1958). Cf. Burkert (1985) 83; Mossé, Schnapp Gourbeillon (1994) 48–49. Cf. also Fisher (2001) 249–250. See especially Ogden (1997) 142–145 (ostracism as 'an early democratic rationalising development of the scapegoat ritual', p. 142); it is the most comprehensive work on this topic, but also verging on free association at times (e.g., 'casting' ostraka into the Bouleuterion enclosure in Vatican Codex 1144 as a lineal remnant of the ritual stoning of the 'scapegoat'). Contrasting with such interpretations are the well-balanced studies by Mirhady (1997) and recently by Reggiani (2016), and an earlier one by Parker (1983) 269–271. On Greek scapegoat rituals (comparatively), see Bremmer (1983), who, significantly, does not mention ostracism in his study at all. See also Burkert (1985) 82–84.

[146] See, e.g., Mossé, Schnapp Gourbeillon (1994) 48–50. This way of thinking is compatible with the increasingly popular 'ritualistic' interpretations of Athenian democracy, especially at its initial stages. Good examples here are Mirhady (1997); Kosmin (2015).

[147] See Bremmer (1983) 301–302, 318–319, with bibliography cited in footnotes.

removing an individual from the *polis*, there is nothing in common between the two regarding their goals and procedure. Ostracism operated, theoretically, with pinpoint accuracy in anticipating and preventing a potential crisis. At the same time, the *pharmakos* ritual was supposed to save the community from general, unspecified, and already widely disseminated evil, or even from problems in a way naturally nested in the life of the *polis*. Ostracism is functionally connected with political power and the scapegoat ritual—defilement and purification. Most importantly perhaps, the essence of the former is a peaceful exile of a powerful citizen for 10 years, but above all, the ability to return to his hometown unthreatened after this period. It is difficult to imagine a sharper contrast between ostracism and the ritual mentioned.[148]

Let us add yet another argument to those presented by Mirhady. The fact that the Athenians resorted to *ostrakophoria* extremely rarely speaks against the idea of associating ostracism with the *pharmakos* ritual. Not only did they not use it regularly, at equal intervals defined by a ritual calendar, but they did not even resort to it in times of a grave threat for the *polis*, particularly an external one, as should be expected if the memory of such ritual roots of ostracism had lived in fifth-century Athens. Neither the war with the neighbours in the early years of Athenian democracy in the sixth century BC, the wars of the 60s–40s of the fifth century BC, nor finally the Peloponnesian War served as a pretext for an *ostrakophoria*.[149] Naturally, this can be considered as resulting from conscious, sensible acting of the Athenian people in this matter, but it seems evident that the decisions of the *dēmos* were not restrained here by any ritual or old custom, or even a general association of ostracism with the scapegoat ritual. As Robert Parker cautiously writes, 'the institution seems [...] to have been functional, if singular'.[150]

Let us move on to a more specific level. While discussing the allegedly very close analogies between ostracism and the *pharmakos* ritual, Daniel Ogden analyses in detail the case of ostracising Hyperbolus, claiming that 'ostracism seems to have returned to its roots in its final and discrediting

---

[148] Mirhady (1997) 15, 17.
[149] The exceptionally high accumulation of ostracisms in the 480s, between the two Persian Wars, as well as their later 'chronological distribution' will be the subject of my consideration further on, at 2.2.3.
[150] Parker (1983) 269: 'It has sometimes been suggested that ostracism is a kind of expulsion of the scapegoat in secularized form. The institution seems, however, to have been functional, if singular; and it is not clear that its symbolic and expressive significance is sufficiently important in contrast to its purely practical effect to make such an explanation appropriate.'

use'.¹⁵¹ At the same time, he reminds us that already Hyperbolus' contemporaries regarded this event as scandalous precisely because of the person exiled, 'unworthy' of the previous (and intended by the lawgiver) victims of this institution.¹⁵² In other words, it is true that, as Ogden shows, the figure of Hyperbolus perfectly illustrates the possible links between the scapegoat ritual and the institution of ostracism. The problem is that it is precisely here where we can fully see the limitations of hypotheses of this kind because already in the view of the Athenians of the second half of the fifth century, this politician was not suited to be a victim of ostracism. Meanwhile, those who were considered 'worthy' of being ostracised, representatives of best Athenian families, and at the same time often people of great merit to the *polis*, do not fit at all the social and political 'profile' of the scapegoat. Despite that, Ogden goes further in his argument, pointing to implicit associations between beggar and king, allegedly occurring in the case of Hyperbolus, despised by the Athenians. In this manner—and, in a way, above the heads of all the fifth-century victims of ostracism, except one—this last and unusual *ostrakophoria* may become an argument supporting ritual origins of the classical and typical ostracism.¹⁵³

One could assume, of course, that the idea to expel outstanding citizens from the *polis* can be fitted into the framework of the logic reflected in myths featuring a community being saved by a sacrifice made (voluntarily) by a king (for instance, the Athenian ruler Codrus) or members of the royal family (for instance, the daughters of king Erechtheus). However, as Bremmer rightly points out in his excellent study of scapegoat rituals in Greece, in the historical material available to us, the role of the *pharmakos* is always played by a wretched and despised member of the community, who, following the logic of the myth, is treated like royalty until the moment of ritual expulsion. It is only in the world of myth where significant figures take on the function of scapegoats, but even then, we are dealing with individuals of a marginal status in the *polis*: girls, young men, or a king.¹⁵⁴ Hence,

---

[151] Ogden (1997) 143-144 (cit. p. 143).
[152] See above, pp. 6-7. For more details on Hyperbolus' ostracism, see below, pp. 240-241.
[153] What is more, through the association with Hyperbolus as a typical demagogue, another argument for the connection between ostracism and the scapegoat ritual, in the view of Ogden (1997) 144-145, becomes Cleon, who (admittedly) was never ostracised, nor was he ever, in all probability, even a 'candidate' for ostracism in *ostrakophoria* voting (see below, pp. 118-119).
[154] Bremmer (1983) 303-307.

Athenian ostracism does not seem likely to have been directly rooted in the Athenian *pharmakos* ritual.[155]

At the same time, I have a strong impression that the way in which Vernant wrote and Louis Gernet spoke about the relationship between ostracism and the scapegoat ritual suggests a link that is more structural or 'dialectic' rather than a direct or 'genetic' descent.[156] From this point of view, even if ostracism was introduced at a particular, and quite late, historical moment, without consciously drawing any inspiration from the *pharmakos* ritual, the observations of both these scholars remain in force, as they refer to the logic of the Athenian collective imagery rather than to the logic of institutions or of Athenian rituals of a particular historical period. It is the attempt at 'historicisation' of this connection by some scholars that I regard as unjustified.

David Mirhady suggests taking a look at ostracism from a slightly different perspective, namely from the point of view of a 'ritual institution' of a hero-athlete, which was recognised in our sources by Joseph Fontenrose. However, Mirhady eventually leans towards the opinion that the 'ritual *aition*' of ostracism with such connotations could have functioned only in the Athenians' imagination, but it was not based on any specific ritual.[157]

In his insightful article on the genesis of Athenian ostracism, Lindsay G. H. Hall points out the possibility of ritual connotations of this institution on a more general level. While the preliminary voting in the ostracism procedure most probably took place during the Lenaia festival, the *ostrakophoria* itself, if it were to happen in a given year, would take place, according

---

[155] To the 'ritualistic' arguments for the existence of historical links between ostracism in Athens and the scapegoat ritual one more can be added. As Bremmer demonstrates, processions leading the *pharmakos* outside the community's boundary obligatorily started at the Prytaneion, as the political–ritual heart of the *polis* (Bremmer (1983) 313). Those giving credence to the version from Vatican Codex 1144 could claim that the role of the Bouleuterion in the procedure of ostracism had its roots precisely in this ritual. However, having excluded this testimony from among our trustworthy sources, we are losing support for such an interpretation.

[156] Vernant, Vidal-Naquet (1973) 125–126: 'Quand [la cité] fonde l'ostracisme, elle crée une institution dont le rôle est symmétrique et inverse du rituel des Thargélies. Dans la personne de l'ostracisé, la cité expulse ce qui en elle est trop élevé et incarne le mal qui peut lui venir par le haut. Dans celle du *pharmakós*, elle expulse ce qu'elle comporte de plus vil et qui la menace par le bas. Par ce double et complémentaire rejet, elle se délimite elle-même par rapport à un au-delà et à un en deçà. Elle prend la mesure propre de l'humain en opposition d'un côté au divin et à l'héroïque, de l'autre au bestial et au monstrueux.' In n. 120 on p. 126 Vernant refers to Gernet's observation that between the antithetical poles of ostracism and the scapegoat ritual there exists sometimes a peculiar feedback loop, as it happened in the case of the ostracism of the 'unworthy' Hyperbolus.

[157] Mirhady (1997) 15–19. Cf. Fontenrose (1968).

to the scholar, during the Dionysia.[158] However, the problem is that the saturation, so to say, of the ritual calendar of the Athenian *polis*, makes such considerations virtually unverifiable.[159] A discussion on this topic would be possible only if we could recognise some Dionysiac elements in the practice of ostracism, directly linking this institution with this deity's festival, but this, I believe, is impossible.

To sum up, I would argue that no convincing arguments can be found for the practice of ostracism, or even the general idea to introduce this institution in Athens, to have derived from the scapegoat ritual or any other specific religious ritual which we know about nowadays. This does not exclude various connections of this institution with Athenian religion or, more generally, with the religious imagination of the Athenian people. Still, it does not allow us to use religious or ritual arguments to explain the genesis of ostracism.

1.3 Conclusions: The Invention of Democratic Athens

What is at stake in the discussion regarding 'ostracism before ostracism' in Athens and beyond is the ability to identify the potential sources of inspiration for the Athenian institution of ostracism. A priori, it is conceivable that Athenian ostracism of historical times could have emerged as a result of the influence of certain widespread political customs or rituals, or perhaps even laws existing in specific *poleis*, or that it could have constituted another stage in the evolution of local Athenian rituals or institutions using ostraka with the name of the citizen threatened with some form of punishment for their behaviour in Athenian public life. However, on the one hand, it turns out that all the *ostrakophoriai* outside Athens attested in literary or archaeological sources are later, and often much later, than the Athenian ostracism, and that in the majority of cases, it can be argued that ostracism or

---

[158] Hall (1989) 99. See, however, below, pp. 127–129.
[159] Carcopino (1935) 71 in turn, saw a connection between ostracism and the Anthesteria, due to the temporal proximity of *ostrakophoria* to the festival. He is followed by Mossé and Schnapp Gourbeillon (1994) 48. The difference lies in the fact that Carcopino did not suggest any ritual or symbolic connections, but only a practical link: the masses of Athenians gathered for the festival guaranteed high attendance at the *ostrakophoria*. Cf. also Hansen (1989) [1983] 81–82.

similar institutions were adopted in various parts of the Greek world following the Athenian model.[160] On the other hand, I have excluded a direct influence of Athenian rituals (such as the scapegoat ritual) on the emergence of ostracism in Athens, and secondly, a decisive role in this matter of an archaic Athenian institution using ostraka.[161]

It should be emphasised here, nonetheless, that my so far negative conclusions are of merely relative value at this point. Being unable to exclude any of the possibilities mentioned above indisputably, I have only endeavoured to demonstrate that particular 'positive' cases of hypothetical sources of inspiration for Athenian ostracism referred to by scholars cannot be used in the discussion about the beginnings of this institution in Athens.

Therefore, it can cautiously be said that we are now entitled to embark on investigating the 'facts' and the procedure, and especially the primary aims of Athenian ostracism, autonomously, regardless of various theories of 'ostracism before ostracism' appearing in scholarship. Perhaps there existed (in or outside Athens) precedents for the ostracism law, but in the light of the material available to us today, one has to conclude that at the moment of the introduction of this law in Athens, the lawgiver was not constrained by any ritual, legal, customary or generally institutional 'straightjacket'; he was making relatively independent decisions regarding the shape of the future law in this matter. He was not following or adapting any specific technical solution (Athenian or foreign) either, even if he might have been superficially inspired by some formal solution, perhaps used in a completely different context.[162] More specifically, we can tentatively assume that the Athenian lawgiver who introduced ostracism (even though his actions must have been determined by various factors, as is usually the case) invented this institution in response to the current and long-term needs of the Athenians, as he understood them at that point. This admittedly very general presumption will allow me to move on to the next stage of my investigation.

---

[160] Nevertheless, it has to be admitted that in the cases of Argos and Tauric Chersonesos, there is still some hesitation in this matter, due to the relatively early dating of ostracisms in these places.
[161] It cannot be excluded that some political–judicial voting with ostraka had taken place before Cleisthenes' time and that he could have followed this model, but cases of such voting were most probably exceptional and carried out ad hoc, without being an element of an obligatory procedure or a particular law.
[162] The latter seems to be evidenced by the (hypothetical) decision to apply a similar procedural principle and a similar technical solution in both ostracism and *ekphyllophoria*. Cf. above, 1.2.2 with n. 129, on the terminology of *ekphyllophoria*. Cf. also Węcowski (2018) 13–15.

However, it should be added that eliminating the testimony of excerpt 213 of Vatican Codex 1144 from the corpus of our sources will have far-reaching consequences for my entire reasoning concerning another fundamental research aim: the search for the primary functions of Athenian ostracism. Methodologically, a definitive exclusion of the historicity of the 'bouleutic' stage in its evolution allows us to preliminarily assume the possibility of a comprehensive interpretation of this institution's function throughout the entire period of its operating in fifth-century Athens. For since, contrary to the view of scholars fascinated by the testimony of the Vatican Codex, no fundamental formal or legal change happened on the way of ostracism's functioning, we can posit a tentative hypothesis that the primary aims of this institution can be studied based on the data available to us from the subsequent decades of its fifth-century history. Minor changes in the organisation of the procedure of ostracism cannot be excluded, of course, but we have rejected the possibility of a takeover of this institution by the Athenian people acting *in corpore* from a narrower group of magistrates in the Athenian *polis*. In this context, we can assess the original intentions of the lawgiver in the light of the way ostracism functioned in later times—or at least, we are allowed to keep doing it until we prove that such a course of action is unjustified.

2
Towards a Reconstruction of Ostracism in Athens
The Facts

In the following chapters, I shall tackle the most important conundrums in studying the procedure of ostracism. In this chapter, I shall consider the facts: dating the introduction of the ostracism law in Athens and the historically attested cases of ostracising Athenian citizens: their overall number and dating (even though the last issue will not be crucial for my argument). In the next chapter, I shall consider the essential issues connected with the procedure of ostracism, looking at its stages and particular issues regarding the topography of ostracism, counting the sherds during *ostrakophoria*, etc. While the first, 'factual' part of this endeavour will require constant assessment of the credibility (and, if possible, of the provenance) of sources offering us detailed information of this kind, in the second part, apart from this problem, we also have to ponder a more general question. For it does not suffice to ask how the sources available to us, especially A.P., know anything about the procedure of ostracism. Most important will be the issue of whether we can at all speak about one ostracism procedure, from the moment of its introduction, through the times of the last *ostrakophoria*, until the moment when Ps.-Aristotle described the elements of this procedure. In other words, whether the way ostracism operated remained virtually unaltered throughout the 90 years of this institution's functioning and then for the subsequent 90 years of its 'fossil-like' existence in the Athenian political system. In the last matter, we are bound to rely on circumstantial evidence because our sources do not provide us with a direct answer to this question. However, essential here will be to decide on one particular detail: whether the two-stage procedure of ostracism existed already in the times when the Athenians used this institution to remove outstanding citizens from the *polis*, or perhaps it was introduced later, after the negative ostracism experience of the second half of the fifth century, to make its 'abuse' impossible.

In many cases, my considerations will illustrate the general problem of the sources and the research method in the study of ostracism, which I mentioned briefly in the introduction. Even the earliest ancient scholars of this institution, working in the second half of the fourth century BC, despite having at their disposal first-hand knowledge about the initial stages of the procedure of ostracism (as they were still carried out in Athens in their times), had little information on *ostrakophoria* because the actual 'voting' with ostraka had already been abandoned two generations earlier, in the last quarter of the fifth century. This is clearly visible in the case of *A.P.*, whose author mentions annual preliminary voting on ostracism (43.5), but in the systematic part of his work he has nothing to say about the organisation of *ostrakophoria*. Nonetheless, the imagination of the fourth-century scholars was sparked, and their attention was attracted by this decisive and final act of each ostracism. Therefore, it is fair to say that from the very beginning, the interests of our ancient authors were incompatible with their knowledge about ostracism, which must have had a significant and naturally negative impact on the content of the earliest testimonies regarding this institution. It can also be assumed a priori that throughout the subsequent centuries in the history of ancient and Byzantine interest in antiquities, such source problems must have been further aggravated. Moreover, also modern scholars, even after the information on ostracism contained in *A.P.*[1] went into circulation, remained focused on the interpretation of *ostrakophoria*, failing to acknowledge the significance of the preliminary stage of ostracism's procedure in Athens, known to us incomparably better, thanks to the description by Ps.-Aristotle. This double 'original sin' regarding the sources and methods committed in the studies on this institution has to be kept in mind by anyone attempting to establish essential facts in its history.

2.1 Cleisthenes or the 'Generation of *Marathonomachoi*'? Dating the Law about Ostracism

2.1.1 Ps.-Aristotle, Harpocration, and Androtion's *Atthis*

One of the most vivid scholarly controversies regarding Athenian ostracism concerns the date when the law of ostracism was introduced in Athens.[2]

---

[1] Cf. Bravo (1997).
[2] Thomsen (1972) 16–60 gave a thorough, systematic and critical, survey of the scholarly positions in this debate since the seminal study of Carcopino (1935). Early in the history of this discussion Cleisthenes' authorship of the ostracism law was supported by (among others):

This discussion is vital in itself, but—as we shall see further on—its results may also have a decisive impact on another crucial issue in the study of 'facts' regarding ostracism, namely on our idea of how often and in what circumstances the Athenians resorted to *ostrakophoria* (see below, 2.2). This, in turn, is of fundamental importance for explaining the mechanisms and aims of this institution's operation in Athens.

The controversy arises principally from the peculiar way in which *A.P.* (22.3–4) speaks about the first ostracism, but also from the juxtaposition of this passage with an entry in Harpocration's lexicon, which is largely concurrent with Ps.-Aristotle. Therefore, it has to be strongly emphasised that the debate regarding the date of the introduction of ostracism in Athens (and, in consequence, regarding the originator of this law) has, as Konrad H. Kinzl brilliantly pointed out in his article of 1991,[3] a completely different status than the other 'factual' discussions which I shall present below, especially the classic scholarly debates on the duration of the 'punishment' for the ostracised Athenians and the geography of their exile. In the dispute regarding the date of the ostracism law, our problem arises not from a discrepancy in the ancient traditions we possess but from the divergence between two extant versions of the same tradition. Let us, then, take a look at the relevant texts.

In the historical part of *A.P.* (22.1)—at the beginning of the section about a new stage in the evolution of the Athenian political system, following Cleisthenes' reforms—the author briefly summarises the impact of this politician on the Athenian *politeia*. He firmly states that Cleisthenes introduced new laws 'with regard to [the interests of] the people' (*plēthos*), and among them the ostracism law (καινοὺς δ' ἄλλους θεῖναι τὸν Κλεισθένη στοχαζόμενον τοῦ πλήθους, ἐν οἷς ἐτέθη καὶ ὁ περὶ τοῦ ὀστρακισμοῦ νόμος). The *A.P.*'s diction here is extremely succinct (some have even suggested a lacuna),[4] but it is indisputable that to this writer, the authorship of the ostracism law is beyond the slightest doubt. What is more, it seems that *A.P.* counts this law among the basic package of Cleisthenes' reforms, considering it as characteristic, or even symptomatic, of his political intentions. In any case, he places it chronologically with complete confidence before the next

---

Wilamowitz (1893) v. 1, 123 n. 3; Seeck (1904) 300–301; and in more recent times, very cautiously, e.g., by Raaflaub (1995) 29 (with bibliography cited in the notes) and Bleicken (1995) 47, 518–519. In favour of dating the introduction of ostracism to the times of the first exile attested in our sources—Beloch (1926) 332–333 (cf. already Beloch (1914) 30, with n. 1); and more recently, e.g., Gouschin (2009), with ample bibliography. Stein-Hölkeskamp (1989) 193–194 (with bibliography cited abundantly) leaves the matter undecided.

[3] Kinzl (1991a) 44.   [4] See Rhodes, *ad loc*.

TOWARDS A RECONSTRUCTION OF OSTRACISM IN ATHENS 69

stages of the evolution of the Athenian political system and definitely before the battle of Marathon, which he briefly mentions further on (22.3). Of course, the concision of *A.P.*'s author is characteristic of his writing style and way of thinking. Still, the almost reflex mention of ostracism seems to suggest that the writer thoughtlessly assumed that his readers would associate this institution with Cleisthenes as well. However, interpretative issues significant for us appear only in the third and fourth paragraph in this chapter of *A.P.*:

[3] ἔτει δὲ μετὰ ταῦτα δωδεκάτῳ νικήσαντες τὴν ἐν Μαραθῶνι μάχην, ἐπὶ Φαινίππου ἄρχοντος, διαλιπόντες ἔτη δύο μετὰ τὴν νίκην, θαρροῦντος ἤδη τοῦ δήμου, τότε πρῶτον ἐχρήσαντο τῷ νόμῳ τῷ περὶ τὸν ὀστρακισμόν, ὃς ἐτέθη διὰ τὴν ὑποψίαν τῶν ἐν ταῖς δυνάμεσιν, ὅτι Πεισίστρατος δημαγωγὸς καὶ στρατηγὸς ὢν τύραννος κατέστη. [4] καὶ πρῶτος ὠστρακίσθη τῶν ἐκείνου συγγενῶν Ἵππαρχος Χάρμου Κολλυτεύς, δι' ὃν καὶ μάλιστα τὸν νόμον ἔθηκεν ὁ Κλεισθένης, ἐξελάσαι βουλόμενος αὐτόν. οἱ γὰρ Ἀθηναῖοι τοὺς τῶν τυράννων φίλους, ὅσοι μὴ συνεξαμαρτάνοιεν ἐν ταῖς ταραχαῖς, εἴων οἰκεῖν τὴν πόλιν, χρώμενοι τῇ εἰωθυίᾳ τοῦ δήμου πρᾳότητι· ὧν ἡγεμὼν καὶ προστάτης ἦν Ἵππαρχος.

[3] In the twelfth year after this they won the battle of Marathon, in the archonship of Phaenippus. After waiting for two years after their victory, when the *dēmos* was now confident, they then first used the law about ostracism, which had been enacted because of their suspicion of the men in powerful positions, because Pisistratus from being a demagogue and general had been established as tyrant.

[4] The first man ostracised was one of his relatives, Hipparchos son of Charmos, of Kollytos; and it was because of him in particular that Cleisthenes had enacted the law, wanting to drive him out. For the Athenians allowed those of the tyrants' friends who had not joined in wrongdoing during the disturbances to live in the city, following the *dēmos*' customary mildness; and the leader and champion of these men was Hipparchos. (tr. P. J. Rhodes, slightly adapted)

The text of *A.P.*, as preserved on the papyrus, does not present virtually any difficulties here.[5] Problems arise when these paragraphs are juxtaposed with

---

[5] As Benedetto Bravo has pointed out to me, the occurrence of the word οτε in front of Pisistratus' name in the third paragraph, as preserved on the London Papyrus, would have substantial consequences for my interpretation. However, it is indisputable that Kenyon's obvious

the already mentioned entry in Harpocration's lexicon to Attic orators (*s.v. Hipparchos*, 161.2 Dindorf). Part of this entry forms a fragment of the Atthidographer Androtion in Jacoby's edition (*FGrHist* 324 F 6). I am quoting below the passage in question in the most recent edition by Hans Taeuber (Siewert, T 31):

ἄλλος δέ ἐστιν Ἵππαρχος ὁ Χάρμου, ὥς φησι Λυκοῦργος ἐν τῷ κατὰ Λεωκράτους. περὶ δὲ τούτου Ἀνδροτίων ἐν τῇ β' φησὶν ὅτι συγγενὴς μὲν ἦν Πεισιστράτου τοῦ τυράννου καὶ πρῶτος ἐξωστρακίσθη, τοῦ περὶ τὸν ὀστρακισμὸν νόμου τότε πρῶτον τεθέντος διὰ τὴν ὑποψίαν τῶν περὶ Πεισίστρατον, ὅτι δημαγωγὸς ὢν καὶ στρατηγὸς ἐτυράννησεν.

Another [man called Hipparchos commonly mentioned by orators – M.W.] is Hipparchos son of Charmos, as Lycurgus says in his speech *Against Leocrates* [§ 117]. Concerning this man Androtion says in Book Two [of his *Atthis*] that he was a relative of Pisistratus the tyrant and was the first to be ostracised, since the law about *ostrakismos* had first been established at that time on account of suspicion (*hypopsia*) of Pisistratus and his circle because, being a popular leader (*dēmagōgos*) and general (*stratēgos*), he had become a tyrant.   (tr. N.F. Jones, *BNJ*; adjusted by L.O.)

It is quite commonly assumed nowadays that the ultimate source of Harpocration's lexicon[6] was the excellent but unpreserved Attic onomasticon, referred to as V[1] since the ground-breaking study by Georg Wentzel.[7] Despite such an excellent source, our Harpocration entry is very chaotic. Other Hipparchoi occurring there (as well as magistrates called *hipparchoi*) have been treated very carelessly. References to authors who allegedly mention them turn out to be completely misleading.[8] Konrad Kinzl has rightly highlighted the misunderstandings and the linguistic and logical flaws of the epitomist of Harpocration, which we can to some extent correct,

---

conjecture ὅτι should be accepted here, even regardless of the fact that we find this word in the version preserved in Harpocration's lexicon (cf. below). Wilamowitz and Kaibel corrected οτε from the papyrus to ὁ γὰρ, which seems to be a slightly less 'economical' conjecture.

[6] Or 'Harpocration', as Kinzl (1991a) puts it: the lexicon has been preserved in two versions, one of which is highly abbreviated, and the other one, fuller, is very corrupt.

[7] Wentzel (1895) (reprinted in *LexGrMin*, pp. 1–11). Its author has been identified as a certain Iulianos, a contemporary of Oualerios (= Valerius) Diodoros; an episode from his life can be dated, thanks to a certain papyrus (*P. Oxy.* 2192), to 173 AD. See Alpers (1981) 120–123 (based on *P. Oxy.* 1904).

[8] Cf. Kinzl (1991a) 30–32.

by comparing the entry *Hipparchos* as it exists in the manuscript tradition and the *Suda* (*s.v. Hipparchos* [I 523 Adler]). Although some of Kinzl's conclusions seem far-fetched (see below), it has to be conceded that Harpocration's entry in its present shape cannot be treated as an authoritative source. Nonetheless, many scholars comparing this entry with *A.P.* 22.3–4 still tend to underplay the significance of Ps.-Aristotle's account, among other things, because this writer (Aristotle himself, according to Wilamowitz) has been considered since the times of Ulrich von Wilamowitz-Moellendorff a rather unremarkable historian.[9] From their standpoint, confirmation of this can be found, for instance, in the fact that *A.P.* does not cite here the authority of Androtion, even though it is undoubtedly following precisely this source. A reference to Androtion would allegedly indicate that Harpocration's source made more careful use of his *Atthis*.

The account of *A.P.* 22.3–4 is, of course, much more comprehensive and includes most of the content of Harpocration's entry. It has been observed (Kinzl 1991a) that the correspondence rate reaches 90 per cent of the vocabulary used in both texts. Therefore, there are two possibilities: either a common source of both these texts (Androtion?) or a direct dependence of Harpocration and his sources on *A.P.* However, the discrepancies between the account in *A.P.* and Harpocration's version are fundamental and clearly meaningful. Hipparchos son of Charmos of Kollytos (it should be pointed out that only *A.P.* gives the politician's *demotikon*) is in both versions a relative (*syngenēs*) of Pisistratus—and it is Hipparchos who was the first to be ostracised in Athens. Nevertheless, while *A.P.* presents him as the first victim of ostracism and claims that he was the reason for the introduction of the ostracism law, it definitely separates the first application of ostracism (τότε πρῶτον ἐχρήσαντο τῷ νόμῳ τῷ περὶ τὸν ὀστρακισμόν), which it dates to 488/487 BC, from the legislation regarding ostracism, which, as we have seen, it ascribes to Cleisthenes and dates to the times of his reforms (22.1), i.e., to the year 508/507 BC. Harpocration, citing Androtion, states (as does *A.P.*) that Hipparchos was the first to be ostracised and that the law was introduced because of him, but at the same time the author affirms that ostracism was then instituted 'for the first time' (τοῦ περὶ τὸν ὀστρακισμὸν νόμου τότε πρῶτον τεθέντος).

The discrepancy between these two sources divided scholars not into two but into several camps, whose representatives have been trying to reconcile

---

[9] Cf., e.g., Wilamowitz (1893) v. 1, 366–367, 373 and *passim*.

the two texts in various ways—each choosing such a manner, however, that would allow them to support one or the other scenario mentioned. For on the entire discussion weighed the authority of the great historian Karl Julius Beloch, who said about ostracism that 'people do not forge such a weapon to let it rust for 20 years in its sheath' (Beloch 1926: 332). In other words, the incessant, and often very inventive, work of philologists on both these texts has been (and still is) determined by—diversely understood—historical probability.

To synthesise this very intensive discussion, one could say that the dispute is focused mainly on the discrepancies between Ps.-Aristotle's τότε πρῶτον ἐχρήσαντο and Harpocration's τότε πρῶτον τεθέντος.[10] Both these expressions, constituting the main difference in wording between these two texts, have been subject of attempts to correct or supplement so that their meanings become mutually compatible; however, it should immediately be added that Harpocration's phrase 'had first been established at that time' does not seem logical in itself.[11]

Another radical hypothesis in this matter was put forward by Konrad Kinzl, who tried to demonstrate that Harpocration's account is entirely worthless. This is because, first, invoking Androtion's authority is fundamentally misleading. According to Kinzl, Androtion must have discussed the genealogy of Hipparchos and Harpocration quoted the Atthidographer exclusively for this reason. The remaining part of the entry and the mention of ostracism would come directly from A.P., even though the entry in the good onomasticon of Attic orators, using Ps.-Aristotle, would have been distorted, corrupt and/or copied without comprehension. Even if the idea that all Harpocration's information about ostracism is wholly detached from Androtion's *Atthis* seems too radical to me, I agree with Kinzl in two fundamental points. This scholar observes, as does P.J. Rhodes (*ad loc.*), that the chapter of A.P. containing considerations on ostracism is very sophisticated in its formal composition (Rhodes recognises a subtle *Ringkomposition* there). We are, therefore, dealing with (1) a deliberate structure in A.P. (including a well-considered picture of ostracism), while

---

[10] See, among others, Schachermeyr (1932) 346, n. 2; Dover (1963); Keaney (1970a) and (1977); Meister (1971); Chambers (1979); Develin (1985b); Musti (1993); Jones (2015). Cf. Kinzl (1991a) and (1991b) as well as Sickinger (2003).

[11] Unless we assume that Harpocration's source knew, e.g., about some act of re-instatement of the ostracism law, which would have then been introduced more than once in the past. However, M. Chambers in *Aristoteles 10.1.*, translates this expression as 'genau dann, gerade dann', referring, i.a., to Thuc. I 96,2 and A.P. 41.2.

(2) Harpocration gives us a view which admittedly is verbally very close to it (or its fragment) but in a corrupt version. At this juncture, I must recall the attempt at explaining the discrepancies between A.P. and Harpocration undertaken by Felix Jacoby (in his edition of fragments of Greek historians). He assumed the existence in fourth-century Athens of two divergent narratives ascribing the authorship of ostracism either to Cleisthenes[12] or to some politician of the 80s, for instance, Themistocles. This discussion allegedly had an ideological background, as it would serve some Athenian writers to take the odium of democratic radicalism off Cleisthenes, the alleged creator of the honourable 'ancestral constitution' (*patrios politeia*).[13] Such would be, according to Jacoby, the stand taken by Androtion, who as if deliberately emphasised that ostracism was established only after the radicalisation of the *dēmos* following the battle of Marathon. Jacoby's hypothesis arises directly from his conviction of an ideological 'profile' of almost every Atthidographer. Androtion would write from the perspective of a moderate conservative, indeed as a follower and propagator of the ideology of *patrios politeia*.[14] The author of A.P., in turn, would go in the opposite direction in his view of the history of ostracism, deriving from the (allegedly) more widespread opinion, which Androtion questioned from an ideological perspective. However, the author of A.P. would not base his view on any sources but would merely use a kind of syllogism: ostracism is a democratic institution, and democratic institutions must come from Cleisthenes, so ostracism must have been his doing as well.[15] It is only very recently that Philip Harding has thoroughly and

---

[12] We know that this is precisely what Philochorus thought, *FGrHist* 328 F 30 (with comm. by Jacoby), and so did Ephorus (in Diodorus, XI 55,1) and some Atthidographic source of his (cf. Jacoby on Hellanicus, *FGrHist* 323a F23).

[13] Jacoby saw in this group the 'people from Theramenes' circle' and Isocrates. Cf. Ruschenbusch (1958) and Hansen (1990).

[14] See Jacoby (1949) 76 and, more generally, 71-78 (see also *FGrHist*, Text, pp. 87-93).

[15] Fornara (1963) made a slightly similar attempt in his article, explaining A.P.'s ascription of the ostracism law to Cleisthenes with a polemic against Androtion. The polemic would not be motivated ideologically but would rather be rooted in political theory (Fornara regards Aristotle as the author of A.P.), according to which Cleisthenes played a key role in the release of the potential democratic powers which were gradually starting to assert themselves with the increase of confidence and self-awareness of the *dēmos*. This is why (Aristotle) had to emphasise the distinction between the moment of introduction of the ostracism law and the time when ostracism was first used in practice. Although I generally disagree with Fornara's interpretation, I believe that he correctly recognised the significance of this chronological discrepancy in A.P., instead of blaming it on a coincidence or the preservation state of the texts of our two sources, as had done many scholars before him. See below.

convincingly criticised this ideological vision of Atthidography.[16] In his view, the Atthidographers' interests were strictly historical and antiquarian, and not political or ideological, as Jacoby claimed. Androtion's *Atthis* was a relatively concise work, without sufficient space for ideological or propagandistic constructs or a re-interpretation of Athenian history from such a point of view.

Relying partly on the observations by Harding and Kinzl, we can now return to the two texts discussed here. The most important conclusion of the scholars mentioned above is that attempts at reconciliation of the testimonies on ostracism by Ps.-Aristotle and Harpocration through emendation or supplementation of one of them are not worth undertaking. Our attention should be focused on the much fuller testimony in *A.P.* For the short excerpt in which both the sources coincide verbally, we can assume either Harpocration's dependence on *A.P.* or a derivation of both these texts from a common source, perhaps Androtion's *Atthis*. It is indisputable, however, that Harpocration gives us a very corrupt version of his source.[17]

The phrase in *A.P.*, 'they then first used the law about ostracism' (22.3), often discussed in scholarship, should be considered crucial for Ps.-Aristotle's line of reasoning. These strong words may at first seem to be expressing a polemical idea.[18] It is continued in the explanation of the reasons for which ostracism was applied so late on, given a bit further (22.4): the Athenians, following the *dēmos*' customary mildness, allowed some of the 'tyrants' friends' to remain in the *polis*.[19] Most scholars did not apprehend the connection between τότε πρῶτον ἐχρήσαντο and this statement in *A.P.*, because in the concise prose of Ps.-Aristotle the phrase about the kindness of the people misleadingly refers at the same time to the fact that some of the

---

[16] Harding, *Introduction, passim*. According to Harding, all the Atthidographers wrote with a democratic tendency, following the political current of their times. Harding, pp. 13–25 (see already Harding (1976); cf. Davies, *APF* no. 913) best demonstrates this on the example of Androtion, about whose long (40-year) and prolific political career in Athens we know most.

[17] This is also the ultimate conclusion of the thorough overview of scholarly debates by Thomsen (1972) 16–60: 'The principal conclusion of our survey of previous research must be that there is only one sound tradition in our ancient sources about the origin of ostracism [...]' (cit. p. 60).

[18] Jacoby saw this as well (comm. on Androtion, *FGrHist* 324 F 6, p. 121), but he ascribed it to *A.P.*'s arguing against Androtion's view, who in turn questioned the popular opinion attributing ostracism to Cleisthenes (see also above).

[19] Some scholars sought the origins of the thought about the alleged inherent kindness of the Athenian *dēmos* in Androtion—in the light of his fragment 46 (*ap.* Paus. VI 7,4–7). However, it seems to me that this passage by no means constitutes sufficient proof that the judgement from chapter 22 in *A.P.* came from Androtion. For the motif of the 'kindness of the *dēmos*', cf. also *A.P.* 16.10; Isoc. VII [*Areopag.*] 67–69; XV [*Antid.*] 20; Dem. XXIV [*Timocr.*] 51. Cf. below, p. 170.

'tyrants' friends' were allowed to remain in Athens after the Pisistratids were exiled (which is, of course, apparent in the text at first sight) and to the argument explaining such a late application of the ostracism law in practice (which is not immediately obvious).[20] However, to the author of *A.P.*, these two ideas were clearly connected, as they both prove the '*dēmos*' customary mildness'. Moreover, they both illustrate—through contrast—the change in the behaviour and position of the *dēmos* within the political system. Thus, we can conclude that the troublesome formulation 'then for the first time' does not have much polemic value, but it places a strong emphasis on the attempt to reconcile two seemingly contradictory pieces of information. Nevertheless, the aim was not to reconcile two alternative versions of dating the ostracism law or to argue in support of one of them, but something completely different. On the one hand, this law was introduced by Cleisthenes in (our) 508/507 BC, and on the other, the first victim of this law was Hipparchos in 488/487 BC. In the corrupt version passed on by Harpocration, at some stage of the development of this tradition, it was lost from sight that all this was about reconciling two seemingly disparate pieces of information; thus, the 'first application' of ostracism naturally became corrupt into its 'first (sic!) establishment'. It should immediately be noted that this corruption might have occurred at any stage of the tradition's evolution when a grammarian (even a very sensible one) was already dealing with merely a snippet of information, a small 'jotting' or note meant to help in formulating a given lexical entry or a piece of commentary on the orators, but did not have access to the whole context of the original account of ostracism. Thus, he could not see that several paragraphs above, his source unhesitantly ascribed the invention of ostracism to Cleisthenes and simultaneously dated it to 508/507 BC.

If we accept this explanation of the discrepancies between *A.P.* and Harpocration and at the same time consider as proven that *A.P.* gives us the original and incorrupt version of our account, we can venture a reconstruction of Ps.-Aristotle's line of thinking. Subsequently, we can draw some conclusions regarding not the knowledge or state of mind of this author in the second half of the fourth century BC, but rather the state of his sources on ostracism, and perhaps even make inferences regarding some historical facts connected with this institution.

---

[20] This observation was also made by Jacoby, even though cursorily and without drawing any further conclusions from it (Jacoby, comm. on Androtion, *FGrHist* 324 F 6, p. 116, n. 24). Cf. also Thomsen (1972) 30.

The attempt at explaining the (seeming) contradiction between the pieces of information available to him was most probably Ps.-Aristotle's own idea. Despite the low esteem in which scholars hold the research skills of *A.P.*'s author as a historian, this argumentatively very successful attempt should not cause distress. On the one hand, the writer was interested precisely in the successive stages of development of the Athenian *politeia* and the increasing participation of the *dēmos* in it. The explanation of ostracism's chronology proposed by him was firmly rooted in his interests. On the other hand, the recognition of the problem discussed here did not require complex historical criticism. We must simply assume that in the main source for these parts of *A.P.*, there were two factual pieces of information given in an annalistic manner: about the place of the ostracism law among Cleisthenes' laws and about the first application of this law 20 years later. Naturally, the best candidate to have been the hypothetical source of this information is Androtion's *Atthis*,[21] which Harpocration's entry refers to anyway. It should further be noticed that both in *A.P.* and Harpocration there recurs the idea of the anti-tyrannical cutting edge of the ostracism law and the clearly related information about Hipparchos' family connections with Pisistratus. It can be presupposed with high probability that this element, perhaps briefly explaining the reasons behind exiling Hipparchos in 488/487, was already present in Androtion.[22] Ps.-Aristotle kept all this information but also added his explanation why, on the one hand, the Athenians did not apply the law instituted by Cleisthenes for such a long time (22.4) and why they put it into practice at this particular moment of their political system's evolution (22.3: θαρροῦντος ἤδη τοῦ δήμου [...]). Whether any answer to these questions could be found in Androtion, is beyond our

---

[21] If the critically important fragment 30 of Philochorus, or perhaps better 'the big scholion about ostracism' (see in general Heftner (2018)), is based on a passage of Theophrastus' *Laws* (see below, pp. 158–160), one of the latter's sources of information for factual matters, as in the case of *A.P.*, could have been Androtion. If so, Androtion must have dated the introduction of ostracism to 508/507 BC, since our two best testimonies of this 'scholion' claim precisely this:... ἀρξάμενον [*scil.* τὸ ἔθος of ostracism—M.W.] νομοθετήσαντος Κλεισθένους, ὅτε τοὺς τυράννους κατέλυσεν, ὅπως συνεκβάλῃ καὶ τοὺς φίλους αὐτῶν. I think that the fact that in this testimony the law of ostracism, explicitly ascribed to Cleisthenes, and the attack against the 'friends of the tyrants' go hand in hand may be yet another important argument in our discussion here.
[22] This thought will reappear in *A.P.*, in paragraph 22.6. It is intriguing how significant a role it plays in Ps.-Aristotle's arranging the list of Athenians ostracised before the Persian Wars. *A.P.* divides them into two distinct groups, ensuing in chronological order: first the 'tyrants' friends', on whose account Cleisthenes had introduced this law 20 years earlier, then the others, 'far from tyranny' (22.6). See also below, 2.2.2.

knowledge—apart from the hint that Androtion could see a link between the fear of tyranny and Hipparchos' exile.[23]

For my present argument, the most important thing is that in his sources Ps.-Aristotle could find both the mention about the introduction of this law by Cleisthenes and about its first application 20 years later. And that both these pieces of information were trustworthy enough for the author of A.P. not to reject either (despite the seeming contradiction between them), but to try and reconcile them.

2.1.2 Cleisthenes, the Inventor of Ostracism?

Hans Taeuber and other commentators in the *Ostrakismos-Testimonien I* deny the possibility that the authorship of ostracism was in the fourth century unambiguously ascribed to Cleisthenes.[24] They emphasise that the first source to mention Cleisthenes by name in this context is A.P. In this matter, they follow Jacoby and those who claim that many details in the fourth-century representations of the more and less ancient history of the Athenian *polis* were a product of political polemics and ideological disputes revolving around the ideal of *patrios politeia*, which had flared up in Athens at the end of the fifth and the beginning of the fourth century. In the matter in question here, I cannot agree with this opinion. Already Herodotus had a detailed vision of Cleisthenes' reforms,[25] and the institution of ostracism widely echoed in the Greek world already in the 480s.[26] In this context, it seems impossible to me that until the first mention of ostracism's author by name in the second half of the fourth century, the Athenians (and possibly also other Greeks) had used in their spirited discussions about this institution merely the anonymous term 'lawgiver', without associating it with a specific Athenian reformer. The absence of Cleisthenes' name in this context in the earlier sources may instead be due to the nature of these sources: none

---

[23] Which may suggest, however, that the chronological hiatus between Cleisthenes' law and the first ostracism did not very much draw his attention. This in turn might have opened the way to the original interpretation in A.P.
[24] Taeubner, in: Siewert, pp. 449–458; cf. also Scheidel, *ibidem*, p. 483. At the same time, scholars attach much significance to the fact that the 'lawgiver' of ostracism appears only anonymously in two instances in the speech by Andocides IV [*Against Alcibiades*] (§§ 4 and 35). See Siewert, T 18, p. 289 (by Brigitte Eder and Herbert Heftner).
[25] Even though, as we know, the things he says about them are highly disappointing in terms of informational value, due to their anecdotal character: Hdt. V 66, 2; 69, 1–2; VI 131, 1.
[26] See above, p. 6, on Pindar (Siewert, T [?] 2).

of them recounts the beginnings of ostracism; they usually discuss only its particular cases or give its overall appraisal. The first extant account of the origins of this institution is found in Ps.-Aristotle. In other words, among the testimonies on ostracism available to us, this was the very first opportunity for Cleisthenes' name to be mentioned. Overall, we can reasonably assume that *A.P.* (and probably already Androtion) relied on a good Athenian tradition while pointing to Cleisthenes as the initiator of ostracism.[27]

A much more complex issue is the historical validity of the information that the first application of the ostracism law took place 20 years after Cleisthenes' reforms. This topic is closely related to how trustworthy the list of ostracism victims provided in *A.P.* is and, more generally, to the 'prosopography' of Athenian ostracism. All these matters will be discussed in the next section.

2.2 Athenian Ostracisms of 508/507 BC–ca. 416 BC

The aim of this section will be not so much to establish a reliable list of Athenian ostracisms as it will be to assess the number of citizens who were ostracised under the relevant Cleisthenes' law. On the one hand, we ought to consider the number of the attested *ostrakophoriai* carried out in Athens. On the other, the question arises how probable is that more of them took place without leaving traces in our literary sources—such cases could conceivably be testified to by the available epigraphic material or other data at our disposal.

2.2.1 The Extant Athenian Ostraka and the Study of the History of Ostracism

Due to the already mentioned scholarly focus on the Athenian *ostrakophoriai*, analyses of ostraka occupy a special place within the studies on

---

[27] The answer to the question whether this was an exclusively oral tradition (including the oral tradition from which the Atthidographers used by *A.P.* derived) or based on some documents as well does not depend on the assessment of the extent to which the text of Cleisthenes' laws was available in Athens of the fifth and the first half of the fourth century. If these laws were partly included in Nicomachus' 'codification', they were most probably not bearing Cleisthenes' name (see below, pp. 123–124 with n. 21). For general information on oral tradition in Athens of that time, see especially Raaflaub (1988); Thomas (1989).

ostracism.[28] However, it should be stressed here that the final scholarly publication of ostraka from Kerameikos was effectuated as late as 2018.[29] Additionally, their number (at least 9376 items catalogued in *Kerameikos 20*) is overwhelmingly higher than that of the finds from other areas in Athens (cumulatively, hardly above 1300),[30] including the Agora and the northern slope of the Acropolis (AO) in particular (see Fig. 3.1).[31] Research possibilities are now open, but it will take many years for scholars to come to terms with this fresh publication fully. The only ostracism 'votes' published and subsequently studied systematically thus far are those from the Agora (1145 items). This excludes 165 ostraka in possession of the American School in Athens, which still have not been catalogued, due to being difficult to identify. As a result, for instance, even in the case of the Athenian Agora, we cannot answer with full confidence whether, among the ostraka found on the site, there are empty 'votes', not bearing any graffiti with an ostracism 'candidate's' name. From the way in which the analysed and catalogued ostraka are being published, one may get an impression that such objects do not exist at all (the last section in various publications of individual deposits usually mentions 'other names'). Still, there is no guarantee that they are not present in the uncatalogued material, described as 'too fragmentary'.[32] What is more, even if we could analyse the uninscribed ceramic sherds from Athenian deposits, we still would not know whether or not they are a result of a later 'contamination' of these deposits with waste which accumulated in the Kerameikos or Agora in a natural way. Meanwhile, from the presence or absence, as well as from the proportion,

---

[28] In general, cf., e.g., Mann (2007) 66–74.   [29] *Kerameikos 20.1–2*, by Stefan Brenne.

[30] For earlier discussions of ostraka and deposits of ostraka from Kerameikos, see especially Thomsen (1972) 71–80, 101–106; Willemsen, Brenne (1991) and (1992); Brenne (1994) and (2001) as well as Brenne in: Siewert, pp. 36–166. Cf. esp. Lewis (1974); Williams (1978). Ostraka from the Agora have been published by Mabel Lang (*Agora 25*); cf. also Lang (1982). Cf. also Guarducci (1995) 524–534. To the figures mentioned above, over 275 new ostraka should now be added, including over 150 found on the Agora; see Sickinger (2017a) and (2017b).

[31] Except for the famous deposit of ostraka against Themistocles, discovered on the Acropolis slope (see below, pp. 150–153; cf. Fig. 3.5), those usually found outside the Agora or the Kerameikos, where ostraka were disposed of after use (see below), are most probably the result of coincidence, such as an ostracism 'vote' dropped by an Athenian citizen.

[32] Even now, in *Kerameikos 20.2*: 7.3.9.6 ('Unbeschriftet', p. 650), S. Brenne registers only two ostraka with 'no recognizable writing', because they belong both to a specific group of ostraka and at the same time are clearly individual objects. As far as I can see, the more detailed criteria of this inclusion (and of excluding others? how many of them?) are not further specified. See, however, *Kerameikos 20.1*, p. 2, where one learns of many sherds (previously) considered 'unwritten' ('als unbeschriftet geltenden Scherben') as being ultimately identified, which suggests, I think, that uninscribed potsherds do not count.

of such empty 'votes' in our corpus, a great deal could be inferred regarding the procedure of *ostrakophoriai*, the sentiments of the Athenians on the voting day and during the time immediately preceding it, as well as more generally—regarding the political climate, which in the year with an *ostrakophoria* would be determined mainly by this event.[33]

Moreover, it was only with the pioneering studies by Stefan Brenne, now culminating in his monumental edition of the Kerameikos material, that research on ostraka moved in the direction of more detailed prosopographic, political, and social considerations.[34] Before the ground-breaking studies of this author, scholarly work was predominantly focused on establishing the chronology of Athenian ostracisms,[35] verifying the credibility of literary sources in this matter, and supplementing the information provided there, with special attention paid to Ps.-Aristotle's *A.P.*

The scholarly effort in this respect, however, should be treated with reserve. Importantly, the methods used in such research took shape before the rapid surge of the number of known ostraka caused by the discovery of the 'Great Kerameikos Deposit' (or 'Great Deposit' henceforward) in 1965–1969 (ca. 8500 items in total).[36] Accordingly, scholars back then made certain general assumptions, which appeared evident to them at the time, but which now seem doubtful. Above all, they treated the entire corpus of ostraka known to us, especially individual deposits or groups of deposits, as representative in various ways of particular Athenian *ostrakophoriai*— even if not fit for exact dating or statistical analysis. Whereas only exceptionally can we date individual deposits by epigraphic or ceramic criteria or based on the entire find's stratigraphy. An absolute exception is the case of the 'Great Kerameikos Deposit'. On the one hand, it includes a sherd of a vessel by the well-known Pistoxenos Painter,[37] which suggests that the dating of this batch should be no earlier than after around 480 BC. On the other hand, we are (almost) certain that this batch belongs to a single *ostrakophoria* because more than ten per cent of ostraka (i.e., 1014 items)

---

[33] Invalid votes (i.e., in this case, blank ballots; for 'spoiled ballots', see below, pp. 218–219 with n. 56) in our contemporary democracies are more and more seriously studied nowadays, opening interesting new insights into socio-demographic, institutional, and political factors (including, importantly, political discontent) involved. In general, cf. Power, Garand (2007); Moral (2016), and esp. Kouba, Lysek (2019). I owe these references to Adam Gendźwiłł.
[34] Brenne (2001) and Brenne in Siewert, T 1 with commentaries and syntheses.
[35] For the Kerameikos material, see now *Kerameikos 20.1*, esp. pp. 43–44.
[36] See, above all, Brenne (2001) 30–48 and Brenne in Siewert, T 1, pp. 40–43.
[37] Willemsen (1991) and *Kerameikos 20.1*, esp. pp. 43–44.

can be fitted to one another or can be interpreted as sherds of the same ceramic vessels or can be somehow related to one another.[38] Faced with this difficulty, for the absolute (but also relative) chronology of individual deposits and their groups, scholars resorted to circular reasoning, linking the prosopographic material from the ostraka with data obtained from literary sources. While the results proved valuable for general outlines, the findings on the detailed level—some of which became axioms in scholarship later on—often have to be treated with caution. To point out the main problems of method in this matter, I am forced to anticipate here my further results and briefly refer to the conclusions from the sections of my work to follow.

First of all, the statistical, prosopographical, and chronological calculations were based on the conviction that in our considerations, we can regard as trustworthy the mention of the threshold of 6000 ostraka, designating either the quorum or the qualified majority in the *ostrakophoria* voting. Therefore, it was speculated, for instance, that in a given deposit or a group of deposits (and thus within a fragmentarily preserved result of a given *ostrakophoria*), there are 'too many' or 'too few' ostraka with a particular name (or with a combination of two or more names on different ostraka) for this material to belong to a given year for which an *ostrakophoria* is attested in literary sources with the name of its victim. The same principle led to the emergence of the phantom of an 'abortive *ostrakophoria*',[39] when a dramatically small number of ostraka (or ostraka with certain names) was observed and ascribed to specific years in Athens' history. Further in my work, I shall try to demonstrate that neither a quorum nor a qualified majority of ostracism ever existed in the number of 6000 'votes' and that our sources (the Atthidographer Philochorus and most probably already his peripatetic predecessor Theophrastus), for reasons important to them but otherwise completely unjustifiably, 'supplemented' the text of the ostracism law available to them with this piece of information.[40]

Secondly, while analysing the content and location of individual deposits or their groups, scholars operated within a tradition formed not only before the discovery of the 'Great Deposit' but also before the identification by

---

[38] *Kerameikos 20.1*, esp. pp. 141–142. Cf. Brenne (2001) 38 and Brenne in: Siewert, T 1, pp. 72–76. See below for possible implications of this fact for our understanding of Athenian *ostrakophoriai*.
[39] *Agora 25*, 22–24, following Vanderpool (1972) 234–235, on the alleged *ostrakophoria* of 483 BC.
[40] See below, p. 170.

T. B. L. Webster of a vase representation with a scene of 'vote' counting during *ostrakophoria* (see Fig. 3.4).[41] I shall discuss and interpret this scene in detail in one of the sections to follow,[42] but I shall refer to my conclusions in this matter already here to cast doubt on some results of the research carried out so far.

Insight into the method criticised here can be gained, for instance, from the highly reliable works by Mabel L. Lang. She assumes that the occurrence of a name of an ostracism victim known to us on ostraka from a given deposit allows us to connect this deposit with the *ostrakophoria* carried out in the year of this politician's exile or one of the several (two?) years before but excludes linking this deposit with any date within the following 10 years after the exile. It is difficult not to agree with this statement, of course. The only problem is that some of the most important Athenian politicians, and thus natural 'candidates' for exile through ostracism, were politically active for decades, as was the case, for instance, of Themistocles, Cimon, and Pericles.[43] Theoretically, then, an ostrakon with such a name may come from the times after the politician's return from exile, which makes our chronological calculations virtually useless. Lang goes further, however (as did many of her predecessors), to exclude the possibility of dating a given deposit to a particular *ostrakophoria* in case of an absence or 'too small a number' of ostraka with the name of the politician exiled in a given year. This conclusion, in turn, seems unjustified, and the elimination of some potential historical identifications of *ostrakophoriai* is not convincing.[44] For Lang assumes that individual large deposits or their connectable groups are more or less proportionally representative of the 'votes' actually cast in a given year.[45] Accordingly, individual deposits can allegedly be ascribed to various historical *ostrakophoriai*.

---

[41] Webster (1972) 142 with Pl. 16b.   [42] See below, 3.2.3.

[43] For example, Pericles could have been indicated by his fellow citizens as a 'candidate' for exile at any point of his career, from its glorious beginning (the successful *choregia* of Aeschylus' *Persians* in 472 BC) up until his death in 429 BC, which is over 40 years.

[44] E.g., *Agora* 25, 23 (it is impossible for the deposit E 2 from the Agora to be dated to 486 BC, when Megakles was exiled, because it would mean that all the 'votes' cast against him ended up in the Kerameikos *en masse* and did not leave any trace on the Agora); 22 (the mutually connected deposits E 1 and E 1a cannot be dated to 487, when Hipparchos was exiled, because there are no ostraka with his name there, and it is not probable that the 'votes' cast against the 'winner' were deposited separately; the same line of reasoning makes it difficult to ascribe this deposit to the year 482, the date of Aristides' exile, who has 'too few' ostraka there, or 'too many' if the 'winning' ostraka were deposited separately).

[45] In *Agora* 25, 22, M. Lang herself, however, notes some methodological problems involved here.

This optimistic assumption can be rejected if we, first, accept my conclusion that on the day of *ostrakophoria*, the Agora was filled with countless crowds of Athenians,[46] far exceeding the number of 6000 mentioned by our sources. Statistically speaking, apart from the 'Great Kerameikos Deposit', all deposits turn out to be dramatically non-representative of the number of the 'votes' actually cast, and even this deposit may constitute, say, merely a half of the ostraka from that year's *ostrakophoria*.[47] As we shall see further, the average number of Athenians voting on the Agora in a given year can be established, through sheer estimation, at 10 000 at least. In some years, it must have been more. On this scale, the randomness of our ostraka finds looks quite dramatic.

Secondly, we have to remember that our deposits are, in fact, 'recycled' batches of ostraka used, after being counted, for instance, to level the area of the Agora.[48] This means that, while analysing our deposits, we are dealing with the byproduct of the activity of the Athenian 'ballot-counting committees'. Therefore, we have to hypothetically reconstruct their method of work before we assume that a given batch of ostraka is to any extent representative of the Athenian *ostrakophoria* in a given year. Thanks to the aforementioned identification of the two representations on a kylix by the Pan Painter (around 470–460 BC)[49] as the scene of ostraka counting, we can try and reconstruct not only the way of functioning of such committees but also the mechanism of 'disposing' of the ostraka already counted (see Fig. 3.4.). I shall discuss these representations in detail further on. Here, it suffices to say that at the moment of voting the Athenians cast their ostraka into a wide 'basin' (*skaphē*), which was then brought to a place where the 'votes' against individual citizens were counted on a special table, or counting board, under the supervision of a magistrate. This calculation was noted down on writing tablets, and all the partial scores were summed up at the end. To make space on the table for the next ones, ostraka were placed in a large ceramic vessel (*lekanē*) and most probably carried away to the place of their disposal or temporary storage before disposal. As the subsequent *skaphai* were brought in, the procedure was repeated however many times it was necessary. It is

---

[46] See below, pp. 156–157.

[47] Problems with dating this *ostrakophoria* are comprehensively discussed by Brenne (2001) 30–46 (with cited bibliography). Cf. also above, on the identification of sherds of the vessel by the Pistoxenos Painter among this deposit. Cf. also below, p. 101, n. 102.

[48] Such a supply of excellent construction rubble left after an *ostrakophoria* must have played a significant role in the city's life. Analogical action was taken in Cyrene (see above, p. 23).

[49] Oxford, Ashmolean Museum 1911.617 (ARV^2 559.152 = *CVA* Oxford III, 1 [Great Britain 99], pl. VII, nos. 3 and 4; Beazley Archive, no. 206398).

almost certain that each Athenian *phylē* had its own table on which ostraka were counted under the supervision of an archon and some members of the Council of Five Hundred.[50]

Thus, in reality, our deposits of ostraka are the contents of one or more *lekanai* with the 'votes' already counted. This means that in a case where very many 'votes' were cast against a specific 'candidate', ostraka with his name filled in one or more vessels, and the 'end' which did not fit into the last one, was placed in the next *lekanē*, containing 'votes' against other Athenians. Therefore, we must conclude that no deposit and no group is in the slightest degree representative of the *ostrakophoria* of a given year or even of the voting of some part of the citizens. The vessels with counted 'votes' were 'packed' not after all ostraka (from a certain *phylē*?) were counted, but entirely at random, as if 'on a conveyor belt', as they were coming in from counting.

Thus, only the 'Great Kerameikos Deposit' can theoretically comprise all or almost all the 'votes' against Megakles (4433 in total) cast (most probably) in the year of his second exile (472/471 BC).[51] All other deposits and their groups are useless for our calculations, even vaguely approximate: for instance, the large deposit (E 1 + E 1a) from the south-western part of the Agora, containing 176 ostraka against Themistocles, 168 against Kallixenos, 49 against Hippocrates, and only five against Aristides, can come from one *lekanē* or from several *lekanai*, one of which contained this 'end' of the set of the already counted ostraka against Aristides, while the rest (filling in entirely one or more vessels) were deposited and disposed of in a place unknown to us. Thus, based on the statistics of this deposit, we cannot even exclude that we are dealing here with ostraka from the year of Aristides' exile (483/482 BC).

Even more problematic are sporadically found ostraka ascribed to a particular *ostrakophoria* on prosopographical grounds. For instance, even if 30 ostraka traditionally associated in scholarship with the exile of Hyperbolus are indeed to be dated to ca. 416 BC, one cannot build too much on the random distribution of the names they bear (Germ. *Splitterstimmen*). It would be

[50] Apart from the descriptions of the organisation of voting in our sources (see below, 3.2.3), this can be supported by an archaeological argument, namely the relatively large proportion (5 to 10 per cent) of ostraka broken off the same vessels in the 'Great Kerameikos Deposit'. Citizens heading together towards the voting spot might have shared ostraka by breaking them up into smaller parts, and their 'votes' ended up in the same 'basins' and on the same counting tables, since we find them in the same deposit, composed of material coming from emptying the same *lekanai*.
[51] See below, pp. 101–102.

far-fetched to take it as representative of the allegedly scattered character of the vote of *ostrakophoria* that year and draw historical conclusions from it.[52] In other words, such 'scattered votes' are not even enough to suggest a particularly scattered vote on this occasion because, in some deposits, we encounter more homogeneous results due exclusively to the procedures of counting and disposing of Athenian ostraka. One should rather posit a relatively high number of such *Splitterstimmen* for every single *ostrakophoria* ever held.

In this context, some conclusions arising from the analysis of ostraka will, naturally, remain valid. A large number of ostraka against a particular politician may (but does not have to) suggest that in a given year, he was a serious 'candidate' for exile, or perhaps that he was even sent into it. The presence of the name itself can be associated with the date (or with several preceding years) of this politician's ostracism attested elsewhere, or—the epigraphic and ceramic features permitting—with the times after his exile, but probably not with the decade when he was outside Attica (even though single ostraka brought by absent-minded or simply exceptionally fierce opponents of his could have happened, of course). On the other hand, no conclusions can be drawn from the absence of a given name even in a large deposit, or a small number of ostraka with this name, or the ratio of ostraka with various names.

The remarks made above clearly indicate that based on the catalogue of Athenian names found on ostraka, we cannot draw perhaps the most important conclusion that we could optimistically expect from it a priori. Even a relatively high number of 'votes' against a politician about whose exile we do not learn from literary sources cannot prove the occurrence of an *ostrakophoria* not attested in our sources. It should be noted that, although more than 270 Athenian names in total appear on ostraka (176 of them targeted as potential victims),[53] ca. 30 among them have over 10 sherds as of today, and only 12 have over 50 ostraka. In the last group, we find only four names unattested for ostracism victims in literary sources, with three of them being (or having been) considered by scholars as potential 'champions' of the ostracism of 486/485 BC, the anonymous 'friend of the tyrants', whose name is not given in *A.P.*[54] On the other hand, the 12-person group of

---

[52] See, however, e.g., Siewert (1999); cf. Heftner (2000a) 49–52.
[53] Precisely 272 names, according to the catalogue by Brenne (2001). However, only 176 belong to the 'candidates' for ostracism, whereas 93 names are their fathers, and a few more are catalogued as 'other' [*sc.* names].
[54] See below, p. 164.

names inscribed on more than 50 ostraka lacks several important politicians about whose exile we read in our literary sources.[55] The only 'statistical' pattern that can be discerned in our corpus is that two politicians with a relatively high number of ostraka within a specific, clearly defined chronological frame must have been regular 'candidates' for being ostracised in several consecutive *ostrakophoriai*. If we exclude from our analysis the ostraka against Megakles from the 'Great Deposit' (as it was most probably a single *ostrakophoria* that sent him into exile), Themistocles is such a figure for the sherds of the 80s and 70s (2175 catalogued ostraka as of today, but perhaps ca. 2240 items in total), and Cimon for the 'mid-fifth century', conventionally defined as the period between the 60s and 30s (472 items out of 647 found for this period in total). In this respect, the ostraka found seem to confirm the information we see in our literary sources, even though they cannot contribute anything new and at the same time secure.

Therefore, we have to accept that the increasingly impressive corpus of Athenian ostraka can, of course, be used to a limited extent for drawing conclusions in specific matters, but a sum of such findings will never form a coherent picture of either the chronology of ostracisms or the results of consecutive *ostrakophoriai*, or even of their total number. Thus, it is most probable that neither the chronology nor the prosopography of ostracism will change significantly in the future due to the constantly growing number of excavated ostraka. The literary sources available to us still occupy a prominent place in the study of ostracism. In the fifth chapter of this book, we shall see, however, that graffiti from ostraka can easily be used to interpret the general political sentiment surrounding the whole procedure of Athenian ostracism. In this matter, their role will prove essential.

2.2.2 The List of Athenian Ostracisms in *Athenaion Politeia* and its Possible Sources

The sizeable material and epigraphic 'corpus' of ostraka used (or prepared for use) during Athenian *ostrakophoriai* turns out to be almost entirely useless for the study of 'facts' regarding ostracism. Ostraka will not help us compile or even verify a list of names of the victims of this institution, nor will they allow us to establish the chronology of individual *ostrakophoriai* or

---

[55] Hyperbolus (Brenne (2001) no. 108) has only three sherds, found on the Agora.

even estimate, no matter how roughly, their total number. In this part, we have to focus on the literary sources available to us and the more or less hypothetical unpreserved sources of these sources.

In his commentary to *A.P.* 22.3, P. J. Rhodes observes that Ps.-Aristotle does not ascribe dates by archon to any of the ostracisms of the 80s, even though he undoubtedly knew them, as he dated in this manner other events taking place in the years of the exiles of Megakles (22.5 *ad fin.*) and Aristides (22.7 *ad fin.*). Rhodes convincingly argues that this form of record is motivated solely by stylistic reasons. The author simply wanted to avoid monotonous repetition here, which is inescapable in creating an annalistic list of events, where each item would begin with the formula 'in the archonship of X...'.[56]

However, it is necessary to ask the question about the source basis of the list of ostracisms in *A.P.* This question appears particularly important because Ps.-Aristotle in chapter 22, quite uniquely for his work, presents a detailed discussion of ostracism in general, but also lists in chronological order the consecutive cases of individual Athenian politicians who were ostracised. It should be noted that in the remaining sections of the historical part of *A.P.*, apart from the cursorily and marginally mentioned 'Damonides [most probably Damon – M.W.] of Oie' (27.4),[57] ostracisms do not appear at all. And this is true even of politicians discussed by Ps.-Aristotle more extensively and about whose exile we hear from other sources, such as Themistocles or Thucydides son of Melesias. Therefore, it may seem that in chapter 22 Ps.-Aristotle closely follows a source conveniently assembling early ostracisms, but only those from the years preceding Xerxes' expedition.[58] And indeed, in 1904, Otto Seeck suggested identifying this source as the document communicating the resolution of the Assembly which, on the one hand, recalled from exile the Athenians specified by name, and on the other hand, enacted new rules of the execution of the ostracism punishment for the future (cf. *A.P.* 22.8). According to him, such a decision might have contained the provision by what period each exile's

---

[56] Rhodes, pp. 266–267; cf. *ibidem*, pp. 42–44.
[57] On this ostracism, questioned by some scholars, see below, pp. 107–110.
[58] The fact that the name of the third successively exiled 'tyrants' friend' is missing should not be a subject of concern. *A.P.* most probably had this name among the ostracisms listed in his source but decided that repeating the archon's name and mentioning a name of an ostracism victim unfamiliar to him would make the narration excessively monotonous (thus Rhodes, *ad loc.*). On the possibility of identifying the exile of 486/485 BC see below, pp. 99–100 with n. 97.

'sentence' was commuted, whence the exact dates of individual ostracisms could be inferred.[59]

Seeck proposed an ingenious solution, but the problem is that the silence of A.P. regarding ostracisms in further sections of the historical part of the work might not have been coincidental (due to the lack of an equally convenient list of the ostracised as that for the times before the Persian Wars). In the case of Ps.-Aristotle, we are definitely dealing with a not-always-careful compiler, but the first part of this work is supposed to illustrate a specific vision of changes in the Athenian political system, in which the successive emergence of institutions marks the successive stages in the 'democratisation' of the *polis*. Therefore, although in chapters 1–41 we are following the evolution of the Athenian *polis* chronologically, Ps.-Aristotle does not relate the political history of Athens. In other words, we must read the parts of *A.P.* dedicated to ostracism in the same way as we study the chronologically arranged mentions of other vital institutions and procedures operating within the system. In chapters 22–23, we learn, in order, about the introduction of Cleisthenes' laws, including ostracism, about the introduction of the oath for the Council of Five Hundred, about the introduction of the election of generals (*stratēgoi*), about the first application of ostracism in practice, about the introduction of the appointment of archons by lot, about the change in the motivation for ostracising Athenian politicians ('tyrants' friends' are replaced from now on by 'also others, if somebody appeared too powerful', 22.6 *ad fin.*), about Themistocles' idea, which allowed the building of the Athenian battle fleet, later on victorious at Salamis, about ostracising Aristides, about recalling from exile all the expelled through ostracism in the face of Xerxes' expedition, and finally about the introduction of an amendment to the ostracism law at this opportunity. The mention of Aristides' exile proves particularly important here (22.7 *ad fin.*) because it is detached from the list of ostracisms in 22.4 and 6. Nonetheless, it is deeply significant, as it is concluded with the note about the recalling of all the ostracised, including Aristides, to Athens in 481/480 BC, which in turn prepares the reader for the information about the essential role played by this politician in the shaping of the Athenian *politeia* later on (23.3–5).

---

[59] Seeck (1904) 301. Interestingly, Seeck suggests that the reason why no earlier ostracisms are mentioned in *A.P.* is the fact that Ps.-Aristotle's list derived from the (hypothetical) *Amnestiedekret*, which did not mention earlier 'victims' (*sc.* as no longer residing in exile).

If we consider the mentions of individual ostracisms in chapters 22 and 23 of *A.P.* in their immediate context, it will become clear that it is not coincidentally that the author abandons his interest in this institution and its victims in further sections of the historical part of this work. Similarly to the procedure of electing generals or archons or to the mechanism of financing the Athenian fleet, ostracism belongs to the democratic institutions, which will be discussed at the relevant stage of the evolution of the *politeia*. And once discussed, they should remain in the reader's memory until their systematic analysis in the descriptive part of *A.P.*, without the necessity of returning to them repeatedly in the historical part, as they reached their 'accomplished' form at a particular moment in history.[60] It should be noted that the final remarks on ostracism in these chapters unambiguously define and date the moment when it took its ultimate political and legal form (corresponding with the Ps.-Aristotelian understanding of the essence of the contemporary Athenian democracy). On the one hand, we learn that beginning with the exile of Xanthippus son of Ariphron in 485/484 BC, the Athenians will 'from now on' subject to ostracism not only individuals suspected of sympathising with the tyrants but also those who seem 'too powerful' (22.6: μετὰ δὲ ταῦτα τῷ τετάρτῳ ἔτει καὶ τῶν ἄλλων εἴ τις δοκοίη μείζων εἶναι μεθίσταντο). On the other hand, we read about a regulation prescribing that 'from now on' the exile should take place within a well-defined geographic area (22.8: καὶ τὸ λοιπὸν ὥρισαν τοῖς ὀστρακιζομένοις, ἐντὸς Γεραιστοῦ καὶ Σκυλλαίου κατοικεῖν, ἢ ἀτίμους εἶναι καθάπαξ).[61] While the passage quoted from paragraph 22.6 demonstrates how *A.P.* understands the practice and political sense of ostracism in the Athenian *politeia* of later times, paragraph 22.8 informs us about a revision (clearly only partial) of Cleisthenes' law about ostracism, which will remain in force until the times of Ps.-Aristotle.

If the above interpretation of information on ostracism contained in chapters 22 and 23 stands, it becomes clear that no source-critical inferences can be made from the silence regarding ostracism further in the historical part of *A.P.* It can merely be stated that the author had a reliable source at his disposal, providing a list of Athenian ostracisms with dating, but it cannot be established with what date the list ended. Its meticulous use for the times

---

[60] Quite similarly, if I understand his slightly 'impressionistic' considerations at this point correctly, Jacoby (1949) 207–208.
[61] It is of no consequence to me here whether the exile was to take place 'within' or 'outside' the Saronic Gulf. On this famous controversy in scholarship, see below, 3.3.1.

until Xerxes' expedition is equally well justified within the general conception of *A.P.* as its (hypothetical) foregoing for later times. Thus, any attempts at determining the character or even identifying Ps.-Aristotle's source based on the level of detail in the account of ostracisms from before 480 BC are absolutely arbitrary. Albeit the existence of a chronological list of ostracisms reaching further back into the fifth century, or perhaps even a complete list of Athenian cases, seems more probable to me than one covering only the times before the Persian Wars.

One positive outcome should be added right here, as it will prove of great significance for my further argument. Regardless of how the geographic aspect at the end of paragraph 22.8 is understood, *A.P.* speaks with exceptional firmness and precision there. We cannot be sure, of course, whether the author had good reasons for that because we are not able to establish indisputably whether he or (slightly more probably) his source or sources had direct access to the actual text of the law about ostracism, revised in 481/480 BC.[62] However, it is beyond doubt that Ps.-Aristotle regarded this revision as final and was not aware of any other important alterations of this law. According to his knowledge, at the recalling to Athens of politicians ostracised before Xerxes' expedition, Cleisthenes' law about ostracism was slightly amended and promulgated in the version which was in force in the times of *A.P.*'s author.

The most likely candidate for the direct source of information in *A.P.* on ostracisms from before 480 BC is, of course, Androtion and his *Atthis*. The question is, however, where he could have derived his knowledge from.

In the already mentioned passage from his commentary to *A.P.*, Rhodes states that every ostracism had equally high chances of appearing in some official document as other events referred to in chapter 22. Scholars have long been wondering what document it might have possibly been and whether, hypothetically, it could have been available to Atthidographers at the end of the fifth and in the fourth century BC.[63]

Rhodes is right, of course, in claiming that each ostracism should have left a trace in the form of a public document. The announcement of the result of an *ostrakophoria*, even if we do not hear about it in our sources, must have had official character; it could not have entered general circulation merely as a rumour, after all. It is not worth speculating whether it was through some resolution of the Assembly or a decision of some other form taken, for

---

[62] It seems very likely to me that they did. See below, 3.1.   [63] See above.

TOWARDS A RECONSTRUCTION OF OSTRACISM IN ATHENS 91

instance, by the Boulē. Such a document would undoubtedly have been archived, for example, by the Council of Five Hundred. The problem is, however, that these would solely be single notes. If the decision of the people made through the procedure of *ostrakophoria* was publicly announced, certainly no complete and 'running' list of individuals exiled in this way ever existed.[64] The 10-year period of ostracism would make such an 'announcement' absurd; besides, *ostrakophoriai* happened too rarely (as we shall see) for it to be possible to maintain such a document.[65] The only conceivable public and widely available document could be a resolution of the people about the recalling of all the ostracised, of the kind proposed by Seeck (see above). Theoretically, such a list would have to be created based on the individual decisions mentioned above after their retrieval. There remains the question of whether in a document recalling the exiles it would be necessary to include a list of individuals whom this decision concerned; in other words, whether such a document would be a roll-call decision. In any case, 'the Decree of Themistocles' (ML 23, ll. 44–47 = Fornara 53 = Siewert, T 26), despite its fragmentary state of preservation, does not refer to individual exiles by name but merely to their categories: those exiled for 10 years (i.e., ostracised), and the *atimoi* (unless other categories followed).[66]

---

[64] Hence, I do not understand what Harding, p. 45 meant by claiming that the list of the ostracised in *A.P.* 22 testifies that Hellanicus or, more probably, Androtion 'consulted these documents [Harding is dealing here with several other examples as well – M.W.] and used the information as the basis of this entry'.

[65] It is only as late as in Lycurgus (*Leoc.* 117–118) that we find a confusing piece of information about a bronze stele with names of 'offenders and traitors' (ἐψηφίσαντο εἰς ταύτην [sc. στήλην] ἀναγράφειν τοὺς ἀλιτηρίους καὶ τοὺς προδότας), which the Athenians made, by the decree of the Assembly, out of the statue of Hipparchos 'son of Timarchos', after melting it down. On the one hand, if the orator means the first victim of ostracism here, he presents a hopelessly confused version of events, ascribing to Hipparchos not ostracism but fleeing the country in fear of a trial for treason, which would induce the citizens to sentence him to death in default of appearance. Thus, in his tirade against the deserter, Lycurgus would use vaguely remembered snippets of information about the first ostracism, but the whole would not be trustworthy, and least the note about the bronze stele. Another possibility, as one of my OUP referees kindly observed, would be that such a stele did exist, but in the form of a fabricated fourth-century document such as those mentioned below. On the other hand, in his recent commentary on Lycurgus' speech, Roisman (2019) 199–200 cautiously accepts the historicity of the stele, but hesitantly opts for another Hipparchos, who 'was not the notorious son of Charmus'. And perhaps rightly so. Be it as it may, even here no collective (and systematically updated) list of the ostracised is mentioned, but merely the inscribing of names of 'offenders and traitors' on a stele.

[66] The first editor of the 'decree', Jameson (1960) 221–222 (based on the possible parallel: the decree of Patrocleides, quoted by Andoc. I [*On mysteries*] 77–79), supposed that in the unpreserved, further part a longer list of categories of exiles must have followed. Raubitschek (1965) 286 logically assumed that further on there must have been regulations for the future, of the kind we know from *A.P.* 22.8.

The 'Decree of Themistocles' can and should be doubted, but I cannot discuss in detail the problems of its authenticity here. I also admit that I do not have a definite opinion on this matter. I am inclined towards the compromise view expressed by Rhodes that this third-century inscription from Troezen can be a 'forgery' in the sense that it merges several authentic documents (and perhaps some inauthentic alongside them) into one.[67] This idea allows us to regard in isolation the lines dedicated to the recalling of the ostracised Athenians. Russell Meiggs and David Lewis (ML, p. 52) point out in their commentary that the forger would naturally call the metics 'metics', and the victims of ostracism—'those ostracised', and not 'those exiled for ten years' as they are called here (l. 45–60).[68] One more fact can speak in support of the historical authenticity of at least these parts of the inscription from Troezen (and more specifically, of their originating from an authentic document). Towards the end of 'the Decree of Themistocles', the ostracised are contrasted with the category of *atimoi* (l. 46–47).[69] A similar opposition appears in the summary of the decision to recall the exiles in the face of Xerxes' expedition in *A.P.* 22.8: 'and for the future they defined for the ostracised that they should settle between Geraestus and Scyllaeum, or else they should be completely (καθάπαξ) *atimoi*' (tr. Rhodes). Although the inscription with 'the Decree of Themistocles' breaks off without allowing us to establish what intentions the Athenians had towards the *atimoi*, in both the cases, the exiles' lot is subject to a similar gradation or is comprised in the contrast between the victims of ostracism and the *atimoi*.

The case of 'the Decree of Themistocles' can be very instructive for our considerations. We learn from Demosthenes that in 348 BC, Aeschines referred to some 'decree of Miltiades and Themistocles'.[70] Meiggs and Lewis claimed that it could not have been much different from the Troezenian inscription of the third century, even though Aeschines most probably quoted publicly only its initial parts. State documents were archived centrally in the Metroon already before the end of the fifth

---

[67] In her edition of the relevant parts of the inscription (Siewert, T 26), Christa Meyer summarises the most important voices and arguments in the famous and infinite debate on the authenticity of 'the Decree of Themistocles'. Raubitschek (1965) 287 conveniently points out verbal analogies between the provisions of this decree and the law of ostracism. This would certainly support the authenticity of the sections of the 'Decree of Themistocles' under consideration here.
[68] The supplementation [δ|έκα] 'at the turn' of line 46 seems to be the sole possibility.
[69] Also here, the restoration [ἀτίμου|ς] seems to be perfectly justified, in the light of Andoc. I [*On mysteries*] 107 (= Siewert, T 17).
[70] Dem. XIX [*On the Embassy*], 303. For ML, p. 50, this was the very 'Decree of Themistocles'.

century,[71] but in Aeschines' times, there were yet no erudite collections of them in Athens, such as the later *Collection of Athenian Decrees* by Craterus.[72] However, it must be assumed that politicians did have the possibility of consulting the authentic or fabricated documents referring to key moments in the early history of the Athenian *polis*, particularly to the events from before the Persian Wars and from around the beginnings of Athenian democracy. It is true that the first Atthidographers did not use to quote texts of this sort word by word in their narration.[73] However, they undoubtedly used them in their work, and they are, in fact, our main suspects of the search for, or even of (creative) compilation or fabrication of, documents of this type for their own use.[74]

If we exclude the existence of an official, publicly available document gathering all the cases of ostracising Athenian politicians—remembering about the traces of a detailed list of those ostracised before the Persian Wars in *A.P.* 22, and at the same time assuming that such a list was most probably available to Androtion, to whom this chapter of *A.P.* owes the information about ostracism (and perhaps available to Ps.-Aristotle himself as well)—we must consider how such a list could have seen the light of day. Given the case of the 'decree of Miltiades and Themistocles', circulating in Athens in the mid-fourth century, I suspect that it would be perfectly natural for the Atthidographic tradition to compile a list of those ostracised.[75] Creating it would require archival research but also rudimentary chronographic and genealogical studies, relying heavily on oral traditions of important Athenian families. After all, such work would result in a list gathering the most accomplished Athenian politicians. Thus, creating it would be in line with Atthidographers' work methods and their interest in Athenian history and *politeia*. It is precisely a list of this kind that might have been used by Androtion, whose narrative of the period between Cleisthenes' reforms and

---

[71] See Boegehold (1972). Cf. Thomas (1989) 38–45.
[72] Cf. the edition of Craterus in *BNJ* by Carawan (2007), with commentary.
[73] But they certainly exploited them thoroughly, contrary to Jacoby's view (e.g., Jacoby (1949) 209). On the use of documents by Atthidographers, see recently Harding, 36–40, especially 43–47. On the most probably quite wide availability of documents from the archaic times in classical Athens, see Stroud (1978).
[74] On Atthidographers and their method in general, alongside the remarks by Jacoby (1949) *passim* (and before him by Wilamowitz-Moellendorff (1893) *passim*, to a large extent rendered out of date by Jacoby), see esp. Harding and Costa's introduction to his edition of Philochorus. Cf. also Pearson (1942).
[75] After all, lists of Athenian kings and archons, although then a subject of an ongoing discussion among Atthidographers, were already complete at that point and constituted a chronological skeleton of all the *Atthides*.

the Persian Wars was conscientiously adopted by the author of *A.P.* An indirect proof that Androtion's work used a complete list of ostracisms, not just those from before the Persian Wars, is found in a scholion to Lucian, *Tim.* 30 (p. 114 Raabe), where Hyperbolus' ostracism is briefly mentioned with reference to Androtion (*FGrHist* 324 F 42) as the source of this note.[76] However, Androtion did not have to create such a list; it might have been produced before him.

It may be revealing to compare the amount of space dedicated to the account of the period in question in the works of first Atthidographers, including Androtion. Among the eight books of Androtion's *Atthis*, only three books covered the mythical and historical past of Athens until the end (most probably) of the Peloponnesian War. This means that the beginnings of democracy were treated very cursorily there, perhaps barely more extensively than the preserved account of *A.P.* Androtion's interests, and the lion's share of his work concentrated on the times when he was active in Athenian politics himself. Hellanicus of Mytilene wrote his *Atthis* in merely two books, structuring one of them according to the chronology of Athenian kings and the other one according to archons, perhaps reaching the end of the Peloponnesian War. This means that he, in turn, focused mainly on the mythical times, dedicating very little space to the period when Athenian democracy was emerging. It is not a coincidence either that none of the preserved fragments that reveal—even though very selectively and haphazardly, of course—how this writer was used by later tradition discusses the history of the Athenian political system. The second Atthidographer, and the first Athenian to write an *atthis* (perhaps entitled *Protogonia*), Cleidemus, arranged it in four books.[77] Interestingly, in the second one, he writes in detail about the 10 *phylai* of Cleisthenes (*FGrHist* 323 F 8), and in his *Nostoi* (?) in turn—about the family and erotic connections of Charmos, incidentally the father of the first ostracism victim, Hipparchos (F 15). Apart from that, for instance in F 22, Cleidemus inquired into the number of Athenians who fell at the battle of Plataea, with the clear intention of

---

[76] If this case may be taken as instructive, Androtion's 'entries' on ostracisms would include the name, the *patronymikon*, and the *demotikon* of a given victim. These would probably be preceded by the archon date, absent from this scholion. I would argue that our hypothetical list of ostracisms used by Androtion might have had a similar, the simplest possible, structure of its entries. Meanwhile, it is less clear whether the brief comment in the scholion ('he had also been ostracized for his worthlessness' [*phaulotēs*]) was not taken from a source different than Androtion.

[77] An edition of Cleidemus in *BNJ* has recently been prepared by Morison (2016). Cf. also McInerney (1994).

complementing Herodotus' account (IX 70,5), establishing that they came from the *phylē* of Aiantis. I would argue that this is precisely the antiquarian sensibility that makes Cleidemus a suitable candidate for the authorship of the list of those ostracised. Additionally, the place where he wrote about Cleisthenes' reforms suggests that merely a half of his *Atthis* covered the period from the Persian Wars (as this is the most plausible caesura) to his own times. It is generally believed that he published his work at some point after 378/377 BC.

A.P. uses Cleidemus' work very infrequently (and when it does, it is mainly polemically),[78] and the basic source for its author was most probably Androtion. However, considering the very high level of detail in the parts of Cleidemus' work dedicated to the beginnings of the democratic system in Athens, we can assume that he was—next to Herodotus—Androtion's most important source for this period. Moreover, Androtion must have treated Cleidemus' narration very concisely in his *Atthis*, most probably reckoning that the latter covered the early history of Athens with sufficient diligence.[79] I suppose it was Cleidemus, the first Athenian Atthidographer, to whom Androtion, and following him also the author of A.P., owed the list of ostracised Athenians. We shall never find out whether this list was trustworthy, even though some considerations in this matter will need to be presented further in this book. Nevertheless, it is evident that for the period before Xerxes' expedition, it reached far beyond the information provided by Herodotus, who mentions only one from among those ostracised at that time, Aristides (VIII 79,1). If we exclude the existence of a unified document gathering names of all the victims of ostracism from before the Persian Wars, created for instance at the occasion of recalling the exiled to Athens, it will testify to the scale of independent research of the author of the list (Cleidemus?) which Ps.-Aristotle used. The list, let us add, which might have been produced already in the first quarter of the fourth century. However, its part covering those exiled after the Persian Wars did not leave any visible traces in the sources available to us (but see below) due to the manner in which the author of A.P. used his sources and organised his material.

---

[78] Cf. *A.P.* 21.5 and *FGrHist* 323 F 8, as well as *A.P.* 23.1 and *FGrHist* 323 F 21.

[79] Slightly similarly (*contra* Jacoby) on the relation between Androtion and Cleidemus, see Harding, p. 27.

Now, there are fundamental differences in the ways in which in the fourth century one could use fabrications, or indeed erudite 'reconstructions' regarding the Athenian history of the fifth century. On the one hand, let us consider the so-called 'Decree of Themistocles', and on the other, the hypothetical list of those ostracised (produced by Cleidemus?). While the 'decree' could be useful to Athenian politicians, perfectly fitting to be quoted in a public speech as a (pseudo)document confirming or illustrating the orator's words, an Atthidographic list of ostracisms was merely a chronographic tool. Thus, it would be helpful exclusively to specialists, other scholars of Athens' past, i.e., principally to Atthidographers. Therefore, such a list would never enter wider circulation, remaining a part of a published *atthis* at best.

In the extant corpus of Attic orators, there are only a few mentions of ostracisms and only of those whose victims were the most important and the best-known Athenian politicians of the fifth century. They appear there accompanied by a few other great Athenians, who were, in different ways, exemplarily punished by the people, such as Aristides[80] and Themistocles.[81] Apart from several mentions by orators, within the remaining non-historiographic prose, there is only one more passage in Plato. In *Gorgias* (516D), as in Demosthenes, Socrates' references to the ostracisms of Themistocles and Cimon, in close relationship with references to Pericles and Miltiades, seem to reflect the popular consciousness of the Athenians, most probably focusing more and more on the great statesmen of the past. In any case, we are dealing here with a very limited 'pool' of merely the four most accomplished Athenians of old: Aristides, Themistocles, Cimon, and Pericles (who was never ostracised).[82] The obvious inference is that only the most famous ostracisms from before and after Xerxes' expedition permanently entered the general and widely spread conceptions of the Athenians regarding their past.

We also hear about Cimon's ostracism in chapter 33 of Ps.-Andocides' speech *Against Alcibiades* [IV], where the matter becomes more complicated. Not unlike in Demosthenes and Plato, this politician remains an example of the justified ruthlessness of the Athenians of old towards the

---

[80] Dem. XXVI [*Against Aristogeiton II*] 6, in one breath with the mention of the punishment imposed on Miltiades and Pericles.
[81] Dem. XXIII [*Against Aristocrates*] 205, alongside the mention of Cimon's trial.
[82] On Miltiades son of Cimon, whose ostracism is referred to by Andoc. III [*On the Peace with Sparta*] 3, see below, p. 99.

offences of their even most accomplished citizens. This time, however, we learn much more; for instance, the reason for Cimon's ostracism turns out to be his 'breaking the law by living with his sister [as wife]' (§ 33).[83] As part of the same argument, the orator also gives another example of a distinguished victim of this institution, Callias son of Didymios, and his merits for the *polis* (§ 32).[84] He does all this to demonstrate the existence of a close connection between ostracism and the target of this speech's attack, Alcibiades, who (as we learn in paragraph 33) is carrying the stigma of ostracism both on the spear and on the distaff side. Both his grandfather, Alcibiades, and his mother's father, Megakles,[85] were exiled—and each of them twice.[86] The double exiles of Megakles and Alcibiades the Elder (*APF* 579) are mentioned, in very similar words, by one more Attic orator, namely the author of the speech *Against Alcibiades I* [XIV] preserved in the corpus of Lysias' speeches (39). The text in the corpus of Andocides' speeches under the same title is undoubtedly a later (fourth-century?) rhetorical exercise.[87] However, the authenticity of the 14th speech in the corpus of Lysias' orations has long been disputed, too.[88] One of the greatest scholars of Attic rhetoric, Friedrich Blass, following an exhaustive formal analysis, concluded that it was irrefutably inauthentic.[89] It seems that the appearance of information about the ostracisms of Alcibiades the Elder (*APF* 579) and Callias son of Didymios and about the second exile of Megakles son of Hippocrates in precisely these two Attic speeches may not be coincidental.

Unlike Plato or Demosthenes, who cited cases widely known to their audience for argumentative or illustrative purposes, in Ps.-Andocides and Ps.-Lysias, we are dealing with different kind of references, namely with (admittedly limited) quasi-erudite effort to embellish a fictitious speech with

---

[83] See briefly below, pp. 220–221, on the ostrakon in *Kerameikos 20.2*, 1336 (= O 68740), for which see S. Brenne, in: Siewert, T 1/67, pp. 92–93.

[84] See below, pp. 105–106.

[85] I shall deal with the disputable historicity of these ostracisms below, pp. 101–102, 104–105.

[86] The mention of the double exile of both of them is due to the emendation by Markland (δίς), which is indispensable in the light of a very similar passage in a speech by Ps.-Lysias, on which see below.

[87] For the discussion and linguistic analysis, see Edwards (1995) 131–136, 208–211. See also the two extensively annotated editions: Cobetto Ghiggia (1995) and Gazzano (1999). Cf. also commentaries in Siewert, T 18–21 (by Brigitte Eder and Herbert Heftner).

[88] Already the ancients must have doubted it (see Harpocration, *s.v. Alkibiades* [22.13 Dindorf]). Carey (1989) 147–148 ultimately defends the authenticity of this speech, but he does it with much hesitation.

[89] Blass (1887) 468–498, esp. 494–495.

interesting details. In other words, it is a properly erudite rhetorical exercise. In both cases, the search for information about the ostracisms of Alcibiades the Elder (*APF* 579) and Megakles seems to be natural, but the mention of Callias son of Didymios[90] in Ps.-Andocides no doubt testifies to a more intensive antiquarian inquiry. The information (repeated in both the speeches) about the double ostracisms of Alcibiades the Elder and Megakles, barely trustworthy to some scholars, is very intriguing in itself. It can be expected a priori that cases of double ostracism of figures of such a stature as Megakles the Alcmaeonid or of an ancestor of such a key hero in the Athenian history of classical times as Alcibiades, must have echoed widely in the public consciousness of the Athenians and been preserved in one of our sources. If Plutarch had had access to such information, he would have certainly used it. However, it did not happen. On the other hand, it should be emphasised that the recurring note about two ostracisms of each of the mentioned figures, even if at this stage the historicity of these events cannot be decided upon,[91] seems to indicate that Ps.-Andocides and Ps.-Lysias (or the one of the two who was the inspiration for the other) had at their disposal a list dating individual Athenian *ostrakophoriai*, and not only a simple enumeration of the ostracised politicians.

If my argument thus far stands, we are dealing here with evidence of the existence—in adequately educated circles of Athenians interested in antiquarian information—of a hypothetical Atthidographic list of ostracisms dated according to archons' years, or more precisely, of this list's part reaching beyond Xerxes' expedition. On such a list, apart from the ostracism of Megakles son of Hippocrates, known to us from *A.P.* 22.5, this politician must have also figured in another place and under a different date, after the Persian Wars. If this was the case, it should be noted that, for the times after the Persian Wars, the compiler went beyond the data provided by Thucydides (who mentions only two ostracisms, that of Themistocles, in I 135,2–3, and that of Hyperbolus, in VIII 73,3). Similarly, for earlier times he did not limit himself to the data provided by Herodotus (see above). All things considered, I believe that the most likely source where an Athenian of the fourth century could find such a list was the *Atthis* by the Athenian Cleidemus, containing much more detail for this period than Androtion's work.

---

[90] See below, pp. 105–106.   [91] Cf. also Bicknell (1975).

2.2.3 Ostracisms Attested in Literary Sources and Disputable Ostracisms

The total number of people who appear in our literary sources as victims of ostracism is not too high.[92] It comprises merely 17 names (or 15, if repeated ostracisms are left out); two of them can be excluded immediately, such as Theseus, who was most probably not associated with this institution before Theophrastus,[93] or Miltiades son of Cimon, whose absence from the list of the ostracised before Xerxes' expedition in *A.P.* finds excellent confirmation in Herodotus' narrative, and who appears in Demosthenes and Plato (see above) in the company of ostracism victims, but is never considered one.[94] Information about five cases from before Xerxes' expedition is supplied, as we have seen, by *A.P.* in chapter 22, and it can be regarded as relatively reliable because it comes from a good Atthidographic tradition, perhaps reaching back to the first quarter of the fourth century BC: [our no. I] Hipparchos son of Charmos of the deme Kollytos in 488/487 BC (*APF* 7600);[95] [no. II] Megakles son of Hippocrates of the deme Alopeke in 487/486 BC (*APF* 9695);[96] [no. III] anonymous 'tyrants' friend' in

---

[92] The (disappointing) contribution of the preserved Athenian ostraka to the 'prosopography' of ostracism has already been discussed above, 2.2.1.

[93] See Theophrastus, F 131 Wimmer = F 638 Fortenbaugh (*ap. Suda, s.v. archē Skyria* [A 4101 Adler]); cf. Theophrastus, *Characters* 26 [*The Oligarch*], 5 (text corrupt, perhaps a lacuna, but the allusion to Theseus as the inventor and the first victim of ostracism is clear); Euseb. *Chron. II*, p. 50 Schoene (as in Theophrastus' *Characters*, the introduction of ostracism by Theseus and his exile are directly connected here with Theseus' synoecism of Attica); Hieron. 58 Helm. Excellent remarks on this tradition are found in Thomsen (1972) 13–16. Recently, see Heftner (2005).

[94] The only source mentioning the ostracism of Miltiades is Andocides, *On the Peace with Sparta* [III], 3, but scholars have long suspected that the formulation 'Miltiades son of Cimon' might have been a simple mistake, faithfully repeated by Aeschines, II [*The Speech on the Embassy*], 172. In fact, it should be 'Cimon son of Miltiades' (which Umberto Albini introduces to the text in his edition of Andocides, despite the unanimity of all the manuscripts), which would perfectly match our 'prosopography' of ostracism. In this context, Miltiades' absence from among the victims of the ostracisms we hear about would arise, on the one hand, from Herodotus' strong authority, and on the other hand, from the influence of the Atthidographic tradition, with the (hypothetical) list of the ostracised (by Cleidemus?) at its source.

[95] Archon of the year 496/495 BC and probably grandson of Hippias (his father Charmos was most probably married to the tyrant's daughter). More on his family connections in *APF* 11793 (IX), p. 451; cf. Brenne (2001) no. 98, p. 161. Apart from Androtion, *FGrHist* 324 F 6 and *A.P.* 22.4, his ostracism is mentioned by Plut. *Nic.* 11 (emphasising, following our tradition, that he was the first ostracism victim), Harpocration, Photius [I 162] and *Suda, s.v. Hipparchos* [I 523 Adler].

[96] More extensively at *APF* 9688 (X), p. 379; cf. Brenne (2001) no. 171, pp. 225–228. Apart from *A.P.*, his (first?) ostracism is referred to by his contemporary, Pindar, *Pyth.* VII, 18–21, at the occasion of his victory in the Pythian Games in 486 BC (see above, p. 6). On the mentions by

486/485 BC;⁹⁷ [no. IV] Xanthippus son of Ariphron in 485/484 BC (*APF* 11169);⁹⁸ [no. V] Aristides son of Lysimachos (*APF* 1695) in 483–482 BC (484/483 BC in Hieronymus 108 Helm).⁹⁹ For the reasons discussed above, all the later ostracisms attested in literature are much more difficult to analyse, and with the sole exception of Cimon's ostracism, their chronology remains highly disputable. Particularly challenging is the ostracism [no. VII] of Themistocles (*APF* 6669; *PA* 6669),¹⁰⁰ for which we have an exceptional abundance of literary mentions (as we do for the exile of Aristides and Cimon), starting with the historians of the fifth century and continuing until the late Byzantine times—due to the significance of these three figures in the Athenian history

Ps.-Andocides and Ps.-Lysias of the double exile of Megakles, see above. Similarly, Harpocration, *s.v. Alkibiades* ([22.13 Dindorf] but without Megakles' name). On the probable historicity of his repeated ostracism, cf. below.

⁹⁷ In earlier scholarship (e.g., Vanderpool (1972) 235–236), due to the large number of ostraka with his name cast in the 'Great Kerameikos Deposit' (at least 720 items), a serious candidate for this place was Callias Kratiou of the deme Alopeke (*APF* 7826 VI; Brenne (2001) no. 119, pp. 179–181). After the 'Great Deposit' was re-dated to the 70s (see above), Callias, known to us only from ostraka, lost his position. In more recent scholarship, he has been replaced by Hippocrates Anaxileo (47 ostraka in total; Brenne (2001) no. 104, pp. 163–166) and Kallixenos Aristonymou Xypetaion (278 ostraka in total; Brenne (2001) no. 124, pp. 186–188). However, they too have ostraka dated to the 80s, coming mainly from the Agora, as well as ostraka from the Kerameikos, which may have come from the late 70s. Therefore, it is theoretically conceivable that each of them, having been exiled in 486/485 BC, would become a 'candidate' for ostracism again after their return to Athens. However, all this makes the above identifications very insecure. For my purposes, the most important thing is that none of the possible exiles of that year (Callias Kratiou, Hippocrates Anaxileo, and Kallixenos Aristonymou Xypetaion) are mentioned in this capacity in the literary tradition, which could explain the absence of his name from *A.P.*, even if Ps.-Aristotle saw this name on the (hypothetical) list of ostracism victims which he was using. See above, 2.2.2.

⁹⁸ For more, see *APF* 11811 (I), pp. 455–456; cf. Brenne (2001) no. 268, pp. 310–312. His resounding marriage to Agariste (the Younger), daughter of Hippocrates the Alcmaeonid, nowadays dated to around 496 BC, is mentioned by Hdt. VI 131,2. Xanthippus' career begins (for us) with his political attack on Miltiades in 489 BC (cf. Hdt. VI 136). The information about his ostracism will be repeated (following *A.P.*) only by Herakleides Lembos, 4 Dilts. An intriguing testimony regarding Xanthippus' ostracism (or perhaps only his 'candidature' for ostracism) is an epigram inscribed on one of the ostraka (Siewert, T 1/153; *Agora 25*, 1065 (P 16873); ML, 21 with p. 42 = *CEG* I 439). Cf. Merkelbach (1969) and recently Zerbinati (2018), discussing, among other things, a new deposit from the Agora containing as many as 56 ostraka against Xanthippus, alongside, i.a., 59 ostraka against Themistocles; cf. Sickinger (2017a).

⁹⁹ Aristides, b. around 520 BC, was archon in 489/488 BC and perhaps *stratēgos* in 490/489 BC. Cf. also Brenne (2001) nos. 31, 32, pp. 114–117. On his ostracism, apart from *A.P.*, see above all Hdt. VIII 79,1; Dem. XXVI 6; Demetr. Phaler., *FGrHist* 228 F 43 (*ap.* Plut. *Arist.* 1.2); Herakleides Lembos, 4 Dilts; Aristodemos, *FGrHist* 104 (= *BNJ* 104; with comm. by Pownall (2020)) F 1.1.4; Plut. *Arist.* 7.

¹⁰⁰ Archon in 493/492 BC. Cf. also Brenne (2001) no. 258, pp. 297–300. On his ostracism, see Thuc. I 135,3; Pl. *Gorg.* 516 D, Cic. *Amic.* 42; Nep. *Them.* 8; D.S. XI 55; Plut. *Them.* 22; Aristodemos, *FGrHist* 104 (= *BNJ* 104; with comm. by Pownall (2020)) F 1.6.1.

of the fifth century. The difficulties in dating Themistocles' exile arise from, first, the hardly reconcilable divergence in its dating by various ancient sources, and secondly, from the troublesome chronological relation between ostracising this politician and convicting him in Athens *in absentia*. Nevertheless, the occurrence of a large number of his ostraka in the 'Great Deposit' (second only to those against Megakles) makes it virtually certain that he was still in Athens in 471 BC (see below). Hence, his ostracism must have happened in 470 BC.

The second ostracism [no. VI] of Megakles son of Hippocrates is alluded to merely in two, most probably fourth-century, rhetorical exercises: Ps.-Andocides and Ps.-Lysias, *Against Alcibiades*. For a long time, there has been a consensus in scholarship that this information should not be taken seriously. The situation radically changed when in the years 1965–1969, German archaeologists found on the Kerameikos the repeatedly mentioned 'Great Deposit'. Its recent editor Stefan Brenne and his predecessor Franz Willemsen have put a lot of effort into making it possible for scholars to familiarise themselves quite thoroughly with the contents of this deposit even before the final publication of *Kerameikos 20.1–2*.[101] Together with the ostraka from the Kerameikos, the Agora or the Acropolis known before, today we have 4433 ostraka in total with the name of Megakles son of Hippocrates (or inscribed in some other form, clearly identifiable with him).[102] At the same time, the 'Great Deposit' from the Kerameikos brings us 4176 of them. The problem is that only a small part of the known ostraka can be securely dated to the times of Megakles' exile in 487/486 BC or allows for a possibility of such dating. The overwhelming majority of ostraka from the Kerameikos, or the 'Great Deposit', are identified today with a single *ostrakophoria* of the late 70s., hypothetically dated to 471 BC,[103] i.e., 16 years

---

[101] See now *Kerameikos 20.2*, 2012–6188.

[102] Themistocles, second to him as regards the number of ostraka (see above), has 2240 of them.

[103] The basis for such dating is three-fold: (1) One of the ostraka against Megakles was a sherd of a red-figure vase by the Pistoxenos Painter, which excludes dating it to the 80s (Willemsen (1991)) (other ceramological indications of a post-80s date, much less conclusive, are mentioned in *Kerameikos 20.1*, p. 43). (2) In the 'Great Deposit', an ostrakon against Menon of Gargettos (see below) has been found, with the comment *hos erchsen*. If the author meant the eponymic archonship, Menon was archon in 473/472 BC (Develin (1989) 69 and no. 1990; *PA* 10055). Thus, the earliest *ostrakophoria* in which he could be so described falls to the year 471 BC. (3) Since Themistocles' ostracism could have happened in 470 BC at the latest (see above), the year 471 BC seems to be a good date for the *ostrakophoria* attested by the 'Great Deposit' from the Kerameikos. However, it has to be noted here that referring to Menon as former archon would be possible for further several years (Lewis (1974) 4), so dating the second ostracism of Megakles to the early 60s of the fifth century is not entirely impossible. For general

after the ostracism discussed by the author of A.P. The issue is quite complicated, but it is indisputable that the burden of proof has shifted to the side of the sceptics and the double ostracism of Megakles seems more probable now than his single exile. Without drawing any statistical conclusions from the deposit of sherds with Megakles' name, it can be said that the number of 4176 'votes' cast against him during one *ostrakophoria* of the late 70s and coming from a single deposit of ostraka 'disposed of' after counting seems to exclude the possibility of this particular voting to have been 'won' by somebody else.[104]

The only literary source of information regarding Menon's ostracism [no. VIII?] is the entry in Hesychius' lexicon (*s.v. Menonidai* [M 866]): Μενωνίδαι· τῶν †εὐφήμων, ἐκ Μενωνιδῶν. τινὲς δέ φασι τὸν Μένωνα ἐξωστρακίσθαι. The last editor of this entry, Kurt Latte, following some hesitation apparent in the critical apparatus,[105] clearly considered its key point as corrupt. He did not accept August Meineke's suggestion, who proposed in his edition of anonymous new comedy fragments of 1841 (*FCG* IV, p. 645, no. 161) to correct εὐφήμων to εὐσήμων, which would allow understanding the opening of the entry in the following way: *Menonidae illustribus gentibus adnumerandi*. According to Meineke, the lexicographer is explaining here the phrase from new comedy: ἐκ Μενωνιδῶν, then adding an erudite comment about the ostracism of Menon. Regardless of whether we accept Meineke's correction or not, it is evident that the lexicographic tradition preserved the information about the group (family?) of 'Menonids', descending from Menon, who was regarded as an ostracism victim by an earlier commentary to some literary work.

This late mention would not have attracted scholars' attention had it not been for the discovery of a large number of ostraka with the name Menon son of Menekleides of Gargettos (or 'Menon', or 'Menon of Gargettos'). We currently have ca. 658 of them, including the ostraka where the name

---

information on dating this deposit, see Brenne (2001) 30–46 (with cited bibliography) and *Kerameikos* 20.1, pp. 43–44. Cf. also Berti (2001), who, however, argues for more than one Megakles as being targeted by the Kerameikos ostraka.

[104] See below, 3.2.5, on the conundrum of the 'quorum' for ostracism and the way of voting in *ostrakophoria*.

[105] K. Latte regarded Meineke's proposition as contradicting the lexicographer's linguistic usage; he considered in turn the possibility of correcting δυσφήμων to συκοφάντων. Latte naturally accepted Meineke's most important correction in this text. In manuscripts we find the probably meaningless ἐκ Μένων ἰδίων. The preservation of this last reading led Raubitschek (1955a) to identify the (perhaps) ostracised Menon with Menon of Pharsalus (Dem. [*Against Aristocrates*] XXIII 199), who came with his own people to rescue the Athenians besieged in Eion in 477 BC, for which act he was later rewarded with Athenian citizenship. See also below.

TOWARDS A RECONSTRUCTION OF OSTRACISM IN ATHENS 103

Menon is accompanied (probably erroneously[106]) by other patronymics or epithets. However, most of them come from the 'Great Deposit' of the Kerameikos, identified with the *ostrakophoria* of Megakles (see above). Of course, even the large number of ostraka cast against Menon son of Menekleides cannot prove that he was ostracised. Antony Raubitschek identified the Menon from Hesychius' entry with the naturalised Athenian Menon of Pharsalus and later (quite hazardously) with Menon son of Menekleides of the deme Gargettos and concluded that his ostracism must have taken place in spring 457 BC.[107] However, if we reject this interpretation, the only remaining option is to identify our Menon with the archon of 473/372 BC (Develin 1989: 69 and no. 1990), whose former office is mentioned on one of the ostraka (Siewert, T 1/117; *Kerameikos 20.2*, 6262 = O 6092).[108]

The note about Menon's ostracism, preserved in the lexicographic tradition and most probably derived from some Hellenistic commentary to a classical Attic poet (according to Meineke) or orator, is worth attention. Although a considerable number of ostraka with his name unquestionably come from Megakles' ostracism in 471 BC, their accumulation testifies to Menon's place among the top political players in Athens of this time. It should be remembered that the only piece of information we have about this politician's belonging to the Athenian élite is due to the *hypothesis* of Aeschylus' *Persians*, which mentions him as an archon. This reference may be merely a result of the chronographer's work on dating the staging of the play based on the list of archons. In this context, it seems hardly conceivable that some comedy writer or Attic orator made up this person's ostracism. Hence, the information about it should be treated seriously, and Menon's exile should be regarded as probable, even if impossible to prove. If it actually took place, it could have happened shortly after the ostracisms of Megakles and Themistocles in the early 60s of the fifth century.

The victim of the next, this time resounding, ostracism was [no. IX] Cimon son of Miltiades from Lakiadai, Philaid (*APF* 8429; 472 ostraka in total, mainly from the Kerameikos), one of the wealthiest Athenian aristocrats of this time and a key figure in the Athenian 'reconquest' from the

---

[106] See Siewert, T 1/115–140, and pp. 44 and 63, with references (by Brenne). Brenne (2001) nos. 183–190, pp. 235–242.
[107] Raubitschek (1955a). Cf. Thuc. I 111,1; D.S. XI 83, 3–4. This already precarious structure collapsed with the reinterpretation of two ostraka directed at Menon, on whose erroneous reading Raubitschek was relying (Siewert, T 1/115–116; *Kerameikos 20.2*, 6857 and 6259 = O 6712 and 6088).
[108] See above, n. 103.

Persians in the Aegean.¹⁰⁹ His ostracism is closely related to Ephialtes' reforms and to the dispute regarding the position of Areopagus in the *polis*,¹¹⁰ so he must have been exiled in 462/461 BC.¹¹¹ Ps.-Andocides and Ps.-Lysias mention a double ostracism [no. X] of Alcibiades the Elder (*APF* 579),¹¹² of whose exile, even if single only, we also hear in Harpocration's entry (*s.v. Alkibiades* [22.13 Dindorf]) and in the scholia to Aristophanes' *Knights* (sch. vet. Tr 855B).¹¹³ However, this information regards a significant politician of the first half of the fifth century, who, as we hear from Thucydides (V 43,2; cf. VI 89,2), at some point in his life, renounced the honour of the Spartan proxeny in Athens. It is precisely this decision (probably quite desperate in a family with traditionally strong Laconian connections) that scholars interpreted as an attempt to repudiate some allegations which ultimately led to Alcibiades' ostracism.¹¹⁴ Cimon also fell victim to ostracism resulting from the suspicion of his Spartan affinities, and the chronology of the life of Alcibiades the Elder (*APF* 579) suggests dating his hypothetical ostracism to around 460 BC, immediately after Cimon's exile. This would fit in with the (hypothetical) political atmosphere of the time in Athens. Today we know 14 ostraka with the name of Alcibiades son of Kleinias, Scambonid: eight from the Agora (dated imprecisely to the mid-fifth century) and six from the Kerameikos (dated to 471 BC), which is, however, not particularly helpful in our considerations.

---

¹⁰⁹ Most probably *stratēgos* in 479/478 and 478/477 BC (thus, born around 510 BC), and definitely in 476/475 (possibly also in the following years, but the available sources do not confirm this), in 469/468 and from 466/465 continuously until 462/461 BC. See Develin (1989) 67–69, 70–73; cf. Brenne (2001) no. 130, pp. 193–195.

¹¹⁰ See, e.g., Sealey (1964); Wallace (1974); Pritchard (1994); Raaflaub (1995) 41.

¹¹¹ The source evidence for Cimon's ostracism is discussed above, p. 103 and n. 109. See also Theopompus, *FGrHist* 115 F 88; Plut. *Cim.* 17,2 and *Per.* 9,4. Cf. Cole (1974); Steinbrecher (1985) 46–49.

¹¹² Cf. *APF* 600 (V), pp. 15–16 (Alcibiades II).

¹¹³ While Harpocration repeats the information after Ps.-Lysias (doubting the authenticity of this speech), scholia to *Knights* provide a very reliable list of the ostracised (exaggerating in saying that almost all the excellent Athenians fell victims of ostracism): Aristides, Cimon, Themistocles, Thucydides, Alcibiades. The scholion clearly dissociates the last one from the ostracism of Hyperbolus, who appears in the following sentence. Thus, this is clearly about Alcibiades the Elder, and the source of this scholion was entirely independent of Ps.-Lysias. Interestingly, it does not follow the tradition descending from *A.P.* (Androtion? and ultimately Cleidemus?) and ignores the first four ostracism victims. It is possible, however, that the original source of this scholion included their names, but they were dropped at some evolution stage of the tradition as not belonging to properly 'potent' Athenians. The name of Alcibiades the Elder (*APF* 579) might have remained on this list through the association with his more famous namesake, Alcibiades the Younger. For this scholion, see now Heftner (2018).

¹¹⁴ See Hatzfeld (1951) [1940] 16; Vanderpool (1972) 8; *APF*, p. 15.

While scholars accept the single ostracism of Alcibiades the Elder (*APF* 579) without major reservations, his second exile mentioned by Ps.-Andocides and Ps.-Lysias [no. X bis], and thus possible around 450 BC at the earliest, is uniformly rejected. In my opinion, rightly so. Ps.-Lysias and Ps.-Andocides (or, more precisely, the one who served as a model for the other),[115] while writing about Alcibiades, most probably resorted to rhetorical exaggeration, transferring the information about the double exile of Megakles onto another ancestor of their protagonist to construct a symmetrical image of Alcibiades' family, doubly defiled with ostracism: in both the male and female line.

The ostracism of Callias son of Didymios [no. XI?] is mentioned only by Ps.-Andocides (IV [*Against Alcibiades*], 32). Callias son of Didymios (*PA* 7823), was one of the greatest Athenian sportsmen of the fifth century, whose career extended from around 480 BC to at least around 450 BC.[116] Today we have 10 ostraka with his name: seven from the Kerameikos (471 BC?) and three from the Agora from the 'mid-fifth century' (see above). Scholars are generally inclined to accept Callias' ostracism as historical and to place this event in the 40s of the fifth century, regarding the politician as a more or less significant opponent of Pericles.[117]

From my point of view, this is far from certain. On the one hand, a famous sportsman of the first half of the fifth century (see Paus. V 9,3; VI 6,1) would be perfectly fit for a rhetorical model of the Athenians' ruthlessness towards the *polis*' benefactors—this time, as Ps.-Andocides emphasises, towards somebody who made Athens famous like no other 'with his own effort'. On the other hand, we do not have any other traces of such a (hypothetical) *topos*. In this speech, Callias' company is limited to Cimon, Megakles, and Alcibiades the Elder (*APF* 579). Interestingly, the flow of Ps.-Andocides' thought leads him from Callias' athletic success and

---

[115] Unfortunately, we do not know the mutual relationship between these two fictitious fourth-century speeches.

[116] A29 in Kyle's (1987) catalogue of Athenian sportsmen (with the bibliography on the topic gathered there). Callias' dedication on the Acropolis (most probably after his victory in the youth competition during the Panathenaia of 480 BC): *DAA* 21 (*IG* I² 608+714). Another one (surely shortly after 450 BC) speaks about his victories at the Olympic and Panathenaic games, five times at the Isthmian, four times at the Nemean and twice at the Pythian games: *DAA* 164 (*IG* I² 606). It is not impossible that he came from the deme Alopeke. He also might have had family connections with the Alcmaeonids or with the family of Callias son of Hipponikos (*APF* 7825), which in turn would link him with Cimon's family circle.

[117] Vanderpool (1972) 239-240; *Agora* 25, p. 65 (ostraka nos. 310-312). Cf. Kyle (1987) 202-203 (A29) and Siewert, T 1, p. 56.

ostracism to Cimon's athletic victory at Olympia and his ostracism (with the mention of his father Miltiades' athletic success added at the opportunity), and then to the ostracism of Megakles and Alcibiades the Elder (*APF* 579) (§§ 32-34). The author of this speech had in mind an apparently not unreasonable association of athletic success, political prominence, and merit for the *polis*.[118] And indeed, as a (retired at that point) sports 'celebrity' of the first half of the fifth century, Callias would have naturally been an object of envy to some of his fellow citizens and a serious political authority to others (cf. the case of the notorious wrestler Thucydides son of Melesias (below) and that of Megakles in Pindar, *Pyth.* VII 18-21). We can probably regard the historicity of his ostracism after 450 BC as likely, even though not proved.

Thucydides son of Melesias (*AFP* 7268; Develin (1989) no. 3012; Brenne (2001), no. 261, pp. 302-303; Siewert, T 1, p. 70) was unanimously considered in ancient tradition a serious (and even the last significant) political opponent of Pericles, and the ostracism of Thucydides [no. XII] was consistently ascribed to his conflict with 'the Olympian'.[119] The unexpected, even though surpassable, problem with dating his exile resulted from the discovery of ostraka targeted at Thucydides (65 in total) on the Kerameikos (two more from the Agora). Admittedly, only one of them ended up in the 'Great Deposit', most probably by coincidence, but we should consider their 'early' (70s?) dating nevertheless. Therefore, it must be assumed that, exactly like Pericles, this politician was a 'candidate' for ostracism from early youth for several decades until the point when Pericles interrupted his long career. The long-lasting (albeit unequal) competition between the two politicians can explain to a certain extent their feelings towards each other, as attested in our sources. And although no statistical conclusions can be drawn here, as we remember, the supply of our epigraphic material indicates that the overwhelming majority of Thucydides' ostraka come precisely from the end of the 70s. Only two come from the 'mid-fifth century' (see above), i.e., from the times of his actual ostracism. From the same period come all the known ostraka (four) against Pericles (Brenne (2001), no. 214, pp. 260-261).

---

[118] For the criticism of an elevated political position of successful sportsmen, see already Xenoph. F 2 W².
[119] See esp. Plut. *Per.* 14,1-2 (cf. also below, pp. 233-234); however, cf. Theopompus *FGrHist* (= *BNJ*) 115 F 91 (*ap.* sch. vet. Ar., *Vesp.*, 947C = Siewert, T 29). On doubtful references to Thucydides' ostracism in comedy, see below, p. 118.

The traditional dating of Thucydides' ostracism to 443/442 BC, shortly after the year when he acted as *stratēgos*, arises from a calculation based on Plutarch's statement (*Per.* 16,3) that after the exile of this politician, Pericles held the office of *stratēgos* uninterruptedly for 15 years, enjoying full power in Athens.[120] Peter Krentz's proposition that this date should be moved to the times after 439 BC is not well-founded.[121]

The ostracism [no. XIII] of Damon from Oa (*APF* 3133 = 3143),[122] mentioned in *A.P.*, is one of the cases vividly discussed in the last decades. This is due to the disturbing preservation state of our main source, *A.P.*, but above all to the strong impression which the information about ostracising a musician and music theorist, one of the greatest Athenian intellectuals in the fifth century,[123] made on scholars. The discussion was heated up by the discovery of four ostraka with his name on the Kerameikos (Brenne 2001, no. 52), one of which, a sherd of a painted vessel, can be dated to the mid-fifth century.

In *A.P.* 27.4, we read:

> Since Pericles' property fell short for that service, on the advice of Damonides of Oë (who seems to have suggested most of Pericles' measures to him: because of that they later ostracised him)[124] that since he was being worsted through private resources he should give the many their own, he devised the payment of a stipend for the jurors. (tr. P.J. Rhodes)

Although this information is perfectly clear, the text preserved on the London papyrus presents two problems. An issue of secondary importance to me is identifying the deme where the protagonist of this sentence came from.[125] The fundamental difficulty is identifying the person involved here.

---

[120] See, e.g., Wade-Gery (1932) 206–208; Frost (1964); Meyer (1967). Cf. also Kienast (1953).

[121] Krentz (1984). Such dating would roughly correspond to one of the possible interpretations of the fragment from Cratinus (fr. 73 K–A) which mentions Pericles becoming free from the fear of ostracism. However, see my interpretation of this passage below, pp. 120–121.

[122] On his family connections (including the cautious suggestion that he was the first husband of Agariste, known from the Hermakopidai affair of 415 BC; cf. Andoc. I [*On mysteries*] 16), see *AFP* 9688 [XIII], p. 383 (bibliography on p. 369).

[123] Wallace (2004) and (2015), supporter of the view that Damon was ostracised, reviews the previous discussion. *Contra*, recently, Raaflaub (2003) (with previous bibliography). Cf. also Meister (1973); Giangiulio (2005).

[124] Original: [...] συμβουλεύσαντος αὐτῷ Δαμωνίδου τοῦ Οἴηθεν (ὃς ἐδόκει τῶν πολλῶν εἰσηγητὴς εἶναι τῷ Περικλεῖ· διὸ καὶ ὠστράκισαν αὐτὸν ὕστερον) [...].

[125] The demes Oa and Oie are regularly confused in our sources. The Οἴηθεν (or Οἰῆθεν, according to Plutarch, *Per.* 9,2, using this passage from *A.P.*) in our papyrus was corrected to

Our sources associate Damon son of Damonides with Pericles, and some sources, including Plutarch (who speaks about Damonides in *Per.* 9,2, quoting precisely this sentence and referring directly to Aristotle), ascribe ostracism to Damonides.[126] A doubling of ostracisms and of cooperation with Pericles by attributing them to both Damon and Damonides is still considered as a possibility by some scholars, even though it appears as a desperate idea. Since the times of Wilamowitz,[127] however, the prevailing (and in my opinion, correct) view was that we are dealing here with a simple corruption of *A.P.* and that the text we received should be supplemented to read <Δάμωνος τοῦ> Δαμωνίδου [τοῦ] Οἴηθεν (or Ὄαθεν). Rhodes (*ad loc.*) observes that it is easy to make a mistake, given the cumulation of genitives. However, since the same kind of mistake occurs both in the papyrus and in the text Plutarch was using, we should assume a very early emergence of this corruption. It could have happened very early in the text of *A.P.* or been copied by Ps.-Aristotle from an already erroneous record in his source.[128]

The debate between scholars supporting the historicity of Damon's ostracism and those opposing it lies in establishing whether the nature of Damon's teaching (passed on to us fragmentarily by ancient sources) justifies Plutarch's strong opinion about the political role of Damon by Pericles' side or not. Settling this dispute will not be facilitated by the four ostraka against Damon son of Damonides found on the Kerameikos and dated to the 'mid-fifth century', i.e., the period between the 60s and 30s (see above). Nevertheless, I believe that Robert W. Wallace's argument regarding close connections between Damon's music theory and a certain model of politics is convincing.[129] Moreover, if the author of *A.P.* was working with a list of ostracisms produced earlier and reaching back to before Xerxes' expedition

---

Ὄαθεν on the basis of Stephanus of Byzantium (*s.v.* Oa [O 1]), whose source for this entry seems to be quoting this passage from *A.P.* as well. Oie is a larger and a better-known deme—hence, the corruption of manuscripts in this direction may seem more probable.

[126] Plut. *Per.* 4,2–3; see also *Arist.* 1,7 and *Nic.* 7,1.

[127] Wilamowitz (1893) v. 1, 134 (cf. already Wilamowitz (1879)).

[128] Meister (1973) 43 and following him Rhodes, *ad loc.*, in quite neutral form, support the former solution (Meister points out that in chapter 22 *A.P.* lists names of ostracism victims with their patronyms, but the author's method and interests are different here; see below), but the latter seems equally probable to me. There is a third possibility, namely a simple mistake made by Ps.-Aristotle, who was using his source (a hypothetical Atthidographic list of ostracisms?) hastily, as in this chapter ostracism is a completely marginal issue for the author. It is simply a distinctive detail adorning the account, and not a significant piece of information which would make the person's precise identification and the chronology of this ostracism equally important as those in chapter 22.

[129] Wallace (2004) and (2015). On Damon's image in comedy, see Schwarze (1971) 160–164.

(see above) in front of him, the probability that another ostracism mentioned by him is historical increases.

Concerning the date of Damon's *ostrakophoria*, two hypotheses have been put forward: the 40s (most probably just after the ostracism of Thucydides son of Melesias) and the late 30s—when Pericles' political influence dwindled, which resulted in court trials against his friends and associates: Phidias, Anaxagoras, perhaps Aspasia (432–431 BC), and finally in Pericles' own trial (430 BC).[130]

Regardless of the reliability of A.P.'s account of the financial competition between Cimon and Pericles, which (on Damon's advice) made Pericles introduce pay for Athenian jurors (27.3–4),[131] Ps.-Aristotle mentions Damon in the context of political struggle between these two great politicians, i.e., before 462/461 BC, but he clearly states that Damon's ostracism took place 'later' (ὕστερον). Pedantically, one could expect that if A.P.'s source placed Damon's exile in the late 30s, i.e., a generation after Cimon's ostracism, Ps.-Aristotle would have written 'much later', but *hysteron* can equally well refer to his ostracism in the 40s or 30s. While choosing between these two hypotheses of dating Damon's ostracism, I am inclined towards the former. In the following section of this chapter, I shall consider, among other things, the image of Athenian ostracism in Attic comedy. I shall point out that in the period of the activity of Aristophanes and other old comedy writers (preserved fragmentarily), allusions to famous historical ostracisms occur on stage only rarely, and solely to one contemporary ostracism, namely to Hyperbolus' exile. Although arguments from silence never have decisive force, it is worth noting that old comedy refers to Damon several times but never alludes to his ostracism. In this light, his *ostrakophoria* in the 40s seems more probable.

Scholars dating Damon's ostracism to around 430 BC invoke the passage in *Life of Nicias* by Plutarch (6,1–2),[132] which gives examples of hazards looming over accomplished politicians on account of the Athenian people. It lists in one breath Pericles' trial (430 BC), Damon's ostracism, the *dēmos*' mistrust towards Antiphon of Rhamnus, and the accusation of the *stratēgos*

---

[130] Ephorus in D.S. XX 39 (*FGrHist* 70 F 196); Plut. *Per.* 31–32. On the political background of these events, see Kienast (1953), who links them with the return from exile of Thucydides son of Melesias, ostracised 10 years earlier. However, Kienast's reconstruction appears slightly too reductionist, despite being very interesting. See Podlecki (1998) 101–117. Cf. Banfi (1999); Raaflaub (2000); Giangiulio (2005).
[131] See Rhodes, *ad loc.*
[132] See already Beloch (1914) 313, with n. 1; cf. Meister (1973) 32.

110   PART I: KEY ISSUES

Paches, conqueror of Mitylene (427 BC). According to Plutarch, Nicias took these cases to heart when he started his political career around 430 BC. Pericles' trial and Paches' case indeed form a certain chronological sequence, but the mention of Antiphon is very general, and it can refer to any point in his career up until 411 BC. I believe that the mention of Damon's ostracism here is similar. In Plutarch's account, it is merely a memorable example from the (recent) past; it was not introduced as a current event, which would allow us to date it precisely. It should be noted that the sequence of names here is rhetorically sound. Plutarch starts with the greatest Athenian politician (who was never ostracised, so his trial was the only possible illustration of Plutarch's thought), then he lists three different 'specialists': the politician and music theorist Damon (concealing his sophistic skill and political influence, in Plutarch's view), the orator and politician Antiphon, and the military commander and politician Paches. All these are examples of the people's envy towards exceptionally accomplished and successful citizens, typical for Plutarch's writing, and not a summary of any particular moment in the history of Athenian politics. In other words, in my opinion, we cannot construct any argument regarding the chronology of Damon's exile based on this passage of Plutarch.[133]

Today nobody questions the historicity of Hyperbolus' (*APF* 13910) ostracism [no. XIV], I think, even though a small number of ostraka with his name used to make scholars sceptical.[134] Vividly discussed in turn continue to be, on the one hand, the dating of this event (and its consequences for our knowledge about the length of the 'sentence' of ostracism), and on the other hand, the political circumstances which led to Hyperbolus' exile; more generally debated is also the mechanism of this particular *ostrakophoria*, which appeared surprising already to the contemporaries of this event. Here I shall briefly address only the dating problem.[135]

Unlike in the case of other Athenian ostracisms, we have a large corpus of sources at our disposal for the last one, beginning with testimonies

---

[133] Norbert Loidol's more recent hypothesis (in Siewert, T 23, pp. 338–339) hesitantly puts Damon's ostracism between 438 BC (because Plato Comicus, fr. 207 K–A, dated at the earliest to 428 BC, is supposed to allude to Damon after his return to Athens) and 432 BC (because after the outbreak of the Peloponnesian War *ostrakophoriai* would be very unlikely, 'aus Grunden der Staatsraison'), but both these assumptions seem doubtful.

[134] Only three ostraka with his name have been preserved, while we have eight against Cleophon, whose participation in these events is not mentioned in literary sources at all.

[135] On the relative chronology of Hyperbolus' fortunes, in relation to the issue of the duration of exile through ostracism, see below, pp. 183–185. On the political circumstances which led to his ostracism as well as on the exceptional place of this *ostrakophoria* and this ostracism among other attested Athenian ostracisms, see below, pp. 240–244.

contemporary with the events.[136] The issue of its dating can be seen as a clear example of irony, if not maliciousness, of the historian's fortune. For we have two contemporary sources: a passage in the greatest ancient historian Thucydides, and lines by a contemporary comedy writer (offering insight into the sentiment in Athens shortly after this *ostrakophoria*), as well as several mentions in Plutarch, who often returned to this issue; finally, a set of ostraka from this voting has been preserved. Despite having access to this evidence, when dating the event, we have to rely on three testimonies of highly doubtful value: a precarious reconstruction of a very badly preserved inscription (*IG* I² 95 = *IG* I³ 85), an undoubtedly very corrupt fragment of Theopompus (*FGrHist* 115 F 96b),[137] and one of the speeches included in Andocides' corpus, *Against Alcibiades* (Andoc. IV), which is most probably a later rhetorical exercise, at an uncertain temporal distance from the *ostrakophoria* of Hyperbolus. If we accept the inscription's supplementation proposed by Geoffrey Woodhead, we could infer that at the end of the year 418/417 BC Hyperbolus was still an active Athenian politician, which makes his ostracism in spring 417 impossible.[138] His exile, in turn, followed by his murder on Samos at the end of 412/411 BC, about which we learn from Thucydides (VIII 73,3), could have lasted six years, in the light of a corrupt fragment of Theopompus. At the same time, it is not clear whether Theopompus' source counted these years 'inclusively' (= 416 BC) or 'exclusively' (= 417 BC).[139] However, while rejecting the last date, we have to consider the testimony from the speech by Ps.-Andocides, which plays with several colourful 'facts' from the times of Hyperbolus' ostracism. They are not entirely coherent chronologically,[140] but if we assume that the author of

---

[136] Plut. *Alc.* 13,4–9; Arist. 7,3–4; *Nic.* 11,1–7 init. (for passages in Thucydides and comedy writers contemporary to the events, see below). The most comprehensive discussion of the discrepancies between various accounts (including the different versions in Plutarch's *Lives*) can be found in Heftner (2000a). Only Bianchetti (1979), writing before the final publication of the ostraka against Hyperbolus by M. Lang in *Agora* 25 (1990), firmly supports the earlier date of this politician's exile—in 418/417 BC. Roobaert (1967) does not tackle the problem of dating this *ostrakophoria* in detail, but he definitely excludes the possibility that ostraka with names attributable to the times of Hyperbolus' political activity (apart from this politician, also Alcibiades, Phaeax, Hippocles, Charias, Phileriphos, Philippos, Cleophon, Philinos) could have belonged to more than one *ostrakophoria*, as is assumed by Hands (1959) 73–74, who believes that another, 'failed' (abortive) *ostrakophoria* took place around this time. On the mirage of 'failed' *ostrakophoriai*, which in fact merely serve the interpretation of this challenging material according to the principle *obscurum per obscurius*, see above, p. 81.

[137] See more on this fragment of Theopompus, below, pp. 183–184.

[138] Woodhead (1949).

[139] I find unconvincing the entirely 'revisionist' interpretation of this fragment by Raubitschek (1955c).

[140] They are diligently analysed by Rhodes (1994) 87–91.

112　PART I: KEY ISSUES

this fourth-century rhetorical exercise was using good sources unknown to us, which he juggled as he pleased but kept the essential factual data, we shall have to date this *ostrakophoria* to 415 BC.[141] Worse still, in a recent restoration of the aforementioned inscription *IG* I² 95 (= *IG* I³ 85), Angelos P. Matthaiou suggested its new reading and a fresh general interpretation of its dating.[142] As a result, once again, one ought to regard as possible all the three years under consideration: 417, 416, and 415 BC. Therefore, I shall be conventionally using the imprecise expression 'around 416 BC' further in my work.

*

As we have seen above, one of the ostracisms passed on in our literary tradition is not trustworthy (no. IX bis; the second ostracism of Alcibiades the Elder (*APF* 579)), and two other remain only probable (the ostracisms of Menon [no. VIII?] and Callias [no. XI?]). The other cases referred to in literary sources of the classical times seem to be certain. This gives us 12 very well-attested and 14 reasonably well-attested cases in total during the fifth century, when *ostrakophoriai* took place in Athens, leading to the exile of Athenian politicians.

Thus, a chronological list of the attested ostracisms reads as follows:

I. 488/487 BC: Hipparchos son of Charmos;
II. 487/486 BC: Megakles son of Hippocrates;
III. 486/485 BC: anonymous 'friend of the tyrants';
IV. 485/484 BC: Xanthippus son of Ariphron;
V. 483/482 BC: Aristides son of Lysimachos;
VI. 472/471 BC: Megakles son of Hippocrates—repeated;
VII. 470 BC: Themistocles son of Neokles;
VIII. (?) Early 60s: Menon son of Menekleides;
IX. 462/461 BC: Cimon son of Miltiades;
X. Around 460 BC: Alcibiades the Elder (*APF* 579);
XI. (?) After 450 BC: Callias son of Didymios;
XII. 443/442 BC (?): Thucydides son of Melesias;
XIII. Before 443 BC or after 442 BC: Damon son of Damonides;
XIV. Around 416 BC (?): Hyperbolus.

---

[141] The divergent scholarly views in this matter have been summarised by Rhodes (1994) 91 n. 36 and now in Rhodes, forthcoming. See also Siewert, T 18–21.
[142] Matthaiou (2015) esp. 710–723.

2.2.4 The End of Athenian *Ostrakophoriai* 'around 416 BC'

One of the rare issues on which scholarly consensus exists in our studies on Athenian ostracism is the end of the Athenian *ostrakophoriai*. Interestingly, the common opinion being widespread, it is rarely argued in any detail, so it is worthwhile to restate the case briefly here. Meanwhile, the problem of the reasons why this particular *ostrakophoria*, the banishment of Hyperbolus in 'around 416 BC', was the last one effectively carried out, as well as the scholarly theories on this matter, will be treated at length elsewhere in my book (see below, in my 'Epilogue and Conclusions').

On the one hand, our ancient sources rather consistently claim that ostracism 'was discontinued' 'with Hyperbolus' (μέχρι δὲ Ὑπερβόλου ὁ ὀστρακισμὸς προελθὼν ἐπ' αὐτοῦ κατελύθη – sch. vet. Ar. *Eq*. 588B; tr. Fortenbaugh) or 'after him' (Philochorus, fr. 30: μετὰ τοῦτον δὲ κατελύθη τὸ ἔθος). The most detailed account is provided, in three different works, by Plutarch. In his *Life of Aristides* (7,4; tr. Bernadotte Perrin), we read that '[t]he people were incensed at this [i.e., the scandalous exile of Hyperbolus – M.W.] for they felt the institution had been insulted and abused, and so they abandoned it utterly and put an end to it' (ἐκ δὲ τούτου δυσχεράνας ὁ δῆμος ὡς καθυβρισμένον τὸ πρᾶγμα καὶ προπεπηλακισμένον ἀφῆκε παντελῶς καὶ κατέλυσεν).[143] A bit different, and less detailed, is Plutarch's comment in his *Life of Nicias* (11,6; tr. B. Perrin): 'And in the end no one was ever ostracized after Hyperbolus, but he was the last [...]' (καὶ τὸ πέρας οὐδεὶς ἔτι τὸ παράπαν ἐξωστρακίσθη μετὰ Ὑπέρβολον, ἀλλ' ἔσχατος ἐκεῖνος κτλ.). Finally, in his *Life of Alcibiades* (13,4–5) Plutarch briefly refers his reader to the two other works on this matter. On the other hand, the systematic part of *A.P.* describes the preliminary vote of ostracism (for this vote, see below, 3.2.1 and 3.2.6): '[During the *ekklēsia kyria* – M.W.] [i]n the sixth prytany, in addition to what has been stated, they also provide a vote on ostracism, whether the assembly should decide to hold one or not (περὶ τῆς ὀστρακοφορίας ἐπιχειροτονίαν διδόασιν, εἰ δοκεῖ ποιεῖν ἢ μή) [...]' (43.5; tr. P. J. Rhodes).[144]

The majority of scholars naturally concluded that the law of ostracism was still 'on the books' in Athens when Ps.-Aristotle wrote his *Politeia* in the

---

[143] Cf. also above, pp. 6–7.
[144] On other ancient testimonies confirming, less univocally though, that the law of ostracism was still in force after exiling Hyperbolus, at least in the fourties and thirties of the fourth century BC, see recently Heftner (2003) 29–32.

320s BC. As P. J. Rhodes writes in his commentary on this passage of *A.P.*, 'presumably the institution was not formally abolished, and the assembly voted each year not to hold an ostracism' (p. 526).[145] In this context, W. Robert Connor and John J. Keaney observed that Theophrastus (or, let me add, Philochorus, most probably following Theophrastus) says that what was 'discontinued' (κατελύθη or κατέλυσεν) was the ἔθος and not the νόμος of ostracism—say, the practice and not the letter of the law—so 'the law was not formally abrogated'.[146]

So far, so good, but the scholarly consensus has not been universal.[147] Two important objections were raised, both resulting from the unease about the quasi-automatical assumption of a necessary historical continuity between the moment of ostracism's (informal) 'abrogation' 'after 416 BC ' and its functioning in the time of *A.P.*, i.e., almost 90 years later. On the one hand, Robert M. Errington (1994) suggested that ostracism was reinstated and put again 'on the books' alongside other and fresh legal measures after the battle of Chaeronea to curb the Macedonian 'fifth column' in Athens. Thus, according to Errington's hypothesis, there is no conflict, but no historical link either, between the accounts regarding the abolition of ostracism 'after Hyperbolus' and the testimony to its existence in *A.P.* On the other hand, Herbert Heftner questioned the idea of *ethos* being a technical term, contrasting with *nomos*, in Theophrastus' *On laws*.[148]

P. J. Rhodes decisively repudiated Errington's general theory.[149] As for the second objection, I think that the wording, technical or not, of our accounts, very probably all stemming from Theophrastus, is of minor significance here. More important are the possible parallels for the existence of laws that were not put into practice or executed for an extended period of time.

---

[145] See also Connor, Keaney (1969) 313; Lehmann (1987) 48–52; Rhodes (1995) 98.
[146] Connor, Keaney (1969) 313 n. 5. They also provide an analogy from *A.P.* 60.2, to which I will return shortly.
[147] M. Chambers in *Aristoteles 10.1*, comm. on 43.5 (p. 352) suggests that ostracism was no longer in use after Hyperbolus, but this plainly contradicts *A.P.*'s practice to describe the institutions still functioning in Athens in his times.
[148] Heftner (2003) 35–36. A third objection to the widespread opinion about the demise of ostracism in Athens 'after Hyperbolus' has been raised by Connor, Keaney (1969), who claimed that ostracism was not so much abandoned but made impossible in practice by the demographic catastrophe of the Peloponnesian War and in particular of the Sicilian expedition. In other words, the high 'quorum' requirement of *ostrakophoria* was simply impossible to meet henceforward. Below, pp. 158–177, I will discuss the issue of the 'quorum' of both the initial *epicheirotonia* and of *ostrakophoria*. There, it will become clear why I take this hypothesis as untenable.
[149] See below, pp. 126–127. More recently, see also Heftner (2003) 27–28.

As Connor and Keaney pointed out,[150] in *A.P.* 60.2, we read of a (seemingly very old) law that 'has nominally remained in force, but the trial [for its violation] has gone out of use' (tr. P. J. Rhodes; ὁ μὲν νόμος ἔστιν, ἡ δὲ κρίσις καταλέλυται). In his commentary on this passage, Rhodes provides us with two more parallels, namely that of *A.P.* 61.2 (οὐκ εἰώθασι δὲ ἐπιβάλλειν), on the possible fines summarily executed by generals when in office ('...but they are not in the habit of imposing penalties'; tr. Rhodes), and the well-known passage 7.4 *ad fin.*, stating the exclusion of the *thētes* from office, but at the same time implicitly assuming it was not executed too scrupulously in his times.[151] As these notes by Ps.-Aristotle only occur because a rule he was interested in opened itself for such a comment, there can be no doubt that the Athenian law and Athenian legal and constitutional practice knew many more such cases.

Of course, there is a significant difference between such situations, and other conceivable cases of the kind, and the vote of ostracism. The former probably resulted from a sort of obstruction, or practice of nonfeasance, by various Athenian legal institutions. In contrast, the latter was a conscious and repeated decision by the majority of voters in the Assembly.

Therefore, if 'the assembly voted each year not to hold an ostracism' for at least nearly 90 years, i.e., between Hyperbolus and Ps.-Aristotle, the question why it was so and why the Athenian people were so steadfast in their negative decisions regarding the practical recourse to ostracism becomes all the more important. A tentative answer to this question will be central to my general conclusions in this book (see below, in my 'Epilogue and Conclusions').

2.2.5 The Issue of Possible *Ostrakophoriai* Unattested in Literary Sources

At the second stage of my work, the question often posed in the previous section of this chapter needs to be reversed. Instead of discussing the validity of particular pieces of information in the sources regarding the ostracism of one Athenian politician or other, we should presently ask whether in Athens of the fifth century there were ostracisms that did not leave any trace in

---

[150] Connor, Keaney (1969) 313 n. 5.
[151] 'Apparently by the time of *A.P.* the law which excluded the *thētes* from all offices had not been repealed but had become a dead letter' (Rhodes, *ad loc.*, p. 146).

literary sources. Such a possibility cannot be excluded. Naturally, any answer can only be hypothetical, and any arguments in this matter are merely circumstantial.

Our literary sources can be divided into several categories as regards the testimonies on ostracisms. First, works offering accounts of ostracisms contemporary to them or taking place during their author's lifetime, as is the case of Pindar and the ostracism of Megakles, or of Thucydides, Plato Comicus, an anonymous comedy writer (*PCG* VIII, Adespota, fr. 363 K–A) and perhaps Aristophanes—all mentioning the ostracism of Hyperbolus. Such cases undoubtedly guarantee the historicity of a particular ostracism, but they will also be helpful indirectly in more difficult cases.

Secondly, there are works by writers of classical times, not very distant from the events they relate. Their authors made an effort to investigate the past using the available methods to establish facts of interest to them (and us); such is the case of Herodotus writing about the exile of Aristides or of Thucydides—about Themistocles. But this is also the case of earlier Atthidographers and their continuators using the findings of their predecessors. Ostracisms found in the works belonging to this group should not arouse our suspicions.

This category comes close to the next one, namely the historians and Atthidographers of the late fourth century, having at their disposal (apart from the accounts by Herodotus and Thucydides, known also to us) the works of early Atthidographers. Let us remember that there was no public document from these times which would establish for them a complete list of the ostracised. All the writers mentioned above, very diverse in their methods of work, must have used chiefly the findings of their predecessors, at times attempting to verify and complement the results of their own inquiries.

Hardly different will be, from our perspective, the status of the information passed on by writers who did not study the past professionally but used the results of such studies in their work for other purposes. To this group belongs, of course, the author of *A.P.*, but also Aristotle. Apart from the 'common' knowledge available to any educated Athenian (in this case a Stagirite), he used the findings of historians, both directly and indirectly, through the corpus of *politeiai*, prepared by his disciples. The ostracism of Damon son of Damonides of Oa, which is probable from the historical point of view, as we have seen, looks plausible also in terms of source criticism. In the same category, if I am correct, we can place so-called Ps.-Andocides and Ps.-Lysias. While composing fictitious speeches in rhetoric schools, they were using popular knowledge and the available erudite material, even though most probably in a limited manner. All the works in this category will naturally manipulate the data on historical ostracisms, tailoring it to their own needs, but they will certainly not attempt to put into circulation non-historical ostracisms, about which no knowledge has been preserved. In the case of the two fictitious speeches mentioned, doing so would harm the rhetorical plausibility of their arguments.

This becomes clear when comparing these works with well-known orators of the fifth and fourth centuries, where information about ostracism is exceptionally sparse. When it appears, it is limited to the most resounding cases, undoubtedly widely circulating in the common knowledge of the Athenians of their times. Our examples include Demosthenes referring to the ostracisms of Aristides and Themistocles, or Andocides mentioning the decision to recall all the ostracised before Xerxes' expedition (I [*On mysteries*], 107) or Cimon's return from exile (III [*On the Peace with Sparta*], 3–4, with the necessary text correction). If we add to this last category the testimony of Plato (*Gorg.* 516D), acknowledging only the ostracisms of Themistocles and Cimon, it will turn out that the Athenians of the classical times were only aware of the ostracisms well-known to us, and that less conspicuous cases (such as Hipparchos son of Charmos, the two ostracisms of Megakles, Alcibiades the Elder (*APF* 579), Callias son of Didymios or Damon of Oa) appear in the analysed texts as a result of the antiquarian work of their authors.

Unfortunately, these source-critical considerations may lead to two entirely divergent conclusions. The *ostrakophoriai* took place in Athens very frequently, but only the most important of them became engraved in the citizens' memory, and the information about the exiles of minor politicians was attained only by the erudite. Or, on the contrary, ostracisms occurred extremely rarely, and the accounts in our sources roughly reflect the level of frequency of historical ostracisms, even though they may skip an *ostrakophoria* or two.

Choosing between these alternative conclusions, I am inclined towards the latter, and so is the majority of scholars today. My reason for this is the following.

A severe complication in our study is the manner in which ostracisms were treated by the two great historians of the fifth century, contemporary to the cases known to us. Herodotus mentions only Aristides, completely neglecting other *ostrakophoriai* from the times before the Persian Wars; he does not say anything about ostracism during the 'Pentekontaetia' before the

Peloponnesian War. Similarly, Thucydides, who refers to the ostracism of the great Themistocles, tells us nothing about the 'Pentekontaetia'; the case of Hyperbolus he mentions (merely marginally) only because his murder was connected with the political events he was describing. For both historians, ostracisms as such were not crucial for constructing a meaningful historical narrative.

Against this background, the image of ostracism in Aristophanes' comedies may be a significant, even though not decisive, argument in our discussion of the issue of ostracisms not attested in our literary sources. All the more so that his plays chronologically span almost the entire period of the Peloponnesian War and reach beyond it. First, as in the case of Demosthenes and Plato, in Aristophanes we find references or allusions to the perhaps most famous ostracism of the fifth century, the exile of Themistocles (*Eq.* 819). Commentators on *Wasps*, staged at the Lenaia of 422 BC, saw in this play an allusion to the ostracism of Thucydides son of Melesias, whose name appears there (*Vesp.* 947, with sch. vet. 947A), but they must have been mistaken.[152] In the same scholion (sch. vet. 947), we read that Aristophanes referred to Thucydides' case elsewhere. Alas, we are not able to identify this passage in his plays.[153] Now, we would expect Aristophanes to allude to ostracisms if they happened during the time of his creative activity. And indeed, in fragment 661 K-A (Siewert, T [?] 13) of an unknown play, in a rather obscure context, we hear about an 'ostracised amphora', but this is hardly enough for us to follow Georg Kaibel in taking this passage as an allusion to the ostracism of Hyperbolus. The exile of this politician is referred to by Plato Comicus (fr. 203 K-A = Siewert, T 12) and perhaps by an unknown playwright (Adesp. Fr. 363 K-A = Siewert, T [?] 14). Aristophanes, in turn, clearly appeals to his public for ostracising Cleon (*Eq.* 855–857). Apart from that, as far as I can see, there are no allusions to particular *ostrakophoriai* in the corpus of Attic comedy writers available to us.[154]

This argument *ex silentio* is not strong enough. However, the lack of such allusions in Aristophanes and other comedy writers—except for the references to the ostracism of Hyperbolus, which we hear about from other sources—may be meaningful. It may suggest that the picture emerging

---

[152] Cf. comm. by Sommerstein (1983) *ad loc.*
[153] Cf. Siewert, T 10, with comm. by Brigitta Eder.
[154] On fr. 73 K-A of Cratinus, see below, pp. 120–121; on fr. 168 K-A of Plato Comicus, see below, pp. 210–211.

from our literary sources is valid at least for the period of the Peloponnesian War. During that time, until 'around 416 BC', the Athenians seem not to have used ostracism even once. The nature of the sources discussed above does not allow us to project this conclusion onto the earlier decades of the fifth century with any degree of certainty. But there are many indications that we have no reason to question the number of Athenian ostracisms in the fifth century implied in our literary sources.

Before discussing the historical usefulness of ostraka (the 'tools' of Athenian ostracism) more systematically further in my book (cf. also above, 2.2.1), I can add that their analysis points in the same direction. Aristophanes, in his *Knights*, aims to persuade his audience to ostracise 'Paphlagon'-Cleon. Regardless of the entirely coincidental or random evidence of the Athenian ostraka, it is striking that not even one ostrakon with the name of a politician so significant, so controversial, and so much hated by some has been preserved.[155] If any *ostrakophoriai* had taken place between the 30s, when he began his political career, and his death at Amphipolis in 422 BC, we would expect him to be one of the most serious 'candidates' for exile at any such occasion.[156] A complete lack of ostraka against Cleon (thus far) may conceivably confirm our hypothesis that no *ostrakophoriai* took place in Athens for over 20 years before 416 BC.

---

[155] Cf. Bourriot (1982).
[156] It is reasonable to suppose that if an *ostrakophoria* had been carried out in 424 BC, shortly after the staging of *Knights* (see above), some part of the Athenian theatre audience would have taken Aristophanes' playful persuasion to heart.

3
Towards a Reconstruction of Ostracism in Athens
The Procedures

In the well-known fragment of Cratinus' comedy entitled *Thracian Women*, quoted by Plutarch (fr. 73 K–A, *ap.* Plut. *Per.* 13,9 = Siewert, T 7), we read: 'The squill-head Zeus!¹ lo! here he comes, | The Odeum like a cap upon his cranium, | Now that for good and all the ostracism is o'er. (ἐπειδὴ τοὔστρακον παροίχεται) (tr. Bernadotte Perrin)'.² Dating this play is a classic example of a vicious circle. We are entrapped while trying to reconcile the 'historical reality' discernible in the literary work with our general interpretation of this text and this very 'reality'. Eduard Meyer and Georg Busolt associated the historical background of the play with the ostracism of Thucydides son of Melesias (see above) in 443 or 442 BC.³ Rudolf Kassel and Colin Austin, in their edition of Cratinus in the fourth volume of *PCG*, point out the references the play makes to the orator Euathlos (fr. 82 K–A) and Callias son of Hipponikos (*APF* 7826) as well as the 'presence' on the stage of Pericles, still alive (d. 429 BC). This may be combined with the fact that the chorus of Thracian women is composed of worshippers of the goddess Bendis (introduced to Athens most probably just before the Peloponnesian War).⁴ All this strongly suggests the time around 430 BC.⁵ The stalemate caused by the discrepancy between the date of the sole evident case of ostracism in the last decades of Pericles' supremacy in Athens and the dating of the characters appearing in the play was brilliantly broken by Wilamowitz. He pointed out that a preliminary vote took place in Athens

---

¹ Cf. Schwarze (1971) 66–69. Other passages containing humorous remarks on the shape of Pericles' head have been conveniently gathered in the edition of *testimonia* PCG K–A. Cf. also Schwarze (1971) index, *s.v. Perikles: Kopfkarikatur*, Bakola (2010) index, *s.v. Pericles: head jokes*.
² Cf. Mosconi (2011).   ³ Busolt (1897) 495 n. 3; Meyer (1901) 43.
⁴ Cf. Garland (1992) 111–114. Alas, I could not use here several studies by A. Blomart on this subject.
⁵ See already Geissler (1925) 21–22. Several other scholars (cited by Geissler in *Nachtrag*, p. XI) suggested various other dates, closer to 440 BC or shortly after, consistently speculating on the ostracism threat to Pericles.

every year to decide whether an *ostrakophoria* should be carried out or not.⁶ In other words, in the eyes of the Athenians and in the playwright's joke, Pericles might have serendipitously escaped ostracism at any point in his career, or even every year after a negative preliminary vote on this matter. Thus, dating the play to just before the Peloponnesian War or even to 430 BC does not present any difficulties.⁷

Even when referring to Wilamowitz's note in their works, most scholars focus so closely on the spectacular voting with ostraka⁸ that they do not draw any conclusions from this priceless testimony of the political tension that must have accompanied the preliminary vote on the ostracism procedure every year. I shall analyse this two-stage process below because it may be key to our understanding of the very idea of this institution and the motives of its inventor, Cleisthenes.⁹

3.1 The Question of the Availability of the Law about Ostracism in Fourth-century Athens

It is slightly surprising that the availability of the ostracism law in Athens in the fourth century BC, when the first accounts of ostracism were emerging, giving rise to the entire later tradition, is discussed in scholarship relatively rarely.¹⁰ Scholars are usually satisfied with general statements, unsupported with a more detailed analysis.¹¹ However, a thorough study of this issue has recently been attempted by Philipp Scheibelreiter.¹² Based on Antony Raubitschek's findings regarding the departure point of all the subsequent

---

⁶ Wilamowitz-Moellendorff (1879) 319 n. 3.

⁷ Furthermore, as one of my anonymous OUP referees kindly suggested to me, given the uproar in Athens caused by the first Spartan invasion of Attica in 431 BC, Pericles might have been threatened by ostracism even more immediately thereafter.

⁸ See, for instance, Schwarze (1971) 67–68 or the discussion in Siewert, T 7 (by Katharina Knibbe) with cited bibliography.

⁹ Forsdyke (2005) 147 suggests two indirect indications of the existence of this two-stage procedure in the fifth century: first, the fact that we only hear of one ostracism per year when it happens at all and secondly, allusions to ostracism in Aristophanes (see below, pp. 127–129) that may be indicative of a fixed time for *ostrakophoria* in the Athenian political calendar. As she admits herself, both these considerations are far from being decisive.

¹⁰ One reason thereof may be the self-explanatory mention of the need to consult, in 411 BC, 'the ancestral laws' introduced by Cleisthenes when establishing democracy (*A.P.* 29.3, with Rhodes, *ad loc.*). However, as pointed out by Lévêque, Vidal-Naquet (1973) 7, this reference is far from proving the availability of the actual texts of the laws ascribed to Cleisthenes at the time.

¹¹ For example, Raubitschek (1958) and Wade-Gery (1933). For 'publication, preservation, and consultation' of Athenian laws in general, see now Sickinger (2004).

¹² Scheibelreiter (2008).

literary and lexicographic tradition about ostracism,[13] he argued that the scholion to Aristophanes' *Knights* (sch vet 855B) preserved a paraphrase of the provisions of this law, which was used (even though not quoted literally) by Theophrastus in his *On Laws*.[14] Ten years later, another Viennese scholar Herbert Heftner made a ground-breaking step forward in our philological interpretation and reconstruction of the text underlying the scholion.[15]

Let us take a more precise look at this paraphrase of the ostracism law, discernible in the text usually edited as Jacoby's fragment 30 of Philochorus (which I shall analyse in more detail further in this chapter: pp. 129–134):[16]

[...] διαριθμηθέντων δὲ ὅτῳ πλεῖστα γένοιτο καὶ μὴ ἐλάττω ἑξακισχιλίων, τοῦτον ἔδει τὰ δίκαια δόντα καὶ λαβόντα ὑπὲρ τῶν ἰδίων συναλλαγμάτων ἐν δέκα ἡμέραις μεταστῆναι τῆς πόλεως ἔτη δέκα (ὕστερον δὲ ἐγένοντο πέντε), καρπούμενον τὰ ἑαυτοῦ, μὴ ἐπιβαίνοντα ἐντὸς Γεραιστοῦ τοῦ Εὐβοίας ἀκρωτηρίου κτλ.

[...] After [the ostraka] were counted, the person for whom the most [ostraka] occurred [i.e., were cast] and not less than six thousand, this man had to tender and exact settlements ['just things'] concerning his personal arrangements within ten days, to relocate from the city-state for ten years (but later it became five), enjoying the use of his property, not overstepping [a boundary] within Geraestus, the promontory of Euboia [...].

(tr. Nicholas F. Jones, *BNJ*)

We find here the famous expression καρπούμενον τὰ ἑαυτοῦ, which occurs throughout the subsequent historiographic and lexicographic tradition about ostracism,[17] but also a series of technical legal formulations (τὰ δίκαια δόντα καὶ λαβόντα and ὑπὲρ τῶν ἰδίων συναλλαγμάτων) as well as details regarding the geography of exile, also provided in *A.P.*[18] Although, as we shall see, Theophrastus added two short 'supplements' here, I believe that

---

[13] Raubitschek (1958); cf. above, 1.2.2.
[14] Theophrastus, fr. 18(b) Szegedy-Maszak (= 640B Fortenbaugh).
[15] Heftner (2018). I will briefly discuss his conclusions in my next sections. Here suffice it to say that Heftner's interpretations do not have direct bearing on the problem of the availability of the original law of ostracism in fourth-century Athens.
[16] In a slightly similar fashion, Heftner (2018) 109.
[17] See already Raubitschek (1965) 287, referring to his earlier work on this matter.
[18] Here, the original wording of the geographical provision of this law is of no consequence to me, but see below, 3.3.1.

we are dealing with a paraphrase of a fragment of the original law about ostracism. It cannot be excluded that also earlier in this scholion and in the fragment of Philochorus further paraphrases or excerpts from this law can be found (for instance, about the magistrates supervising the *ostrakophoria* voting), but the passage quoted above seems to be based directly on a coherent fragment of this law.[19]

In this context, the question should be asked how Theophrastus (as the ultimate source of this tradition, see below, pp. 158–160) could have gained insight into the text of the ostracism law. I think that the most probable explanation is that Cleisthenes' law was included, at least partly, in a compiled 'revision' of the Athenian law created by the team of *anagrapheis* working, with changing competences, in the years 410–399 BC, and featuring Nicomachus.[20] After the re-establishment of democracy in Athens, this 'codification' was probably subject to two further revisions. Its final version was perhaps inscribed on the walls of, or close to, the Royal Stoa.[21]

---

[19] Following Brigitta Eder and Herbert Heftner's commentary on the fourth speech by Ps.-Andocides, Philipp Scheibelreiter comments that the verb μεταστῆναι used there could not have occurred in the original text of the law. In earlier prose he would rather expect a form of the verb φεύγειν as equivalent of ὀστρακίζειν. Such use of the word μεταστῆναι can be found in fourth-century authors and in the 'Decree of Themistocles' (Scheibelreiter (2008); cf. Eder, Heftner in: Siewert, T 18, pp. 287 and 292. Cf. also the discussion of these verbs in the debate on the authenticity of the 'Decree of Themistocles' (see above, pp. 91–93): Siewert, T 26, pp. 357, 360). Scheibelreiter infers from this that Theophrastus used the verb μεταστῆναι in a natural way, paraphrasing the provisions of the ostracism law, but I think another explanation can be proposed. Aleksander Wolicki pointed out to me that what should be expected in the original text of the law is precisely a periphrasis such as μεταστῆναι. This is because the peculiarity of this law laid exactly in the difference between the traditional forms of exile (*phygē*) applied thitherto and the new solution, much milder because it reduced the number of victims, the duration, and the general conditions of this form of banishment.

[20] This is also implied by Scheibelreiter (2008) 136. It is possible that for some areas of the Athenian law, this 'codification' was one of the bases (if not the sole basis) and a natural source of the data contained in Theophrastus' *On Laws*. His knowledge about the text of the ostracism law must have stemmed precisely from there.

[21] For general information, see Clinton (1982) (with earlier bibliography on the 'codification' by Nicomachus' committee); cf also MacDowell (1986) 46–48, Stroud (1978), Todd (1996), and Carawan (2013) esp. 233–250 with Canevaro (2015). Contrary to the erroneous but widespread conviction, K. Clinton emphasises that this 'codification' was not complete: it did not rescind all the previous laws not included there, nor did it gather all those which were in force at the time, but only those introduced by Solon which were 'still in force' (cf. *A.P.* 8.3). However, the last expression must be understood quite broadly because many of the laws ascribed to Solon must have admittedly had a Solonian 'core' but were subject to numerous modifications afterwards (see Scafuro (2006)). True, Sickinger (2004) 100 with n. 41, following Robertson (1990), is sceptical about the historicity of the publication of the revised law-code. Robertson's minimalistic hypothesis has been soberly answered by Rhodes (1991). Meanwhile, even if the task of Nicomachus' committee did not involve publishing the revised 'law-code' but only 'to provide a full and reliable collection of texts for Athens' central archive, which was installed during these

Alongside the most important provisions of the still-in-force laws of Solon and the amendments introduced to them later on (for instance, regarding the prerogatives of the Boulē—see below, pp. 173–174), this publication must have included laws devised later (for instance, by Cleisthenes), 'which applied to the whole community of Athenian citizens',[22] and concerning the same aspects of the functioning of the Athenian *polis*.[23] The 'political' laws must have ultimately been among them. After all, one of the primary reasons for the revision (or at least inspection or adjustment) of laws after the overthrow of the oligarchic régime was the fact that many citizens were then considered 'liable under' (*enochoi*) 'many of the laws of Solon and Draco', 'owing to previous events' (Andoc. I [*On mysteries*] 82: . . . τῶν πρότερον ἕνεκα γενομένων), namely to the period of oligarchic power. And Cleisthenes' law about ostracism belonged to the set of regulations still in force in Athens and regarding (among other matters) *atimia*, exile, tyranny prevention, and *stasis*.

3.2 The Procedure and Chronology of Ostracism

3.2.1 Between *Epicheirotonia* and *Ostrakophoria*

Our sources for the study of the procedure of ostracism may appear reliable and unambiguous at first sight. On the one hand, the passage in *A.P.* 43.5 mentions the annual preliminary voting on ostracism at the main Assembly session (*ekklēsia kyria*) in the sixth prytany.[24] On the other hand, the famous

---

very years' (Robertson (1990) 45), this was where Theophrastus and others could consult Cleisthenes' law about ostracism, most probably integrated into political laws ascribed to Solon. See below.

[22] See Rhodes (1991) 91 and *passim*.

[23] That the law about ostracism was available in such a form is also supported by the fact that Cleisthenes' name as its author appears relatively late in our sources (cf. above, pp. 77–78). The Athenians, or at least those more inquisitive among them, naturally knew who they owed ostracism to, but the law regulating it was included in the 'codification' of laws generally ascribed to Solon.

[24] ἐπὶ δὲ τῆς ἕκτης πρυτανείας πρὸς τοῖς εἰρημένοις καὶ περὶ τῆς ὀστρακοφορίας ἐπιχειροτονίαν διδόασιν, εἰ δοκεῖ ποιεῖν ἢ μή ('In the sixth prytany, in addition to what has been stated, they also provide a vote on ostracism, whether the assembly should decide to hold one or not' – tr. P.J. Rhodes). I shall briefly discuss below (pp. 176–177) the widely debated issue whether this text should be read with the word *epicheirotonia* as preserved in the papyrus, or with the correction *procheirotonia*, proposed and later withdrawn by Wilamowitz and Kaibel (based on the corresponding verb in Philochorus, F 30, below), or possibly with the correction *diacheirotonia*, suggested by Rhodes (*ad loc.*). However, it does not have much impact on the interpretation of this passage here.

fragment of Philochorus (*FGrHist* 328)²⁵ describes the *ostrakophoria* procedure. It begins with a peculiar sentence,²⁶ which (with Jacoby's correction) seems to be indicating that *ostrakophoria* took place in the eighth prytany. Thus, everything is seemingly clear: the preliminary vote on ostracism was carried out in the sixth prytany, and *ostrakophoria* in the eighth. However, interpretation of both these testimonies presents many difficulties. The most significant problems connected with understanding the passage from *A.P.* are two technical details: the mention of *ekklēsia kyria* and the chronology according to the prytany system. In short, the question arises whether Ps.-Aristotle's words can be understood as referring to earlier times, given that the 'main Assembly session' was certainly introduced much later than Cleisthenes' reforms, as was most probably the public calendar dividing the year into prytanies. While reading the fragment of Philochorus' in turn, we have to consider correcting or supplementing it, or at least infer what is not directly stated there. Moreover, the value of this entire testimony can be questioned due to the obvious errors and distortions, which are easily noticeable in its further parts (see below). Therefore, before we embark on reconstructing the procedure of Athenian ostracism, we need to consider the reservations regarding both our sources mentioned above.

Taking this scepticism as our point of departure, we could claim that (1) the procedure of ostracism described in *A.P.* is completely anachronous and in the early times (until when?) the preliminary vote on ostracism did not take place or was carried out simultaneously with the *ostrakophoria* (the day before?).²⁷ Alternatively, (2) despite the anachronistic terminology, the principle of separating the preliminary vote from *ostrakophoria* was in force from the very beginning, even when the 'main Assembly session' was not formally distinguished yet and the prytany calendar was not yet in use. Due to the preservation state of the available sources, our reasoning in this matter must be circumstantial and cumulative, even though we know that the sum of many weak arguments is not equal to the strength of one indisputable proof.

---

²⁵ With other testimonies, in poorer preservation state, coming from the same fragment of Philochorus—see below, pp. 158–160.

²⁶ προεχειροτόνει μὲν ὁ δῆμος πρὸ τῆς ὀγδόης πρυτανείας, εἰ δοκεῖ τὸ ὄστρακον εἰσφέρειν. ὅτε δ' ἐδόκει ἐφράσσετο σανίσιν ἡ ἀγορά κτλ. ('Before the eighth prytany the People conducted an advance vote, whether it is deemed good to introduce "the *ostrakon*". Whenever it was so deemed, the Agora was fenced with planks...' – tr. Nicholas F. Jones, *BNJ*). I shall return below to this passage, the proposed emendations, and its general interpretation.

²⁷ Thus, for instance, Carcopino (1935) 70.

In 1994 Robert M. Errington hypothesised that the obligatory annual preliminary vote on ostracism described in *A.P.* was introduced in Athens only in 338/337 BC. After the defeat at Chaeronea, the Athenians, driven by the fear of Macedon and its Athenian 'fifth column', invented, re-instated, and adapted various solutions to protect democracy (cf. Eukrates' law on tyranny: *SEG* XII 87). That was when the order of Assembly sessions described in *A.P.* was introduced, which can be inferred from the fact that only from that time on did the Athenians regularly use the term *ekklēsia kyria* in their decrees.[28]

However, against this hypothesis speaks the fact that the Athenians never voted for carrying out ostracism in this difficult period.[29] Moreover, if we assume that their intention was fighting internal enemies with ostracism, introducing the two-stage procedure at this particular point would be counter-effective. Furthermore, as we have seen above, the logic of Ps.-Aristotle's account in chapter 22 of *A.P.* indicates that the writer was convinced that the law about ostracism was not altered significantly after Xerxes' expedition. Ps.-Aristotle could naturally be mistaken in this matter, but the silence of *A.P.* about a decision potentially so fundamental to the Athenian political system, which its author would have witnessed himself, strongly undermines Errington's hypothesis. P. J. Rhodes points out that in the political campaigns in Athens before and after the battle of Chaeronea, so well-known to us, none of our sources mentions a possibility, or even a suggestion of carrying out, introducing or re-introducing ostracism.[30] Most importantly, however, if my interpretation of fr. 73 K–A of Cratinus (proposed already by Wilamowitz in 1879) is accepted, it will constitute a strong argument that preliminary voting on ostracism took place in Athens already around 430 BC, hundred years before the hypothetical reform of the whole procedure postulated by Errington. Overall, Rhodes' arguments in his response to Errington's article of 1994 must be fully accepted here:

> The rubrics *ekklesia* and *ekklesia kyria* do not supplant old rubrics which have become incorrect, but give information of a kind that had not

---

[28] Errington (1994); see also Errington (1995). Rhodes (1995) responded to Errington's ideas decisively, in my opinion. Cf. also below.

[29] The explanation that the fast-unfolding political events, especially the death of Phillip II, made this hypothetical element of the new political provisions in Athens insignificant (thus, for instance, Siewert, T 14, p. 466, chapter by Walter Scheidel and Hans Taeuber, who accept Errington's ideas as a 'probable theory') only dodges the question about *A.P.*'s understanding of the entire procedure of ostracism as still in operation.

[30] Rhodes (1995) 197.

previously been given at all. It may be, then, that the decision to include these rubrics does not reflect a change which for the first time made these rubrics possible, but is simply an instance of the tendency with the passage of time to give more information in the prescripts of decrees [...].[31]

It would be, of course, absurd to claim that the procedure described by *A.P.* functioned without changes since the times of Cleisthenes. However, for my argument, it suffices to assume that already around 430 BC we have evidence for the existence of preliminary voting on ostracism in Athens. If so, we can use Ps.-Aristotle's testimony as an indication that such voting had an assigned place in the traditional 'calendar' of political business of the Athenian democracy already in the fifth century BC. The passage from *A.P.* (43.5) read in this way in its immediate context suggests that to the key problems which need to be voted on during the most important session of the Assembly in each prytany, should be added at some point of the year (incidentally, in the middle of this calendar) a series of particularly important polls,[32] with that on ostracism among them. We do not know whether the list of these polls was always the same and whether ostracism was 'always' the first item on such or a similar list.[33]

The question of whether it is possible to establish when the preliminary voting on ostracism took place during the periods when we cannot be confident of the prytany calendar being in use will lead us in a promising direction.

Scholars have repeatedly attempted to deduce the place of ostracism in the annual sequence of political activities of the Athenian democracy and in the calendar of Athenian festivals.[34] Bernhard Palme[35] has recently discussed the testimony from Aristophanes' *Knights* which mentions Themistocles' exile (l. 819). He tried to find a correlation between the possible date of the preliminary vote at the beginning of the sixth prytany and the time of the staging of this play, which elsewhere quite openly calls on the Athenian people to ostracise Cleon (ll. 855–857). Palme concludes that this play by Aristophanes—staged during the Lenaia in mid-Gamelion of

---

[31] Rhodes (1995) 189.   [32] Cf. Christ (1992).
[33] Rhodes (1995) 192–193 emphasises that already in Dem. XIX [*On the Embassy*] 185 it is clear there was a strict order of proceedings during particular sessions of the Assembly scheduled to discuss specific issues determined by law.
[34] Cf. already Busolt–Swoboda (1926) 990, with n. 2.
[35] Siewert, T 8, pp. 213–214; cf. also comm. to Siewert, T 9 by the same scholar.

424 BC (perhaps Gamelion 12–21;[36] roughly, in January)—was a good moment for such a call, given that the sixth prytany corresponds to some period in late winter. At the time of the Lenaia of 424 BC, the Assembly about to gather at the beginning of the sixth prytany would be voting literally within several days or weeks.

Palme's reasoning is naturally based on the assumption that the prytany calendar was already in use at that time and that the preliminary voting on ostracism was already taking place. The latter is quite secure, on the condition that we regard fr. 73 K–A of Cratinus as referring to such a situation. It should also be noted that a call to ostracise a politician would not be out of place even several months before the potential ostracism. However, Palme does not point out that such a call itself constitutes indirect proof that in 424 BC there existed a practice of preliminary voting. As we remember, we do not know of any instances of *ostrakophoria* around the time of staging *Knights*.[37] In other words, for reasons which are still to be investigated, ostracisms did not happen in this period. However, a call for ostracism coming from the stage during the Lenaia of that year indicates that it was apparently conceivable to Aristophanes and his audience that in the nearest time (not necessarily in the nearest days, but certainly within months or a year) a vote would take place which could ultimately lead (in the comic convention) to ostracising 'Paphlagon'.

Unfortunately, we do not know at which Athenian festival Cratinus' *Thracian Women* were staged. This is where fr. 73 K–A comes from, which alludes, as I believe, to recent preliminary voting on ostracism. Given that Pericles survived it safely, it probably did not set in motion the *ostrakophoria* procedure. I am naturally tempted to date the staging of this play to the Great Dionysia of 430 BC (or one of the preceding years). Cratinus' jokes must have been particularly resounding in the Athenian ears in the month of Elaphebolion (10–16?)[38] late in March, several weeks after the Assembly vote at the beginning of the (hypothetical) sixth prytany. In such a case, Pericles would have escaped ostracism quite recently. However, it is impossible to further our considerations regarding the trustworthiness, or rather relevance, of the testimony from chapter 43.5 of *A.P.* to the procedure of ostracism. Even if we accept as proven the place of the

---

[36] Mikalson (1975) 109–110 and 201.
[37] The last one took place most probably around 442 BC or (less probably) around 430 BC (Damon's ostracism), and the following one did not happen until 'around 416 BC' (Hyperbolus' ostracism).
[38] Mikalson (1975) 125–130, 137, and 201.

preliminary vote on ostracism in the political 'calendar' of around 430 BC, dating the introduction of the bouleutic calendar in Athens presents a serious difficulty here. Rhodes dated this reform to the times of the attack on the prestige of the Areopagus and on the position of archons at the point of Ephialtes' reforms.[39] Nevertheless, from the same perspective, this reform could be placed at the moment of introducing the archons' selection by lot in 487/486 BC (cf. A.P. 22.5). Few scholars would support ascribing this decision to Cleisthenes,[40] but from their point of view, the year 503/504 looks equally plausible, as that was when the Council of Five Hundred was ultimately constituted (cf. A.P. 22.2). In this context, given the silence of A.P.—let us emphasise this again—regarding the changes in the law about ostracism, we can assume only tentatively the possibility that the point of the year at which the *ekklēsia kyria* of the sixth prytany gathered, during the times when the procedure described by Ps.-Aristotle was in operation, roughly corresponds to the stage at which such voting had occurred earlier on. For my purposes, it suffices if, with this assumption made, the model of ostracism's functioning, which I shall propose below, proves effective. To quote Rhodes' words again, which contradict Errington's theses, 'Where proof is impossible, we have to resort to conjecture; Errington's disbelief is no less conjectural than my belief, and we must leave it to readers to judge which conjectures are more likely to be right'.[41]

Let us now move on to our second testimony on the procedure of ostracism, fragment 30 of Philochorus:[42] προεχειροτόνει μὲν ὁ δῆμος πρὸ τῆς ὀγδόης πρυτανείας, εἰ δοκεῖ τὸ ὄστρακον εἰσφέρειν. ὅτε δ' ἐδόκει ἐφράσσετο σανίσιν ἡ ἀγορά κτλ. ('Before the eighth prytany the People conducted an advance vote, whether it is deemed good to introduce "the *ostrakon*". Whenever it was so deemed, the Agora was fenced with planks...'—tr. Nicholas F. Jones, *BNJ*). Felix Jacoby (in his commentary on this passage: *FGrHist* 328 F 30) described this way of referring to the time

---

[39] Rhodes (1972) 17–19, 225, with earlier bibliography. See also Rhodes (2015) 61.

[40] For instance, Bicknell (1972) 36.

[41] Rhodes (1995) 191, n. 18. Ultimately, as one of my anonymous OUP referees points out, 'one could imagine that the two votes might have been initially dated by reference to the festival calendar (e.g., before the Lenaia and Dionysia) but that once the bouleutic calendar came in this was naturally formalized in those terms because of the responsibility of the *bouleutai* in both cases, and that would have carried over in the recodification'.

[42] On the text or texts underlying this 'fragment' (partly corresponding to F. 640B Fortenbaugh of Theophrasus [= sch vet 855B]), in its fundamental new interpretation by Heftner (2018), see more below. For the time being, I am leaving aside the issue of slightly divergent readings of several versions of this text in our tradition. Here, these divergences have no bearing on my argument.

when *ostrakophoria* was carried out as surprising. He interpreted it as an abridgement of a more detailed text, which (after the necessary supplementation) could have read for instance like this: προεχειροτόνει μὲν ὁ δῆμος <ἐπὶ τῆς ζ' πρυτανείας> εἰ δοκεῖ τὸ ὄστρακον εἰσφέρειν. ὅτε δ' ἐδόκει <ἐπὶ τῆς η' πρυτανείας> ἐφράσσετο σανίσιν ἡ ἀγορά ('In the sixth prytany the People conducted a preliminary vote, whether it is deemed good to introduce "the *ostrakon*". Whenever it was so deemed, the Agora was fenced with planks in the eighth prytany...'). However, such a far-reaching interference with the text (let us remember, however, that Jacoby did not implement this 'supplementation' in his edition of this fragment) has been deemed inadmissible by the majority of scholars. Nonetheless, Jacoby's reservation itself seems valid. Dating the preliminary vote on ostracism to the time 'before the eighth prytany' is a bizarre idea or at least a very imprecise formulation.

The text under scrutiny here (with Herbert Heftner, I will call it for convenience 'the great scholion about ostracism') is known from five different excerpts. The most complete is the text preserved in *Lexicon rhetoricum Cantabrigiense* (see below).[43] All these texts most probably derive ultimately from a common source—Didymus' commentary to one of Demosthenes' speeches, quoted as belonging to Book Three of Philochorus.[44] The method of work of this author of excerpts explaining the 'way in which ostracism functioned' consisted in abbreviating the commentary quoting—presumably also without major textual changes—a certain passage or passages from his source or sources.

Importantly, in the passage used by Didymus, the Atthidographer was not describing the whole ostracism procedure, including *epicheirotonia*, but merely the day of voting with sherds. This is clear in the opening of the quotation from Philochorus (ὁ δ' ὀστρακισμὸς τοιοῦτος, in Heftner's 'Komposit-Text'), where 'ostracism' denotes *ostrakophoria* exclusively. If this was the case, the current wording of the Atthidographer's fragment might be following quite closely the original here. Philochorus did not intend to date the preliminary vote but merely emphasised in a slightly cursory manner that it took place some time in advance of the vote deciding

---

[43] All these texts are meticulously studied, and compared with one another, by Herbert Heftner (2018), who ultimately comes up with a 'Komposit-Text' possibly corresponding to the 'Urtext' of our tradition (see esp. Heftner (2018) 105–106, for the edition and translation).

[44] Interestingly, Heftner (2018) 108 plausibly argues that one of these excerpts (sch Lucian, *Tim.* 30 Rabe, p. 114) may derive from Didymus' other commentary—on Aristophanes. On Didymus, cf. Dickey (2007) 51–52.

on exile.⁴⁵ Thus, the expression 'before the eighth prytany' is entirely natural because it simultaneously allows us to place the *ostrakophoria* in the eighth prytany (most probably at its beginning) and to generally indicate its removal in time from the first step in the entire procedure. Therefore, A.P.'s testimony on the time of the preliminary vote and Philochorus' account providing the time of *ostrakophoria* are fully compatible.

It should be emphasised here that Philochorus wrote perhaps 150 years after the last *ostrakophoria* known to us, but also that in his times (unlike in the case of A.P.'s author), the preliminary vote (an element of the Athenian *politeia* still alive for Ps.-Aristotle) did not take place any more either. As a result, while detailed information on *epicheirotonia* could be found in Philochorus' times, for instance in A.P., he must have derived the precise dating of the *ostrakophoria* from some other good source, most probably from Theophrastus' *On Laws* (see below), or from one of his predecessors Atthidographers (Androtion?).⁴⁶ In this context, the 'supplementation' of Philochorus' text proposed by Jacoby ('In the sixth prytany the People conduct an advance vote, whether it is deemed good to introduce "the *ostrakon*". Whenever it was so deemed, the Agora was fenced with planks in the eighth prytany...') is convincing, but in reference to a hypothetical, unpreserved source of the Atthidographer. However, the existence of such a source at the time is beyond doubt.

Therefore, we can assume that the opening of Philochorus' account of the procedure of ostracism provides us with exceptionally valuable information, perfectly compatible with other testimonies discussed above. Nevertheless, the remaining part of the text discussed here—whence almost the entire later tradition derives, including the absurd Byzantine speculations⁴⁷—is highly suspicious. Let us first quote the entire fragment from Philochorus in Jacoby's edition (*FGrHist* = *BNJ*) and then discuss the most important problems with its interpretation ([A] *Lexicon rhetoricum Cantabrigiense*, pp. 23-24 Houtsma [*LexGrMin*, pp. 83-84]; [B] Claudius Casilon, p. 398 [E. Miller, *Mélanges de literature grecque*, Paris 1868, p. 398]; [C] *Lexicon*

---

⁴⁵ In a similar vein, cf. already Rhodes (1995) 197–198, accepted by W. Scheidel and H. Taeuber, in Siewert, T 41, p. 467 n. 4.
⁴⁶ This is less likely, given the extremely cursory form of Androtion's work.
⁴⁷ See above, 1.2.2 and already Węcowski (2018).

Demosthenicum, Against Aristokrates [= *P. Berol.* 5008, B 27–40 Blass = Diels-Schubart, p. 82], s.v. ὀστρακισμοῦ τρόπος):[48]

ὀστρακισμοῦ τρόπος· Φιλόχορος ἐκτίθεται τὸν ὀστρακισμὸν ἐν τῇ τρίτῃ γράφων οὕτω· «ὁ δὲ ὀστρα[κισμὸς τοιοῦτος]· προεχειροτόνει μὲν ὁ δῆμος πρὸ τῆς ὀγδόης πρυτανείας, εἰ δοκεῖ τὸ ὄστρακον εἰσφέρειν. ὅτε δ' ἐδόκει, ἐφράσσετο σανίσιν ἡ ἀγορά, καὶ κατελείποντο εἴσοδοι δέκα, δι' ὧν εἰσιόντες κατὰ φυλὰς ἐτίθεσαν τὰ ὄστρακα, στρέφοντες τὴν ἐπιγραφήν· ἐπεστάτουν δὲ οἵ τε ἐννέα ἄρχοντες καὶ ἡ βουλή. διαριθμηθέντων δὲ ὅτῳ πλεῖστα γένοιτο καὶ μὴ ἐλάττω ἑξακισχιλίων, τοῦτον ἔδει τὰ δίκαια δόντα καὶ λαβόντα ὑπὲρ τῶν ἰδίων συναλλαγμάτων ἐν δέκα ἡμέραις μεταστῆναι τῆς πόλεως ἔτη δέκα (ὕστερον δὲ ἐγένοντο πέντε), καρπούμενον τὰ ἑαυτοῦ, μὴ ἐπιβαίνοντα ἐντὸς Γεραιστοῦ τοῦ Εὐβοίας ἀκρωτηρίου». *** μόνος δὲ Ὑπέρβολος ἐκ τῶν ἀδόξων ἐξωστρακίσθη διὰ μοχθηρίαν τρόπων, οὐ δι' ὑποψίαν τυραννίδος· μετὰ τοῦτον δὲ κατελύθη τὸ ἔθος, ἀρξάμενον νομοθετήσαντος Κλεισθένους, ὅτε τοὺς τυράννους κατέλυσεν, ὅπως συνεκβάλοι καὶ τοὺς φίλους αὐτῶν.

The procedure of ostracism: Philochorus in his third (book) sets out (the procedure for) ostracism, writing thus:

'*Ostra[kismos* is of such kind]: Before the eighth prytany the People conducted an advance vote, whether it is deemed good to introduce "the *ostrakon*". Whenever it was so deemed, the Agora was fenced with planks, and ten entrances were left (open) through which the people, entering by *phylai*, cast the ostraka, turning (i.e. downwards) the inscription. The nine archons and the Council were in charge. After (the ostraka) were counted, the person for whom the most (ostraka) occurred (i.e. were cast) and not less than six thousand, this man had to tender and exact settlements ("just things") concerning his personal arrangements within ten days, to relocate from the city-state for ten years (but later it became five), enjoying the use of his property, not overstepping (a boundary) within Geraestus, the promontory of Euboia'.

*** Hyperbolus alone of undistinguished citizens suffered ostracism, on account of the wickedness of his ways, not on account of suspicion of (aiming at) tyranny. And after him* (Hyperbolus), the practice was

---

[48] In Heftner's (2018) interpretation and edition of a 'Komposit-Text', two more texts are taken into consideration: [D] sch vet Aristoph. *Eq.* 855B; [E] sch Lucian, *Tim.* 30 Rabe, p. 114 (cf. already Heftner (2005) 156–157).

abolished, having begun when Cleisthenes enacted legislation, after he had abolished the tyrants, in order to cast out their friends as well.

(tr. Nicholas F. Jones, *BNJ*)

In this quotation, several elements of a different character, both in terms of style and 'content', are discernible. The first introductory sentence, discussed above, may be ascribed to some good but unpreserved source of the Atthidographer.[49] Jacoby suspected a lacuna after the mention of Geraestus, the promontory of Euboea.[50] What follows in the text is not reported in the same manner as the previous part. Nicholas F. Jones argues in his commentary in *BNJ* that a different source may be suggested here by the abrupt shift from a detailed account of the *ostrakophoria* procedure to a specific case of ostracism and the note about its abandonment by the Athenians, as well as by the fact that the information about Hyperbolus' ostracism should have appeared in the fourth and not in the third book of Philochorus' *Atthis* (Jones 2016). However, these objections lose weight when we realise that we are not dealing with short chronographic notes but with a more extensive erudite account. The remark about Hyperbolus' ostracism perfectly corresponds with the image he regularly receives in the entire ancient tradition, beginning with its part contemporary to the event.[51] The final statement about Cleisthenes' authorship of the law about ostracism and the original intentions of the lawgiver is thoroughly consistent with the versions in *A.P.* and Androtion, so it does not need to be dealt with here either.

Most important for our considerations is the description of the procedure of ostracism, undoubtedly belonging to the quotation from Philochorus' work. However, also in these sections of our text, we must distinguish two separate parts. I have argued above that the closing sentences of this description (consubstantial with sch vet Aristoph. *Eq.* 855B) provide us with a series of technical pieces of information, most probably deriving (directly or indirectly) from the provisions of the law about ostracism:

---

[49] More extensively on the issue of the ultimate source of this tradition, see below, pp. 158–160.

[50] Nicholas F. Jones, in comm. on *BNJ* 328 F 30, suggests as an alternative, 'a break marking the end of the quotation from Philochorus'. Jacoby's suspicion seems to be supported by the fact that the quotation from Philochorus gives only one border point in the 'geography of exile', which will be discussed in more detail below, 3.3.1.

[51] But see above, pp. 6–7 and below, pp. 240–244.

[...] τοῦτον ἔδει τὰ δίκαια δόντα καὶ λαβόντα ὑπὲρ τῶν ἰδίων συναλλαγμάτων ἐν δέκα ἡμέραις μεταστῆναι τῆς πόλεως ἔτη δέκα (ὕστερον δὲ ἐγένοντο πέντε), καρπούμενον τὰ ἑαυτοῦ, μὴ ἐπιβαίνοντα ἐντὸς Γεραιστοῦ τοῦ Εὐβοίας ἀκρωτηρίου.

I shall return to this essential passage further in this book. In the two following sections of this chapter, I shall focus on the description of the *ostrakophoria* procedure, analysing two of its elements: the topography and the 'setting' of voting with ostraka on the Athenian Agora, as well as the puzzle of the 'quorum' for ostracism, vividly discussed by scholars.

3.2.2 The Topography of Ostracism

ὅτε δ' ἐδόκει [sc. τῷ δήμῳ τὸ ὄστρακον εἰσφέρειν], ἐφράσσετο σανίσιν ἡ ἀγορά, καὶ κατελείποντο εἴσοδοι δέκα, δι' ὧν εἰσιόντες κατὰ φυλὰς ἐτίθεσαν τὰ ὄστρακα, στρέφοντες τὴν ἐπιγραφήν· ἐπεστάτουν δὲ οἵ τε ἐννέα ἄρχοντες καὶ ἡ βουλή. διαριθμηθέντων δὲ κτλ.

Whenever it was so deemed, the Agora was fenced with planks, and ten entrances were left (open) through which the people, entering by *phylai*, cast the ostraka, turning [i.e., downwards] the inscription. The nine archons and the Council were in charge. After (the ostraka) were counted [...]. (tr. Nicholas F. Jones)

The information about *ostrakophoria* being supervised by nine archons (plus their secretary, as may be assumed) and members of the Council of Five Hundred can only be taken on trust. However, it looks sensible if one assumes that archons were responsible for counting the votes and council members were assigned the task of carrying out a basic verification of personal identity, and thus of the right to vote, among the members of their *phylai* entering the area where the voting was taking place. Hence, we should begin our considerations precisely with the topography and 'setting' of the *ostrakophoria*.

While discussing these issues, scholars have been focusing on identifying the spot on the Agora where *ostrakophoriai* took place.[52] To me, however,

---

[52] See esp. Carcopino (1935); Martin (1951) 315–327 (cf. already Martin (1942)); Wycherley (1955) and *Agora 3*, 162–164; *Agora 14*, 50–51; Kolb (1981) 53–58. Cf. Ehrenberg (1962) 339–342. For general information on the Athenian Agora, see the very outdated but classic

the stakes in this discussion are much higher than that. The challenge is to investigate the character of the gathering of the Athenian people on the last day of the ostracism procedure and, ultimately, to understand why this voting was never moved to a more convenient venue, such as the Pnyx. In other words, why the Athenians decided to continue carrying out *ostrakophoriai* in the place where they were arranged, or rather planned, by Cleisthenes. In the lawgiver's times—before the Pnyx was adapted to accommodate the Assembly[53]—they were to be held where the *dēmos* customarily gathered *in corpore*. But in later times, there must have been important reasons for the last stage of the ostracism procedure to happen still in the Agora, even though it must have presented many technical difficulties, as we shall see. The apprehension of these reasons may allow us better to understand the nature of ostracism and its primary aims.

The debate regarding the spot in the Agora where *ostrakophoriai* took place has been principally relying on two sets of data (see Fig. 3.1 and 3.3). On the one hand, it has been dominated by attempts to identify two toponyms attested in literature: the so-called Orchestra and the so-called Rope Enclosure (*Perischoinisma*). On the other hand, specific technical solutions or single topographic elements of the Agora were vividly discussed, such as the enigmatic 'gates of the Agora' or the 'planks' (*sanides*) appearing in our sources as part of various structures in this area.[54]

We know that in the Agora, there was a structure called the Orchestra, preceding the Theatre of Dionysus on the southern slope of the Acropolis as a venue for 'music' and theatre (or 'Dionysiac') performances.[55] It was most probably a large wooden structure, undoubtedly permanent,[56] and perhaps in later times fitted with temporary benches (called *ikria*),[57] according to needs: for the audience of the Panathenaic contests or processions, for instance. The Orchestra was generally defined as the place where Athenian 'festive assemblies' (*panegyreis*) were held. Admittedly, our sources do not

---

account by Travlos (1980) 1–5. Cf. also Camp (1992); Hölscher (1994); Longo (2007); and a very useful recent overview by Di Cesare (2020) esp. 196–198 (however, I admit that his thesis regarding the placement of the Tyrant-Slayers' group by Kritios and Nesiotes as 'linked to the use of the spot for *ostrakophoriai*' (p. 197) may seem far-fetched given the rarity of *ostrakophoriai* after the Persian Wars). Recently, see in general the rich collection of essays in Ampolo (2012), especially in its first part.

[53] On the history of the Pnyx as venue for the Assembly, see generally Hansen (1983) 25–33 and (1989) 129–141, 143–153. Cf. also Węcowski (2009) 393–396. Recently, see Moretti (2019).

[54] A bit further on (3.2.3), I shall present the third type of data, or rather a single hypothetical iconographic source to this effect.

[55] See *Agora* 3, no. 276, 520, 524–526. [56] Cf. Pl. *Ap.* 26D-E (= *Agora* 3, no. 527).

[57] Cf. esp. *Agora* 3, no. 276, 528.

Fig. 3.1 General plan of the Agora showing distribution of ostraka. Agora Image: 2002.01.2660 (Agora Drawing: PD 2660 (DA 3941); artists: R. C. Anderson, J. Travlos, W. B. Dinsmoor, Jr.). Courtesy of The American School of Classical Studies at Athens: Agora Excavations.

present the Orchestra as the place of gathering of any political or judicial institutions. Still, scholars readily assume that it must have been functioning as such. The *Perischoinisma*, in turn, was a particular area within the Agora,[58] termed so regardless of the Athenian custom of closing (or 'sealing') off with ropes an area or building at occasions of paramount significance.[59] Frank Kolb, who pondered the idea that the Orchestra and the *Perischoinisma* may have been one and the same thing, inventively proposed to recognise there a pristine 'sacred tribunal' of the Agora and so later on a natural venue of the *ostrakophoria*.[60]

Interestingly, the *Perischoinisma*, or more precisely a *perischoinisma*, was identified recently in the Agora (see Fig. 3.2). As John McKesson Camp II puts it, '[i]n 1972, just east of the Altar of the Twelve Gods, five stone sockets were found in a row [...]. Set ca. 1.86 m apart, center to center, they were designed to hold a square wooden post measuring ca. 0.11 m on a side.'[61] Recently, consecutive excavations discovered a second and the third line of identical sockets to the south and to the west of the first one, thus forming an area of ca. 12×15 m, i.e., close to 180 m².[62] In different parts of this 'enclosure', the sockets were dated, respectively, to the early and to the second half of the fifth century BC. Hence, their chronology needs to be more securely established. Another problem is that this enclosed area cuts into the course of the Panathenaic Way and, when in use, simply seems to block it. Therefore, the relationship between the two needs to be studied further.

About the *Perischoinisma* as such, we learn only from writers of the Roman period: Alciphron and Ps.-Plutarch.[63] The latter uses this toponym (as well as the Altar of the Twelve Gods) to determine the location within the Agora of Demosthenes' statue sculpted by Polyeuktos. However, they are both erudite texts deeply anchored in the Atticising culture of the Roman

---

[58] See *Agora 3*, no. 529–536.
[59] E.g., when the Athenian court was deciding on issues connected with the Eleusinian mysteries, ropes were attached at the distance of 50 feet from the tribunal to keep the non-initiated away (Pollux, 7.123-124 = *Agora 3*, no. 535). Cf. also 'roping' off the Areopagus tribunal gathering in the Royal Stoa (Dem. XXV [*Aristog.* I], 23).
[60] Kolb (1981) 53–55.
[61] Camp (2015) 473. Cf. already, perhaps, Kolb (1981) 53 n. 239. Recently, see R. Di Cesare, in Greco (2014) 1065–1067 and Lippolis (2019) esp. 106–110. The first to ascribe these stone sockets to Athenian *ostrakophoriai* was to my knowledge Rausch (1999) 34–35. He posited that for earlier *ostrakophoriai* simple holes were dug into the ground to accommodate wooden posts of this hypothetical enclosure (cf. also Lippolis (2019) 108).
[62] See Saraga (2013) 134–137 and Camp (2015) 473–475.
[63] Alciphr. *Ep.* IV 18, 11 Schepers (= II 3, 11 Meineke); Ps.-Plut., *X orat.* 847A.

Fig. 3.2 The so-called 'Perischoinisma' in the Athenian Agora, Panathenaic Way, East Trench. Agora Image: 2013.18.0029 (photographer: Craig Mauzy). Courtesy of The American School of Classical Studies at Athens: Agora Excavations.

imperial times, so their references, presented to their audience as self-evident, most probably go back to explicit indications in, or commentaries on, Attic orators of the classical period. This goes well with the fifth-century date of the enclosure found in the Agora. Of course, before this dating is more securely established and (if) corroborated, we find ourselves on a slippery ground here. However, if the enclosure (or some parts thereof) was—no doubt only periodically—functional late in the fifth century BC and if it was referred to as somehow operational in the fourth century by Attic orators, the active use of this structure does not agree with the history of Athenian *ostrakophoriai*, abandoned for good 'around 416 BC' and carried out only this one time after the 40s of the fifth century. The temporary nature of this enclosure, blocking the crucial Panathenaic Way when in use, seems to exclude the possibility of it being a spot still famous for its long past glory. Simply put, to be visible, let alone prominent, it must have still been used from time to time. One cannot exclude that it might have been used at some point for some activities related to an *ostrakophoria*, but making it an established element of the topography of ostracism would be far-fetched.

Now, only one source speaks explicitly about 'roping off' some part of the Agora (περισχοινίσαντας δέ τις τῆς ἀγορᾶς μέρος κτλ.) in connection with ostracism (Pollux, 8.20 = *Agora* 3, no. 534): 'They roped off a part of the agora and any Athenian who wished (to vote) had to take into the place so marked off a sherd inscribed with the name of the man who was to be banished by ostracism' (tr. Wycherley). However, one manuscript gives an alternative and perhaps better reading, namely περισκηνήσαντας, 'having tented off', at any rate, a clear *lectio difficilior*.[64] Meanwhile, as I have already argued above (1.2.2), all the late reports referring to 'fencing off', 'roping off', and here perhaps 'tenting off' some particular place in the Agora for the Athenians to bring, or throw, their ostraka there (be it an improvised enclosure or, for instance, the Bouleuterion) seem to have stemmed, indirectly, from the traditions about ostracism we possess.[65] In this case, therefore, we are left with the question about the function of the archaeologically

---

[64] Cf. *Agora* 3, *ad loc.* and (1955) 163–165. Similarly, Kolb (1981) 53 n. 235. *Periskēnia* were used as 'balustrades' in theatres (*E.M.* 743.30 Gaisdorf; one manuscript gives here *paraskēnia*).
[65] Thus Pollux, 8.20, discussed above; Plut. *Arist.* 7,4 (ἦν δὲ τοιοῦτον, ὡς τύπῳ φράσαι, τὸ γινόμενον. ὄστρακον λαβὼν ἕκαστος καὶ γράψας ὃν ἐβούλετο μεταστῆσαι τῶν πολιτῶν, ἔφερεν εἰς ἕνα τόπον τῆς ἀγορᾶς περιπεφραγμένον ἐν κύκλῳ δρυφάκτοις); *E.M.*, *s.v. exostrakismos* (349.15 Gaisdorf): πῆγμα δὲ γίνεται ἐν τῇ ἀγορᾷ. See also Timaeus the Sophist, *s.v. exostrakismos* (ed. Ruhnken), and above, 1.2.2, on the Byzantine consequences of this picture. Philochorus' version corresponds to the testimony of sch. Ar., *Eq.* 855B.

attested *perischoinisma*, whereas the connection between the *ostrakophoria* and the *Perischoinisma* referred to in our literary sources, or some other particular form of enclosure, seems to have originated in the vision of 'fencing the Agora off with planks' in our fragment of Philochorus.

The Orchestra also seems simply an unnecessary entity as far as the space of *ostrakophoria* is concerned. Regardless of this structure's (unattested) political and/or judicial function in the archaic and early classical times, the Orchestra was naturally unsuited for carrying out the ostracism procedure. Briefly speaking, voting with ceramic sherds without any deliberation did not require the participants to be seated. It must have consisted in solely approaching the voting 'poll', or the area where ostraka were placed. What it required was merely a number of well-defined 'gathering points' for the members of a given *phylē* as well as a security or control system for the crowd of assembled citizens. It is precisely the latter we need to address in our interpretation, without any illusions that we shall be able to point to a specific spot of *ostrakophoria* in the topography of the Athenian Agora.

The idea of 'fencing off' the Agora or its part with 'planks' frequently recurs in our sources,[66] especially in the fragment of Philochorus discussed here. And it is crucially important to stress at this point the chronological priority of Philochorus' version, from which all other versions of our tradition stemmed. Meanwhile, surrounding the entire central square of Athens tightly with some sort of fencing which would effectively hold anybody back is, I think, absolutely inconceivable. Apart from the ridiculously high construction expense and effort in such a vast space, this enterprise could not possibly succeed due to the nature of the Athenian Agora. A horde of guardians would be required to prevent the nearby houses, artisan and trade workshops, finally, the trees planted there in large numbers by Cimon (see below) from making it possible for the unauthorised to sneak into the voting space.[67] Naturally, it cannot be excluded that only the area assigned for vote counting, where the archons proceeded, was tightly fenced off, but this seems unnecessary in turn, given that they had roofed offices and religious buildings at their disposal (for instance, the *stoai*, the Prytaneion, the Old Bouleuterion) as well as some 'commercial' structures

---

[66] See also above, p. 135 and the previous note.
[67] Cf. Fig. 3.3. However, it should be noted that the model of the Agora is very schematic—it does not include temporary structures or trees in the square itself.

TOWARDS A RECONSTRUCTION OF OSTRACISM IN ATHENS 141

in the Agora, which would be perfectly suited for the purpose.⁶⁸ Anyway, the image of (some part of) the Agora being tightly surrounded with boards could have had its indirect source in concrete practice. Both the *Etymologicum Magnum* and the scholia to Aristophanes' *Ploutos* mention a place in the Agora called Telia—an enclosure made of tightly connected planks ([. . .] περίφραγμα σανίδων ἐν τῇ ἀγορᾷ) on a square plan, where flour was sold. Allegedly, it periodically served as an arena for cockfights.⁶⁹ The tight arrangement of the boards had a specific purpose, of course, and the area enclosed in this manner was small. Telia would naturally be well-suited for ostraka counting, but its existence clearly illustrates how absurd would be the idea to organise in this way the entire, vast and very irregular area of the Agora.

The note by Philochorus saying that the entire Agora was tightly fenced off with 'planks' for the duration of the *ostrakophoria* was perhaps derived from his source (very probably Theophrastus) or else devised by himself. It was later repeated and reinterpreted by many ancient writers and lexicographers. All things considered, I think that in its original version it should be regarded as a desperate attempt by a regular visitor of the Athenian Agora a century or more after the last effective *ostrakophoria* at imagining how this area—full of permanent and improvised structures, and usually congested—could be arranged and organised so that the voting with ostraka could take place undisturbed. The only reliable piece of information underlying this speculative vision of Theophrastus (or Philochorus himself) seems to have been that of the existence of 10 entrances for 10 Athenian tribes because it goes well with the role supposedly played in *ostrakophoria* by the archons and by the Council. It might have been, but more probably was not, mentioned in the text of the law of ostracism.

Therefore, another element of the topography of the Agora worth attention in this context is the 'gates of the barley' which Raubitschek recognised in a passage from Aristophanes' *Knights* (ll. 850, 855–857; tr. Alan

⁶⁸ Without any serious commitment to this idea, but merely for the sake of giving an example, let us think of the famous Circle (*kyklos*, or Circles, *kykloi*), which is alluded to already by Aristophanes in his *Knights* of 424 BC (l. 137) in the playful name Kykloboros (as if 'Circle-Devourer'), whose function and origin was explained by ancient commentators in a variety of ways (see *Agora* 3, 616–622). Allegedly, there was a special 'table', on which stood the slaves put up for sale. We shall see shortly that a special, improvised table for vote counting was an essential element of the *ostrakophoria* equipment.

⁶⁹ Cf. *Agora* 3, 632 and 633. This space should not be identified with the Stoa Alphitopolis mentioned by Aristophanes (*Eccl.* 686), which most probably was not a wooden building on a square plan and which was identified by Raubitschek (I am not sure whether correctly or not) with the so-called South Stoa I (Raubitschek (1956) 279, n. 1). See also below.

Fig. 3.3 Model of the Athenian Agora *c.* 400 BC, by P. Demetriades and K. Papoulias, Athens, Agora Museum; Agora Image: 2004.02.0083 (LCT-6) (photographer: Craig Mauzy). Courtesy of The American School of Classical Studies at Athens: Agora Excavations.

H. Sommerstein):[70] 'It's a cunning scheme, Demos, so that if you want | to punish this man you won't be able to. | [...] with the result that if you were to start making menacing noises and looked like playing the potsherd game (καὶ βλέψειας ὀστρακίνδα) | they'd take those shields down under cover of darkness and run | and occupy the entry-points for ... our daily barley ([...] θέοντες | τὰς ἐσβολὰς τῶν ἀλφίτων ἂν καταλάβοιεν ἡμῶν).' Through the allusion to the children's game 'ostraka',[71] this passage plays with the motif of the potential ostracism of Cleon. All the scum of the city—here embodied by representatives of various professions based in the Agora— stand up for him, having taken up the shields won from the Spartans at Pylos. As Raubitschek points out, following one of the interpretations of the scholion to this line (sch vet 857), the language of the Sausage Seller, who utters these words, is playfully military. *Eisbolai* means either the enemy's invasion or the place through which they violate the border,[72] or an isthmus

---

[70] Raubitschek (1956).   [71] For details see below, pp. 210–211.
[72] As in Hdt. II 75,2 (although this passage may be interpolated).

(of land or sea)—and thus a potential defence point of the *polis*' borders.⁷³ However, I am not sure what the 'barley breach' or 'corn isthmus' was supposed to mean.

Admittedly, the scholion mentioned here explains ἐσβολαὶ τῶν ἀλφίτων as granaries (which Raubitschek interprets as a reference to the doors or doorframes of granaries), but it could equally well be understood as meaning the main corn supply routes of Athens or Attica. In this situation, it is best to follow Aristophanes' tracks, who in the *Acharnians* (ll. 1073-1077; tr. Sommerstein) makes the Athenians hasten 'and keep watch on the passes in the snow. Someone's reported to them that there will be an incursion by plundering Boeotians about the time of the Pitcher and Pot Feasts' (κἄπειτα τηρεῖν νειφόμενον τὰς ἐσβολάς. | ὑπὸ τοὺς Χοᾶς γὰρ καὶ Χύτρους αὐτοῖσί τις | ἤγγειλε λῃστὰς ἐμβαλεῖν Βοιωτίους). In the light of this passage, it seems pointless to seek in the lines from *Knights* analysed by Raubitschek an allusion to the (otherwise completely unknown to us) hypothetical 'gates of ostracism'.⁷⁴

Nevertheless, Raubitschek claims that Aristophanes playfully replaces the 'gates of ostracism', allegedly underlying here, with 'gates of the barley'—or more specifically, that in his joke Aristophanes draws on the fact that the Athenians used the same (hypothetical) gates in the Agora in the ostracism procedure and in corn distribution. On both these occasions, the identity of citizens entitled to participate in *ostrakophoria* and food distribution would be verified in a similar way. The scholar associates with these two procedures several quite mysterious inscriptions, found mainly in the Agora and analogical to the inscriptions from Piraeus (better-known to us) using the following formula: 'Here ends phyle A and [its] trittys X and begins phyle B and [its] trittys Y.'⁷⁵ I must admit that in neither of these points do Raubitschek's conclusions seem convincing to me. As we have seen, the existence of the 'gates of ostracism' cannot be inferred from Aristophanes'

---

⁷³ Cf. *LSJ*⁹ s.v. A2.
⁷⁴ Similarly, Sommerstein (1981) *ad loc*. It should be noted that *A.P.* 43.4 lists 'business about grain and about the defense of the territory' (περὶ σίτου καὶ περὶ φυλακῆς τῆς χώρας; tr. P.J. Rhodes) among the first and foremost items on the agenda of the 'main session' of the Assembly. In the minds of the Athenians, both these spheres are inherently connected, even though they do not overlap entirely.
⁷⁵ See Siewert (1982) 10–13 and 16. They belong to Siewert's 'Poros-Gruppe' and are markedly different from those of his 'Marmor-Gruppe'; the latter were most probably originally situated in the Assembly venue on the Pnyx. See also *Agora 19*, H 36–42.

passage quoted above. The wit shall be even sharper if at the end, there appears a surprising turn of thought and a military act of separating the people (or Demos) from food supplies by a random bunch of dodgy sellers decked out in Spartan equipment. Neither can I accept (in either of the hypothetical functions) the identification of the inscriptions mentioned. As in the attempts to connect the Orchestra with the Athenian *ostrakophoria*, we must keep in mind that corn distribution and voting with ostraka required arranging the Athenians entitled to participate in a queue and not gathering them for a certain amount of time in a particular place.[76] It seems that an interpretation compatible with the situation, which we can deduce in the case of Piraeus, is more justified here. Stelae arranging the Athenian *phylai* and their *trittyes* in a specific space would be most natural in a military context, during mobilisation of contingents of particular organisational units of the Athenian citizen body. Incidentally, these inscriptions are not placed at gates or passages leading somewhere but at border points between the units. In short, the alleged 'gates of the Agora' must share the fate of the illusory 'boards' as well as the Orchestra and the 'Rope Enclosure' in the main square—real but most probably unrelated to ostracism.

Nonetheless, as if on the margin of these considerations, Raubitschek made several crucial observations. Here, I must refer back to the idea of 'roping off' some part of the Agora on the day of *ostrakophoria*. In his reconstruction, Raubitschek assumed that some temporary fencing made of light material joined with strings was stretched out between some permanent topographic elements of the Agora (including the hypothetical 'gates of ostracism').[77] This hypothesis seems entirely convincing, on the condition that we find a purpose which such a 'roping' or fencing off would serve. On the one hand, its role would be guiding the Athenians towards the voting place in a relative order; on the other hand, it would separate them from the site, or places, of vote counting.[78] The orientation point would be some improvised 'entrances' (10 in number), at which, or more precisely, behind

---

[76] Unlike in the case of Roman voting, according to Philochorus, the Athenians did not have to await their turn in predefined groups. They only had to pass through some 'entrances' and leave their ostrakon.

[77] Raubitschek (1956) 280 n. 2.

[78] For the latter function, cf. Pollux 7.123–124 and Dem. XXV [*Aristog.* I], 23, referred to above.

which (from the perspective of the Athenians approaching the voting area) the 'ballot boxes' would be placed.[79]

An analogy for such a form of space organisation in the Agora to carry out a particular procedure is provided, of course, by the aforementioned cases of 'roping off' Athenian offices or tribunals. However, those situations were similar only regarding the (hypothetical) function of separating the space for 'vote' counting during *ostrakophoriai*. For this reason, all the more interesting seems to be the passage from Demosthenes' speech *On the Crown* (XVIII 169). The *prytaneis*, upon hearing the news about the fall of Elateia, instantly rose from the table (most probably in the Tholos), cleared the stalls in the Agora of the people, and unfolded the wicker (τούς τ' ἐκ τῶν σκηνῶν τῶν κατὰ τὴν ἀγορὰν ἐξεῖργον καὶ τὰ γέρρ' ἀνεπετάννυσαν). In our manuscripts, we find the expression 'set on fire (ἐνεπίμπρασαν) [the wicker]',[80] absurd in this context. Girard rightly emended this verb based on a passage from Ps.-Demosthenes' speech *Against Neaera* (LIX 90), where the *prytaneis* 'raise *gerra*' (τὰ γέρρα ἀναιρεῖν) in preparation for an Assembly voting, as well as based on a scholion to Aristophanes' *Acharnians* (sch vet 22A) explaining the well-known image of citizens running away from the 'red rope' in the Agora to avoid being driven onto the Pnyx.[81] The ancient commentary preserved in this scholion mentions an alternative means of coercion: a temporary trade ban on the Agora and precisely the unfolding of wicker (*gerra*), used for blocking the routes leading to the Assembly.

If Girard's emendation is accepted, the succinct expression in Demosthenes' speech *On the Crown* could turn out to be of great significance: the orator would then be assuming that such a functional re-organisation of space in the Agora is, in the eyes of his audience, a most obvious task of the magistrates if the need arises. In all the testimonies cited

---

[79] These 'entrances' could have been located in a particular area of the Agora, but they could have equally well been scattered all over the place. What was important was only that their location is not in conflict with the task of allocating some space for the archons to count the ostraka. Moreover, during the urban evolution and the development of the Agora both the workplace of the 'ballot counting committee' and the location of particular 'entrances' for Athenian *phylai* could have changed, making use of new, characteristic or for some reason convenient topographic elements of the Athenian Agora. At some stage the 'votes' could have been counted in the Bouleuterion, for instance, and on another occasion in a different building, or in the open air. After all, let us remember how infrequently the Athenian *ostrakophoriai* took place.

[80] Setting fires on the main marketplace of the already panicky Athens would be preposterous, as would be the supposition that the *prytaneis* in fact intended to send a fire signal. Cf. *Agora* 3, 263–264.

[81] Ar. *Acharn.* 22: τὸ σχοινίον φεύγουσι τὸ μεμιλτωμένον.

above, this prerogative belongs to the *prytaneis*, which perfectly corresponds to the role of the members of the Council of Five Hundred in the *ostrakophoria* procedure. This is precisely how I think we ought to envisage the preparation of the Agora by the Athenians: determining (most probably the day before) voting spots ('entrances' from Philochorus' fragment) for members of the Athenian *phylai* and separating them from the place, or places, where the ostraka will be counted.

3.2.3 The Pan Painter and the Day of *Ostrakophoria*

We can venture even further in our reconstruction, bringing in a sensational source, which entered the discussion on *ostrakophoriai* relatively late: a red-figure kylix by the Pan Painter, dated with caution to the first half of the fifth century BC (ca. 470–460 BC? Oxford, Ashmolean Museum 1911.617; see Fig. 3.4).[82] In 1972, T. B. L. Webster recognised a possible representation of the vote-counting procedure during *ostrakophoria* in the tondo and on the outer side of the body (side 'A') of this vase.[83] In the lack of any convincing alternative interpretation of these images, unprecedented in vase painting iconography, Webster's idea seems to be worth our greatest attention. Inside the kylix, a naked youth is represented (his *himation* wrapped around his hips) carrying with apparent effort a large basket or basin (*skaphē*?) containing small rounded objects irregular in shape, painted in red. To his right is an adult man wearing a *himation* and holding a set of writing tools in his left hand: a stylus with closed writing tablets. On the vase's external side (side 'A'), a youth similar to the one described above brings his basket full of identically painted objects to a low central stone or wooden table, improvised, supported by two rocks. A bearded adult man fully dressed and standing in a commanding pose, with a stylus in one hand and an open set of writing tablets in the other, supports his right leg against the table. The characteristic, quite unusual position of the man's body suggests that he may be indicating to the youth where he should place the basket[84] and most probably simply empty its contents. Next to the man's leg, on the right side of the table, irregularly shaped objects are piled, clearly

---

[82] *ARV*² 559.152 = *CVA* Oxford III, 1 [Great Britain 99], Pl. VII, nos 3 and 4 (formerly in Antikenmuseum of the University of Leipzig). See Siewert, T (?) 4.
[83] Webster (1972) 142, with Pl. 16b.
[84] This is pointed out by Brenne, in: Siewert, T (?) 4, p. 174.

identical with the contents of both the youths' baskets. To the man's left, behind the table, there is another half-naked youth, extending his arms towards the man to show him similar objects he is holding in his right hand. Below is a large ceramic vessel (*lekanē*) full of identical objects, placed centrally on the table already with some of such objects still on the table. It is essential that the small objects are arranged in this vessel much more regularly than those in the baskets and on the table. In my view, the youth's gesture can be interpreted as a sign of a completed task or work done. Thus, all this seems to indicate that the objects in the *lekanē* have been subject to some action, most probably counting. Further to the left, flanking the entire representation, stands another adult man, depicted in a way suggesting elderly age in the Attic artistic convention; he is holding a writing-set in his right hand, extended towards the table, and supporting himself with the left hand on a knotty cane, an attribute of citizens in Attic vase painting.

Interpretation of these representations should begin with the observation that the corresponding scene on the opposite side of the kylix (side 'B') is very solemn. It is quite a typical sacrifice scene, with two adult offerers and two assisting youths.[85] There is a fire burning on a low stone altar in its centre, while two (or three) participants pour a liquid libation onto the altar, where the remnants of the sacrifice victim are charring.[86] This alone suggests that the 'mirror' representation on the other side of the vessel must have been intended by the painter as analogically ceremonious, or at least formal. Furthermore, as in the libation scene, the adult men and the youths in the representations in question wear wreaths around their heads, which indicates a formal, official, or perhaps even duly ritual, character of the depicted activity.

In his comprehensive analysis of these representations, Stefan Brenne pointed out that the only known to us vase painting representations analogical to the irregular objects visible in the tondo and side 'A' of the Pan Painter vessel are small items doubtlessly identified as *psēphoi* cast in several painted voting scenes. In some of them, the *psēphoi* are counted on tables or altars not dissimilar to the one described above.[87] It is worth adding that the

---

[85] See also *ThesCRA* I pl. 32.GR569 (A, B) and *ThesCRA* V pl. 57.1198 (I); Van Straten (1995) fig. 145 (I, A, B).
[86] Cf. Ekroth (2005).
[87] See, e.g., the famous red-figure Douris kylix (ca. 500–490 BC) in the collection of Osterreichisches Museum in Vienna (Kunsthistorisches Museum, 325). Cf. also the red-figure kylix attributed to the Louvre Painter G 265 (ca. 480–470 BC) in the collection of Rijksmuseum

Fig. 3.4 Attic red-figure *kylix* of the Pan Painter (*c*. 470–460 BC; H. 8.5 cm, 26 cm in diameter), Oxford, Ashmolean Museum, 1911.617 (= The Beazley Archive, no. 206398). Image © Ashmolean Museum, University of Oxford.

comparison with the *psēphoi* from these representations reveals the difference between them and the ostraka identifiable on the kylix by the Pan Painter, diligently depicted as relatively large objects, varying in size and irregular in shape.

Brenne interpreted the representation on the kylix by the Pan Painter as referring to *ostrakophoria*. Linking it with other sources available to us, including fragment 30 of Philochorus, he proposed the following reconstruction of the manner of voting with ostraka in the Agora. The voters

---

van Oudheden in Leiden (PC 75): in the tondo Athena is supervising a voter and on side 'A' four voters are placing their *psēphoi* on an altar under her vigilant eye. Representations of this kind are usually interpreted as referring to the scene of voting on the lot of the armour of the fallen Achilles. *Psēphoi* are particularly clearly visible on a fragment of a red-figure kylix attributed to the Painter Douris, currently in the Vatican, Museo Gregoriano Etrusco Vaticano, 35091 (now AST 132). For a brief interpretation of such images in the context of vote counting, see Boegehold (1963) 369–370, who underlines the combination of pebbles (*psēphoi*) and 'a complete lack of secrecy' (cf. also a superb treatment of this series of images by Spivey (1994)). This is exactly how it worked in *ostrakophoria*, when the citizens were supposed, as we shall see, to place their ostraka in an open-shaped vessel, and not on a reckoning board, as is the case in these images. On the other hand, however, the ostraka were cast with their inscriptions turned downwards (see above) and all were put in one vessel, because there could be no clear divide between the votes 'for' and 'against' put in separate urns, as in Athenian law courts.

underwent identity control (most probably visual) before entering the Agora through the 10 gates. At the same time, they handed in or cast their ostraka into vessels assigned to their *phylē, trittys*, or deme. Then, an official representative of the *polis* supervised the transport of subsequent vessels containing votes (cf. the tondo of the kylix) to the place where they were officially counted (cf. side 'A' of the kylix).

This interpretation can be enriched with several details. Apart from the youths, here playing an exclusively ancillary role and perhaps representing slaves, worth noticing is the hierarchy among the adult men, clearly of citizen status. Two of them (one in the tondo, the other on the body of the vessel) are depicted as citizens in the prime of life, directly overseeing the youths carrying baskets with ostraka. At the same time, another one, represented at a distance from the place of vote counting, assumes a more formal position of authority, analogical to that of the citizen-orator in vase painting. Conventionally, he is also intended by the painter to represent the elders participating in this procedure. I am tempted to tentatively identify the men in their prime with the *prytaneis* and the council members and the older man with the archon from our literary sources. In the 'synoptic' artistic convention, which synthesises several stages of a given activity into one image, the latter seems to be announcing the result (a partial result?) of the ostraka counting,[88] while the others seem to be supervising the process of calculation (side 'A' of the vessel) or the transport (tondo) of the 'votes'.

If we assume that it is correct to identify the representations on the kylix by the Pan Painter from Oxford as a scene of the Athenian *ostrakophoria*, it seems pretty natural to interpret the *lekanē* placed on the table, or better: counting board, as a vessel filled with ostraka arranged in neat layers. As I have already suggested, it is conceivable that the painter intended to represent the result of vote counting: a set of sherds with the name of a particular Athenian politician or a combination of sets with names of several politicians. In other words, it would be a simplified image of a deposit (or its part) ready for 'disposal' after the *ostrakophoria* day, which would correspond, for instance, to the 'Great Kerameikos Deposit'. The fact that each of our archaeological deposits contains a large number of ostraka with the

---

[88] As Carcopino (1935) 89 supposed, probably correctly, the announcement of the result of the *ostrakophoria* (most likely by the archons), after the votes had been counted, must have taken place on the Pnyx.

same name evidently indicates that the 'ballot-counting committees' proceeded precisely in this way.

It is also worth considering briefly the possible function of the baskets carried by the two youths. Stefan Brenne interprets them as vessels for transporting 'votes'. However, it seems more probable to me that they were of double use. Considering the quite chaotic circumstances of voting in the Agora on the day of *ostrakophoria*, which I shall return to a bit further on, it is difficult to accept that the porters (properly overseen, as was necessary) first emptied the contents of some 'ballot boxes' into these baskets and only then carried them over to the place where the ostraka were counted. Transferring the 'votes' between vessels multiple times and the considerable number of people required to run such a multiple-stage procedure would pose too grave a risk. It seems more natural to assume that the baskets served at the same time as 'ballot boxes' for voting and transport vessels for the 'votes', which were successively carried away to be counted as they filled up, and as new vessels appeared to replace them.

The considerations on the topography and the procedure of *ostrakophoria* presented so far should be completed with the implications of another unique set of our data, namely the famous deposit found in 1937 and containing 190 ostraka against Themistocles.[89] Unlike all other deposits, discovered much closer to the spot where voting took place and resulting from the 'disposal' of ostraka used during *ostrakophoria*, this one was found in a well on the north slope of the Acropolis. The epigraphic analysis shows that this assemblage of ostraka was prepared by merely 14 securely identified scribe 'hands' (with 11 ostraka impossible to ascribe with certainty), which indicates an attempt to manipulate the vote by Themistocles' political enemies (see Fig. 3.5).[90] They had meticulously prepared this set of ostraka for a particular *ostrakophoria*, using a special precise technique to cut the feet of *kylixes* off their bodies, as Kathleen Lynch

---

[89] For general information, see *Agora 25*, 142–161. On the find, cf. Broneer (1938) 228–243.

[90] The number of scribes may not be insignificant here. An average dining room where members of the élite gathered for an all-night *symposion* was sometimes called *heptaklinos oikos* (room of seven couches), which means it could accommodate 14 participants. Letting imagination run wild, one could conceive of a banquet in one of the rich houses on the southern edges of the Agora during which members of a *hetaireia* hostile to Themistocles make an attempt at manipulating the vote by dedicating some time at the *symposion* to preparing this set of ostraka, an activity potentially entertaining in itself.

TOWARDS A RECONSTRUCTION OF OSTRACISM IN ATHENS 151

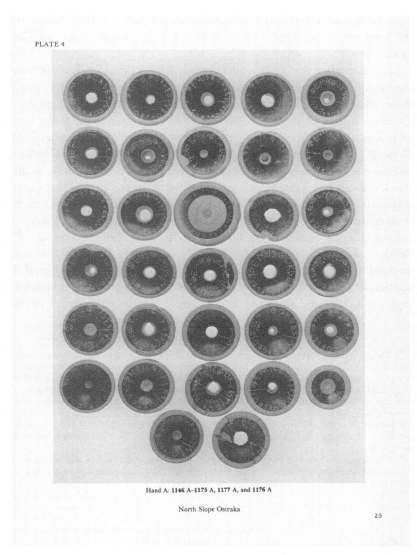

Fig. 3.5 North-Slope ostraka of the 'Themistocles Deposit', after *Agora 25*, Pl. 4. Courtesy of Ephorate of Antiquities of Athens-Ancient Agora/American School of Classical Studies Archive. Image © Hellenic Ministry of Culture and Sports/Organization of Cultural Resources Development (H.O.C.R.E.D.).

informs me in a personal communication (29 July 2021).[91] Moreover, this batch was most likely never used, as it was abandoned (concealed?) by its creators.[92]

Most important for our considerations is naturally the question of how the 'conspirators' intended to use their ostraka. Did they intend to hand them out at the Agora entrance to the Athenians who had not brought duly prepared 'votes' with them,[93] or did they aim to add them to the 'ballot box' or several 'ballot boxes' during the voting? The famous anecdote from Plutarch (*Arist.* 7,7–8; cf. also *Apophteg.* 196E), which used to be vividly discussed in the context of the rate of literacy among Athenian citizens of the classical times, supports the first interpretation.[94] In the light of the recent epigraphic discoveries, particularly the so-called 'herders' graffiti' from sixth-century Attica, the conviction about a remarkable scale of illiteracy among Athenian citizens of the fifth century seems no longer sustainable.[95] Besides, an attempt to hand out such a number of ostraka at the very moment when the citizens were voting would have surely triggered a reaction of the *prytaneis*, the council members or simply of Themistocles' supporters, resulting in a riot and perhaps in a major political affair.

---

[91] The current widespread idea of sourcing the vases from the supply of 'production discards' from a certain ceramic workshop is thus discarded. Another crucial piece of information provided to me by Kathleen Lynch is her opinion that the vases should be dated to some time after (and not before, as it is usually assumed) the Persian Wars, which would link this deposit with the *ostrakophoria* successfully banishing Themistocles in 470 BC. Slightly similar, even though smaller, groups of ostraka prepared for use have been identified in the Agora and in the Kerameikos (*Agora 25*, 13–14 (cf. *Agora 25*, p. 161); see also Brenne (2001) 28 and Brenne, in Siewert, T 1/24–34, pp. 78–79). However, save for *Agora 25*, 13–14, those ostraka were evidently used in voting.

[92] The distance of this find from the Agora evidently indicates that we are not dealing here with the result of the offenders having been caught in the act by Athenian magistrates or political opponents.

[93] This is how this deposit has been interpreted by the majority of scholars since its first publication by Broneer (1938) 243. Cf. also below, n. 110, for the idea of selling inscribed ostraka on the spot.

[94] Examples of interpretations of Plutarch's anecdote in this context abound. See, e.g., with some hesitation, Carcopino (1935) 84–87 and Boegehold (1963) 368.

[95] See Langdon (2015). It may also be instructive to confront the strikingly high number of ostraka physically fitting one another, or stemming from the same vessel, in the 'Great Deposit' (1014 items, i.e., ca. 1/9 of their total number) with the number of ostraka that can be fitted to one another based on epigraphic criteria (80 items in total). If one additionally considers the number of the 'prefabricated' ostraka of the 'Themistocles deposit' (190 items), it seems natural to conclude that the extent of professional scribal assistance to the voters during *ostrakophoriai* was very limited. Last but not least, the very idea of a vote of the entire citizen body in a way requiring writing on ostraka testifies that Cleisthenes expected a relatively high literacy rate among the Athenian *dēmos* (I owe this idea to Aleksander Wolicki). In general, cf. also Missiou (2011) 36–55.

TOWARDS A RECONSTRUCTION OF OSTRACISM IN ATHENS 153

Therefore, the second possibility seems much more likely, namely that the intention of the 'conspirators' was to add the entire set of ostraka to particular vessels for 'votes' (*skaphai*?) at the moment of voting, most probably taking advantage of a brief confusion in the queue for the 'ballot boxes' or even provoking it. The citizens, entering the Agora wearing *himatia*, would undergo (visual) identification by their *prytaneis* and the council members of their *phylē*, of course, but they would certainly not be searched, so smuggling some additional ostraka, even in considerable number, would be possible.[96] I suppose that this is what the enemies of Themistocles were counting on.

The 'deposit of Themistocles' allows us to make another statement crucial for my argument. The very laconic testimonies on the course of *ostrakophoria* available to us seem to suggest that every Athenian came to vote with their own ostrakon. Such a solution is naturally catastrophic for the order and validity of the voting. Every person could easily smuggle at least one additional ostrakon, thus doubling the vote. There are also many ostraka broken off the same vessel,[97] which indicates that this is exactly what would occasionally happen. Another solution would be for magistrates to give out ostraka to citizens already in the Agora, expecting those interested to 'fill in' such a 'form' on the spot. However, the sources do not mention such a procedure, and the set of 190 ostraka against Themistocles prepared in advance seems to exclude such a possibility.[98] Hence, we must conclude that the Athenians treated this vote (although theoretically a secret ballot) much less rigorously than others (secret or open) involving the use of 'tokens' of various kinds.[99] The question of why they did so is closely related to the usefulness of the Athenian Agora as a voting place in the *ostrakophoria* procedure.

---

[96] This idea may be further confirmed by the fact that the deposit contains ostraka of similar shape and dimensions; their regular and uniform shape would probably facilitate hiding and smuggling them in numbers. Moreover, since many of them are pierced, one can think of the intention to thread them on a string and thus sneak them into the vote.

[97] See Brenne, in: Siewert, pp. 79–80 and above, p. 81 with n. 38 and p. 84 with n. 50.

[98] Apart from that, such a procedure would be in itself counter-effective. Every Athenian could break his ostrakon into two or more votes. Another argument against this method can be the slight number of uninscribed ostraka in the *ostrakophoria* deposits in the Agora and on the Kerameikos (if this is indeed the case; see above, pp. 79–80). If the sherds were officially distributed among the voters, we would expect a significant number of 'empty' votes. However, it seems that those who voted were dedicated and came prepared to express their opinion.

[99] Cf. Boegehold (1963) 367–368, where Athenian fifth-century problems with secret ballot are briefly discussed (as the reason why the system was changed in the fourth-century BC).

As I have pointed out, in the fifth century BC, the Agora was already surrounded and increasingly filled with subsequent buildings (see Fig. 3.1 and 3.3). Some were also located in its central part and were permanent wooden structures, such as the aforementioned Orchestra. Others, such as the hypothetical 'enclosures' used as venues for the proceedings of certain Athenian tribunals, or the recently identified mysterious 'Perischoinisma', could have been temporary, and some of them changed their shape and size depending on the occasion.[100] Some others still were erected seasonally, for instance, to accommodate the audience of the Panathenaic contests.[101] On a daily basis, in turn, the Agora was probably filled with irregularly scattered temporary trade and artisan structures, stalls, workshops, tents, etc. They were, however, stable enough for our sources to distinguish them from portable stalls or various devices for itinerant trade.[102] The majority of these structures were probably removed for the duration of *ostrakophoria* (and other festive occasions), but we know that some of them were merely closed or blocked with the 'wicker' mentioned above. We also hear that Cimon adorned the Agora with plane trees,[103] undoubtedly to create a large amount of shaded space on the sun-scorched square.[104]

Therefore, there is every indication that the area of the Agora was exceptionally difficult to adapt to the needs of ostracism and that the voting taking place there (whatever the manner of carrying it out) was difficult to oversee in a space full of various recesses. To understand the challenges which the Athenians faced on the day of *ostrakophoria*, it suffices to compare this area with the voting place of the massive *comitia centuriata* of the early Roman Republic: the diligently arranged 'enclosures' and 'bridges' of the Roman *ovilia* on Campus Martius—a vast empty area outside the city centre, making it possible to control the crowd of voters and to carry out the voting procedure in an orderly way.[105]

However, regardless of how accurately we envisage the manner of voting and the possibilities to manipulate it, there is no doubt that such manipulations—reaching hundreds of ostracism 'votes', so potentially

---

[100] Cf. Dow (2004) [1939] 80–84.   [101] See above, pp. 135–137.
[102] Cf., e.g., in a comic convention, Ar. *Eq.* 1245-1247. See R. Di Cesare, in Greco (2014) 1068-1070.
[103] See the testimonies gathered in *Agora* 3, nos. 717 and 718.
[104] Regardless of the groves dedicated to various deities, we also hear about planes and (black) poplars growing on the Athenian Agora: cf. *Agora* 3, no. 715–728.
[105] See, e.g., Liv. XXVI 22,11. Cf. Taylor (1966) 34–58, 107–113 and recently Humm (2019) 271–273.

impacting the ultimate result in a significant, if not decisive, way—were indeed possible and practised during Athenian *ostrakophoriai*.[106]

3.2.4 Interim Conclusions: *Ostrakophoria* and the Agora

The conclusion that the Agora was not suited for orderly voting on the day of *ostrakophoria* has to be slightly relativised, of course, by taking a diachronic perspective. It is indisputable that at the moment of Cleisthenes' reforms, it was a natural and the only possible area for (future) *ostrakophoriai*. Back then, it was essentially an empty space where such activities could be easily controlled. However, we should remember that the first case of an *ostrakophoria* occurred 20 years later, and that the Athenians did not move the voting elsewhere, for instance, to the usual venue of the Assembly, for the entire period when ostracism was applied. During this time, the Agora was gradually becoming increasingly difficult to control effectively on the voting day.

Moreover, the character of the Agora underwent large-scale changes, including the planting of trees by Cimon when the Pnyx had already taken over its former function as the place of the Assembly.[107] This may not have been a coincidence. It can be supposed that it was precisely at this moment when it was decided that the Agora had lost its fundamental political function as the gathering place of the people. Hence, the question of why the Athenians never moved *ostrakophoriai* to the Pnyx (or to some other place) is of great significance, provided that it is asked with regard to the times when ostracism was actually applied: after Cleisthenes, beginning in the 80s, 70s, and 60s of the fifth century BC.

There are two alternative ways of considering this issue: focusing on the pragmatic reasons on the one hand, and the symbolic ones on the other. In both these approaches, however, we remain within the framework of a general conception (undoubtedly correct, even though insufficient in itself)

---

[106] If the 'Themistocles' deposit' is to be dated to the seventies of the fifth century BC, as Kathleen Lynch tentatively suggests, i.e., to the *ostrakophoria* which actually sent Themistocles to exile, this batch of nearly 200 'votes' was most likely but a part of a coordinated political campaign that ultimately put an end to Themistocles' political position in Athens. If this was the case, we are entitled to assume that other batches of the kind were used successfully by the enemies of this politician.

[107] See above, p. 135. It cannot be excluded that the Pnyx had taken over this function already earlier, during the times of Cleisthenes or shortly after. It certainly happened by the time of Ephialtes' reforms.

of the natural conservatism of the Athenian *dēmos*. Moreover, it has to be taken into consideration that such gatherings took place infrequently enough for the difficulties connected with them not to be regarded as indeed burdensome.

Students of the Athenian democracy following the increasingly popular ritualistic approach will point out that *ostrakophoria* is first and foremost an act of symbolic control by the Athenian 'masses' on the community leaders coming from the uppermost social strata.[108] From this point of view, a chaotic gathering of the people, full of anger and extremely negative emotions, is of utmost significance in itself. A more orderly gathering, for instance on the Pnyx, would take away much of the violent practice and symbolism, which the *dēmos* must have valued highly. This explanation seems quite convincing, even if insufficient. On the other hand, more pragmatic reasons can be sought. One of them has been suggested to me by Prof. Judy Barringer. She pointed out that sherds, essential for *ostrakophoria*, were widely available to those interested in large amounts precisely in the Agora, where a particular market 'zone' hosted stalls with ceramic products.[109] Additionally, in the northwest, the Agora was directly adjacent to the Kerameikos and its ceramic workshops. But even without such specialist assistance, as Kathleen Lynch observes, '[f]rom excavation, it is clear that sherds could be found on every surface of the Agora. This would explain why voters found older sherds to use as ostraka. They didn't always need to fabricate them, just pick them up' (*per litteras*, 30 August 2021).[110] Thus, while everybody would have to carry their own ostrakon to the Pnyx, prepared in advance, with the forgetful being deprived of a vote, in the Agora the voting instruments could be supplied even at the last moment.[111] This pragmatic explanation of why the Agora remained the site of the *ostrakophoria* voting also seems convincing but still insufficient.

I believe one more factor should be considered here. If, following Mogens H. Hansen, we reject the increasingly widespread 'minimalistic' convictions regarding the degree of political engagement among the Athenians (i.e., mainly regarding the scale of participation in the Assembly),[112] we shall

---

[108] Recently, cf. esp. Kosmin (2015). In general, cf. Forsdyke (2005) esp. 161–164. This scholar interestingly emphasises 'the visual spectacle of ostracism' in the Agora (p. 164).

[109] Cf. *Agora 3*, 221–224 and generally *Agora 14*, 185–190.

[110] In a similar vein, *Kerameikos 20.1*, p. 203. Incidentally, these remarks seem to seriously undermine the idea of (some) ostraka of ostracism being prepared for sale (thus, e.g., M. Lang in *Agora 25*, p. 161).

[111] This must have generated additional chaos during the voting.

[112] See, above all, Hansen (1983) 1–20 (an article first published in 1976).

find the answer we are seeking here. The indeterminate nature of the physical boundaries of the Agora (not to be confused with its precise ritual delimitation), its irregular shape, as if 'blending into' the paths and streets leading to it, and especially its vast dimensions gave it an almost infinite capacity as a venue for gatherings of the Athenian people (cf. Fig. 3.1 and 3.3). A quick comparison of the total area of the Agora (ca. 40 acres, i.e., ca. 12 hectares) with the space available on the Pnyx (so-called 'Pnyx I', where the capacity in the fifth century BC is estimated at ca. 6000 persons) reveals a figure many times higher in the case of the Agora.[113] Thus, in extreme compactness, the Athenian Agora could perhaps hold the majority of the entire male citizen population of the *polis*, and a gathering of 10000 would have some freedom of movement there. As Ps.-Andocides puts it (IV [*Against Alcibiades*], 4), '[...] but in this decision [sc. on the day of *ostrakophoria* – M.W.] all Athenians have a voice' (ἀλλὰ τούτου τοῦ πράγματος ἅπασιν Ἀθηναίοις μέτεστι). At least in theory.[114]

This, I believe, is precisely the answer to our question.[115] The Agora remained the venue for *ostrakophoriai* principally because, on that day, it could be expected that the crowd would reach a size unparalleled at other occasions and significantly exceeding the capacity of all other conceivable gathering spots.[116] Granted, citizens were supposed to just pass through their entrances and the Agora itself, in relative order, and not stay there in groups. But lining up in long queues was inevitable, so the bigger the area available the better.

Given the exceptional infrequence of *ostrakophoriai* and the fact that it never became a regular element of the community's political life, the Athenians of the fifth century were able, as it appears, to accept the organisational challenges, the potential chaos, or perhaps even—*horribile dictu!*— the compromised reliability of the vote, inevitably resulting in such

---

[113] From this point of view, the Theatre of Dionysus in its fifth-century form would be more capacious than the Pnyx, but still significantly less capacious than the Agora.

[114] Meister (2020) 343–346 convincingly argues for a high mobilisation of the civic rural population at *ostrakophoriai*. As Forsdyke (2005) 163 points out, a high turnout was ensured by the fact that 'this period [early March – M.W.] corresponds to a low point in the agricultural year'. Cf. already Siewert, T 41, pp. 467–468 (by W. Scheidel and H. Taeuber).

[115] Cf. already Carcopino (1935) 74–76. If I am not mistaken, such an idea is implicitly present in Gauthier (2011) [1990] 424 n. 8. In a similar vein also Forsdyke (2005) 162–163.

[116] The hypothesis about the overwhelming turnout at the Athenian *ostrakophoria* seems to be supported by the case discussed above of a single ostraka deposit (the 'Great Kerameikos Deposit') which rendered much more than 4000 'votes' cast against just one 'candidate' and more than 2000 against another one, during just one *ostrakophoria*. These two 'sets' of 'votes' exceed the turnout of even the most crowded session of the Athenian Assembly.

circumstances.[117] This last inconvenience must have been of lesser importance in the prospect of granting the people the right to decide about the life and (political) death of the most accomplished representatives of the Athenian élites.

This conclusion naturally leads to another serious problem in the study of Athenian ostracism, namely to the issue of the so-called 'quorum' of *ostrakophoria*.

3.2.5 The Conundrum of the 'Quorum' of Ostracism and the Issue of Ineffective *Ostrakophoriai*

In this section, we shall remain within the same set of data offering insight into Athenian ostracism. The text usually edited as fragment 30 of Philochorus has a special place among them. However, while in the matters of topography and procedure of *ostrakophoria* our sources presented a reasonably consistent picture (even though not entirely reliable, as it turned out), in the case of the 'quorum' of ostracism, according to many scholars, the same testimonies seem to be unclear, self-contradictory, or even corrupt. The relevant parts of the fragment of Philochorus and the sources connectable with it seem to contain, as we remember, snippets of the text of the law about ostracism. This makes the analysis of these testimonies an even more interesting challenge.

But before embarking on this enterprise, at this juncture, we ought to clarify the status, and so the potential utility, of the text referred to as Philochorus' fragment 30. As mentioned above, Herbert Heftner has recently meticulously commented on a group of five texts forming the 'great procedural-historical scholion about ostracism' ('Das Große verfahrenstechnisch-historische Scholion'), i.e., Philochorus, *FGrHist* 328 F 30 also known as Theophrastus, fr. 640A–B Fortenbaugh. Heftner's goal was establishing a 'Komposit-Text' of this 'scholion' underlying the whole and slightly divergent tradition represented for us by the five aforementioned texts, which he most spectacularly did (Heftner (2018) 105–106). Ultimately, Heftner's ingenious idea was also to tentatively ascribe the

---

[117] However, we should remember that the political sensitivity of the Athenians on this point could have been lesser than that of citizens of modern democracies. For it seems that during a vote by a show of hands at the Athenian Assembly, the majority was merely assessed visually (and often contested, as a consequence), and the result of a vote with *psēphoi* was traditionally 'rounded off'. See Hansen (2004) [1977] and below, n. 173.

scholiastic or lexicographic work underlying this group of texts to Didymus, as had done many scholars before him (see above, p. 130), albeit not to just one of his learned commentaries but two. In Heftner's opinion, while the four major texts in this group follow Didymus' commentary on Demosthenes, the last one, a short scholion to Lucian's *Timon* 30, may be based on Didymus' commentary on Aristophanes. Didymus would simply use one and the same note he compiled about ostracism in two of his works (Heftner (2018) 107–108).

So far, so good. Meanwhile, when eventually considering the ultimate source of information for Didymus' 'note' on ostracism, Heftner concludes that the first and procedural-historical half of the scholion is a verbatim quotation from Philochorus (quoted as source by three texts of our group), while its second and historical-political part, much more succinct and most probably abbreviated, may be drawn from an author from the Peripatetic circles (Theophrastus' *Nomoi* are quoted as the source of information in the shortest text of this group). And indeed, one may ponder the following alternative. Either the entire 'scholion' is based on Book Three of the *Atthis* by Philochorus, who follows here his own source, the *Laws* of Theophrastus, or the first part of the 'scholion' is quoted from Philochorus, whereas the second one is an abbreviated note based on Theophrastus. After careful consideration, H. Heftner hesitantly opts for the latter solution.[118]

My reasons for hesitantly choosing the former alternative are as follows. First, it seems that the source of the first and procedural-historical part of the scholion is erudite or antiquarian and not chronographic. The dependence of these sections on an earlier *Atthis* seems unlikely.[119] Secondly, the fact that this part was placed in Philochorus' Book Three suggests that the description of the 'procedure of ostracism' belonged with its first occurrence (and not with the banishment of Hyperbolus), giving rise to an erudite excursus based on a specialised piece of information. Thirdly, the formal or stylistic difference between the two parts should not be overestimated. They might have simply been due to the fact that Didymus was much more interested in the detailed erudite information regarding the procedure of *ostrakophoria* and its consequences and much less focused on the historical-political notes he must have also known from other sources. His understandable selectivity here determined the succinct and truncated style of this part. Fourthly and most importantly, the 'great scholion' taken as a whole

---

[118] Heftner (2018) 109–111.
[119] See also above (p. 76 n. 21), on the 'entries' about ostracism in Androtion.

corresponds very well to the nature of the entries of Theophrastus' *Laws* as thoroughly analysed by Andrew Szegedy-Maszak.

'For Theophrastus a complete notice of law includes a statement of its terms, a specific example of its use, and an explanation of its intent'.[120] Studying Theophrastus' discussion of the law of homicide, Szegedy-Maszak argues that its disproportionate length 'was due to the unique importance of the crime and the uniquely elaborate measures devised to deal with it'.[121] Ultimately, when commenting on usual scholarly complaints about 'stylistic inelegance' and 'the chaotic presentation of the material itself', Szegedy-Maszak, based on the case of the long fragment 21 regarding contracts, points out that '[t]he fragment does not represent a brief prepared by a lawyer. Rather, it is a study conducted by an intelligent and inquisitive layman who has explored widely in the field of law and is reporting his findings'.[122]

All in all, I would argue that underlying the 'great scholion about ostracism' was a fragment of Didymus' commentary on Demosthenes (and perhaps on Aristophanes as well). Its immediate source was a lengthy treatment of ostracism (understood as *ostrakophoria*) from Book Three of Philochorus, cited as such at the beginning of Didymus' entry. Philochorus in turn based these passages of his work on the note on *ostrakismos* in the *Laws* of Theophrastus, mentioning him as his source at the end of his treatment of ostracism. Didymus, vividly interested in the erudite and detailed first part of Philochorus' fragment, quoted it *verbatim* while cutting and abbreviating (what is now) the second part. Henceforth, then, I will refer to the 'great scholion about ostracism' as 'fragment 30 of Philochorus' without reservations. With this in mind, we may resume our interpretation.

[...] διαριθμηθέντων δὲ ὅτῳ πλεῖστα γένοιτο καὶ μὴ ἐλάττω ἑξακισχιλίων, τοῦτον ἔδει τὰ δίκαια δόντα καὶ λαβόντα ὑπὲρ τῶν ἰδίων συναλλαγμάτων ἐν δέκα ἡμέραις μεταστῆναι τῆς πόλεως ἔτη δέκα (ὕστερον δὲ ἐγένοντο πέντε), καρπούμενον τὰ ἑαυτοῦ, μὴ ἐπιβαίνοντα ἐντὸς Γεραιστοῦ τοῦ Εὐβοίας ἀκρωτηρίου [...].

[...] After [the ostraka] were counted, the person for whom the most [ostraka] occurred [i.e., were cast] and not less than six thousand, this man had to tender and exact settlements ['just things'] concerning his personal

---

[120] Szegedy-Maszak, p. 65.   [121] Szegedy-Maszak, p. 84.
[122] Szegedy-Maszak, pp. 84–85 (quotation on p. 85).

arrangements within ten days, to relocate from the city-state for ten years (but later it became five), enjoying the use of his property, not overstepping (a boundary) within Geraestus, the promontory of Euboia [...].

(tr. Nicholas F. Jones, *BNJ*)

The corresponding parts of the scholion to Aristophanes' *Knights* (sch vet 855B 6–8) give a slightly diverging version and read as follows: '[...] After [the ostraka] were counted, the person for whom the most were cast, and not less than 6000, had to relocate from the polis within ten days. If there were not 6000, he did not relocate.' (ἀριθμηθέντων δέ, ᾧ πλεῖστα γένοιτο καὶ μὴ ἐλάττω ἑξακισχιλίων, τοῦτον ἔδει ἐν δέκα ἡμέραις μεταστῆναι τῆς πόλεως. Εἰ δὲ μὴ γένοιτο ἑξακισχίλια, οὐ μεθίστατο). The version preserved in Pollux's lexicon (8.20) in turn says: 'the person for whom 6000 ostraka were cast had to go into exile' (ὅτῳ δὲ ἑξακισχίλια γένοιτο τὰ ὄστρακα, τοῦτον φυγεῖν ἐχρῆν). The same piece of information is delivered in a slightly different way by the *Etymologicum Magnum* (s.v. *exostrakismos* [349.15 Gaisdorf]): ἑξακισχιλίων δὲ γινομένων, φυγὴ δεκαετὴς ψηφίζεται τοῦ κρινομένου. It should be noted that the concision of the last lexicon entry allows for two interpretations: 'when there were 6000 [ostraka]' can refer equally well to the number of 'votes' cast against one Athenian or to the 6000 ostraka in the total vote. Regardless of this ambiguity, it is certain that all these testimonies are variants of the same tradition, which is most fully represented in fragment 30 of Philochorus.

Two other sources stand out against this background. Diodorus (XI 55,2) writes simply that 'he whose name figured on the largest number of ostraka was obliged to go into exile from his fatherland for a five-year period' (tr. Peter Green) (ᾧ δ' ἂν ὄστρακα πλείω γένηται, φεύγειν ἐκ τῆς πατρίδος ἐτέτακτο πενταετῆ χρόνον).[123] Plutarch in turn presents the entire procedure in his *Life of Aristides* in a way fundamentally different from the other accounts (*Arist.* 7,6; tr. Bernadotte Perrin):

οἱ δ' ἄρχοντες πρῶτον μὲν διηρίθμουν τὸ σύμπαν ἐν ταὐτῷ τῶν ὀστράκων πλῆθος· εἰ γὰρ ἑξακισχιλίων ἐλάττονες οἱ φέροντες εἶεν, ἀτελὴς ἦν ὁ

---

[123] The correction made by Jacoby (*FGrHist* IIIb Suppl. I 316), who added ἑξακισχιλίων after πλείω, was clearly motivated by an attempt at reconciling this account with those quoted above (the genitive is by no means required here, as Develin (1985b) 25, n. 2 points out). For now, I am leaving aside the information about the five-year exile; I shall return to it later on, 3.3.2.

ἐξοστρακισμός· ἔπειτα τῶν ὀνομάτων ἕκαστον ἰδίᾳ θέντες τὸν ὑπὸ τῶν πλείστων γεγραμμένον ἐξεκήρυττον εἰς ἔτη δέκα, καρπούμενον τὰ αὑτοῦ.

The archons first counted the total number of ostraka cast. For if the voters were less than six thousand, the ostracism was void. Then they separated the names, and the man who had received the most votes they proclaimed banished for ten years, with the right to enjoy the income from his property.

Diodorus' version could be regarded as a highly abridged variant of the dominant tradition,[124] followed also by the entry in the *Etymologicum Magnum* quoted above (in an equally reductive manner), which gave rise to the ambiguity mentioned there. This ambivalence is completely absent from Diodorus, where it is replaced by an unambiguous statement about the majority of votes against a given 'candidate'.[125] Plutarch's account manifestly differs from other testimonies.[126]

Nonetheless, most of the available sources regard the 6000 ostraka as the qualified majority required for ostracism to be effective, but there also appears the conviction that 6000 votes were actually the 'quorum' of *ostrakophoria*, which needed to be reached before the simple majority of ostraka indicating a given 'candidate' decided about his exile. Faced with the close similarities but also with the fundamental discrepancies between the sources, scholars have referred to two theoretically complementary but nevertheless separate interpretation strategies, which, as we shall shortly see, may turn out to be completely irreconcilable. On the one hand, they have tried to establish the most homogenous or 'best' text within this dominant tradition,[127] assuming that this would be the 'primary' and thus historically reliable one, while all the versions regarded as 'departing' from it have been seen as worthless results of this tradition's corruption. On the other hand, scholars have considered the probability, or rather the potential practical effectiveness of *ostrakophoria* in one and the other procedural

---

[124] A marginal remark about a five-year exile can also be found in Philochorus; however, it is presented there as amendment to an earlier law.

[125] However, it should be emphasised that this is due to the lack of a numeral in Diodorus as well as to the syntax in both the testimonies. The relative clause in Diodorus simply does not allow for ambiguity, which is created by the genitive absolute in the *Etymologicum Magnum*.

[126] Even though the final quotation from an archaic-sounding fragment of the law about ostracism (incidentally, cited enthusiastically by many sources) links it with Philochorus.

[127] From a certain point of view, Heftner (2018) is the climax of this approach. In his subtle and meticulous study, he does not, however, directly address the problem of the historical reliability, or the sources, of his 'Komposit-Text'.

variant. Moreover, it should be emphasised that both these interpretation strategies involved making a crucial presumption, which is largely out of date today, even though not all scholars have realised the implications of this. It was assumed that 6000 ostraka cast during a single *ostrakophoria* was a very high figure, extremely difficult to achieve in practice—either for the quorum or for the simple majority of votes. However, today we know for sure that this premise was erroneous. This conclusion can be drawn from the discovery of the 'Great Kerameikos Deposit' and the reasoning presented in the previous section of this work, which indicates a very high turnout expected of the Athenian citizens on the day of *ostrakophoria*.

Therefore, in the interpretation which follows, I shall give priority to textual features when studying what I take as Philochorus fragment 30 based on a note in Theophrastus' *Laws*. The appearance of extracts from the law about ostracism there should theoretically make it possible to achieve a higher than usual degree of probability in our considerations. Let us begin, however, with an overview of the most important arguments related to the pragmatic aspect (diversely understood) of activities connected with *ostrakophoria*.[128]

The most detailed description of this procedure is provided by Plutarch, as we have seen. It is precisely the level of detail in this digression that rightly aroused the suspicion of Jérôme Carcopino.[129] He emphasised that such a doubled procedure would very much hamper *ostrakophoria*, or at least prolong it unnecessarily, without being of any particular use. The scholar ultimately assumes (based mainly on speculations on the Athenian demographics in Cleisthenes' times) that the 6000 votes required to exile an Athenian citizen, roughly equivalent to two-thirds of the total number of those having the right to vote, is the qualified majority.[130] On the other side of this dispute are the interesting remarks by Gianluca Cuniberti, who argues, based on the case of the last Athenian *ostrakophoria* known to us, that the only possible way to interpret the tradition as we received it is to regard the requirement of 6000 ostraka as the required quorum. Otherwise, it would be impossible to explain the very hazardous political deal made last-minute between Nicias and Alcibiades (and perhaps also Phaeax), which consisted in the united voting of their supporters against their common

---

[128] I am presenting here a selection from among the abundant bibliography of voices which, in my view, are most characteristic.
[129] See Carcopino (1935) 91–97. Staveley (1972) 90–91 simply takes Plutarch's version as reliable.
[130] Carcopino (1935) 87–110.

enemy, Hyperbolus. Had the 6000 votes been the qualified majority required to ostracise an Athenian politician, it would have been much safer and easier to simply count on the wide distribution of votes, with as many as three (or even four) serious 'candidates' for ostracism.[131]

In my view, Cuniberti's argumentation strikes the decisive blow against the conception of the qualified majority. Regardless of my assumption of a very high turnout at *ostrakophoria* and of the proven possibility that a single candidate would obtain a large number of votes (cf. the case of Megakles in the 70s), the extremely wide variety of names found on the Athenian ostraka (272 names in total, but only 176 names of 'candidates') allows us to suppose that the dispersal of votes was usually quite wide. The requirement of the majority of 6000 votes cast against one 'candidate' would every now and then have to lead to a situation when the 'winner' of the *ostrakophoria* could not be identified. However, it should immediately be added that a similar argument could be used against the conception of the quorum of 6000 cast votes. Most probably while instituting ostracism, Cleisthenes could not know for certain that the Athenians would turn up for *ostrakophoria* in large numbers every time. It was possible to see this in practice only 20 years later.[132] Such a high quorum would entail the risk of indecisive ostracism.

It should be noted that the first possibility is considered by the scholion to Aristophanes' *Knights* (Εἰ δὲ μὴ γένοιτο ἑξακισχιλία, οὐ μεθίστατο), while the second situation is mentioned as a perfectly natural fact by Plutarch (εἰ γὰρ ἑξακισχιλίων ἐλάττονες οἱ φέροντες εἶεν, ἀτελὴς ἦν ὁ ἐξοστρακισμός). The problem is that Plutarch's idea of a 'void' (ἀτελής) ostracism has no parallel in any other testimony regarding this institution.[133] I would venture to regard it as impossible that the anecdotal tradition about Athenian political life did not record even a single case of an Athenian politician escaping exile on the day of *ostrakophoria*. Its focal point were stories about dramatic fortune changes of great (and lesser) Athenians of the fifth century, and it

---

[131] Cuniberti (2003) 119. This interpretation is seconded, as one possible explanation, by Costa, p. 231 in his commentary on fr. 20 of Philochorus.

[132] And, naturally, the demographic situation of Attica must have been different than, say, half a generation later, and still different even later on.

[133] The only parallel is found in the scholion to the *Knights* of Aristophanes (855B: εἰ δὲ μὴ γένοιτο ἑξακισχίλια, οὐ μεθίστατο), but these words, absent from all other testimonies of the 'great scholion about ostracism', are most probably a gloss by a late commentator or scholiast of Aristophanes working on the commentaries prepared by Didymus. Scholars hardly notice the fact that 'void ostracism' is absent from the good sources available to us. However, see the merely cursory remarks by Cuniberti (2003) 119, n. 26. Cf. also above, on the idea of 'abortive' ostracism, p. 81.

TOWARDS A RECONSTRUCTION OF OSTRACISM IN ATHENS 165

was created by contemporary authors (mainly Stesimbrotos of Thasos, but also Ion of Chios and Critias the Athenian). If indecisive *ostrakophoriai* had indeed happened, we would expect such anecdotes (about Themistocles, for instance) to exist. Whereas, as we have seen above, the only possible mention of this kind (by Cratinus in the *Thracian Women*, fr. 73 K–A = Siewert, T 7), referring to Pericles, concerns not an *ostrakophoria*, but a preliminary vote in the ostracism procedure. In my opinion, the complete lack of information about 'void ostracism' constitutes a strong argument in support of the view that every *ostrakophoria* ended with a decisive result. This, in turn, not only disproves the conception of a 6000 qualified majority but also seriously undermines the idea of a 6000 quorum of the vote.

In this situation, I believe we should embark on the analysis of the available testimonies from this perspective, beginning with the seemingly most precise among them, namely with Plutarch (*Arist.* 7,6; tr. Bernadotte Perrin):

> The archons first counted the total number of ostraka cast. For if the voters were less than six thousand, the ostracism was void. Then they separated the names, and the man who had received the most votes they proclaimed banished for ten years, with the right to enjoy the income from his property.

The detailed character of this account misled Raubitschek, who gladly recognised here a description of the (alleged) quorum of ostracism. Consequently, based on this testimony, he tried to emend, or rather interpret in his own way, the text of our fundamental source: fragment 30 of Philochorus.[134] The problem is, of course, that Plutarch's account is not only late but also completely isolated.[135] However, at a closer look, it may turn out priceless for our analysis.

I believe that Plutarch's digression does not actually depart from the information he found in some version of the tradition represented most fully (from our perspective) by Philochorus. The characteristic phrase closing this testimony: καρπούμενον τὰ αὑτοῦ, derived from the law about ostracism, is not the sole indication of that. The mention of archons counting the votes is trivial, but it could have been taken from Philochorus. What is most important for me is that the idea of double

---

[134] Raubitschek (1955b).   [135] Cf. above, on the criticism by Carcopino (1935) 91–97.

counting of votes might have been inferred from the same tradition. It should be noted that the crucial phrase in Plutarch (ἔπειτα τῶν ὀνομάτων ἕκαστον ἰδίᾳ θέντες) may arise simply from the interpretation of the gesture of voting, described by Philochorus: '[10 entrances] through which the people, entering by *phylai*, cast the ostraka, turning [i.e., downwards] the inscription' ([...] ἐτίθεσαν τὰ ὄστρακα, στρέφοντες τὴν ἐπιγραφήν).[136] I suppose that Plutarch, while reading Philochorus or some other version of this tradition, imagined that the ostraka left by the Athenians (most probably on some tables or other flat surfaces)[137] were still turned with the uninscribed side up at the stage of the preliminary counting by archons. Thus, the magistrates could embark on counting the votes cast against individual Athenians only at the next stage, after a 'blind' assessment of their overall number, once the ostraka have been turned over and the names inscribed on them have become visible. In other words, I think that the picture of a two-stage procedure of vote counting, created by Plutarch, is his ingenious but pedantic interpretation of the tradition originating in Philochorus (or rather in Theophrastus);[138] it does not contribute any new information. The question remains for what reason, or better: for what purpose Plutarch carried out such a profound interpretation of Philochorus (or some other text representing this tradition).[139]

It seems to me that the answer to this question can be of great significance to us. At a closer look, it becomes clear that the image constructed by

---

[136] In our tradition, this remark is missing from the scholion to Aristophanes. In general, cf. Heftner (2018) 91–92.

[137] Cf. the painted voting scenes in the dispute regarding Achilles' armour—above, pp. 147–148 n. 87.

[138] More precisely, it is Plutarch's historical reconstruction based on the same tradition. However, it should immediately be added that Philochorus' information about casting votes with the inscribed side facing down cannot refer to placing them on tables or some other flat surfaces. Given that the voting was happening in 10 places simultaneously and that it entailed thousands of citizens voting one by one, such a procedure seems to be impossible to carry out from the organisational point of view. After the voting finished in turn, the ostraka already transported to the counting spots (most probably also in 10 separate areas of the Agora) would need to be placed one by one with their uninscribed side up, and only then would it be decided (after a consultation between the 10 'commissions' counting votes simultaneously) that they would need to be counted again, this time according to the names inscribed on them. Besides, Philochorus' account is not of the moment of counting the votes but rather of casting them. Therefore, I believe that Philochorus merely meant (in the simplest possible way) that in principle, the voters hid their decisions from the sight of the magistrates overseeing the voting and thus, that it actually was a secret ballot. At the same time, it has to be remembered that in the Athenian practice the use of some kind of 'tokens' did not mean a secret ballot in itself because such objects could be placed, for instance, on one or the other side of the voting table, according to the intention of expressing a 'yes' or 'no' in a given matter.

[139] Raubitschek (1958) 97–100 points out that Plutarch quotes Philochorus only once, so the source here was probably Theophrastus himself.

Plutarch was aimed to reconcile two contradictory (in his opinion only seemingly) pieces of information regarding *ostrakophoria*, which he found in the tradition available to him. He found himself in a situation not dissimilar to that of modern scholars, who deliberate whether to relate the information about 6000 ostraka to the qualified majority of *ostrakophoria* or to its quorum. His version is nothing else but an attempt at reconciling these two variants: at the first stage, the ostraka were counted to check whether the quorum was reached, and then again to establish who obtained the majority.

Let us try, then, returning to the departure point of our tradition (i.e., to Philochorus' account) to consider on the textual level the possible origin of the contradiction, or rather ambiguity, which Plutarch was facing already then. Looking from the perspective of Plutarch's version, Raubitschek pointed out the awkward syntax in Philochorus' fragment. For the sentence to be understood as it usually is (after [the ostraka] were counted, the person for whom the most were cast and not less than 6000), we would rather expect a more natural syntax: ὅτῳ πλεῖστα καὶ μὴ ἐλάττω ἑξακισχιλίων γένοιτο. According to Raubitschek, the present syntax (ὅτῳ πλεῖστα γένοιτο καὶ μὴ ἐλάττω ἑξακισχιλίων) seems to be treating the phrase καὶ μὴ ἐλάττω ἑξακισχιλίων as an addition, allowing us to understand the whole in the following way: 'after [the ostraka] were counted, the person for whom the most were cast, provided that not less than 6000 were cast overall.'[140] This would remove the contradiction between Philochorus and Plutarch, making the latter correct. I do not think that Raubitschek's reasoning is entirely convincing. However, Robert Develin, who rejected it, had to content himself with the conclusion that Philochorus completely misunderstood his source (here the text of the law about ostracism) and simply erred in his description of the *ostrakophoria* procedure, ascribing to it the prerequisite of a qualified majority of 6000 votes.[141]

On a different occasion, Raubitschek spotted another syntactic issue impacting our understanding of another passage in Philochorus' fragment, namely the phrase stating the duration of exile: [...] τοῦτον ἔδει τὰ δίκαια δόντα καὶ λαβόντα ὑπὲρ τῶν ἰδίων συναλλαγμάτων ἐν δέκα ἡμέραις μεταστῆναι τῆς πόλεως ἔτη δέκα (ὕστερον δὲ ἐγένοντο πέντε)—'[...] this

---

[140] 'Nach einer Zählung, wem die meisten (Stimmen) zukamen und *von* nicht weniger als sechstausend...', a translation of this ambiguous passage equally possible as 'Nach einer Zählung, wem die meisten (Stimmen) zukamen und nicht weniger als sechstausend...' (Raubitschek (1955b) 120).
[141] Develin (1985b).

man had to tender and exact settlements concerning his personal arrangements within ten days, to relocate from the city-state for ten years (but later it became five)'.[142] Raubitschek pointed out that the phrase in brackets (ὕστερον δὲ ἐγένοντο πέντε) should grammatically refer to the number of days allowed for the settlement of the prospective exile's commitments in Athens, and not to the alleged five-year duration of exile (unattested otherwise). Thanks to this observation, the scholar restored order, making Philochorus' text compatible with our idea of the ostracism procedure.

This conclusion of Raubitschek's was also criticised by Develin, who admits that the use of a plural verb with a neuter plural noun increases gradually, beginning in the Hellenistic times,[143] but at the same time finds classical analogies to this structure.[144] Having thus defended the widely accepted interpretation of Philochorus' text, Develin had to conclude again that the writer made a serious factual error, given that we know that the duration of the exile of the ostracised was never reduced by half (see below, section 3.3.2). Such a solution was rightly opposed already by Felix Jacoby. He excluded the possibility of such an error made by Philochorus but admitted the possibility of him misunderstanding his (hypothetically divergent) sources of information.[145]

Meanwhile, the formal observations made by Raubitschek in both these cases deserve attention, but on the other hand, based on them, he seems to make historical inferences that are too far-fetched. I believe that the syntax imperfections in the text of Philochorus' fragment had an entirely different origin. Both the phrases suspected by Raubitschek could have simply been parentheses, breaking the natural flow of Philochorus' (or his source's) prose in an unfortunate way. In the light of my considerations presented up to this point, I suggest that the text of the relevant parts of fragment 30 of Philochorus could be read in the following way:

[...] διαριθμηθέντων δὲ ὅτῳ πλεῖστα γένοιτο (καὶ μὴ ἐλάττω ἑξακισχιλίων), τοῦτον ἔδει τὰ δίκαια δόντα καὶ λαβόντα ὑπὲρ τῶν ἰδίων συναλλαγμάτων ἐν

---

[142] Raubitschek (1958) 102–103.
[143] Develin (1985b) 30. Cf. Schwyzer (1950) 607–608.
[144] E.g., Thuc. VI 62,4. Theoretically, such 'Hellenistic' grammatical phenomena could indicate a later interpolation in a given passage of Thucydides' text; regular occurrence of interpolations in this author (and Herodotus) has been studied and presented in a series of articles by Benedetto Bravo (see, e.g., Bravo (2000)). However, in this case such suspicions would be groundless. The present form of this sentence can admittedly be due to a simple scribal error, but with this word order, the syntax looks convincing.
[145] Jacoby, FGrHist IIIb Suppl. I 317. In general, cf. Heftner (2018) 95–96.

δέκα ἡμέραις μεταστῆναι τῆς πόλεως ἔτη δέκα (ὕστερον δὲ ἐγένοντο πέντε), καρπούμενον τὰ ἑαυτοῦ, μὴ ἐπιβαίνοντα ἐντὸς Γεραιστοῦ τοῦ Εὐβοίας ἀκρωτηρίου [...].

[...] After [the ostraka] were counted, the person for whom the most [ostraka] were cast (and not less than six thousand) had to, after tendering and exacting settlements concerning his personal arrangements within ten days, relocate from the city-state for ten years (but later it became five years), enjoying [during this time] the use of his property [in Attica], but staying outside [the territory delineated by] Geraestus, the promontory of Euboia [...].

Let us take another look at the two (hypothetically) parenthetic sentences (καὶ μὴ ἐλάττω ἑξακισχιλίων[146] and ὕστερον δὲ ἐγένοντο πέντε). I believe that Theophrastus, Philochorus' immediate source, used in his part of the account the text of the original law about ostracism, still available back then, most probably in the version inscribed in stone.[147] Showing a strong interest in the institutions and legal procedures in the Athenian *polis*, he decided to supplement in two places his quotation, or perhaps rather the paraphrase, of the relevant passage of this law with erudite glosses, which I put here in brackets.[148] Apparently, he considered such complementation necessary. On the one hand, he saw fit to include the gloss about the tempering of the original law,[149] and on the other hand, he added the note

---

[146] The phrase (εἰ δὲ μὴ γένοιτο ἑξακισχίλια, οὐ μεθίστατο – 'if there were not six thousand [ostraka], he did not leave'; tr. W. W. Fortenbaugh) regarding the so-called 'void ostracism' (actually, only repeating the note on the 'quorum' of 6000) can be read in the scholion to Aristophanes' *Knights* (855B) exactly where the three other longer testimonies of the 'great scholion about ostracism' give the provisions of the law regarding the terms of the exile. These excerpts from the law of ostracism are here missing. It looks as if, when abbreviating Didymus' notice, a later commentator or scholiast of Aristophanes, uninterested in the details of the historical law, replaced its provisions by the repetitive and platitudinous words quoted above.

[147] See above, pp. 123–124, with n. 21, on the 'codification' of Nicomachus.

[148] It cannot be excluded that the same author also made a third intervention, altering the 'geography' of the exile of the ostracised from 'within' to 'beyond' the Geraestus promontory (see also below, 3.3.1). Especially if we agree that Philochorus' text is complete here and do not assume a lacuna where information about the other, opposite geographical border would be expected, we could conclude that somebody purposefully introduced a correction into the text of the ostracism law (or its paraphrase), assuming that a natural place of exile for wealthy Athenians would be the area to the north of the southern end of Euboea, thus encompassing Thessaly, Thrace, and finally Macedon. For this was exactly where many famous Athenians of the fifth and the beginning of the fourth century BC went: Thucydides, Critias, Euripides, tragedians, but also more recently Demosthenes and Aristotle.

[149] We shall never know for certain whether this information was true or arose from the ideological conviction about the fundamental 'mildness' of the Athenian people, held by

about the 6000 ostraka. This last insertion was ambiguous from the beginning (i.a. because of the series of unconnected genitives it created) and could have referred equally well to the quorum or to the qualified majority, even though I suspect that the author meant the 6000 quorum of *ostrakophoria*. Intellectually, the two (hypothetical) glosses seem mutually consistent. These 'supplementations' were probably motivated by the author's erudite and ideological profile. The unverified piece of information about reducing the traditional ostracism sentence appeared to him plausible enough.[150] In a similar vein, writing about an institution which ceased to be used around 100 years before his times, Theophrastus—convinced of the inherent 'mildness' (*praotēs*) of the Athenian *dēmos*[151]—must have been seriously disturbed by the thought that an Athenian citizen could be 'sentenced' to long-term exile without a court trial.[152] Therefore, he assumed that ostracism operated on the principle which he knew very well from the practice of the fourth-century Athenian democracy. Granting citizenship, granting *adeia*, and applying the law *ad hominem* to individual citizens all required reaching the quorum of 6000 votes at the Assembly—always in voting with *psēphoi*, and not by a show of hands.[153] Naturally, regarding *ostrakophoria* as a type of secret ballot using *psēphoi*,[154] he concluded that also here the rule of 6000 votes must have been in force. It is worth emphasising that the expression added by Theophrastus, καὶ μὴ ἐλάττω ἑξακισχιλίων, also occurs in the fragments of two laws quoted by Demosthenes in his speech *Against Timocrates*.[155] This

---

Aristotle and his disciples. I am inclined to believe in an arbitrary decision of Philochorus' source, possibly guided here by the analogy with the Syracusan *petalismos*, which must have been regarded as an institution fundamentally similar to the Athenian ostracism. And rightly so.

[150] Cf. below, 3.3.2, on the duration of the exile.
[151] Cf. above, pp. 74–75.
[152] Cf. a similar concern of a certain fourth-century Athenian orator, the author of the speech ascribed to Andocides, IV [*Against Alcibiades*] 3.
[153] The relevant testimonies have been conveniently gathered and engagingly discussed by Hansen (1983) 10–16. Cf. already Fränkel (1877) 14–19. Meiggs (1964) very tentatively suggests that 6000 might have originally been used as being a fifth of 30000 'Athenian adult males enrolled on the deme registers at the time of Cleisthenes' reforms', but this inference looks rather far-fetched.
[154] A similar association may be found in Pollux, 8.16–20, esp. at 8.19.
[155] Dem. XXIV, 45 (granting *adeia*: [...] ἐὰν μὴ ψηφισαμένων Ἀθηναίων τὴν ἄδειαν πρῶτον μὴ ἔλαττον ἑξακισχιλίων, οἷς ἂν δόξῃ κρύβδην ψηφιζομένοις) and Dem. XXIV, 59 (the law *ad hominem*: <ἐὰν μὴ> ψηφισαμένων μὴ ἔλαττον ἑξακισχιλίων οἷς ἂν δόξῃ κρύβδην ψηφιζομένοις) (see also Andocides [I], *On the mysteries*, 87; cf. Dem. XXIII, 86 and Dem. XLVI, 12 *ad fin*.). The fact that the latter passage of Demosthenes XXIV might have been a result of a forger's work (thus Canevaro (2013) 145–150) should not alarm us. It is only natural that the erudite forger had to pattern his text on the passages from orators known to him (e.g., Dem. XXIV, 45) or, as in the case of Theophrastus, on some other law known to him.

seems to confirm that specific provisions of Athenian laws provided the inspiration for one of the glosses.[156]

In the light of the results I have obtained so far, the original provisions of the law about ostracism regarding *ostrakophoria*, while consulted and quoted but before being glossed upon by Theophrastus, might have been formulated in the following or similar manner:

> After the votes [are] counted, the person for whom the most ostraka [were] cast [has] to, after legally settling his business, relocate from the *polis* within ten days for the period of ten years, enjoying [during this time] the use of his property [in Attica] [...].

In other words, there was no quorum in the procedure of *ostrakophoria*, but only the principle of the simple majority of votes cast against the 'sentenced' through ostracism. The version cited very briefly by Diodorus (XI 55,2), following his source (Ephorus? Theopompus?), proves to be correct in this respect.[157]

Although the lawgiver expected that on the day of *ostrakophoria*, the turnout on the Athenian Agora would be very high, the core of this idea was to efficiently carry out a kind of voting which, regardless of the turnout or distribution of votes, would result in the exile from Athens of one of the accomplished citizens. It is worth noting that the one-stage character of *ostrakophoria*—i.e., the fact that the Athenians did not choose from among a pre-determined pool of 'suspects', nor did they allow for defence or even provide an opportunity for specific accusations to be formulated—could in extreme situations lead to a completely random selection, regarded by the citizens themselves as wrong, as it was in the case of Hyperbolus. This shows that the lawgiver did not have a just sentence for the guilty in mind, but something entirely different.[158]

---

[156] Heftner (2003) 30, the other way around, thinks that it was this provision of the ostracism law that inspired the lawgiver who introduced the law quoted by Demosthenes and by Andocides.

[157] Cf., however, below, 3.3.2, on the issue of the duration of the exile through ostracism.

[158] I think it can partly be explained through an analogy. Slightly similar might have been the situation of voting on the winning play in the Athenian theatre. Ultimately, only five out of 10 votes cast by the judges were selected and counted to come up with the results, with more votes chosen if necessary to break a tie. To put it coarsely perhaps, what was important was reaching a clear result and not doing justice to the actual value of the performances involved as evaluated by the judges. For technical details of the process of judging dramatic contests in Athens and for competing scholarly theories on how to understand our ancient testimonies on the matter, see Csapo, Slater (1995) 157–165, esp. 158–160 (recently, see also a reassessment of this procedure

This observation should encourage us to return to the Cleisthenian idea of a double procedure of ostracism, consisting of the preliminary vote at the Athenian Assembly and the decisive vote with ostraka on the *ostrakophoria* day.

3.2.6 The Hypothetical 'Quorum' of the *Epicheirotonia* of Ostracism in the Fifth Century BC

If my conclusions stand, on the one hand, there was no prerequisite of a quorum or a qualified majority during *ostrakophoria*. On the other hand, one might usually expect a high turnout on the day of *ostrakophoria*. If so, my earlier results become even more striking, namely the hypothesis that throughout the (roughly) 90 years of the history of ostracism, merely 14 cases at most (and probably only 12) of ostracising an Athenian politician actually occurred. In other words, it becomes a burning issue why a procedure so important to the Athenians—and one arousing so strong (negative) emotions, as we shall see in the final chapter of this book—ended up being carried out effectively so rarely. Surprisingly, this question, as far as I can see, is never asked by scholars studying ostracism, even though it may be of fundamental significance for understanding the lawgiver's primary intentions.

As R. Develin rightly pointed out in his analysis of fragment 30 of Philochorus, the aforementioned Athenian laws requiring the quorum of 6000 *psēphoi* in matters such as *adeia* (or indemnity), granting citizenship, and several other regulations *ad hominem* (νόμοι ἐπ' ἀνδρί) 'fall in the same conceptual area as ostracism'.[159] However, these observations should not be regarded as referring to *ostrakophoria* (as they were by this scholar) but to the preliminary vote at the Assembly.[160] If we consider the rarity of the actual application of ostracism in Athens as proven, we are forced to assume

---

by Marshall, van Willigenburg (2004)). Incidentally, E. Csapo and W. J. Slater interpret these procedures simply as 'enormous precautions taken by the state' against corruption, bribery, and manipulation in the process.

[159] Develin (1985b) 26. See already Carcopino (1935) 98–99.

[160] Gauthier (2011) 425–435, interestingly discusses parallels between three 'democratic institutions' for which the number of 6000 votes (or 6000 citizens) is attested, namely the 'six thousand Athenians' serving as heliasts, the vote of *ostrakophoria* (in the majority interpretation), and the aforementioned decisions of the Assembly ('but there may have been others [of the kind]', as Gauthier (2011) 427 soberly observes). This scholar, however, rightly points out the exceptional character, in such a context, of the (hypothetical) *ostrakophoria* vote ('[...] la

that the Ekklēsia gathering annually in the sixth prytany (or on a day equivalent to this date in the times preceding the introduction of the prytany calendar) almost always voted against carrying out the ostracism procedure and that it decided to execute *ostrakophoria* only in exceptional situations.

I think that the only technically viable explanation of such a state of affairs is a very high quorum, or rather, what we would today call a 'quorum', required for such a decision to be made. The 'conceptual' similarity between ostracism and various other regulations or decrees *ad hominem* in the fourth-century Athenian law may suggest an analogical rule applied in the fifth century in the preliminary vote of the ostracism procedure. Our sources, including *A.P.*, are silent on this topic, of course, but detailed information of this kind can be found almost exclusively in random mentions by fourth-century orators. *A.P.* never engages with such details, probably considering them too obvious and/or of secondary importance. Significantly, as already mentioned above, a quorum as high as 6000 (Dem. XXIV [*Against Timocrates*] 45 and 59) in the fourth century, perhaps existing in the Athenian law already at the end of the fifth century BC (Andoc. I [*On mysteries*] 87)[161] corresponded with the conviction about the (symbolic) participation of 'all the Athenians' in the vote (Dem. XXIV, 48: [...] εἰ πᾶσιν Ἀθηναίοις ἐδόκει [...]).[162] I think that the 'quorum' of the preliminary vote in the ostracism procedure was perceived similarly.

Is it possible to see a fifth-century equivalent of the fourth-century quorum of 6000 in an enigmatic epigraphic formula attested only in one Attic inscription, *IG* I³ 105 (see also the commentary on this inscription in the AIO edition)? It is the text of laws regarding the Council of Five Hundred of ca. 409 BC, most probably included in the 'codification' by Nicomachus. There appears several times the negative formula, 'without [the

---

distinction nécessaire entre voix exprimées et voix hostiles ne permet pas, à elle seule, de rendre compte de l'ostrakophorie de manière satisfaisante', Gauthier (2011) 427). In his conclusions, logically, he finds the vote of *ostrakophoria* ultimately unsuitable for the functions he ascribes to other parallel cases he studies, and hence, in his opinion, it must have been abandoned by the Athenians (Gauthier (2011) 453). It must be said that these ingenious analyses by Gauthier would excellently fit in with the vote of *epicheirotonia* in the Assembly instead of *ostrakophoria* (save for one aspect, the open character of the former).

[161] It should be remembered (see above, pp. 170-171 with n. 155) that Canevaro and Harris (2012) 116-119 (see also Canevaro (2013) 'Index locorum', *s.loc.*) regard the quotation from the law in Andocides (and in Dem. XXIV 59) as a late insertion. However, if they are right, this passage was probably modelled on Demosthenes' text.

[162] Cf. Gauthier (2011) 432.

decision of] the Athenian people gathered *en masse*' (ἄνευ τō δέμο τō Ἀθεναίον πλεθύοντος).[163] It restricts the actions of the Boulē with regard to individual Athenians, but also in matters of utmost importance to the state, such as starting or ending a war. For a long time, scholars interpreted this formulation as identical with the concept of a 'plenary session' of the Ekklēsia, but Hansen effectively questioned this view, claiming instead that this formula reflects merely the idea of the decision being made by the Assembly (and not the Boulē).[164]

Even if we accept that the phantom of 'plenary assemblies' as distinct from ordinary assemblies (and from *ekklēsiai kyriai*, or 'main sessions' of the Assembly; cf. above, pp. 124–127) needs to be put out to pasture, the formula ὁ δῆμος πληθύων seems to be too sophisticated an expression to just denote the Assembly. 'People gathered *en masse*' is not quite a proportional opposition to the Boulē either.[165] Further on, the inscription mentions simply the Boulē and the Ekklēsia (for instance, ll. 53–55). Moreover, the set of restrictions imposed on the Council of Five Hundred through this formula may be an indication that the *dēmos* limited the Boulē's prerogatives in exceptional situations, such as matters of fundamental importance to the entire community (for instance, war or peace) or issues critical for individual citizens (for instance, death penalty or a fine imposed on somebody, perhaps a significant amount). Furthermore, it seems that one of the restrictions in this inscription (preserved only in fragments, unfortunately) applies at the same time to the Boulē and to the *dēmos* ([...] τὸν δὲ δῆμον μὲ ἔναι [...]), i.e., the Assembly, most probably, I think, contrasting with the prerogatives of the 'people gathered *en masse*' (ll. 39–41).

Meanwhile, Françoise Ruzé has studied two inscriptions (and referred to a third one; see below) from outside the Athenian *polis*, which offer close analogies with *IG* I³ 105.[166] Two of them, coming from Olympia from the end of the sixth century BC (*IvO* 3 = *Nomima* I.108 and *IvO* 7 = *Nomima* I.109),[167] establish a special condition for a particularly important decision

---

[163] For δῆμος πληθύων as 'the people in the assembly' in general, see esp. Rhodes (1972) 197–198 (with earlier discussions); Ostwald (1986) 31–42 and more recently Valdés-Guía (2021) 210–211, with further bibliography. But cf. Ruzé (1997) 412–416.
[164] Hansen (1983) 7–8, 140–141.
[165] Ruzé (1997) 412 is similarly critical in this matter.
[166] The inscriptions have been mentioned in this context already by Rhodes (1972) 197 n. 3.
[167] But cf. *LSAG*², 220, nos. 9 and 5 (with Pl. 42,5), for the date ca. 475? BC and ca. 500 BC, respectively.

to be valid, most probably under special circumstances. Namely, a decision (or some other negative provision, in the case of the very fragmentary inscription *IvO* 3) will only be made in the presence of the Council and the 'people gathered *en masse*'.[168] In the light of the inscriptions from Olympia, the Attic formula may be deemed fairly traditional and rendering the idea of a massive 'quorum', albeit not expressed in numeral terms.[169] It can be assumed that the concept of a high 'quorum' required at the Assembly for matters of exceptional importance existed already in the fifth century and definitely in the times when the oath of the Council members was formulated. Oswyn Murray suggested to me that the formula τοῦ δήμου πληθύοντος could visually express the idea of the Assembly's quorum, analogically to the formula ἀγορῆς πληθυούσης, referring to the time of day when the market is filled with the crowd of people doing business.[170] It is a situation where 'people [tightly] fill in' the gathering place (such as Pnyx I, for instance), which might have served as an 'optical quorum' of the Assembly.[171] It is precisely the kind of formula expected in the original law about ostracism to denote the requirement[172] which made the decision to activate this procedure extremely difficult. It would be dependent on a very high turnout at the Assembly, i.e., on a large-scale mobilisation of the Athenian *dēmos* already

---

[168] Ruzé (1997) 413. *IvO* 7 l. 4: σὺν βολαῖ πεντακατίον ἀϝλανέος καὶ δέμοι πληθύοντι δινάκοι ('[...] qu'on le change en toute securité avec le conseil des Cinque-Cents et le peuple en masse', tr. F. Ruzé) and *IvO* 3 l. 8) ἄνευς βōλὰν καὶ ζᾶμον πλαθύοντα ('... sans le Conseil et le peuple en masse', tr. F. Ruzé).

[169] Ruzé (1997) 413–414 argues hypothetically for the reasons why the numeric 'quorum' would be difficult in the fifth century BC and why the Athenians might have felt the need to use this formula in 409 BC.

[170] See *LSJ*⁹, s.v. Agora IV.

[171] And indeed, a fourth-century honorific inscription from Delphi (*Syll*³ 257, l. 15, of 340/339 BC) mentions special honours for the citizens of Histiaea voted 'in the full agora' (πληθούσης ἀγορᾶς), thus confirming, I believe, the visual origins of this formula, which at the time might have no longer been clear to the Delphians, though. It seems that in standard formulas of full decrees, 98 in total between the third century and the first half of the first century BC, this expression is perhaps mirrored by another one: ἐν ἀγορᾶι τελείωι σὺμ ψάφοις ταῖς ἐννόμοις, 'in fully constituted/valid agora, with the number of votes required by laws' (tr. D. Grzesik). Cf. Grzesik (2021). I thank Dominika Grzesik for our discussion of these formulae.

[172] Cf. already Glotz (1968) [1928] 180. As Hansen (1983) 122 rightly points out, H. Thompson and R. E. Wycherley in *Agora 14*, 51 abuse the evidence by ascribing the quorum of 6000 both to the preliminary vote on ostracism at the Assembly and to *ostrakophoria* without any arguments.

at the preliminary stage of the ostracism procedure (at the extreme, two months in advance of the potential vote on the actual exile on the day of *ostrakophoria*).

Having accepted this interpretation, we need to note the critical difference between the 'high quorum' of the Assembly in the fifth (and already at the end of the sixth) century on the one hand and in the fourth century on the other. It would not be surprising that the more politically formalistic Athenians of the fourth century replaced with *psēphoi* voting one by a show of hands, hypothetically applied in similar matters in the previous epoch.[173] In the case of the 'political fossil' (see above, 2.2.4), which the preliminary vote on ostracism in the sixth prytany was, the traditional solution remained in force, even though from 'around 416' BC it did not entail any practical consequences.

It may not be insignificant here that the terminology of this voting, still in use when *A.P.* (43.5) was written, does not correspond to the more general fourth-century usage. The London papyrus of *A.P.* has ἐπιχειροτονίαν [διδόασιν] in this place, which Kaibel and Wilamowitz-Moellendorff corrected in their edition to προχειροτονίαν.[174] Rhodes (*ad loc.*) states that he would rather expect διαχειροτονίαν here (as in *A.P.* 49.2)[175] because it was actually a choice between two alternatives. The use of the term ἐπιχειροτονία a bit earlier in *A.P.* 43.4 (and 37.1) to mean 'a vote approving a proposal' is radically different than a vote for or against applying the procedure of ostracism in *A.P.* 43.5.[176] All things considered, I believe that the terminology of the last passage corresponds to the earlier use, less systematic than that of the fourth century. The decision to keep this terminology could have been motivated by the same political conservatism which made the Athenians repeatedly vote against ostracism every year (but see below, 'Epilogue and Conclusions'). Perhaps in the law about ostracism

---

[173] Especially given that, as Hansen (2004) [1977] convincingly argued, in the case of voting by a show of hands at the Assembly, the vote counting was merely an estimate and the result was decided based on visual majority by *proedroi* in the fourth century, and earlier by the *prytaneis*. Cf. also Boegehold (1963).

[174] In the edition Kaibel-Wilamowitz, following the wording of F 30 of Philochorus (and more precisely, the relevant text in the *Lexicon rhetoricum Cantabrigiense*) and sch Ar. *Eq.* 855; however, later on they withdrew from this view.

[175] Similarly, Mortimer Chambers, following Rhodes, in the critical apparatus to his edition of *A.P.*, even though he keeps ἐπιχειροτονίαν in the text.

[176] Cf. Rhodes, *ad* 43.4 and *ad* 37.1.

available back then (within Nicomachus' 'codification'?) the relevant passage still read ἐπιχειροτονίαν (*vel sim.*).

3.3 The Issue of the Potential Evolution of Ostracism in Athens in the Fifth Century BC

As I have already emphasised, the question about the possible evolution of the law about ostracism, i.e., the changes it was subject to throughout the 90 years when it was in use, is of fundamental significance to my argument. I believe that in this chapter, I have managed to establish the most important and consequential fact. The two-stage procedure of this institution was not a result of a late modification of this law but was already in place in the 30s of the fifth century at the latest—i.e., before the scandal of 'around 416 BC', which could have theoretically induced the Athenians to implement legal changes to prevent deviations in its working in the future. Therefore, it is very probable that this principle was in force from the very beginning, especially given that, as we have seen, the author of *A.P.* was convinced that the law about ostracism was altered only once, right before Xerxes' expedition. Ps.-Aristotle could have been mistaken, of course, but the burden of proof rests now rather upon the supporters of the thesis about a significant evolution of this law.

Nevertheless, the account of *A.P.* should encourage us to investigate one more issue, of lesser importance, namely the possible evolution of the geography of exile under the law about ostracism. On the other hand, the silence of *A.P.* in another matter, combined with a cursory mention of this issue in a different source (or rather a set of sources of common origin), forces us to consider the possibility of a change in the duration of the exile threatening the victims of Athenian ostracism.

3.3.1 The Puzzle of the Geography of Exile in the Law about Ostracism

The geography of exile in the law about ostracism has been studied from two different points of view so far, with the naturally accompanying search for a way to reconcile them. On the one hand, the analyses focused on philological problems in texts providing information on this topic (mainly, but not exclusively, *A.P.*). On the other hand, on the possible motivations of the

Athenians imposing restrictions on the exiled regarding their movement outside Athens during the 10 years of forced absence from their homeland.[177] Admittedly, the pictures emerging from these two perspectives are not always reconcilable. In such a situation, the final say belongs to our ancient texts and establishing the only possible reading should theoretically settle the argument decisively. However, the matter is not so simple. In *A.P.* 22.8, we read (tr. P. J. Rhodes, slightly modified):

> In the fourth year they received back all the men who had been ostracised, in the archonship of Hypsichides,[178] on account of Xerxes' campaign; and for the future they defined for the ostracised that they should settle between Geraestus and Scyllaeum, or else they should be completely *atimoi*.

In the London papyrus (and perhaps also in the Berlin one), we find the following definition of the area where the exile is supposed to be spent: ἐντὸς Γεραιστοῦ καὶ Σκυλλαίου κατοικεῖν. Already in 1891, in a collective note suggesting emendations to a newly discovered text of *A.P.*,[179] William Wyse proposed a change to ἐκτός, 'outside' (p. 112, cf. p. 274 in the same issue of 'Classical Review'), arguing that Argos is to the west of the Scyllaeum promontory and Samos is to the east of Geraestus. Since both these places became exile destinations for Athenians expelled after the Persian Wars (Themistocles and Hyperbolus, respectively), a trivial mistake must have crept into the text of *A.P.* John E. Sandys supported Wyse's remark in the same note, referring to *Lexicon rhetoricum Cantabrigiense*, or one of the texts of our 'great scholion about ostracism' (= fragment 30 of Philochorus), which says: μὴ ἐπιβαίνοντα ἐντὸς Γεραιστοῦ τοῦ Εὐβοίας ἀκρωτηρίου ('not overstepping (the boundary) within Geraestus, the promontory of Euboia')—even though this passage is a result of an audacious but ingenious emendation by Peter Dobree, as in the manuscript we read ἐντὸς πέρα τοῦ.[180] Thus corrected, the text was accepted in the editions by Frederic G. Kenyon (in his first edition), Sandys, Mortimer Chambers, and most editors in general. Kaibel, in turn, proposed keeping the ἐντός from the papyrus but adding the negation <μή>, also based on the cited fragment of Philochorus (μὴ ἐπιβαίνοντα ἐντὸς [...]), against his co-editor of *A.P.*, Wilamowitz.[181]

---

[177] See esp. Figueira (1987).
[178] The date of this archonship is vividly debated—see Figueira (1987) n. 2.
[179] 'Notes on the text of the *ΑΘΗΝΑΙΩΝ ΠΟΛΙΤΕΙΑ*', CR 5 (1891), 105–119.
[180] Dobree suggested this emendation in the text of *Lexicon rhetoricum Cantabrigiense*.
[181] Cf. Wilamowitz-Moellendorf (1893) v. 1, 114.

On the strictly philological level, the arguments presented by both parties to the dispute seem to remain in balance. As Rhodes (*ad loc.*, p. 282) points out, it is difficult to use the lexicographic tradition (especially given that it has been emended)[182] to correct *A.P.*, mainly because it is precisely in this tradition where there appears only one reference point in the geography of ostracism, which may indicate that this tradition has been corrupt.

For this reason, scholars have to use historical arguments, and more precisely, hypotheses regarding the possible motivations of the Athenians to change or supplement the law about ostracism on the eve of the war against Xerxes. Two schools of thought can be distinguished here. One of them—with Wilamowitz as a pioneer (Wilamowitz-Moellendorf (1893) v. 1, 114)—points out that at that time the Athenians would have cared mainly to cut off important Athenian politicians who fell out of favour with the people from any possible contact with the Persians. Others, including the author of a recent extensive study on the topic, Thomas Figueira, argue the opposite, pointing out the necessity to make it impossible for the exiles to influence Athenian politics.[183] Both the parties can refer here to an additional source, the 'Decree of Themistocles' (discussed above), ordering the victims of ostracism to gather on the island of Salamis and await the decision of the *dēmos*. It can be argued that since this document (inscribed in Troizen in the third century, compiled in the fourth century BC, but most probably using the fifth-century original one or ones) sends them to Salamis, the Athenians assumed that the majority of those ostracised thitherto were in the area of the Saronic Gulf, most likely in Aegina. Thus, decreeing that the exiles should be staying outside this area would be a novelty in the law about ostracism (Figueira). Or, on the contrary, summoning them to Salamis may already be the first step in the change aimed at taking more control over the actions of the ostracised politicians.

Investigating the fortunes of exiles from the times after the Persian Wars will be of little help to us either. Cimon indeed stayed on Aegina, but we do not know for how long. We hear that Themistocles, in turn, stayed in Argos and Hyperbolus on Samos. Cimon allegedly appeared at some point also near Tanagra in Boeotia. However, as Figueira brilliantly observes,[184] the manner in which the restriction is formulated (two promontories on two

---

[182] The Berlin papyrus of the *Lexicon Demosthenicum* (see above) is hopelessly corrupt in this place and we cannot verify the text of the *Lexicon Cantabrigiense*.
[183] Figueira (1987), with earlier bibliography on the topic.
[184] Figueira (1987) 289–290.

edges of an area encompassing the Attic shore and the Saronic Gulf) indicates that the lawgiver assumed that the ostracised leave Athens by sea, which must have been more practical and easier to control. Although Figueira claims that we shall reach decisive conclusions by studying exiles' destinations, his observation undermines our confidence in this matter. Namely, on the eve of Xerxes' expedition, a restriction he postulates would have a completely different meaning than later on, after the Persian Wars. Before, it would be about cutting off the sentenced from any contact with the Athenians and preventing them from impacting the political life in Athens in any way; even though we hear about Athenian exiles staying mainly on the Peloponnese, this provision would be in force wherever they went, in compliance with its (hypothetical) aim. After the Persian Wars, in turn, as the Athenian *archē* was expanding in the Aegean and as Athenian cleruchies were established and Athenian magistrates increasingly managed the maritime 'empire', a law formulated in such a manner would lose its *raison d'être*. Besides, it would probably require another change, which is precluded by the discourse in *A.P.*

One can add another element to this discussion. The fragmentarily preserved provisions determining the lot of the ostracised politicians abroad ('[...] enjoying [during this time] the use of his property [in Attica]') indicate that the lawgiver assumed their constant (even though not personal, of course) contact with their city. In my view, this is the only way to understand the clause that they can enjoy their property during all this time. According to this logic, their residence at a relatively small distance from Attica seems more probable. Then again, also from this point of view, this provision would have a diametrically different meaning before and after the Persian Wars.

Yet another argument can be added, this time source-critical, for maintaining the reading of the *A.P.* papyrus (or papyri) and concluding that the exiles were supposed to remain in the future under the vigilant eye of the Athenians within the boundaries of the Saronic Gulf, i.e., most probably mainly on Aegina, perhaps also in Troezen or Megara. Unlike Figueira, I suppose that the manner in which *A.P.*, on the one hand, and Philochorus as well as the lexicographic tradition on the other, speak about this matter might have arisen from their divergent sources, and not from a single source, which this scholar identifies with an Atthidographer, perhaps Androtion. It should be noted that Philochorus and his successors mention the geography of exile under the ostracism law in connection with the general appraisal of this law (unavoidably referring to the scandalous case of expelling

Hyperbolus) and/or with the selective list of the Athenians ostracised during the entire period when this law remained in force (sch vet Ar. *Eq.* 855B 10: Aristides, Cimon, Themistocles, Thucydides, Alcibiades). If the departure point of this tradition was Theophrastus, he could have been tempted to reconcile the widely available pieces of information regarding the fate of Themistocles (Argos and the Peloponnese) and Hyperbolus (Samos) with the text of the relevant provision within the law about ostracism. Whereas *A.P.*, most likely following Androtion, placed the Athenians' decision in this matter in the context of recalling the exiled (probably from various parts of the Greek world) to the vicinity of Athens, disregarding the places of residence of the politicians exiled in later times, and thus not committing the (hypothetical) anachronism to which Theophrastus and his successors fell victims. However, against this last idea an objection can naturally be raised. Namely, if this was the case, two coevals, colleagues, and collaborators in the circle of Aristotle, Theophrastus and the anonymous writer of *A.P.* would radically differ on that matter, however minor for them. This is, of course, not inconceivable.

Therefore, even though it is not possible to state with certainty whether the exiled were henceforth supposed to reside 'within' or 'outside' the Saronic Gulf, I am, hesitantly, inclined towards the first option. However, most important for my considerations is that the author of *A.P.* regarded the amendment to the earlier law about ostracism as final and theoretically still remaining in force in his times. I suppose that such was the version his source found in the legal regulations in this matter still available in Athens back then. I have already emphasised that in the *A.P.* narrative it seems to be the only substantial change in this law, according to Ps.-Aristotle's knowledge. We have to keep this in mind while considering our next problem.

3.3.2 The Duration of Exile from Athens in the Law about Ostracism

The question about the length of the period of exile resulting from the people's decision in *ostrakophoria* arises from the existence in our corpus of sources of two 'exotic' testimonies, clearly contradicting the main current in the tradition about ostracism. If we were able to assess the historical reliability of sources representing this variant, we should theoretically be able to solve this problem. However, it does not suffice, even if many scholars are content with such conclusions. It needs to be established as well where the alternative version comes from. This question, in turn, naturally led some scholars of ostracism to assume an evolution of this institution and a hypothetical change in the length of the 'sentence' at some point in its history.

Our sources consistently state a 10-year ostracism 'punishment'. Only Philochorus, in a 'supplementation' of the ostracism law inherited from Theophrastus,[185] and Diodorus mention a five-year exile. The latter does it in a brief discussion of this issue accompanying the story about ostracising Themistocles (XI 55,2). On the one hand, he mentions a five-year exile there, and on the other hand—a simple majority of ostraka required in *ostrakophoria*. While the latter piece of information is confirmed by the analyses I have carried out above, the former contradicts what we know about ostracism from elsewhere, so it begs all the more so an investigation of the possible sources of this version.

Diodorus is probably following in his story his main source for these parts of the *Library*, i.e., Ephorus.[186] However, it is intriguing that the brief description of the character of ostracism (beginning with the words: ὁ δὲ νόμος ἐγένετο τοιοῦτος) is concluded with a general thought suggesting that the Athenian ostracism was not a punishment for offences, but a preventive mechanism aimed against 'people of excessive prominence' in the *polis*,[187] which very much resembles Aristotle's views on this topic.[188] I cannot see a good solution to this aporia unless by ascribing to this passage in Diodorus an inquisitiveness not particularly characteristic for him, which made him reach for an additional source coming from the peripatetic circle. However, this does not seem very probable, so perhaps it would be better to assume that by Diodorus' times, this simple idea had already been appropriated by the majority of educated Greeks taking an interest in the history of Athens. However, for my considerations, it suffices to note that Diodorus returns to

---

[185] Raubitschek (1958) 102–103 proposed to understand the 'five' in Philochorus' text as referring to the number of days allowed for the settlement of the exile's commitments, and not to the duration of exile. Such an interpretation seems very tenuous to me, particularly in the light of the existence of a certain tradition about a five-year exile, which Philochorus' source might have known.

[186] Raubitschek (1958) 93–96 unconvincingly argued that Diodorus' source here must have been Timaeus of Tauromenium. Werner (1958) in turn claimed that the entire ancient tradition about ostracism originates in Ephorus, which cannot be excluded, but neither can it be proven. See below.

[187] D.S. XI 55,3: [...] οὐχ ἵνα τὴν κακίαν κολάζωσιν, ἀλλ' ἵνα τὰ φρονήματα τῶν ὑπερεχόντων ταπεινότερα γένηται διὰ τὴν φυγήν.

[188] See Raubitschek (1958) 93–97.

his thought slightly further in the same book while drawing a comparison between Athenian ostracism and Syracusan *petalismos* (XI 87, 1–2). To both the institutions he ascribes the same motive of protecting the *polis* against the citizen who threatens the city with tyranny most.

Whatever Diodorus' source here, it is clear that the historian is using the same 'note' once again. A comparison of the manner in which Diodorus writes about ostracism and *petalismos* reveals[189] that the five-year exile from Athens in XI 55,2 is patterned on the Syracusan case. I have to admit that verbal analogies between Diodorus' phrase referring to *petalismos* (XI 87,1: διαριθμηθέντων δὲ τῶν πετάλων τὸν πλεῖστα πέταλα λαβόντα φεύγειν πενταετῆ χρόνον) and the tradition originating in Theophrastus and most fully known to us from fragment 30 of Philochorus (διαριθμηθέντων δὲ [sc. τῶν ὀστράκων] ὅτῳ πλεῖστα γένοιτο καὶ μὴ ἐλάττω ἑξακισχιλίων, τοῦτον ἔδει [...] μεταστῆναι τῆς πόλεως ἔτη δέκα [ὕστερον δὲ ἐγένοντο πέντε]) seem quite close, albeit rather trivial. Meanwhile, our attention is drawn by the fact that the number of years of exile in both the versions is exactly the same. Perhaps one possible solution would be to assume that the confusion of the duration of the 'punishment' imposed by ostracism and *petalismos* had happened earlier, for instance in Ephorus' work, and that Theophrastus appropriated it when 'supplementing' (for the reasons already discussed above) the paraphrase of the law about ostracism in what we have today as fragment 30 of Philochorus. However, this is merely a very far-fetched supposition.

Faced with the inconclusiveness of the source-critical and strictly philological analyses, scholars naturally turned to consider the 'facts' (as they did in the case of the geography of ostracism) in search for evidence among the known ostracism cases that the 10-year punishment was commuted to five years. Cuniberti has recently done it with the case of Hyperbolus, arguing that the fact that this politician was murdered on Samos towards the end of 412/411 BC, having had to leave Athens in 416 or 415 BC, definitely proves that the 10-year period of exile was not in force any more at that point—and hence, that the law about ostracism had been modified earlier on.[190] This reasoning does not seem convincing because the division between the Athenian forces on Samos and the oligarchs in Athens certainly made it easier for the exile to reduce his 'punishment' by himself. Moreover, a (very

---

[189] Cf. D.S. XI 55,2 with XI 87,1.
[190] Cf. Cuniberti (2000) 134–147 and Cuniberti (2003). See also above, pp. 110–112, on the dating of Hyperbolus' ostracism.

corrupt) fragment of Theopompus (*FGrHist* 115 F 96b), in connection with Thucydides' manner of speaking about the murder of Hyperbolus (VIII 73,3), may suggest that the choice of Hyperbolus for a victim of an act of mutual trust (*pistis*) of oligarchic conspirators (*synōmotai*) was not coincidental. Of course, political motivations could be claimed here (Hyperbolus was perceived as a contemptible demagogue),[191] but Theopompus' version deserves attention. According to him, the murderers cast the victim's body into the sea in a bag, or rather a wineskin, which some scholars associated (perhaps correctly) with the scapegoat ritual.[192] This anecdote about the disposal of his corpse may be of no historical value. It may not accurately describe the circumstances of this politician's death and the disappearance of his corpse. However, the account of the circumstances of his death, both in Thucydides and in Theopompus, seems to be meaningful. If Hyperbolus indeed left on his own initiative the area where he should have been staying (see the previous section), it would automatically make him *atimos*[193] and thus a convenient because legitimate victim for the conspirators. Therefore, generally speaking, Hyperbolus' case cannot prove a change in the law and reduction of the exile period for those ostracised. What is more, it can perhaps even testify to the contrary.[194]

Ultimately, we must return to the state of knowledge of the authors from whom we received the tradition about ostracism. Meanwhile, it is worth noticing that the text (or fragments of text) of the law about ostracism available to them must have contained unambiguous information. The law must have stipulated the duration of the 'punishment' to be either five or 10 years. It would not record previous changes in the law, making its old

---

[191] Cf. Rosenbloom (2004a) and (2004b).
[192] See above, 1.2.3. See in general, Siewert, T 30, by W. Scheidel.
[193] Cf. above on the 'Decree of Themistocles', pp. 91–92. Cf. generally MacDowell (1986) [1978] 73–75; Parker (1983) 'Indexes', *s.v. Atimia*. Cf. also recently van 't Wout (2013).
[194] However, if we assume, following Figueira, that the exiled had to reside outside the Saronic Gulf (see above), the status of the ostracised staying in the *poleis* of the Athenian 'empire', and particularly those in the main military camp of the Athenians on Samos, would be quite ambivalent anyway. As I have noted above, a law regulating the geography of ostracism in this way would cause problems after the Persian Wars. For as long as the exiled were restricted to the Peloponnese and Thessaly, e.g., their contact with the Athenians and Athenian politics was indeed limited. However, if they happened to be within the area of intensive political activity of the Athenians in their Aegean *archē*, they would admittedly comply with the provisions of the law about ostracism, but they would be openly acting contrary to the lawgiver's intention by maintaining (out of necessity) close contact with Athenian citizens and participating in the Athenian political life from a distance. In such a case, Hyperbolus' status on Samos would also be very hazardous.

provisions void. In this context, the manner of Philochorus' speaking in fragment 30, where the change in the duration of exile is mentioned merely in brackets, seems to indicate that Theophrastus, his source having access to the text of the law, read about a 10-year period there. In the light of the above considerations, a 'later' change in this law appears radically less probable than maintaining the original legal *status quo*.

3.4 Conclusions: A Reconstructed Procedure of Athenian Ostracism

Let me briefly summarise our conclusions thus far as regards the procedure of Athenian ostracism. Every year, since the reforms of Cleisthenes in 508/507 BC, at some point in late winter (matching the time of the *ekklēsia kyria* in the sixth prytany of later times), the Assembly convened to decide on ostracism that year. The vote by a show of hands, or *epicheirotonia*, was valid only if a high number of Athenians showed up, which was probably decided based on the high 'visual quorum', rendered by the formula 'when the *dēmos* gathered *en masse*'. This decision was rarely positive, so usually, the negative *epicheirotonia* was the last step of the ostracism procedure that year.

If the vote proved positive, *ostrakophoria* took place two prytanies (or their earlier temporal equivalent) later. On this day, at some point in the eighth prytany, masses of Athenian citizens arrived in the Agora. Its area was reorganised and prepared, most probably by the prytans, using a system of 'wicker' (or *gerra*) to delimitate paths of admission, and so the waiting lines, leading to 10 'entrances' assigned to the members of 10 Athenian tribes. The voting process was supervised by archons and members of the Boulē of Five Hundred. Upon recognition by the *bouleutai* of his tribe, every citizen cast his ostrakon, turning it upside down, as a sort of secret ballot, placing it in a basket or basin (*skaphē*?) by the entrance prepared for his *phylē*. When such basins were full, servants carried them to the spots where the ostraka were counted on improvised tables (in permanent structures or impromptu areas, fenced or 'roped off'), perhaps by the members of the Council. Once each batch of ostraka was processed, the votes were put in vessels (*lekanai*?), carried away by servants, and disposed of to be later used for diverse practical purposes (for instance, as building material in Athens). The whole procedure of counting ostraka was overseen by the archons, who added the partial results on writing tablets and calculated the ultimate outcome. A simple majority of ostraka cast against one citizen was enough to send him into exile for 10 years. The decision was presumably announced at a special gathering of the Assembly.

The 'convicted' Athenian had 10 days to settle his personal arrangements and was henceforward supposed to reside for 10 years within the area between the Scyllaeum and the Geraestus promontories, i.e., roughly within the confines of the Saronic Gulf (the diametrically opposite interpretation is less likely, but possible), albeit his whereabouts were not supervised strictly. During this period, he could enjoy the use of his property in Attica.

PART II
TOWARDS AN INTERPRETATION OF THE ORIGINAL AIMS OF ATHENIAN OSTRACISM

4
The Historical Context of the Cleisthenian Law about Ostracism

4.1 Cleisthenes' Reforms or 'Athenian Revolution'?

Various schools of interpretation of Cleisthenes' reforms have recently been oscillating between two extremes. On the one hand, there is a vision of a comprehensive, very complex but at the same time very coherent reform, which the Athenian *polis* owed to the political genius and personal ambition of Cleisthenes.[1] On the other hand, there is a picture of a popular revolt, which admittedly gave the reformer power and enabled him to act, but which already in the last decade of the sixth century BC sealed the political dominance of the *dēmos* in Athens.[2] It should be noted here that, even

---

[1] Most expressly formulated perhaps in the classic chapter by Martin Ostwald (1988) 309 in *CAH*[2]. See also the most vocal work in this approach emphasising a deeply intellectual, if not philosophical, background of the reforms by Cleisthenes: Lévêque, Vidal-Naquet (1973). Cf. the studies recently gathered in the collected volume edited by Azoulay and Ismard (2011). See also Meier (1980) 91–143. The main works arguing for an egoistic and to a large extent manipulative character of Cleisthenes' reforms include Bicknell (1972) 1–53 and Martin (1974) 12–22. On the other extreme are studies stressing the military and mobilisation dimension of these reforms, such as the pioneering article by Van Effenterre (1976); see also Bradeen (1955); cf. Traill (1975) and Siewert (1982). Lewis (2004) [1963] presents Cleisthenes as both a politician-opportunist and a far-sighted statesman and patriot. Cromey's (1979) hypothesis about a voluntary 'retirement' of Cleisthenes after the introduction of reforms, indirectly indicating his noble intentions, must remain unverifiably speculative. This author also decisively criticises the ancient traditions explaining the disappearance of Cleisthenes from our sources after implementing the reforms as well as the modern guesses in this matter. Cf. also the survey of scholarly opinions in Thomsen (1972) 121–125, ultimately invoking natural causes of Cleisthenes' 'sudden disappearance from history'. Most insightful and at the same time most concise account of the possible motives of the politician is presented in the classic study by Lewis (2004) [1963] and in Loraux (1996).

[2] See esp. Ober (2007) and earlier works, esp. Ober (2004) [1993]; but cf. Karpyuk (2000) 93–96 commenting on the role of 'crowd' in Ober's interpretation of these events. More generally, see Loraux (1996) esp. 1083–1089 with n. 22 and Raaflaub (1998a) 41–44 for their criticisms of Ober's hypothesis (cf. his reaction in Ober (1998) and the response to it in Raaflaub (1998b)); cf. also briefly Rhodes (2015) 52–53. Interestingly, for Rhodes (1992) and Giangiulio (2015) 49–54, 'the Athenian revolution' proper is to be dated after the Persian Wars

though a certain compromise is possible between these two visions,[3] the ultimate interpretation of the primary aims of ostracism critically depends on which side of this debate we take. More specifically, it is predictable that supporters of the theory about a reform initiated by one of the most accomplished among the Athenian aristocrats will tend to interpret ostracism as (speaking in most general terms) a tool in the competition between the aristocratic leaders of the Athenian *polis*. In contrast, supporters of the thesis about an 'Athenian revolution' will almost naturally regard this institution as an instrument of the actual or symbolic (or even 'ritual') dominance of the people over the aristocratic politicians.[4]

I cannot engage here in the complex discussion on the political history of Athens during the 10 or even 15 years after the fall of the Pisistratid tyranny. However, it is worth noting that in our comprehensive interpretation of Cleisthenes' reforms, much depends on the reconstruction of the chronology of events between 511/510 and 507/506 BC, particularly on establishing whether this politician was able to present to the people a most general outline of the reform plans before his exile from Athens and the Spartan intervention in the summer of 507 BC.[5] The account in *A.P.*, which suggests a simultaneous implementation of all of the Cleisthenes' reforms in the year of Isagoras' archonship (*A.P.* 21.2–6 with 22.1),[6] is not entirely

---

(but cf. Davies (1993) 51–63). The true constitutional and political breakout, and the true beginning of Athenian democracy, would thus be dated to the time of the reforms of Ephialtes (cf. also above, p. 13 n. 42 and p. 104 n. 110, with relevant bibliography). From my perspective in this study, however, the debate about the true starting point of democracy in Athens is not a central issue (see also the provocative paper by Eder (1998)). Cf. Cartledge (2007) 163–167 and esp. Osborne (2006). See below.

[3] It is indisputable that the direct and long-term success of Cleisthenes' reforms would not have been possible had this politician's brilliant plan not fallen on a fertile ground. It gained the support of the Athenian people, ready to receive the reforms of the Alcmaeonid as theirs and to stick to them all throughout the political turmoil of the end of the sixth and the first decades of the fifth century BC. See also below, pp. 193–194. For ostracism more specifically, cf. esp. Forrest (1966) 201–203.

[4] For a reassessment of the notion of 'revolution' as applied to Athenian democracy, see Osborne (2006).

[5] A thorough discussion of the problems of the Athenian chronology in this period can be found, e.g., in Knight (1970) 15–24. Cf. also Martin (1974) 3–22. Andrewes (1977) 246 convincingly argues that Cleomenes' intervention in Athens took place 'not too long before mid-summer' in 507 BC (i.e., shortly before the end of Isagoras' archonship)—contrary to the thesis proposed by Busolt (1895) 403 n. 6 that it must have happened in spring, during the customary period of Spartan military expeditions.

[6] Cf. Hdt. V 66,2 with 69,2. Contrary to Hignett (1952) 332–336, Seager (1963) claims a complete compatibility between *A.P.* and Herodotus regarding the sequence of these events, i.e., the commencement of Cleisthenes' reforms before Isagoras' summon of the Spartan forces.

trustworthy.⁷ However, this version might have arisen from a tradition ascribing some decisive actions (which would determine further evolution of the Athenian political system) to Cleisthenes' activities before his exile, forced by the Spartan king Cleomenes.⁸ Only assuming such a sequence of events, I think, can we fully grasp the meaning of the desperate decision to call for a foreign intervention, made by the archon then in office Isagoras, who should theoretically have had at his disposal all the tools necessary to hinder the actions of his political enemy. In other words, Cleisthenes' very first steps towards reform must have already undermined Isagoras' political position enough for him to resort to such extreme means.⁹

This already traditional interpretation was challenged in 2007 by Josiah Ober. He postulated the approach focusing on the institutional aspects of the Athenian breakthrough and the role of a great individual there be abandoned. Without depreciating the significance of Cleisthenes' activity, he regarded it instead as a very inventive reaction to the fundamental change which must have taken place earlier in Athenian politics, namely the profound revaluation in the manner of thinking, acting, and public speaking in Athens. Thus, the 'democracy of the Athenian type' proved not to result

---

⁷ The slightly pedantic discussion in Knight (1970) places all of the Cleisthenes' reforms in an even shorter period, between Isagoras' election for archonship in spring 508 BC and his taking the office in July. Traditionally, scholars (e.g., Wade-Gery (1933) 24–25; Hignett (1952) 332–336; Rhodes, *ad A.P.* 21.1, p. 249) argued that voting on a series of reforms at the Assembly before Cleisthenes' exile and already during Isagoras' archonship was one thing, quite another was their implementation after the defeat of the Spartan intervention and the return of Cleisthenes from exile (according to Rhodes, *ibidem*, the process of introducing the reforms lasted until 501/500 BC; cf. also below, p. 196 with n. 23). This discussion seems to be of no use for my purposes here. Whatever the truth, the direction in which Cleisthenes was heading with his plans must have been clear from the very beginning, regardless of the schedule of the reforms' implementation (and the forced interruption in its course). Cf. also generally McCargar (1976b).

⁸ Naturally, the question as to how Cleisthenes carried out the implementation of his reforms remains open. Wilamowitz-Moellendorf (1893) v. 1, 6 believed that he must have been holding some office after the eponymous archon Isagoras was expelled. According to Busolt (1895) 402, Cleisthenes was 'most probably' an extraordinary and plenipotentiary *thesmothetēs*, accredited by the Delphic oracle. Wade-Gery (1933) in turn argued that *psēphismata* were proposed to the Boulē and the Assembly as a motion by Cleisthenes as a private citizen, in spite of a strong opposition of the archon in office (similarly Hignett (1952) 127–128). Cf. also the previous note. See also below, on the revolutionary circumstances of Cleisthenes' reforming activity (cf. already Wade-Gery (1933) and Lewis (2004) [1963] 307).

⁹ It is sometimes suggested that Isagoras made this move induced by the election of Alcmaeon (hypothetically: Cadoux (1948) 114, based on Pollux, 8.110), i.e., an Alcmaeonid and supposedly Cleisthenes' supporter, as archon for the next year (507/506 BC). For cautious arguments supporting this thesis, see Andrewes (1977) 247. Cf. also below, on the probable motives of Isagoras' actions. Forsdyke (2005) 137–138 suggests that before his exile Cleisthenes appealed to the *dēmos* not by promising some radical political agenda but taking the credit for the fall of the tyranny in Athens.

from a political system foundation act but a pragmatic and experimental entity, subject to constant revision.[10] Institutional changes or reforms would occur there from the very beginning, following events that crystallised new ways of thinking and acting among the Athenians. More specifically, it was not Cleisthenes but the *dēmos* who should be regarded as the main protagonist of the historical drama which we conventionally call the rise of the Athenian democracy. The best proof of this is that the real revolution happened in the absence of the exiled Cleisthenes, when the Council and the entire Athenian *dēmos* consciously opposed Isagoras and removed the Spartan military garrison from Athens with the force of the whole community.[11]

As a result of such an interpretation, in Ober's view, the Athenian ostracism turned out to be one of the institutional innovations in the 'first generation' of democracy, or even one of the most significant among them, as it was a 'frank assertion of the power of the *dēmos* as a political collectivity to judge the public behaviour of each prominent member of the community, and to gather for the express purpose of voting to expel an individual from the community'.[12] The improvised ostraka would be a metaphorical weapon of ostracism against the public enemy, and the entire process 'could be seen as a political ritual that allows for (although does not mandate) the annual reperformance of the revolutionary moment itself'.[13] Ober compares here the Athenian revolution of 508/507 BC to the French Revolution. Admittedly, both found space for the execution of individuals considered 'public enemies', but the Athenian revolution did not evolve into an organised terror aimed at the 'counter-revolutionaries'. In other words,

> [o]stracism channelled what could have become a nasty habit of venting demotic ire in acts of mass violence into a carefully delimited institutional exertion of the 'power to exile'. The object of that power was limited to one prominent individual each year, and punishment was limited to temporary banishment.[14]

---

[10] In a slightly similar vein, cf. Davies (2003) and below, pp. 231–232. This last conclusion seems entirely convincing to me. Cf. Węcowski (2009) 383–390 and *passim*.
[11] See Ober (2007) 83–88.
[12] Ober (2007) 98. Similarly, Forsdyke (2005) *passim*. Cf. also Kosmin (2015).
[13] Ober (2007) 98/99.
[14] Ober (2007) 99. For the last statements, Ober refers to Forsdyke (2000) and (2005).

Although Ober cautiously notes that this hypothetical 'ritual' of 'reperformance of the revolutionary moment' was not obligatory but merely optional, this very observation should make us aware of the weakness of the 'ritualistic' interpretation of ostracism as a ritual that is enacted only sporadically, and in very clearly defined situations, remaining entirely dependent on the circumstances and arbitrary political, and so pragmatic, decisions of the community—in this case, on the result of the preliminary voting at the Assembly.[15] The less strict and thus merely metaphorical understanding of ostracism as ritual naturally takes away from the 'ritualistic' aspect of this institution's interpretation. In other words, the comparison with the French Revolution would be valid if *ostrakophoria* had taken place annually or if exiling one accomplished citizen per year had been inextricably connected with the functioning of the democratic system. However, this was not the case. The only element of the system that remained essential was the community's decision whether *ostrakophoria* should be carried out in a given year and whether anybody at all should be expelled from the country.[16]

Nevertheless, Ober is undoubtedly correct in observing that Cleisthenes' reforms were an expression of a profound political breakthrough in Athens, a historical moment that can safely be called revolutionary. However, even though spectacularly manifest in the activity of the Council and the People in the summer of 507 BC, this revolution should be dated to earlier times, when Cleisthenes initiated these transformations. As H. Theodore Wade-Gery and David M. Lewis pointed out,[17] executing a series of reforms during Isagoras' archonship (however we envisage the historical sequence of Cleisthenes' activity) entailed the necessity to take revolutionary actions, to comply with the will of the *dēmos* while acting on the fringes of the law in force (for instance, by violating or compromising the Assembly's procedures, no doubt supervised by the archon) or even against it (for instance, by intimidating or domineering the opponents or at least exerting relentless public pressure on legitimate institutions of the *polis*).[18] This is how I understand the famous statement by Herodotus that Cleisthenes 'took

---

[15] Cf. also the criticism of such interpretations by Mann (2007) 62–64. See also the thought-provoking considerations by Bremmer (1998) 12–24 on the 'genealogy' of the concept of ritual.

[16] For Forsdyke (2005) esp. 158–161, this annual repetition of the preliminary vote is enough to interpret the entire procedure of ostracism as a form of collective ritual.

[17] Wade-Gery (1933); Lewis (2004) [1963] esp. 306–309.

[18] It is true, as one of my OUP referees points out, that '[o]n the question of legality, much would depend on the role and prerogatives of the (Solonian) bouleutai, and whether *probouleusis* was already a strict requirement'.

the people into his party' (Hdt. V 66,2).[19] Thus, the Athenian revolution could have happened, or rather could have been happening already before the exile of Cleisthenes and his supporters, and its lasting effects could have been revealed to the Spartans at the moment when the Athenian people reacted to their intervention with military resistance.

It is essential to properly understand the motives of both the parties to the conflict, which form the background of this 'Athenian revolution of 508/507 BC'. It is very likely that in his consecutive actions after his return from exile—including the introduction of the institution of ostracism in Athens—Cleisthenes benefited from his own experience of the times when the Athenian political community was facing mortal danger. Throughout the year when he was holding his office, Isagoras must have been merely a ghost archon, since he could not use the political instruments available to him to hinder the actions of Cleisthenes and his supporters. At the same time, the increasingly frustrated archon must have regarded these actions as alarmingly resembling the behaviour of populist tyrants, who sought (as had Pisistratus, not long before) the support of the *dēmos* against the members of the *polis*' élites hostile towards the prospective tyrant. Isagoras most probably feared that what was unfolding in front of his eyes was nothing other than preparing the ground for the restitution of tyranny in Athens, this time under the leadership of the Alcmaeonid Cleisthenes. Under the circumstances, Isagoras appealed (in much the same way as had the Alcmaeonids, fighting against Pisistratus and the Pisistratids with the help of external forces, such as the Delphic oracle or the Spartans) to the Spartan king Cleomenes, whose immediate and eager assistance must have been motivated not only by the alleged personal connections with Isagoras but perhaps also by the desire to complete the mission of liberating Athens from the tyrants and their supporters.

The autonomous action taken by the people in Cleisthenes' absence was naturally a turning point and a true revolution in that it lastingly changed the rules of the political game. Regardless of the earlier motives of the politician, by some considered as manifestly egoistic, from that moment on, he was doubtlessly acting according to a far-sighted plan to improve the position of the *dēmos* and to invest them with expanding prerogatives in ruling the *polis*. In other words, the military action of the *dēmos* against Isagoras and the Spartans decisively ended the politics of gaining

---

[19] Cf. *A.P.* 20.1 and 20.4, with comm. by Rhodes, *ad loc.*

momentary favour of the people by powerful Athenian leaders, who could subsequently consolidate their influence in Athens. In this sense, we are indeed dealing here with a 'democracy's revolutionary start', as J. Ober and Sara Forsdyke saw it.

As I have already mentioned, we should assume here that the details of the ideas put forward to the *dēmos* by Cleisthenes and his supporters after his return from exile must have appeared—both to himself and to the people—to offer adequate protection against the most severe threats which had emerged in the recent past: the excessive growth of individuals' power, the devastating internal political conflict, finally the potential threat of external intervention being called in by one of the parties to the conflict. Therefore, the introduction of ostracism should also be interpreted in the overall context of the experiences and fears of the Athenian people and their leader at the time, Cleisthenes.[20]

4.2 The Law about Ostracism within the System of Cleisthenes' Reforms

Some aspects of Cleisthenes' reforms must indeed have instantly appeared to the Athenian people as immediately beneficial, and perhaps even necessary—for instance, the idea of a new territorial organisation of Attica, with the effect of a remarkable increase of the mobilisation resources of the *polis* at the time when it was threatened with external military interventions. The series of spectacular Athenian victories over their neighbours in the first years after expelling the Spartans must have promptly proved the thoughtfulness of Cleisthenes' actions.[21] However, other reforms had a more long-term character, and the appraisal of their effects did not happen until much later. In the latter case, persuading the Athenians must have been much more challenging.[22] If scholars who ascribe some of the reforms (at least partially) to the egoistic political motives of their author are correct, we have to assume that the *dēmos*, for some reasons (usually elusive

---

[20] One way to put it, as Wade-Gery (1933) 24 emphatically said, 'It seems that Kleisthenes (like Sulla) sought to guarantee that his *coup* should not be copied by other men [...]'.
[21] In a famous passage, Herodotus formulates this idea very clearly (V,78).
[22] As Lewis (2004) [1963] shows, some long-term reforms were successful (demes), others not so much (*trittyes*, as well as citizenship being based on demes rather than phratries). For what Cleisthenes 'did and did not change in the *polis* structure with regard to the criterion of descent for citizenship', see Blok (2017) 116–126.

to us), perceived these changes nevertheless as beneficial in the long run. The success of Cleisthenes' reforms, measured with their radical character as well as the people's determination in the process of their introduction over at least several years, indicates that even if the egoistic motivation was apparent (or at least clear to some), he managed to achieve some sort of balance in the political conflict between the powerful representatives of the Athenian élite and the interests and satisfaction of the *dēmos*. We can assume a priori that such logic must have operated in the case of the implementation of the law about ostracism.

Thanks to the information in *A.P.* (22.2) about the date of the introduction of the oath for council members (501/500 BC?),[23] it is possible to assess the scale of the long-term reforms initiated by Cleisthenes. The Athenian Boulē was supposedly constituted in its new form after the territorial reform of Attica had been completed, several years after the transformation began. The 20-year period of waiting for the first Athenian *ostrakophoria* to happen may induce us to regard ostracism as yet another element of the new system which for some reason could or should be effectively used only after years.[24] In other words, it would be another example of the far-sightedness of Cleisthenes' policy, who would perhaps not have lived to see this part of his reforms implemented. However, such an interpretation would be erroneous. In the light of my conclusions so far, it must be taken into account that placing the 'starting point' of ostracism in 488/487 BC results from a misunderstanding or a mistaken perspective. If the procedure of ostracism had two stages from the beginning, ostracism, as designed by Cleisthenes, functioned very well all the time, from the moment of his reforms' implementation. However, only after 20 years did the people deem as necessary to apply the second and final element, *ostrakophoria*.

As we have seen, the stalemate in the study of ostracism arose from ignoring this last fact and from focusing on the spectacular voting with ostraka and its possible implications. In the next chapter, I shall depart from this time-honoured approach perpetuated in scholarship to establish instead the primary aims of ostracism by considering its entire procedure, beginning with the preliminary voting at the Assembly.

---

[23] Thus, among others, Rhodes, *ad loc.*, based on Kenyon's emendation of the numeral in *A.P.* See, however, M. Chambers in *Aristoteles 10.1, ad loc.*, for the year 503/502 BC.

[24] Among various ways to explain this (apparent) chronological discrepancy, see, e.g., Carcopino (1935) 27, for the leniency of the Athenian people that prevented ostracism from being used 'prematurely' (thus following, in a way, *A.P.* 22.4). In general, scholars used to explain the gap between the introduction of the ostracism law and the first *ostrakophoria* by variously interpreting (hypothetical) political circumstances in Athens after 508/507 BC. For a solid survey of such theories, including his own, see Thomsen (1972) 116–135.

5
The Prisoner's Dilemma—Ostracism and Competition among Athenian Political Élites

5.1 The 'Theory of Cooperation' as a Possible Explanatory Model

In my attempt to explain the primary and intended purpose of Athenian ostracism, I shall use some elements of the 'theory of cooperation', formulated in the 1980s by an American mathematician and political scientist Robert Axelrod based on the classic 'prisoner's dilemma' from the game theory.[1] Since the first edition of Axelrod's book, this theory has been widely applied in mathematics, political science, and evolutionary biology. At the end of the 90s, Gabriel Herman used it for the first time, if I am not mistaken, in his studies on ancient Greece, while analysing strategies of behaviour in Athens, visible in Athenian court orations.[2]

Naturally, Axelrod's theory will not constitute a fully fledged study tool here. It will not serve, as some anthropological or sociological theories do, as a model filling in gaps in our source material, leading to definite or tentative historical conclusions.[3] The value of this theory to me will be more limited. I shall need to verify my hypotheses using a probabilistic argument, proving solely the possibility that the historical conclusions achieved through other means are correct or plausible. Namely, that the group behaviour and individual calculations underlying the invention of Athenian ostracism, as I argue in this book, do exist in nature and in social relations. Perhaps they can even be intuitive. They do not necessarily require subtle and long-term intellectual analysis (even though they do not preclude it), nor do they

---

[1] Axelrod (2006) [1984].   [2] Herman (1998) and (2006) esp. 398–414.
[3] Incidentally, this procedure is not entirely legitimate either (see my remarks in Węcowski (2014) 4–7 and *passim*).

demand an external authority to impose such solutions, approaches, and calculations on individuals or communities.

In general, Axelrod's theory can be described as one more solution to the 'collective action problem'. The basis of the 'theory of cooperation' is the fundamental question of how cooperation between individuals can emerge in a world which is often described by modern scholarship in (simplified) 'Darwinist' terms—in a world where only the strongest and the fittest individuals (and their genes) can survive, in a world where the 'law of the strongest' and egoistic calculations of individuals prevail; thus, in a world where we would a priori expect a general triumph of extreme egoism in relations with others or at least where self-interest seems to prevail over the considerations such as shared gain. Meanwhile, it is doubtless that cooperation strategies are discernible not exclusively in interpersonal relations but also in the animal realm, where they are not only successfully applied but even dominating in some situations. How can this be explained without assuming the necessity of some external coercion, such as decisions of some authority or pressure of the objective reality?

In the classic 'prisoner's dilemma,' each of two detained accomplices is presented during the interrogation with a choice of two strategies whose effect depends prevailingly on which of them will be applied by the other prisoner. Suppose the first one decides to testify (i.e., 'defects') while the other persists in silence. In that case, the first one will have his sentence commuted in exchange for cooperation with the law enforcement authorities. Thus, the first one will gain the maximal benefit, while the second will incur a maximal loss, ending up denounced and sentenced to the full-time penalty. However, suppose both decide to testify, incriminating each other (i.e., both 'defect'). In that case, both will be imprisoned, most probably with a slightly milder than a maximal penalty, but still convicted because the 'defection' of neither of them will prove sufficiently precious for the judicial system. Nevertheless, 'defection' will still be a much safer solution for each, regardless of what the other one does. If, in turn, both decide to remain silent (i.e., they start 'cooperating'), it becomes highly probable that neither of them will be convicted due to the lack of evidence of their guilt. Hence, such 'cooperation' would theoretically be the strategy most beneficial to both of them. At the same time, it is the most hazardous one because they do not know each other's decisions. Thus, if one cowers, the other will get the maximal penalty instead of an acquittal.

All this takes an entirely different turn when the so-called 'iterated prisoner's dilemma' is involved, i.e., when the situation discussed here becomes repetitive, and the accomplices start learning each other's previous decisions, albeit remaining unaware of each other's moves in real time. Then, factors such as gratitude, reciprocity, trust or vengeance come into play. The choices will still be made 'shooting in the dark' because it cannot be known how the other criminal will act this time, but each of them will have a certain set of experiences and expectations at their disposal. As a result, under certain circumstances (or in some aspects), the 'cooperation' strategy, even though still hazardous, will be much safer than in the case of the classic 'prisoner's dilemma', where the choice of strategy is a one-time decision. Moreover, in the 'iterated prisoner's dilemma', this choice is not final and can be altered at various stages, not only according to the previous experiences and expectations (i.e., in reaction to the 'co-prisoner's' actions) but also in line with more long-term plans of the individual.

Robert Axelrod's book of 1984 resulted from a series of international computing tournaments, meant to select a computer program guaranteeing the best result in a game based on repetitive application of the scenario of the 'iterated prisoner's dilemma'. Each program participating in the competition had to play against every other one and against its own 'clone': a program operating on principles identical to its own. The programs were created by scholars and scientists of various disciplines (mathematicians, sociologists, psychologists, political scientists, economists, biologists, and others) and laypeople, including young amateurs of computer games from various countries.[4]

The outcome of the first tournaments organised by Axelrod, later on verified in many ways by representatives of various scholarly disciplines, was surprising. It turned out that the best result in the first two tournaments, and one of the best in several further ones, was repetitively achieved by the program TIT FOR TAT, created by a psychologist from the University of Toronto, Anatol Rapoport and based on the most straightforward possible strategy. The program always decided to 'cooperate' in the first move of the game. In each of the following ones, it always copied its opponents move: so it 'defected' or 'cooperated' depending on the decision of the 'co-prisoner'.

---

[4] One may add that the tournaments took place in the midst of the Cold War, when, following the Soviet Union's invasion of Afghanistan in 1979, American political scientists were haunted by the question whether there exists an optimal strategy against an opponent who does not respect the widely accepted rules (i.e., systematically 'defects' in the international political game). On the horizon of such considerations there shimmered the potential consequences of the ultimate mutual 'defection' of nuclear superpowers, which would bring about a total thermonuclear destruction. It is sad to conclude that we are back to this question nowadays AD 2022.

Much less successful were programs applying different variants of the strategies 'always cooperate' or 'always defect' ('strategies ALL D').

Interestingly, TIT FOR TAT won the first computer tournament organised by Axelrod and the next one, which the participants entered with the knowledge of the results of the first one. However, most of them supposed that by optimally dosing 'defection' and 'cooperation', they would take advantage of the perceived weaknesses of TIT FOR TAT. However, this was not the case, and Rapoport's program became the winner again.

Reflecting on the sources of its success, Axelrod described the strategy applied by TIT FOR TAT as 'nice' (because it never resorted to 'defection' first) or 'forgiving' (because regardless of the previously registered cases of its opponent's 'defection', it always returned to 'cooperation' whenever the 'co-prisoner' decided to cooperate).[5] Another strength of this strategy was its 'clarity', or rather its predictability and recognisability of its behavioural pattern. The game partner could always be confident that they would be punished for 'defection' and rewarded for 'cooperation', which allowed them to influence the other player's moves to some extent.

Thus, the simplest recipe for the best possible playing strategy in the 'iterated prisoner's dilemma' is the following: always assume the possibility of cooperation and always begin with cooperation ('don't be the first to defect'); always reciprocate the opponent's actions but do it predictably ('reciprocate both cooperation and defection'). In the long run, strategies based on systematic 'defection' and deception or provocation have a worse effect than 'cooperation' and predictability. At the same time, it is not worth analysing all the possible motivations of the opponent because they remain hidden from us, given that even with the ability of statistical analysis of the behaviours so far, one has to factor in the possibility of a trick or trap. In other words, the player should not be excessively preoccupied with calculations ('don't be too clever'). What is important is to care for one's own score in the game without measuring one's own success with the opponent's success—i.e., do not act jealously ('don't be envious'). Mutual envy always leads to rivalry, resulting in 'defection' and escalation of the conflict, which is difficult to overcome due to the mutual lack of trust of the players. Thus, it

---

[5] In slightly modified versions, this program punished 'defection' a bit more severely (by returning to cooperation after a strictly defined 'period') or was more determined to mitigate the conflict and refrained from punishing for 'defection' for a strictly defined, small number of moves (e.g., 'tit for two tats', which incidentally is the strategy identified by Herman (2006) 402–410 as what (p. 402) 'the Athenians appear to have developed [as] an ideal of reciprocal interaction').

proves destructive to both parties. In short, be 'nice', 'forgiving', and 'clear', never allow envy of the opponent's success to get the better of you, and in the long run, you will be successful in the game of the 'iterated prisoner's dilemma'.

Understandably, this result must have appeared as highly surprising to the fundamentally pessimist, 'Darwinist' scholars analysing the course of the tournaments described here from the perspectives of various disciplines.[6] However, there is a 'catch' in this result: the viability of assuming the 'nice' strategy depends on the prospect of future interactions with the 'co-prisoner'. For if the interaction is to be limited in time, and not prospective, the most beneficial solution is naturally 'defection' and taking maximal advantage of the opponent in a single or limited-in-time interaction, as opposed to cooperation, potentially leading to further collaboration in the future and building mutual trust.

Axelrod illustrated the functioning of the principles revealed in the computer tournaments with the example of group behaviours of the Members of the American Congress. Despite stark political differences between the parties (and within them), they cooperate profitably, counting on a future reciprocation of their political 'favours'. However, this principle naturally does not apply to the Members of Parliament, who cannot be sure of their election for the next term. It has also been noted that the prevalence of cooperative behaviours in Congress is a relatively recent phenomenon. Historians of the American political system point out its egoistic, violently 'Darwinist' environment of the nineteenth century.[7] This last observation lies at the foundation of the question essential for Axelrod: how can the cooperation principle spread in an environment where the dominant strategy has so far been 'always defect'?

An even more striking example where neither formal nor informal agreement between the 'co-prisoners' could be assumed was an intriguing episode of World War I.[8] The soldiers on both sides of the trench warfare purposefully missed their targets in their everyday shooting to avoid losses caused by the adversary's shooting, and their artillery abstained from firing at mealtimes or in the quartermaster's area. At the same time, a breach of this rule by the opponent entailed an immediate retaliation with double the

---

[6] Cf. already the classic remarks by Simmel on the alternative, ethical or pragmatic, approach to conflict in social sciences: Simmel (1904).
[7] Cf. Axelrod (2006) [1984] 5–6. Incidentally, one cannot be certain if Axelrod's example is still valid in the current American political climate. See also above, p. 2.
[8] Axelrod (2006) [1984] 73–87.

strength. For every soldier lost, two enemies were supposed to be killed. It should be emphasised that in this case, the 'players' not only could not agree on a mutually beneficial strategy or endow the adversary with trust. They had to act in the context of mutual hostility within a military conflict (they were constantly 'defecting' by killing their opponents at other war occasions) and under pressure from their superiors, to whom such behaviour was unacceptable, of course.[9]

Thus, we could be dealing here not only with a cooperation strategy, assumed without any mutual guarantee or long-term calculation by a conscious individual, but also with an informal collective action, a series of automatic and almost intuitive reactions to the behaviour of the hostile 'co-prisoner' in the trenches. The principal factor facilitating this (limited) cooperation between the enemies was long-term interaction with a 'player' whose situation is analogical to one's own. This 'cooperation' was not hindered even by the rotation of troops because the trench wisdom was immediately transferred down to the newly arriving soldiers and units on both sides.[10]

Venturing even further in generalising the results of his experiment, Axelrod looked into the functioning of the 'theory of cooperation' in the realm of animals and plants, inviting the evolutionary biologist William D. Hamilton to join him in his study. They dedicated a relevant chapter in the book to a kind of complementation of Darwin's theory of natural selection, describing it in terms of the game theory and establishing the contexts in which the cooperation principle may operate within biological systems based on reciprocity.[11] Their conclusions are essential to my considerations. They prove that the cooperation discussed here in terms of the 'iterated prisoner's dilemma' can exist even without any consciousness, or rather 'foresight', of the participants in the 'game'.

The chapter in Axelrod's *The Evolution of Cooperation* crucial to me is a sort of guide for a reformer aiming to promote cooperation in a given social environment.[12] As we remember, usually, cooperation turns out more profitable to both parties than mutual 'defection' only if the number of predictable moves (interactions with the 'co-prisoner') is sufficiently high.

---

[9] On trench warfare, see generally Bull (2014).
[10] This 'cooperation' strategy was ended only by the tactics of unexpected raids on the enemy trenches, imposed by the commanders, which ultimately broke up the bond of mutual trust by introducing unpredictability into the relations between the hostile armies.
[11] Axelrod (2006) [1984] chapter 5 ('The Evolution of Cooperation in Biological Systems').
[12] Axelrod (2006) [1984] chapter 7 ('How to Promote Cooperation').

The reformer's task is to change the strategic situation that the players are facing to prevent this principle from working. There are two factors usually discouraging individuals from cooperating. First, the chance that interaction with the partner in the future is not very probable, and secondly, prioritising immediate benefit over long-term profit. These are precisely the factors that need to be modified by the reformer (connectedly or separately) for the 'cooperation' to become more appealing than 'defection'. In the first matter, Axelrod advises applying one (or both) of two techniques of 'enlarging the shadow of the future'. The interaction between the players can be either intensified or prolonged. In its simplest version, the extension of the scope of interaction can, for instance, take the form of a marriage between lovers. However, it is possible even between enemies, which is clearly illustrated by the aforementioned example of the long-term co-existence of two parties to the conflict in trench warfare. The interaction can be intensified in turn in several ways. First, through the 'territorialisation' of such relations: delineating a strict spatial framework of actions will force the players to interact more frequently. Secondly, through specialisation of behaviours, which will have the same effect. Thirdly, by introducing a hierarchy and organisation, or at least some form of bureaucracy.[13] Intensification of interaction can also be achieved by dividing common actions into several specialised stages, which will also increase the effectiveness of the principle of reciprocity between the players, at the same time making them dependent on the mutual trust realised on the level of partial decisions. Such a division of interaction into smaller components promotes stability of cooperation because the immediate profit gained from 'defection' becomes lesser than the benefit gained from further cooperation at later stages of this game. All this leads to making 'defection' less attractive at a given stage than the overall interaction of the players in the future.

Another basic way of modifying the strategic situation of the players is a radical change in the value of their 'payoffs'. If the imposed punishment for 'defection' exceeds the possible immediate profits, then long-term 'cooperation' becomes a more beneficial strategy. Governments and lawgivers have legal tools, of course, allowing them to take such actions in some areas.[14] Still

---

[13] Axelrod (2006) [1984] 131: 'By binding people together in a long-term, multilevel game, organizations increase the number and importance of future interactions, and thereby promote the emergence of cooperation among groups too large to interact individually'.
[14] The best example here will be the radical increase of the penalty for avoiding taxes, stealing or breaching contracts. All these situations can be regarded as exemplifying the functioning of a monumental 'prisoner's dilemma', with many players involved.

another way is educational effort directed at schoolchildren, for instance, designed to teach them to care not only for their own good but also—at least to a certain extent—for the good of others. The altruism achieved in this way will naturally foster cooperation in situations of the 'iterated prisoner's dilemma', regardless of the strategic position of the players. However, altruistic behaviours can result from other motivations as well, such as blood relations or seeking social acclaim. The problem here, of course, will be the possibility that an altruistic attitude may remain unrequited, which (treated as 'defection' in the game) will lead to the altruist's detriment. In such circumstances, the principle must be to begin the game with an altruistic attitude ('cooperation') and then react to the partner's moves according to the TIT FOR TAT strategy. This, in turn, brings us to the fundamental task of any educational activity promoting cooperation, namely to teach the players the principle of reciprocity. TIT FOR TAT again proves to be an excellent conception for a community of players lacking an external authority which could impose a penalty for attitudes and actions potentially harmful to the community of all the game players. Encouraging attitudes based on the principle of reciprocity proves beneficial both for the 'learner' and to the community as a whole, but indirectly also to the 'teacher'. Punishing players inclined to 'defect' gradually removes attitudes of this type by making them unprofitable. The only problem is that strategies such as TIT FOR TAT can infinitely prolong the chains of mutual vengeance for 'defection' on the successive stages of the game. A strategy reacting to 'defection' with 'defection' slightly less frequently than TIT FOR TAT, i.e., a somewhat more 'forgiving' one, would undoubtedly be a bit more beneficial to the whole community of players.

Effective fostering of the principle of reciprocity is conditioned by yet another educational activity, namely cultivating in the players the skill of recognising in the future a partner with whom one has already dealt and remembering the characteristics of the previous interactions. In other words, slightly paradoxically, the effective application of the principle of reciprocity depends on the skills of correct recognition and definition of the previous 'defections' of other players.

It should be added that this is where a significant weakness of simple strategies based on the principle of cooperation surfaces. In real (as opposed to theoretical) life situations, their effectiveness admittedly depends largely on the players' psychology, on whether the players apply objectively rational tools of interaction. Their decisions arise directly from subjective (and non-rational) decisions, conditioned by limited perception and ability to assess the opponent's behaviour. In short, there is a high risk of a punishing reaction to the 'co-prisoner's' move erroneously interpreted as 'defection'. Naturally, in some social situations it is possible to define the framework of the players' interaction to make 'defection' easily (or more easily) recognisable in given, institutionalised behaviours of the participants.

*

Every profound conflict and social or political crisis can be interpreted in terms of the consequences of an unfavourable unfolding scenario of the 'iterated prisoner's dilemma' having influential individuals or social groups as 'players'. Therefore, it has probably already become apparent to the reader that almost every case of a sweeping reform of the principles ruling a political community aimed at limiting egoistic behaviour strategies of one or more participants in social and political 'interaction' can be considered, in the light of the 'theory of cooperation', an activity encouraging a practical harmonisation of mutually contradictory strategies of the 'players'. Both Solon's reforms and the so-called 'Spartan revolution' can be thus viewed, but also Cleisthenes' reforms. Answering the question whether this perspective will allow us to understand better this historical phenomenon resides, of course, with the reader of the last chapter of my work.

5.2 The Mechanism and the Primary Aim of the Law about Ostracism—A Reconstruction Attempt

In previous chapters, I endeavoured to answer some essential questions regarding the way Athenian ostracism worked. I believe the most important conclusion was that while considering the aim of this institution, one has to resist the tendency, widely spread in scholarship, to focus on the day of *ostrakophoria* and the evidence of the preserved ostraka. The symptomatic statement by Stefan Brenne that 'the law about ostracism was only applied between 487 and 416 BC'[15] is erroneous in that this law was actually in force every year from the moment of its introduction at the time of Cleisthenes' reforms. The problem here is that we tend to notice its working only when *ostrakophoria* actually happens. In this chapter, I shall propose an interpretation of the original goal of this law, taking into consideration the entire

---

[15] Brenne (2001) 22. By formulating his thought in this way, Brenne dodges the question when this law was introduced. See above, 2.1.

procedure of ostracism, beginning with the annual preliminary vote at the Assembly. I would also like to break here with the aforementioned tendency prevailing in scholarship or even (paradoxically, at first sight) reverse our usual way of thinking. Let me suggest that *ostrakophoria* happening in a given year can be an indication of a failure or a flaw in this law's functioning and not its natural consequence.[16] The infrequency of carrying out *ostrakophoriai* and the fact that the first one did not happen until after 20 years may suggest that such is the correct line of thinking.[17] And its ultimate confirmation may be that the Athenians did not abandon ostracism but kept on with it in the meantime.

An important caveat needs to be made here. In my interpretations to follow, I have to assume without ample discussion that it is possible to approach ostracism and (more broadly) Athenian political life at the initial stages of democracy in Athens not solely in view of the sentiments, actions, and interests of the *dēmos*. Equally important must have been the political game and play of interests of the members of the Athenian élites and the political support groups led by them. This game would often, albeit not always, be played by two hostile political groups gathered around two prominent politicians of a given time. Such an approach has recently been questioned quite often.

Christian Mann's fundamental work, *Die Demagogen und das Volk. Zur politischen Kommunikation im Athen des 5. Jahrhunderts v. Chr.* (2007), is particularly important here.[18] In his book, on the one hand, Mann strongly emphasised the continuity in Athenian 'rules of political communication' throughout the fifth century BC, thus questioning widespread scholarly ideas of two important historical watersheds, the reforms of Ephialtes in 462/461 BC and the death of Pericles. In his opinion, the rules of political engagement and, in particular, the interplay between the *dēmos* and its politicians (his 'Demagogen') did not change profoundly in the fifth century before the last phase of the Peloponnesian War. On the other hand, Mann questioned the scholarly idea of 'aristocratic politics' in Athens. Both these important theses have a direct bearing on the possible interpretation of Athenian ostracism

---

[16] Grote (1907) v. 3, 376 already pointed this out in a way: 'We must recollect that it [*sc.* ostracism – M.W.] excercised its tutelary influence not merely on those occasions when it was actually employed, but by the mere knowledge that it might be employed, and by the restraining effect which that knowledge produces on the conduct of great men.'

[17] Recently, Zerbinati (2019) argued that the time-gap between the introduction of ostracism and the first *ostrakophoria* might have been due to the instability of the *polis* precluding the application of this law.

[18] See esp. Mann (2007) esp. 58–74 and *passim*; cf. also Mann (2008) and (2009).

and its functions. As he points out, although leading Athenian politicians might well have been interested in exiling their opponents, the decision of who will be ostracised was entirely in the hands of the Athenian *dēmos*. When considering the testimony of Athenian ostraka, we find that it was not feasible for an Athenian politician to have another politician ostracised. Ultimately, Christian Mann interprets ostracism as a tool for disciplining Athenian politicians by the *dēmos*—whatever the original intention of the law about ostracism.[19]

I would argue that one may have two crucial reservations here.[20] First, Mann's criticism of the idea of ostracism 'als Instrument aristokratischer Parteikämpfe' (Mann (2007) 72) is too clear-cut because the notion of 'aristocratic politics' may not necessarily be radically antithetical to the more democratic 'rules of political communication' he postulates for the fifth century BC (see below).[21] Secondly, his interpretation of ostracism is too narrowly focused on the vote of *ostrakophoria*. Therefore, I subscribe to Mann's general interpretation of ostracism, but only as far as its final chord, the *ostrakophoria*, is concerned. If one broadens the scope of our analysis to include the whole two-stage procedure of this institution, its goal looks more complex and, as we shall see below, there is additionally more room for the Athenian élite interplay in our interpretations. Provided, of course, as Mann rightly emphasises, that we do not take fifth-century Athenian ostracism as a tool of 'aristocratic party infighting', but, as I would provisionally suggest, as an expedient possibly devised in response to severe problems with and within Athenian élites at the time when this mechanism was introduced.[22]

I also believe that there are two specific reasons for a bipolar, or better 'personalistic', perspective on ostracism to be still valid, at least to some extent. First, this is how our ancient sources usually present the political context of ostracism of one or other Athenian politician.[23] It could obviously be blamed on the particularly biographical treatment of such events by Plutarch, our main and very late source in this matter. However, much

[19] See esp. Mann (2007) 72–73. In a similar vein, see also Paiaro (2012).
[20] My third doubt regarding Mann's criticism of the idea of a remarkable change occurring in Athenian politics after the death of Pericles will become clear below.
[21] Cf., e.g., Meister (2020) esp. 336–349, following Georg Simmel's model of competition ('Konkurrenz') as an indirect rivalry between competitors for the favours of a 'dritte Instanz', of the *dēmos* in the case of Athenian democracy. In general, see also Meister, Seelentag (2020).
[22] Incidentally, as Chr. Mann is focused on the *praxis* of the fifth-century Athenian democracy, he is not particularly interested in the circumstances or even the date of the introduction of the law about ostracism (cf., e.g., Mann (2007) 59 and 61).
[23] Particularly telling here is Plutarch's mention of an alternative account of the political background of the *ostrakophoria* of 'ca. 416 BC' (*Nic.* 11.10), where Phaeax becomes Alcibiades'

alike seems to be the presentation of the political mechanisms operating in Athens by the witness closest to the times, Herodotus, who describes the political struggle of the end of the sixth and the fifth century BC in precisely the same 'personalistic' or even bipolar way. True, Herodotus is describing here Athenian politics of the pre-democratic era, but the self-explanatory manner in which he does so strongly suggests mechanisms that should look self-evident or even natural to his contemporary public (V 66,1–2).[24]

It is also important to bear in mind that, as far as ostracism is concerned, tentative statistical or historical conclusions drawn from the bulk of the extant ostraka, and especially from particularly 'scattered votes' hypothetically associated with historical *ostrakophoriai* and allegedly suggesting more than two leading 'contenders', have no bearing on this issue for purely methodological reasons.[25]

Additionally, as John K. Davies observed some time ago, 'the informal networks of influence' and 'social control', in other words, Greek and especially Athenian 'patronage' (broadly conceived), has 'only recently begun to attract the attention it deserves'.[26] The data preliminarily gathered by Paul Millett is particularly revealing.[27] The *locus classicus* in this respect is the much-discussed passage of Theopompus (*FGrHist* 115 F 89), the anecdote referred to also in Plutarch's *Life of Cimon* (10,1–2; cf. *A.P.* 27.3), regarding Cimon's magnanimity towards his (most probably) fellow-*dēmotai* and

---

main political contender. This version is unambiguously ascribed by Plutarch to Theophrastus. It is important to note (with Heftner (2000a) 36) that Phaeax is no doubt introduced here as replacing Nicias and not as the third of the leading political players of the time (but cf. Plut. *Alc.* 13,1–2, which is, however, an alternative account devised by Plutarch, perhaps following, indirectly, Ps.-Andocides, *Alc.* [IV] 2; cf. Heftner (2000a) 42–45). In general, cf. already the list in *A.P.* 28.2 (with Rhodes, *ad loc.*), however schematic in its opposition between the alleged leaders of the 'nobles' (*gnōrimoi*) and of the *dēmos*: Xanthippus vs. Miltiades, Themistocles vs. Aristides; Ephialtes vs. Cimon, Pericles vs. Thucydides son of Melesias. In a similar vein, cf., in Thucydides, Nicias vs. Alcibiades.

[24] ...ἐν δὲ αὐτῇσι [sc. in Athens—M.W.] δύο ἄνδρες ἐδυνάστευον...οὗτοι οἱ ἄνδρες ἐστασίασαν περὶ δυνάμιος, ἐσσούμενος δὲ ὁ Κλεισθένης τὸν δῆμον προσεταιρίζεται (on Cleisthenes and Isagoras).

[25] Important though 'scattered votes' may be for our understanding of the day of *ostrakophoria* (see below). In general, see my arguments above, 2.2.1. *Contra*, e.g., Heftner (2000a) 52; cf. Mann (2007) 71–73.

[26] Davies (2003) 331. But see already Cartledge (1987) 139–159.

[27] Millett (1989). More recently, see, e.g., Zelnick-Abramovitz (2000) and Alwine (2016). See also Simonton (2017) 168–185, on oligarchic 'clientelism' (as a 'hypothetical model' not supported straightforwardly by historical sources for oligarchic regimes) distinguished from 'patronage' in that the former 'is a political strategy instituted by an authoritarian government to ensure its rule' (p. 168). For 'racketeers and patrons', and in general for a 'mafia-style regime' (this aspect, however, seems over-emphasised in this essay) in archaic Greece, see van Wees (1999) esp. 29–35; cf. also van Wees (2007).

Athenian citizens at large.[28] As far as I can see, one crucial passage, albeit not infrequently commented on by scholars, has been neglected in this context. In Book VII of Herodotus (tr. Robin Waterfield), one reads that

'[...] [o]n the Greek side, battle honours went that day [sc. in the battle of Artemisium – M.W.] to the Athenians, and among the Athenians to Cleinias the son of Alcibiades,[29] who provided two hundred men and his own ship, all at his expense, for the war effort' (... ὃς δαπάνην οἰκηίην παρεχόμενος ἐστρατεύετο ἀνδράσι τε διηκοσίοισι καὶ οἰκηίῃ νηί – VIII 17).[30]

This passage has been discussed as a piece of information on 'private financing of ships [that] was later formalized by the "liturgy" system'.[31] To me, the most salient feature of this account is the presence of 200 decently trained men, who seem to be Athenian citizens and, in one way or another, may be considered as a group of Cleinias' followers. If we assume such an interpretation of this passage, we obtain a vital testimony of the existence of significant—military, but in peacetime most probably also political—'support groups', which could be mustered by prominent Athenians in the period under scrutiny here.[32]

Mogens H. Hansen denied the existence of substantial groups of voters in the Assembly or in the Boulē that would be controllable by individual politicians.[33] However, P. J. Rhodes pointed out that both descriptive and normative data regarding sitting together of, as it seems, organised groups of citizens in the Assembly, in the Council, and the courts are not uncommon.[34] One crucial passage deserves our particular attention. In Thucydides VI 13,1 (tr. Rex Warner), Nicias complains about seeing 'this

---

[28] Millett (1989) 23–25; cf. Whitehead (1986) 306–308; van Wees (1999) 34–35, and Simonton (2017) 171–173.
[29] See *APF* 600, p. 15; incidentally, he was perhaps the father of Alcibiades the Elder (*APF* 579), a victim of ostracism later on, above, pp. 104–105.
[30] Cf. also Hdt. V 47, on Philippos of Croton and his 'private ship'.
[31] Bowie (2007) *ad loc.*
[32] Plutarch's account (*Cim.* 17.6–7) about as many as 100 of the *hetairoi* of Cimon killed in the battle of Tanagra, although most probably historically unreliable, follows an earlier tradition regarding Cimon and his supporters. It is worthwhile to observe that his *hetairoi* here do not belong to his own *phylē* or his own deme, so the idea is that a considerable number of citizens from all over Attica might have been loyal to this politician. Valdés-Guía (2019) interestingly discusses source material and scholarly theories regarding 'private' (i.e., aristocratic) or 'collective' nature of war effort in archaic Athens.
[33] Hansen (1983) 219–222 and Hansen (1999) [1991] 277–287 (but cf. Hansen (1999) [1991] 137–138).
[34] See Rhodes (1994) 93–94, with further references.

same young man's [sc. Alciabiades' – M.W.] party sitting at his side in this assembly all called in to support him' (οὓς ἐγὼ ὁρῶν νῦν ἐνθάδε τῷ αὐτῷ ἀνδρὶ παρακελευστοὺς καθημένους φοβοῦμαι). Even if Nicias' alarm is intended to tell us more about his character or rhetorical tactics than about the actual course of events in this assembly, the image depicted here must have been plausible enough to Thucydides' public.

Now, my interpretation of such bands of followers (not to be confused with very restricted circles of one's political friends and *hetairoi*) does not necessarily imply the idea, conclusively criticised by Hansen, of the existence of long-lasting, relatively stable, and organised 'parties' or 'factions' in Athenian democracy. Rather, such groups of supporters would be fluid to some extent, mobilised momentarily, some of them more and some less permanently loyal to their leaders, based on selfish interests, political calculations, diverse obligations, personal and family links, local connections, but most of all attracted by lasting or temporary charisma of a given leader rather than constantly approving his policies.[35] The point is that such groups might have been mobilisable whenever it was crucially important to such a politician and whenever other important circumstances, such as the negative political atmosphere surrounding him, did not impede it.

Secondly, we have a priceless testimony at our disposal indicating that this is how the Athenians perceived ostracism at the time when *ostrakophoriai* still took place. In the famous passage from Aristophanes' *Knights* (l. 855), referred to several times above, the playwright mentions the children's ostraka game, *ostrakinda*, putting into the Sausage Seller's mouth the remark that, given the prevalence of various dodgy supporters of Paphlagon, it would be futile for the People to 'look like playing the potsherd game' (see above, pp. 141–143). Aristophanes is playing with the association between the children's game and the *agōn* of ostracism. Plato Comicus elaborates on this comparison in the play *Symmachia*, staged around 416 BC (fr. 168 K-A = Siewert, T [?] 11). Politicians fighting during an *ostrakophoria* (it cannot be excluded that the poet is commenting here on the recent case of Hyperbolus)[36] resemble children playing *ostrakinda*, who first draw a line on the ground and then split into two groups taking their positions on either side of the line. Then one of them, standing in between the groups, throws

---

[35] In general, cf. Rhodes (1986) and (2015) 55–56. Very cautiously, for a conceivable kinship dimension of ostracism (including the so-called 'Cylonian curse' of the Alcmaeonids), see now Humphreys (2018) vol. 1, 488–496.

[36] Cf. also below, p. 241 (where Plato Comicus speaks about the ostracism of Hyperbolus).

an ostrakon high into the air. If it falls on the ground turned with the light (lit. 'white') side up, one group has to run away fast (*pheugein*), and the others have to chase them (*diōkein*).[37] The context in which Plato Comicus used this image is unknown, of course, but the comparison of a children's game with ostracism, or perhaps even *ostrakophoria* itself, is beyond doubt. True, the game had a well-defined loser one could associate with the victim of ostracism. Namely, the child caught first by the chasing team was called 'the donkey',[38] just as in the Greek dodgeball game we hear of in Plato (*Tht.* 146A). However, the *ostrakinda* seems to be all about teamwork and group success. It should be noted that the chase is not after one of the participants of the game (although there will be a random victim of the game) but involves the entire group. Therefore, it is difficult to resist the impression that the poet and his audience could have interpreted ostracism as a kind of 'tug of war' (to use a contemporary concept) between two political groups in the Athenian political game. In the light of the images from comedy contemporary to the phenomena in question described above, it can be stated, I believe, that the Athenians perceived ostracism as an obvious element in the struggle between (relatively loose) political groups. Perhaps in much exaggerated terms, this is explicitly described by Ps.-Andocides (IV [*Against Alcibiades*] 4-5; tr. Michael Edwards), '[...] in such circumstances those who have political friends and confederates have an advantage over the others' (ἐν τοῖς τοιούτοις οἱ τοὺς ἑταίρους καὶ συνωμότας κεκτημένοι πλέον φέρονται τῶν ἄλλων). Aristotle presents its aberrations in much the same manner.

5.2.1 Ostracism—Against Tyranny or Aristocratic *Stasis*? Prevention or Punishment?

A separate type of interpretation of the origins of ostracism is the line of study ascribing mainly ideological motives to ostracism from its very beginning and regarding it as a way (to some extent ritualised) of manifesting the power or domination of the *dēmos* over the Athenian élites. Herbert Heftner rightly emphasises the strictly symbolic functioning of *ostrakophoria*, which

---

[37] It should be added on the margin that the terminology used there may evoke associations with judiciary procedures. See also Pollux, 8.111–112 and Eustathius, 1161.37–46; cf. Pl. *Phdr.* 241 B.
[38] Thus Pollux, 9.112.

sent into exile only one citizen a year,³⁹ regardless of the actual scale of the threat that ostracism was reacting to or preventing in a given year. I already mentioned in my Introduction that such interpretations might arise from certain desperation of scholars over the fact that no single motive (nor even several strictly defined motives) explaining the application of ostracism is clearly stated in the ancient literary sources or suggested by the corpus of Athenian ostraka.

For the sake of a more pragmatic view of the primary aims of Athenian ostracism, some scholars suggested various incidental reasons. They referred either to the egoistic and at the same time short-sighted intentions and interests of Cleisthenes or to various political events and episodes occurring later on in Athenian history, in the first two decades of the fifth century BC (if they did not ascribe the introduction of ostracism to this politician). To this current belongs the proposition by Donald W. Knight that ostracism should be regarded as an *ad hoc* political means directed against Isagoras, which was supposed to protect Athenian reforms even before he took his office as archon.⁴⁰ On the other side, Wade-Gery has a more 'systemic' interpretation, claiming that Cleisthenes intended (as did Sulla later on) to guarantee that no one in the future would repeat his own coup d'état. Ostracism would be a kind of 'safety fuse', completed soon afterwards by the oath of the members of the Council of Five Hundred, which in turn prevented the *prytaneis* from presenting to the Assembly for discussion any motions undermining the Athenian political system.⁴¹ In a slightly similar way, the law about ostracism was associated with the election of archons or generals in the new democratic system.⁴²

However, the two lines of interpreting the origins of ostracism prevailing in scholarship refer to a mechanism protecting Athens from tyranny on the one hand,⁴³ and to an instrument meant to curb aristocratic *staseis* on the other hand.⁴⁴ The common denominator of these two approaches is the conviction that in the eyes of the Athenians, removing an excessively influential politician from the *polis* would prevent others from further growth in power, threatening their fellow citizens, and/or internal

---

³⁹ Heftner (2012) 26. Cf. also Mann (2007) 62–64.
⁴⁰ Knight (1970) 21–23. Cf. also Stanton (1970).   ⁴¹ Wade-Gery (1933) 21.
⁴² Ostracism was associated with elections of archons for instance by Raubitschek (1951) 222–221, and with elections of generals for example by Hignett (1952) 165 and more recently by Phillips (1982) 34, with n. 8. Cf. generally Badian (1971).
⁴³ See especially Raaflaub (1995), with cited bibliography.
⁴⁴ Ostwald (1969) 155–157; Develin (1977) 21; Bleicken (1995) 47, 519; Stein-Hölkeskamp (1989) 194.

destabilisation of Athens resulting from political conflicts between the powerful competing for dominance in the city.

In my Introduction, I showed that the roots of such interpretations reach as far back as ancient discussions of ostracism.[45] I pointed out the main reservations which can be held concerning this tradition. The most fundamental one is, at the same time, the most general. Cleisthenes' law, introduced in 508/507 BC, did not work for the first 20 years in the way modern scholars expect it to have worked. The potential suspects of tyrannical inclinations or destabilisation of the *polis* were removed for the first time 20 years later, in 488/487 BC. Thus, it is immediately apparent that a proper interpretation of the aims of ostracism should consider this temporal distance between the moment of implementation of the law and the first *ostrakophoria*. Secondly, in the times of Cleisthenes and afterwards, Athens had a specialised legal 'path' meant to protect it against tyranny.[46]

However, the most important thing is that in the classic understanding of ostracism as a preventive means against tyranny but also against *stasis*, the result of *ostrakophoria* would exacerbate and not alleviate such perils. A politician enjoying strong support, already threatening the system, or merely inciting internal conflicts, would have a great chance to survive the vote with ostraka. Moreover, having escaped exile, he would become even more dangerous because he would have got rid of his weaker rival for 10 years. This is how we could interpret the political conflicts between Pericles and Thucydides son of Melesias, or between Themistocles and Aristides, both of which ended in the ostracism of the 'defeated'.[47] The case of Hyperbolus' ostracism of 'ca. 416' BC shows even more clearly that the weaker, or even the weakest, contender for leadership of the Athenian *dēmos* in principle lost in *ostrakophoria*.[48]

From among the attempts at defending the honour of the Athenians and their ostracism as a rational institution, I shall mention two exceptionally original interpretations, which deserve special attention. One of them

---

[45] See above, pp. 2–9.
[46] See *A.P.* 16.10 with Rhodes' commentary *ad loc.* Cf. also Hdt. VI 104,2 on the accusations against Miltiades. On the uselessness of ostracism from this point of view, see already Raubitschek (1951). Cf. generally Ostwald (1955). Cf. also Schmitz (2011); Heftner (2012); Gouschin (2016). See also the ingenious, even though not entirely convincing to me, reinterpretation of Solon's law about *stasis* by van 't Wout (2010). More recently, see Valdés-Guía (2021) for an interesting reassessment of the issue.
[47] It should be pointed out that both Pericles and Themistocles were occasionally accused of tyrannical inclinations.
[48] This has been observed by (among others) Martin (1974) 25; Rhodes, p. 270; Stein-Hölkeskamp (1989) 195; Bleicken (1995) 47.

appeared in scholarship relatively recently (even though it was written several decades ago); the other one, in turn, we owe to a scholar and thinker who died almost a century and a half ago.

In a posthumously published article entitled *Cleisthenes II: Ostracism, Archons and Strategoi*, Geoffrey E. M. de Ste. Croix put forward the hypothesis that a 'proper candidate' for ostracism was a politician who led a group of citizens opposed to the views or plans of the majority in some crucial matter.[49] Thus, ostracism would be a means of ridding the *polis* of individuals who jeopardised the 'unity of the State', mainly in the field of foreign policy and particularly in difficult times[50] (such as just before Xerxes' invasion, when the Athenians ostracised a powerful politician year after year).

This interpretation seems extremely interesting, but its principal weakness needs to be emphasised here. In critical moments of the Athenian history (which are exactly the times when ostracism was resorted to, according to the scholar), there might not have been a definite majority or an obvious leader, or even less so a 'Leader of the Opposition' clear to everybody. Thus, the rationality of the Athenian ostracism in critically dangerous situations would still be doubtful. As we shall see further on, the vulnerability of Ste. Croix's conception lies in the fact that this scholar focused exceedingly (as had almost everybody before him) on the exile and the *ostrakophoria* leading to it instead of analysing the entire two-stage procedure.

The same can be said about the other exceptionally inspiring interpretation, formulated by George Grote in the third volume of his *History of Greece* (first published in 1847).[51] According to Grote, the general strategy of Cleisthenes' activity aimed at protecting the democratic system was fostering among the Athenian people an emotional attachment to the new system, and indirectly, through the pressure of the *dēmos*, imposing on the leaders of the community a 'constitutional morality', or a 'great respect for the institutions of the system as well as obedience to the authorities acting in accordance with them and within them'. However, this was supposed to be inextricably linked with freedom of speech and freedom of action within a clearly defined legal framework as well as with unlimited control of these

---

[49] Ste. Croix (2004) 205–206.
[50] Ste. Croix (2004) 201 and *passim*. In a similar vein, cf. already Lugebil (1861). Recently, cf., e.g., Schmitz (2014) 53–54 and, in a somewhat paradoxical way, Eder (1998) 118–120.
[51] Grote (1907) v. 3, 372–380.

authorities as regards their entire public activity—all combined with the absolute conviction of every citizen that even among violent factional struggles these institutional forms will remain equally sacred to their political opponents as they are to themselves (Grote (1907) vol. 3, 372).

These words sound like Grote's political credo, but he saw analogies to this type of 'constitutional morality' (consisting in 'a combination of freedom and voluntary self-restriction') in the system of values of the English aristocracy after the Glorious Revolution of 1688 and in the American democracy. The lack of such morality, in turn, he regarded as a source of 'numerous acts of violence' characteristic of the French Revolution. He understood Cleisthenes' law about ostracism as a way of imposing on the 'first generation of leaders' in a democratic *polis* such 'constitutional morality', or in their case, a voluntary restriction of their ambitions. For this purpose, the lawgiver instituted a mechanism compelling the Athenians to assess the prospects of the future actions of prominent politicians based on their public activity thitherto and the character of a given individual revealed through it. Moreover, Cleisthenes forced all the Athenian citizens to choose between two, usually competing, aristocrats. In this, he followed the example of Solon, who in his law about *stasis* ordered the Athenians to forsake neutrality when the state's integrity is threatened (Grote (1907) vol. 3, 373).

Interestingly, among the safety means preventing abuse of this subtle political mechanism, Grote particularly distinguished the need to mobilise large numbers of citizens to ostracise an Athenian, through the two-stage procedure of ostracism, in which the Assembly voting for the application of this mechanism did not have the power to send anyone into exile, but the threat of ostracism was pending over all the citizens without exception until the moment of *ostrakophoria* (Grote (1907) vol. 3, 374–375). As we shall see, many of Grote's observations and intuitions find confirmation in my further analyses.

*

Finally, there remains the most fundamental question worth keeping in mind in other parts of this chapter. Was ostracism indeed a preventive means, as it has been seen ever since the times of Aristotle, and if so, how did it work? Or was it supposed to serve as punishment for some offences,[52] and if so, to punish whom and for what?

---

[52] It should be noted that such motivation is ascribed to the lawgiver—in a properly rhetorical form—by Ps.-Andocides IV [*Against Alcibiades*], 35, who argues that excessively

5.2.2 The Athenian 'Prisoner's Dilemma', or Ostracism and Athenian Political Life

In the preceding part of my work, I tried to establish some fundamental 'facts' regarding Athenian ostracism and its procedure which are unclear in our sources and/or have eluded modern scholarship. Most important among them are the following.

First, there was no 'ostracism before ostracism', either in Athens (I have demonstrated that the ghost of the so-called 'bouleutic ostracism' before Cleisthenes was born from a misunderstanding of late Byzantine times) or outside Athens (institutions of this kind known to us in the Greek world postdate the Athenian case). While introducing the law about ostracism, the Athenians did not pattern it on any local ritual (I have rejected interpretations of ostracism in terms of the 'scapegoat ritual'), even though some earlier customs or legal solutions might have inspired them in general.

Secondly and relatedly, the 'inventor' of the law about ostracism was Cleisthenes, who introduced it in 508/507 BC, most certainly in reaction to the political problems of the day and those he expected to emerge from his reforms.

Thirdly, the first *ostrakophoria* and the first case of exiling an Athenian politician in the ostracism procedure happened 20 years later, in 488/487 BC. The discrepancy in this matter between the account in *A.P.* and the testimony of the Atthidographer Androtion, which we received from a careless summary of his thoughts in Harpocration's lexicon, arises from a misunderstanding and negligence of Harpocration or his close source or, more probably, of the epitomist of Harpocration's lexicon.

Fourthly, there are very few cases of ostracising an Athenian politician: merely 12 (the remaining two mentioned in literary sources are more than doubtful). It seems quite improbable that there were *ostrakophoriai* which we do not hear about in literary sources. Such cases cannot be inferred from studying the Athenian ostraka. Therefore, in our considerations, we should a priori connect the infrequency of Athenian *ostrakophoriai* with the 20-year 'delay' of the first one in relation to the date of the introduction of the law about ostracism.

---

powerful individuals are mightier than magistrates and laws, so they cannot be effectively indicted for their crimes by private citizens. It is precisely for this reason that the mechanism of 'public vengeance/punishment' (*timōria*) was introduced. Cf. also Schreiner (1970).

Fifthly, apart from the exceptional and historically last *ostrakophoria* of Hyperbolus around 416 BC, all the remaining cases of ostracising Athenian politicians show a clear tendency to be condensed in time. The first five are 'serial' events, with only one year's break in the series. The ostracisms of the 70s, the end of the 60s, and the second half of the 40s of the fifth century seem to have occurred 'in pairs', most probably year after year or one shortly after another. Thus, it can be supposed that *ostrakophoriai* happened only in times of exceptional tension and that consequently the political life returned to normal.

Taking into consideration the last two points, we can venture the hypothesis that the situation in which the Athenians decided not to carry out ostracism in a given year was the norm in Athenian political life.

Sixthly, most probably already in the 30s of the fifth century, and perhaps right from the beginning of the functioning of the law about ostracism, this institution had a 'two-instance', or better two-stage, procedure. First, in the period equivalent to the sixth prytany in the political calendar, there was a vote at the Assembly (without any deliberation) whether *ostrakophoria* should happen at all in a given year. Then, at the time equivalent to the eighth prytany, there was a vote with ostraka in the Athenian Agora.

Seventhly, during the preliminary vote at the Assembly, a very high quorum was most probably required for the decision to carry out ostracism to be valid. Only in this way can the infrequency of Athenian *ostrakophoriai* mentioned above be explained.

Eighthly, during *ostrakophoria* neither a 'quorum' nor a qualified majority of 6000 ostraka applied. (Such information in our sources, usually ambiguous, comes from a late 'supplementation' of the law about ostracism, arising from the views of the peripatetic school on the nature of Athenian democracy.) Whoever obtained the largest number of 'votes' automatically went into a 10-year exile.

Ninthly and consequently, there were no historically attested cases of a void *ostrakophoria*—a situation when nobody is sent into exile due to an insufficient number of 'votes' cast against individual people or due to an insufficient number of voters. In other words, in a year when the vote at the Assembly was positive, it was inevitable that somebody would be expelled from the *polis* for 10 years.

Tenthly, on the day of *ostrakophoria*, the Athenians participated in the vote in great numbers. The only place that could accommodate such a large crowd of citizens was the Agora. Due to the large turnout, this procedure was never moved to the Pnyx or any other place easier to control, even though the Agora presented severe organisational problems. Cheating and manipulation attempts were also involved, one of which (failed) is attested by the famous deposit from the Acropolis slope containing 190 ostraka against Themistocles, prepared in advance (see Fig. 3.5). Another one (this time successful) is evidenced by a similar phenomenon noticeable in the material from the so-called 'Great Kerameikos Deposit'. A third one is perhaps visible in the example of the roof tile from the Agora divided into two ostraka directed against Alcibiades.[53]

*

In Chapter Two of the previous part of this work (2.2.1), I pointed out the negligible value of the ostraka from the Athenian *ostrakophoriai* available to us for the study of facts regarding ostracism (for instance, its chronology and prosopography) or its procedure. Here, I would like to consider the role of ostraka for our knowledge about Athenian political life.

Each year when the Assembly voted for carrying out the ostracism procedure, for up to two months (in our calendar), the political life must have been determined by the approaching *ostrakophoria*. Only a small proportion of the total number of ostraka bring us more than merely the name or some more precise, formal reference to the 'candidate'.[54] In these rare cases, the sherds usually contain accusations (sometimes in pictorial form, not always clear to us),[55] indicating why the Athenian voter would like to send somebody into exile using his ostrakon. The small number of such ostraka should not discourage us from treating them seriously.

I suppose that an analogy with modern election habits can be applied here. Also today, some citizens put on their ballot additional comments or remarks (thus falling into the category of the so-called 'spoilt ballots').[56] This analogy is of course flawed, and of psychological rather than political or socio-economic character. In the case of Athenian ostracism, 'spoilt ballots' are not 'protest votes' in that they still target specific 'candidates'.[57] Therefore, I would be tempted to interpret such 'spoilt ballots' in terms of

---

[53] See also *Agora* 25, 13–14; cf. Phillips (1990) 135–136.
[54] E.g., only 101 items in the *Kerameikos 20.1*, 5.1. (pp. 124–126) and eight more with figurative drawings in the *Kerameikos 20.1*, 5.2. (p. 126).
[55] Cf. Siewert, pp. 41–47.
[56] See esp. Alvarez, Kiewiet, Núñez (2018) on 'protest voting' and in particular on 'BNS protest voting', as in 'blank, null, or spoiled protest voting' (Alvarez, Kiewiet, Núñez (2018) 144–147).
[57] We can also assume that such ballots were handled as valid by the Athenian 'administrators.' See, however, above (pp. 79–80 with n. 33), on the problem of 'blank ballots' of ostracism.

'angry voting'.[58] They may arise from voters' psychological profile, personality, a momentary state of agitation, etc. At the same time, one may suppose that many voters could express, even if in a milder form, similar views or emotions in private conversations, when asked about their opinion on their disliked candidate. Thus, we may assume that the comments on ostraka actually illustrate the negative emotions of a considerable part of citizens participating in a given *ostrakophoria*.

Moreover, if we accept as proven that an exceptionally high turnout could be expected on that day in the Agora, exceeding all other gatherings of citizens for the usual political business, the fact that the Athenians flocked there must have been a result of strong agitation among them. We can be confident that an opportunity to immediately decide the fate of a hated politician through one vote automatically sending him into exile, without any possibility of 'appeal' to a higher instance, constituted a powerful incentive to participate in this exciting gathering.

Not infrequently, the ostraka would just expressly add 'let him go!'.[59] One, hypothetically, demands punishment (*tisis*) for Hippocrates (?).[60] Yet another ostrakon speaks against Isthmonikos 'on behalf of his demesmen' (τὸν δὲ[μο]τευτὸν hισθμόνικος Κοθοκίδες [...]).[61] Meanwhile, it is difficult to interpret declarations such as 'I ostracise...famine' (τὸν λιμὸν ὀστρακίδō,[62] and Λιμὸς Εὐπατρίδες,[63] which Stefan Brenne hesitantly deciphers as 'Highborn' ('Hunger, hochwohlgeborener (?)'). And sometimes we are simply not aware of the specific context: '[I ostracise] Megakles because of Rhoikos' ('Ροίκω χάριν).[64]

---

[58] Cf. Alvarez, Kiewiet, Núñez (2018) 152.
[59] E.g., *Agora* 25, 356 (Agora P 17772); *Agora* 25, 647 (P 29073); *Agora* 25, 1184 B (AO 49); 1191 B (AO 88); 1199 B (AO 147); 1200 B (AO 152); *Kerameikos* 20.2, 1336 (O 6874); cf. Siewert, T 1/67, with commentary by Brenne, in Siewert, pp. 92–93. Cf. also Siewert, T 1/85 (*Kerameikos* 20.2, 3981 (O 2738)).
[60] Siewert, T 1/42; *Agora* 25, 1097 (Agora, P 15594).
[61] Siewert, T 1/44; *Kerameikos* 20.2, 315 (O 5740).
[62] Siewert, T/79 and 80 (*Kerameikos* 20.2, 1786 and 1787) with Siewert, T/81 (*Kerameikos* 20.2, 1784); cf. also T 1/76–78. See the cautious considerations by Brenne (2001) 158 (?), pp. 214–216. But cf. the ritualistic perspective on this topic: Kosmin (2015) 133–134.
[63] Siewert, T 1/75; *Kerameikos* 20.2, 1781 (O 5886).
[64] Siewert, T 1/86; *Kerameikos* 20.2, 1811 (O 5156). Cf. also Siewert, T 1/107 (*Kerameikos* 20.2, 3539), T 1/108 (*Kerameikos* 20.2, 3593), T 1/109 (*Kerameikos* 20.2, 5126), T 1/110 (*Kerameikos* 20.2, 5453), T 1/112 (*Kerameikos* 20.2, 2019). See also the ostraka against Menon 'the simple-minded' (? ἀφελής): Siewert, T 1/119–130 (*Kerameikos* 20.2, 6247, 6265, 6278, 6284, 6300, 6473, 6477, 6499, 6577, 6657, 6726, 6837), with S. Brenne's remarks in Siewert, pp. 125–126.

220   PART II: ORIGINAL AIMS

At this juncture, let us take a closer look at specific accusations, allegations or plain gossip encountered on the Athenian ostraka. Sometimes, it is enough to accuse one's potential victim of a non-Athenian pedigree[65] or belonging to the uppermost social circles associated, for instance, with horse-breeding.[66] But some accusations are more specific. A group of ostraka alludes to religious guilt (*agos*), including the 'Cylonian sin'.[67] Others seem more banal. 'Arist[—] [i.e., Aristides?], brother of Datis';[68] 'Aristides son of Lysimachos, who rejected the suppliants' (... hòs τὸ]ς ηἱκέτας [ἀπέōσ]εν);[69] 'Habronichos, a supporter of the Medes';[70] 'Callias son of Kratios, Mede' (or 'from Media'), appearing on as many as 19 ostraka (one accompanied with a picture of a Mede on the reverse);[71] 'Kallixenos, traitor' (ho πρ]οδότες);[72] 'Leagros son of Glaucon, because he betrayed';[73] '[—]s, *atimos*' (fragmentary);[74] and 'Leagros son of Glaucon, sorcerer' (βάσκανος);[75] 'Menon, the most corrupt' ([δōρο]δοκότατος);[76] 'Megakles son of Hippocrates, avaricious' (φιλάργ[υρος]);[77] 'Megakles son of Hippocrates, adulterer' (μοιχός).[78] And finally, the ostrakon against

---

[65] See Siewert, T 1/66 (*Kerameikos 20.2*, 1110: '...from Skiathos'); Siewert, T 1/68 (*Kerameikos 20.2*, 1624: '...from Byzantion'); Siewert, T 1/82 (Kunsthistorisches Museum in Vienna: '...from Megara'); Siewert, T 1/131–140 (*Kerameikos 20.2*, 6431, 6628, 6735, 6736, 6737, 6738, 6739, 6740, 6741, 6742: '...from Lemnos', but see S. Brenne, in Siewert, p. 128). See perhaps Siewert, T 1/154 (*Kerameikos 20.2*, 8790, if we were to read here the word 'Thracian').

[66] Siewert, T 1/101–102 (*Kerameikos 20.2*, 3221 and 4213); Siewert, T 1/104–105 (*Kerameikos 20.2*, 5463 and 5462); Siewert, T 1/103 (*Kerameikos 20.2*, 5186b) and *Kerameikos 20.2*, 2044. See the drawing of a horse on Siewert, T 1/158 (*Kerameikos 20.2*, 2623). Perhaps cf. also Siewert, T 1/147 (*Kerameikos 20.2*, 8463: '...because of *timē*').

[67] Siewert, T 1/91 (*Kerameikos 20.2*, 3984). See also Siewert, T 1/92–93 (*Kerameikos 20.2*, 2126 and 2028), with S. Brenne, in Siewert, pp. 134–139, commenting on the famous elegiac couplet against Xanthippus (Siewert, T 1/153; *Agora 25*, 1065 (P 16873), with *Agora 25*, Fig. 27 and Pl. 3; cf. ML, p. 42; see also above p. 100, n. 98). Cf., perhaps, Siewert, T 1/149 (*Kerameikos 20.2*, 7544).

[68] Or even 'of Darius'. Siewert, T 1/37; *Agora 25*, 56 (Agora, P 9945).

[69] Siewert, T 1/38; *Agora 25*, 44 (Agora P 5978).

[70] Siewert, T 1/41; *Kerameikos 20.2*, 249 (O 5511).

[71] *Kerameikos 20.2*, 321, 351, 363, 369, 373, 391, 405, 915, 1062, 1065, 1066, 1067, 1068a, 1068b, 1069, 1070, 1071, 1072, 1073. Cf. Siewert, T 1/45–61. For the drawing, see Siewert, T 1/156 (*Kerameikos 20.2*, 405).

[72] Siewert, T 1/65; *Agora 25*, 589 (Agora P 3786).

[73] Siewert, T 1/71; *Kerameikos 20.2*, 1745 (O 5854).

[74] Siewert, T 1/155; *Agora 25*, 1071 (P 17615).

[75] Siewert, T 1/72; *Kerameikos 20.2*, 1741 (O 5847).

[76] Siewert, T 1/118; *Kerameikos 20.2*, 6202 (O 6589).

[77] Siewert, T 1/111; *Kerameikos 20.2*, 5916 (O 4825).

[78] Siewert, T 1/106; *Kerameikos 20.2*, 3773 (O 2514).

Cimon, alluding to his allegedly incestuous relation with his sister Elpinike.[79]

Looking at the array of accusations inscribed on the ostraka, we should emphasise right away that they are not particularly helpful in interpreting Cleisthenes' motivations for introducing ostracism in Athens. This is simply a catalogue of allegations and gossip circulating in the community about well-known individual citizens. This set is essential to us not due to any details of such accusations, but because it offers us insight into the atmosphere of the Athenian political life in the period preceding *ostrakophoria*. From my point of view, most significant here is that it shows what kind of attitudes and opinions of fellow citizens the most prominent Athenian politicians were facing, being conscious that on that day, their 'negative electorate' would be endeavouring to eliminate them from the political life in the *polis* for 10 long years. Thus, the allegations from Athenian ostraka give us indirect insight into the possible calculations of the political leaders facing *ostrakophoria*.

On the other hand, regardless of the relatively small number of such ostraka, we can be sure that the allegations inscribed on them must have circulated in Attica particularly intensively during the time just before *ostrakophoria*. Moreover, we can be sure that their emergence was not exclusively spontaneous.[80] Political groups able to commit electoral fraud on the voting day, such as the one behind the famous 'Themistocles' deposit' of ostraka, must have also been able to run smear campaigns directed against their opponents. Such activity could have been carried out at the Assembly, during gatherings of individual demes or tribunals, but before all in the streets of Athens, in the Agora, and all over Attica.[81] The public life and the city (and country) life must have been exceptionally dramatic in the period between the sixth and the eighth prytany (or the periods matching them before the times of the bouleutic calendar) of the year in which *ostrakophoria* was to happen.

One can surmise the lack of a 'quorum' (or a qualified majority) in *ostrakophoria* made the possibly widest canvassing the only reasonable

---

[79] Siewert, T 1/67; *Kerameikos 20.2*, 1336 (O 6874).
[80] See, e.g., Plut. *Cim.* 15; 17; *Arist.* 7. Cf. Carcopino (1935) 70–72. Recently, see in general Surikov (2006) 356–379.
[81] Cf. Siewert (1991); Hunter (1990). Forsdyke (2005) 162 with n. 90 interprets the same dynamics in terms of 'some informal debate about who should be ostracised'. I consider this view too optimistic. See also Humphreys (2018) vol. 1, 490. Cf. generally Herman (1994); Loomis (2003); Fisher (2008), and recently Gottesman (2014). In general, cf. also, for the fourth-century Athens, Matuszewski (2019).

survival strategy of every influential Athenian politician. One must have encouraged one's supporters to participate and consolidate them against a particular enemy. It was probably a time of ruthless and shameless struggle for one's support, but also striving to disgrace a particular political opponent. *Ostrakophoria* was to seal the fate of the defeated. Every significant politician would fear the dispersal of 'votes' cast against his opponents, which would automatically work against him. Accordingly, the hatred campaign run by each of them must have been targeted against a particular victim because only in this way could the threat be warded off. To save one's skin, a specific person had to be fed to the Athenian people. Therefore, we ought to envision short-lived 'coalitions' of slanderers, abrupt shifts in political alliances, brutal provocations and every public occasion being used to propagate hatred towards particular individuals.

In other words, the period between the preliminary vote at the Assembly and *ostrakophoria*, which could last up to around 60 days, can be described in terms of permanent *stasis*. It would be different from other known situations of violent political struggle in the Athenian *polis* in that in this case, the conflict was not between two or three groups of followers centred around leaders, but it was a fight of everyone with everyone, even though in such a conflict there were obviously two or more politicians with relatively large 'negative electorates'.

Why, then, was no immediate action taken to remove from Athens the potential threat if the Assembly had preliminarily decided that such a threat exists? As Jérôme Carcopino pointed out, '[i]t is good to allow people time for reflection. It is bad to allow them time for becoming anxious.'[82] Written in 1908, these words are still valid as an apt response to different scholarly explanations of the two stages of the procedure of ostracism. The time needed to spread the word about the incoming *ostrakophoria* and to mobilise masses of the citizenry (thus S. Forsdyke), to 'make hot-headed decisions influenced by ephemeral passions if not impossible, then at least less likely' (L. Hall), or the delay for informal deliberation and campaigning (S. Brenne)[83]—all seem sound guesses. However, such considerations do not

---

[82] Carcopino (1935) 68–69. Consequently, the scholar argued unconvincingly for a shorter time lapse between the two votes (Carcopino (1935) 70–71).
[83] Forsdyke (2005) 162–163; Brenne (1994) 13; Hall (1989) 95. Cf. also Hansen (1999) [1991] 209–210, for similar considerations regarding the procedure of *graphē paranomōn* (cf. below, p. 243 n. 9, on *graphē paranomōn* functionally replacing ostracism in the last quarter of the fifth century): '[d]ealing with the matter twice [*sc.* in the Assembly and then in the courts if a decree

outweigh the potential dangers of a 60-day time gap between the *epicheirotonia* and the *ostrakophoria*.

Naturally, the question must be posed here about the conceivable intentions of Cleisthenes, who, while introducing the law about ostracism, must have accounted for the possibility that the *polis* may teeter on the brink of a destructive *stasis* for tens of days as a result. In the light of the above considerations, the law about ostracism could seem completely irrational or even detrimental to the community. However, Cleisthenes, for some reason, did implement it, and the Athenians, for some reason, did not decide to rescind it for many decades. Therefore, it can be supposed that the positive impact of this law should not be sought in *ostrakophoria* itself and in the inescapable consequences of the decision to apply it made by the *dēmos* in the sixth prytany (or the period matching it before), but in the overall effect of the entire procedure of ostracism.

*

I think that it is worth starting a comprehensive interpretation of ostracism (which has many alarming features and some intriguing aspects) with the material from Athenian ostraka quoted above. More specifically, one needs to consider the possible emotional but also pragmatic reactions of the Athenians to the subsequent stages of the ostracism procedure.

Let us look at the functioning of this system in practice from this very perspective. The fundamental difference in the political situation in Athens at each of the stages of the ostracism procedure lies in a radically distinct political atmosphere in Attica then. On the day of the Assembly vote (and the day before), during the sixth prytany (or equivalent), ostracism was a very distant prospect for the Athenian people, not particularly stirring their imagination. The temperature of the political life must have been as usual. The Assembly had many other issues on the agenda, perhaps essential, but voted on routinely, in a long succession of points which needed to be addressed.[84] In contrast, if the result of the vote on carrying out *ostrakophoria* was positive in a given year, then that very day during the eighth prytany (or at an equivalent time) must have looked utterly different from the point of view of the *dēmos*. The comments and allegations on ostraka

was scrutinised as unconstitutional – M.W.] gave them a breathing-space to overcome the effects of mass psychosis such as a skilful orator could whip up in a highly charged situation' (p. 209).

[84] We can assume it was so even if—which seems obvious—we do not think that the programme of this Assembly session in Cleisthenes' times was exactly equivalent to the programme described in *A.P.* 43.5.

indicate an extremely high level of agitation in individuals and the entire community. A huge crowd of citizens, attracted to the Agora not necessarily by the desire to strike a particularly hated politician, arrived there in excitement, awaiting with curiosity, fear or hope the decision about the exile and the accompanying public humiliation of a powerful political leader. To the majority of citizens, this was not only an exciting but also a solemn and satisfying act, in which the *dēmos* enforced its utmost political rights, its ultimate dominance or hegemony over the most potent fellow citizens. From an individual but also group perspective, this was at the same time the supreme example of 'helping friends and harming enemies', as many Athenian writers defined one of the most important ethical principles of that time.[85] However, perhaps most importantly, from the point of view of individual and group psychology, on that day ostracism was no more an abstract matter to anybody. It was a very concrete choice between two (or more) 'candidates' of flesh and blood, 'candidates' about whom the people of Attica (and not only Athenian citizens) had talked, whom they had praised, smeared, or complained about for the past two months (by our calendar), and among whom were the greatest Athenians: the Megakleses, Themistocleses, Cimons, Alcibiadeses, and even leading representatives of the cultural and intellectual life in Athens, such as Damon, an associate of the great Pericles.

Let us now observe that from the perspective of the most prominent Athenian politicians, naturally threatened with exile through *ostrakophoria*, the situation at each of the stages of the ostracism procedure looked utterly different. For them, the day of *ostrakophoria* was a time of fear, but mainly of insecurity. Jan B. Meister pointed out that extreme uncertainty brought by prospective *ostrakophoriai* was partly due to the fact that on such occasions the social composition of the gathering of the *dēmos* must have been very different from the usual make-up, however changing, of the Athenian Popular Assemblies. Hypothetically, a high mobilisation of the rural population of citizens would unsettle whatever more or less regular line-up of the Assembly might have been at any given time.[86] Therefore, the people's sentiments were entirely unpredictable and could shift even at the last moment due to a more successful mobilisation of one's supporters,

---

[85] See Blundell (1989). See also generally Mitchell (2009). Cf. also Herman (1987) *passim* and Konstan (1996).
[86] Meister (2020) 343–346. For local divisions and forms of organisation of the Athenian *dēmos* in Attica, see, e.g., Osborne (1990).

provocation by political opponents, objective external factors, independent of human decisions, etc. Admittedly, powerful Athenians were not facing (as they had been before the introduction of the law about ostracism) a threat of death, property confiscation or lifetime exile, which they could return from only with a proper military force. Cleisthenes ensured that the 'punishment' resulting from ostracism was not final and did not induce the endangered politicians to desperate actions. However, it should be appreciated that a 10-year honourable exile shattered—or at least was very likely to ruin—the political career the ostracised had patiently been building during his entire life. His influence on the *polis*' matters decreased dramatically. At the same time, backbiting in the home city could use his behaviour abroad and his political alliances and friendships in exile to further weaken his position, impacting his ability to act after his return to Athens 10 years later. The exile's helplessness must have been a particularly poignant punishment for ambitious Athenians.

Briefly put, on the day of *ostrakophoria*, all the prominent Athenian politicians could and should have felt endangered, as the result of the people's vote was unpredictable, and the threat to each of them was almost equal.

However, the reality looked completely different just before the vote at the Assembly at the time equivalent to the sixth prytany. On the one hand, anything was still possible and the threat of *ostrakophoria* could still be avoided, provided that the vote on ostracism was negative. On the other hand, the feelings and calculations of influential Athenian politicians were utterly different from those of the *dēmos*, for whom, as we remember, ostracism was a distant and abstract matter at this stage. To the leaders of the Athenian community and even to its slightly better-known representatives, *ostrakophoria* was a genuine threat. It would also become unavoidable if the result of the vote were positive.

The high 'quorum' of ostracism's *epicheirotonia*, which I postulate (above, 3.2.6), is worth attention here as a mechanism functioning in a way precisely opposite to *ostrakophoria*, executed, as I argued, without a 'quorum' or a qualified majority. While the latter, with the additionally very high turnout of the *dēmos*, was bound to result in the exile of one of the prominent Athenians, the preliminary vote in normal circumstances must have necessarily ended with the lack of a positive decision regarding ostracism. This was due not only to the high threshold of the validity of the people's decision but also to the fact that on that day, the Athenian *dēmos* was usually not particularly determined to carry out an *ostrakophoria*. The majority of the voters were most probably quite indifferent to this issue, and the more responsible individuals realised how much chaos a positive vote might cause in the community. Therefore, it can be assumed that obtaining approval for applying the ostracism procedure required considerable effort on that day and suitable preparation of the political ground for such a decision.

It can be assumed that it usually sufficed if none of the community's leaders undertook such an effort.[87] If no one took action to bring about a positive vote result, everybody could stay safe. This required only a silent agreement between the most potent Athenians at a given point.[88] However, if, for reasons independent of the logic of ostracism, the atmosphere in Athens happened to be heated up to the level at which the people's excitement could predictably lead to the decision to carry out an *ostrakophoria*, the potentially endangered politicians were still able to prevent it: either through concertedly voting against this proposal or—if they expected such effort to conceivably fail—by concertedly breaking the Assembly's 'quorum', which would make such a decision void. Whatever the social composition of the meetings of the Assembly, intensely discussed in scholarship, one thing is certain. The majority, or at least a substantial part, of those attending, were simply citizens determined enough, for various reasons, to be there. I think it is safe to assume that followers of powerful and therefore endangered Athenian politicians were represented considerably among those motivated to attend on that day.[89]

---

[87] This is implied in the manner Plutarch writes about the circumstances of Hyperbolus' actions leading to the positive *epicheirotonia* in the Assembly in 'ca. 416 BC' (*Nic.* 11.4; tr. B. Perrin): 'This fellow [*sc.* Hyperbolus – M.W.] at that time thought himself beyond the reach of ostracism, since, indeed, he was a likelier candidate for the stocks; but he expected that when one of the rivals had been banished he might himself become a match for the one who was left, and so it was plain that he was pleased at their feud, and that he was inciting the people against both of them' (παροξύνων τὸν δῆμον ἐπ' ἀμφοτέρους).

[88] Judging by the analogy with the fourth-century Assembly (cf. Aeschines, *Against Ktesiphon* [III], 3), one can also think of the possibility of manipulating the estimation of the vote and/or of group pressure on the voters exercised by those truly determined to pass (or to stop) a particular decision (cf. also Thuc. VI 24,3–4).

[89] Any precise calculations must be deemed superfluous, but just to realise the order of magnitude of such potential manipulations, we may consider the following. On the one hand, if the maximum capacity of the Pnyx I was ca. 6000 persons or slightly more, the 'optical quorum' (*ho dēmos plethyōn*; see above, pp. 175–176) might have been, say, no less than ca. 4000. On the other hand, when we remind ourselves of the number of military-age and body-abled 'followers' of Cleinias, father of Alcibiades the Elder at Artemisium in 480 BC, i.e., 200 men, we may postulate, say, twice this number as possible to be mustered by the most powerful Athenians in peaceful and physically less demanding circumstances. But even if not, two such political leaders might have been able to mobilise at least 10 per cent and perhaps much more of

I posit that the legal construct which defined ostracism as a two-stage procedure, entailing two votes with a completely different logic and taking place in entirely different circumstances, was intended to put prominent Athenian politicians in a situation resembling the 'prisoner's dilemma'.[90] Even though in practice they were always in danger of losing effective control of the Assembly, in principle each of them could either 'cooperate' at the stage of *epicheirotonia* to ensure safety for himself and his political enemies in a given year, or 'defect' at this point, putting himself and his political opponents at risk of an unavoidable exile of one of them.

The problem was, of course, that the community's leaders were actually in the situation of the 'iterated prisoner's dilemma', as all the participants in the Athenian political game had to take into account not only the current situation but also their past experiences connected with the behaviour of their political opponents as well as the future plans and long-term calculations which could be expected of them. The factors in play were infinite, such as the age and experience of the political rivals, their family and social relations, etc. Thus, on the one hand, the sense of impending threat could induce individuals to 'cooperate', but on the other hand, such a decision required a minimum of mutual trust between the most powerful politicians at a given point. For according to the logic of the 'prisoner's dilemma', the decision to 'cooperate' could be mercilessly used by an unscrupulous opponent, who could attack his enemy publicly with populist allegations. It was enough, for instance, to take advantage of the concerted absence of one of the politicians and his supporters, aimed at breaking the Assembly's 'quorum', or of his manifest efforts to bring about a negative result of the vote. If the people received such populist actions well, they could give one a decisive advantage at the very start of the smear campaign before the *ostrakophoria*. The natural mistrust of the people towards wealthy citizens,

---

the citizens required to break the quorum or to tip the vote in their favour. In general, as Ps.-Andocides (already quoted above) puts it (*Alc.* [IV], 4; tr. Michael Edwards), 'in such circumstances those who have political friends and confederates have an advantage over the others.' Even if what the writer had in mind here was simply *ostrakophoria*, this judgement is no doubt valid for *epicheirotonia* as well. Cf. also 100 of Cimon's *hetairoi* at the battle of Tanagra *Cim.* 17.6–7 (see above, n. 32).

[90] Interestingly, Simonton (2017) esp. 67–68 and *passim*, 'conceive[d] of stable oligarchic government as the cooperative solution to an "iterated" Prisoner's Dilemma'. To him, '[o]ligarchs resemble participants in such a game' (both citations on p. 68). In my present case, the 'stable government', and so the ultimate authority in this game, is that of the *dēmos*. And while striving, alongside the *dēmos*, for stability, leading Athenian politicians do not struggle for domination, but for mere political survival to fight another day.

so clearly visible in the accusations on the ostraka and the anecdotal material about Athenian politicians of classical times, made such provocations very easy.[91]

Such treacherous behaviour of a politician or politicians choosing the 'defect' strategy would, of course, have its price, as it would diminish their trustworthiness in the future and thus put them (together with others) at constant risk of *ostrakophoria*. It should be noted that 'cooperation' between politicians seeking safety could take the form of silent agreement, but in more challenging situations or to make the effect more secure, also more concrete forms could be used, such as backroom negotiations or informal alliance sealed with the word of honour and requisite oaths. It is easy to imagine, for instance, negotiations crowned with joint participation in a *symposion*, where the communal and religious aspects could increase the reliability of such momentary political proximity.[92]

For such contacts, indispensable once a year for saving one's skin from the risk of *ostrakophoria*, to be possible at all, representatives of Athenian élites had to maintain a certain level of mutual trust throughout the entire year and avoid behaviours and actions which potentially precluded future negotiations. It is difficult to say, of course, where the boundaries of behaviours acceptable in the common 'code of conduct' of Athenian élites were at that time. They must have been fluid at any point of the game and changeable depending on the overall political situation in Athens, more or less distant family connections between such potential partners, etc. Importantly, each participant of the game would be able to define them at a given point, which was necessary for making individual decisions to 'cooperate' or 'defect', when faced with the procedure of ostracism.

The most important and ultimate effect of keeping the representatives of Athenian élites in readiness for negotiation or even for momentary silent 'cooperation' in the *epicheirotonia* vote was maintaining during the year (between the yearly Assemblies in the sixth prytany or equivalent) the

---

[91] Among possible examples of such political manipulations, of a quasi-theatrical character at that, one may quote an episode of Xenophon's *Hellenica* (I 7,8); cf. also D.S. XIII 101,6. In 406 BC, Theramenes and his supporters (οἱ... περὶ τὸν Θηραμένην) persuaded a large group of citizens at the festival of Apatouria to come to the Assembly in mourning garments and pretend to belong to the grief-stricken families of those who perished in the battle of Arginusae. All this in order to prepare the emotional ground for condemning the generals of this battle in the Assembly.

[92] As I have tried to show (Węcowski (2014) esp. 74–78), such social occasions would traditionally serve as hubs of the natural selection of Greek aristocracies, integrating successful arrivistes into local élite circles. This traditional function of the *symposion* would hypothetically favour negotiating temporary alliances between prominent politicians.

Athenian political life and the political competition between 'players' at a level guaranteeing the possibility for two or multiple parties to hold reliable negotiations at least once a year. The unwritten political code of conduct of the Athenian élites was what normally guaranteed the stability of domestic policy or at least cooled down the political struggle in the first decades of the Athenian democracy's functioning.

It would be reasonable to ask if clear traces of such backstage negotiations and deals, and those of cooperation between influential leaders in fifth-century Athenian assemblies, can be found in our historical data.[93] Although occurring at a later stage, before the *ostrakophoria*, the pact of 'ca. 416 BC' between Nicias and Alcibiades, bitterly fighting each other at this time, is a good case in point.[94] In general, solid indirect evidence for a possibility of such arrangements may be provided by political marriages occurring not infrequently between representatives of otherwise competing élite families in Athens.[95] No doubt, political 'channels of communication' were open for discreet parleying at any given moment of the year—when it really mattered for the leading Athenian politicians.[96]

From the perspective of the 'prisoner's dilemma', a long-term and immediate success (or safety from the risk of exile) depended on the simultaneous concerted choice of the 'cooperate' strategy by two or more important Athenian politicians. The ultimate 'judge' in this game was the *dēmos*, who inexorably punished 'defection' on the day of *ostrakophoria*. We could even pose a hypothesis that the Athenian people perceived the possibility of sentencing someone to an exile not only as an exciting opportunity to harm a particular Athenian politician but also as punishment to the

---

[93] Hansen (1999) [1991] 280–281 gives some examples of collaboration between two or more political leaders 'and the formation of small political groups' (p. 281) in the late fifth and in the fourth century.
[94] See esp. Plut. *Arist.* 7,3 ([*sc.* Alcibiades and Nicias—M.W.]... διαλεχθέντες ἀλλήλοις καὶ τὰς στάσεις ἑκατέρας εἰς ταὐτὸ συναγαγόντες κτλ. – '...they came to terms with one another, united their opposing factions...' [tr. B. Perrin]); *Alc.* 13,4 ('Alcibiades had a conference with Nicias' [tr. B. Perrin]: ...καὶ διαλεχθεὶς πρὸς τὸν Νικίαν); *Nic.* 11,4 ('...they secretly gave their word to one another [καὶ λόγον δόντες ἀλλήλοις κρύφα], united and harmonized their factions...' [tr. B. Perrin, adapted]). In general, cf. below.
[95] In general, see *APF*, *passim*, esp. p. 119 on a 'virtual Whig aristocracy' created by the marriages between the families of Pericles, Teisandros, Callias, Cleinias, Glaukon, and Andocides between the 450s and the 420s of the fifth century; more recently see Harris (2013) 312. See also Connor (1992) 15–18.
[96] Cf. also, e.g., the tradition about the secret agreement between Pericles and Cimon, made through the agency of Elpinike, Cimon's sister, regarding the return of Cimon from exile (Plut. *Per.* 10,4). The anecdote may be historically worthless, but it may be due to an early attempt at explaining not only the (short) peaceful coexistence of those powerful enemies in Athens but also the granting of a crucial military command to Cimon during Pericles' leadership in Athens.

entire group of leading politicians for their quarrelsomeness and lack of cooperation, which exposed the *polis* to political chaos for dozens of days. This period could also be seen—in almost ritual terms—as a peculiar 'safety fuse' and a time to purify Athens from negative political emotions for the sake of the future.

By putting the quarrelsome Athenian élites, to whom he consciously belonged himself, in the situation of the 'iterated prisoner's dilemma', Cleisthenes was drawing on his experience (mentioned above) from the times of tyranny, and above all from the times of his brutal competition with Isagoras. Both by diminishing the 'stakes' of the game through limiting the 'punishment' for the defeated rival (10-year honourable exile instead of death, property confiscation or exile for indeterminate time) and by introducing a procedure forcing political leaders to cooperate, Cleisthenes prevented potential attempts at an extreme violation of the rules of political play by a defeated or weakening populist appealing to the people (as he had once done, and Pisistratus before him) or seeking support abroad and betraying fellow citizens (as he had once done, as had done Isagoras, and finally also the Pisistratids). He was thus preventing the endemic and well-known vulnerability of the Athenian political life of the archaic times. He could have rightly believed that it was precisely a mechanism such as ostracism that was needed, and missing, in the times of his strife with Isagoras and of the 'Athenian revolution of 508/507 BC',[97] when only exceptional serendipity and extreme determination of the *dēmos* (factors non-legal and perhaps inimitable) saved the Athenian *polis* from tyranny and foreign dominance.

*

On the face of it, in the most general outline, the scholars who regarded ostracism primarily as a preventive means against *stasis* and divisions among the citizens were correct—whether they understood it in purely pragmatic terms or as 'a collective ritual', whose 'fundamental significance [...] for the Athenians was its role as a deterrent to violent intra-elite conflict' by the *dēmos* symbolically monopolising the power to impose exile.[98] Of course, contrary to such interpretations, all this would be achieved not through the vote of ostraka itself but through the entire two-stage procedure of ostracism, putting the most prominent Athenians in the situation of the 'prisoner's dilemma'. However, I think our interpretation ought to be more nuanced.

---

[97] In a similar vein, Forrest (1966) 202.   [98] Thus Forsdyke (2005) 161 and *passim*.

In a broader perspective, I would argue that Cleisthenes' ingenious idea, rooted as it was in his own political experience, to introduce ostracism into the Athenian political system, fits in with John K. Davies' interpretation of 'democracy without theory'. No theory or democratic ideology was needed here since ostracism, one of the crucial mechanisms of control in Athenian democracy, was in fact 'basically negative'—i.e., it was 'designed to prevent, or to minimise the impact of, behaviour which is adjudged to be a danger to the community and to its polity'.[99]

Davies singles out 'the seven dangers and their prevention' to interpret the development of Athenian democracy: (1) 'how to prevent regional links and loyalties from escalating into civil war'; (2) 'how to prevent, or to control, or to prevent the re-emergence of, tyranny';[100] (3) 'how to ensure that smaller corporate bodies within the polity [...] do not usurp power to the point of overshadowing and even controlling the Assembly'; (4) [how to prevent] 'the danger of the arbitrary exercise of power by magistrates'; (5) [how to prevent] 'embezzlement of public monies';[101] (6) 'how do we deal with untrustworthy judges (bribable, prejudiced, vindictive)?'; (7) 'how does a community deal with the informal networks of influence, social control, and differential resource allocation which we normally group together under the loose title of "patronage"?'[102]

Interestingly, it can be argued that more than just one of those factors, or 'dangers', were in practice prevented, at least in some circumstances and to some extent, by the subtle mechanism of Athenian ostracism. Or rather, that by imposing mechanisms of (however limited and unstable) compromise among the Athenian leading politicians, more than one of the needs above were or could be met. In time, ostracism happened to be a very flexible political and legal tool. In its long history in the fifth century BC, it proved applicable, at least subjectively in the minds of the Athenians, to various serious political problems. Hence, on the one hand, as one may surmise, its political longevity, but on the other hand, the embarrassing array of its ancient interpretations and the wild range of accusations and gossip one finds on Athenian ostraka.

*

In this context, one needs to consider two conceivable objections to the idea of Cleisthenes consciously introducing into the Athenian polity a law that,

---

[99] I quote here Davies (2003) 327.   [100] Davies (2003) 327.
[101] Davies (2003) 328–330.   [102] Davies (2003) 328–331.

first, could endanger the community by exposing it to the danger of a 'controlled *stasis*' year by year and, secondly, was in fact designed not to be implemented to its full extent in normal circumstances. As to the first objection, briefly put, it is worth emphasising that *stasis*, or civil dissent, was not regarded as absolute evil in sixth-century Athens. If we take the so-called Solon's law against political neutrality as authentic, what was condemnable at times of internal strife was the apathy of citizens that could pave the way for a determined and well-organised minority to seize power.[103] In this respect, Cleisthenes' law about ostracism would, to some extent, follow the logic of the Solonian law.[104] As to the second objection, one may be tempted to draw an analogy between, on the one hand, the two-stage procedure of ostracism with *ostrakophoria* to be activated only as a final resort and, on the other hand, the famous *antidosis*, or property exchange, in Athenian law.[105] In both cases, the goal of their first procedural step was to impose negotiations on those involved for the procedure to be ultimately beneficial to the *polis*. In the case of *antidosis*, the actual exchange of property between two citizens in Athens might well have never happened.

5.2.3 Athenian Ostracism and the 'Theory of Cooperation' I: A Historical Approach

The above hypothesis explaining the aim and functioning of ostracism can be expressed in terms of the 'theory of cooperation' by Robert Axelrod. Namely, the most significant Athenian politicians at a given time, clearly enjoying the support of various groups among the *dēmos*, were put by Cleisthenes in the situation of the 'iterated prisoner's dilemma', in which the Athenian people were the last instance judging their behaviour and ultimately imposing 'penalty' on the defeated 'player'.

In the previous section, I tried to understand the two-stage procedure of ostracism as a tool that Cleisthenes used to achieve the effect of the Athenian 'prisoner's dilemma'. It is worth considering now whether the 'cooperative'

---

[103] See in particular Leão, Rhodes (2015) 63–66, where the authenticity and conceivable logic of this law are discussed at length with relevant bibliography (against its authenticity, famously, Bleicken (1995) 365–366 and 637–638); see also Rhodes, *ad.* 8.5. Recently cf., however, van 't Wout (2010); Schmitz (2011) and (2014) 50–53; Heftner (2012); Gouschin (2016) and Valdés-Guía (2021).
[104] See also above, on George Grote's interpretation of ostracism. Cf. Carcopino (1935) 109.
[105] I owe this idea to Kostas Apostolakis (*per litteras*, 28 September 2017). In general, see Apostolakis (2006) esp. 93–94, for relevant bibliography.

interpretation of how ostracism worked provides a better explanation than those proposed so far of the aspects of this institution discussed above.

Let me recall the famous words by Karl Julius Beloch, who said about ostracism that 'people do not forge such a weapon to let it rust for 20 years in its sheath'.[106] In the light of the above interpretation of ostracism in terms of the 'theory of cooperation' and the 'prisoner's dilemma', the 20-year gap between the introduction of this law in Athens and the first *ostrakophoria* becomes entirely understandable. The Athenians simply used ostracism year after year from the very beginning. However, as long as this 'weapon' worked properly, by its mere prospect forcing the Athenian élites to act together and cooperate, there was no opportunity for its violent use on the day of *ostrakophoria*. Moreover, the vote with ostraka and the exile of the first ostracism victim in 488/487 BC testify, from the perspective of Athenian leaders, that the mechanism designed by Cleisthenes 'seized up', given that one of them decided to 'defect' instead of 'cooperating'. However, from the perspective of the Athenian people, it proves the necessity to resort to a preventive means which would allow them to appropriately punish a representative of the élite for refusing to cooperate.

Based on the same principle, it is possible to explain why the Athenians applied *ostrakophoria* extremely rarely. As we remember, this happened merely 12, or at most 14 times during the nearly 90-year history of this institution. Briefly speaking, the proper functioning of ostracism can be recognised when *ostrakophoria* is unnecessary, and the preliminary vote at the Assembly ends in a negative result.

The Athenian 'prisoner's dilemma' also allows us to understand why *ostrakophoriai* have a clear tendency to be condensed in time in the history of ostracism. The first five of them came in a series, year after year, with only a year's gap: 488/487 [Hipparchos son of Charmos], 487/486 (Megakles son of Hippocrates), 486/485 ('the tyrants' friend'), 485/486 (Xanthippus son of Ariphron), and 483/482 BC (Aristides). The subsequent ones occurred 'in pairs': 471? (Megakles again) and 470? BC (Themistocles), 462/461 (Cimon) and 460? BC (Alcibiades the Elder), 443? (Thucydides son of Melesias) and shortly before or shortly after (Damon). Only the last and the most peculiar case of Hyperbolus' ostracism (ca. 416 BC) is entirely isolated.

Considerations of this pattern must take into account two factors, well defined by Plutarch, who wrote about ostracising Thucydides son of

---

[106] Beloch (1926) 332.

Melesias (*Per.* 14.2), 'and finally he [Pericles] ventured to undergo with Thucydides the contest of the ostracism, wherein he secured his rival's banishment, and the dissolution of the faction which had been arrayed against him (tr. B. Perrin)' ([...] εἰς ἀγῶνα περὶ τοῦ ὀστράκου καταστὰς καὶ διακινδυνεύσας ἐκεῖνον μὲν ἐξέβαλε, κατέλυσε δὲ τὴν ἀντιτεταγμένην ἑταιρείαν). Plutarch rightly emphasises Pericles' hazardous decision, but he naïvely adds immediately afterwards that in consequence of Thucydides' exile, the political struggle within the *polis* ceased altogether, and internal peace prevailed (15.1). However, in reality, the powerful 'Olympian' most probably had to live with the consequences which his mentor Damon had to bear as a result of the *ostrakophoria* of the following year[107] and which exposed other associates and friends of Pericles to attacks made with the use of political instruments other than ostracism.[108] Thus, according to the logic of the 'iterated prisoner's dilemma', a single choice of the 'defect' strategy brings about the revenge of other (political) players. In the Athenian context, this revenge could cease after eliminating the opponent for 10 years, as in Thucydides' case. However, also here vengeance of the allies and supporters of the defeated, even though on a smaller scale, had to be taken into account. Moreover, in the circumstances different than Pericles' domination in Athens, there might have been several strong political players, so the chain of 'defections' and acts of revenge could be quite long, as was the case of the series of the first five *ostrakophoriai* in the 80s—most probably until the most fierce enemies were eliminated or until mutual trust was rebuilt by those less intransigent. Interestingly, Pericles decided to use ostracism as a political tool only once. The comic playwright Cratinus presents him as relieved at the 'passing of ostracism' in a particular year, which refers to the negative result of the preliminary vote.[109]

For the procedure of ostracism to be applied, a politician was needed who was apt to take the risk, but also relentless and uncompromising, not inclined to make deals with other leaders of the community, but endeavouring to eliminate them and convinced of his dominance over them, mainly due to the exceptional support of the *dēmos*, which should translate into the result of the vote on the day of *ostrakophoria*. Such must have

---

[107] However, it cannot be excluded that the sequence of events was reverse. See above, pp. 109–110.
[108] See the bibliography referenced above, p. 109, n. 130.   [109] See above, pp. 120–121.

been the case of Themistocles,[110] a regular 'candidate' in the *ostrakophoriai* of the 80s and the beginning of the 70s, who after the battle of Marathon, most probably intending to realise his political strategy for Athens without compromise,[111] presumably repeatedly pressed for ostracism, armed with the people's support. However, after a shift on the political scene (and perhaps due to some fraud over the ballot box, as is suggested by the 'Themistocles ostraka' from the slopes of Acropolis), he also fell victim to *ostrakophoria*, according to the logic of revenge of the 'fellow players', for consistent application of the strategy ALL D, or 'always defect'. Not dissimilar could have been the case of the two ostracisms which happened towards the end of the 60s. The first of them was caused by the radical populist Ephialtes and his young associate Pericles, but the political life at that time was heated up to an unprecedented degree. Ephialtes was (allegedly) secretly murdered, which is an extreme case of breaking the rules of the political game. The following year must have seen another *ostrakophoria*.

It was pointed out long ago that the majority of the Athenian ostracisms took place during the times which were particularly turbulent in terms of Athenian foreign policy, in situations that stimulated one of the community's leaders to make an unyielding choice of political course. Not only did such times influence the extreme calculations of some Athenian politicians, but they also (due to the general tension) made the people more susceptible to radical propaganda (negative at the personal level, but sometimes positive from the perspective of political plans for the entire community), which additionally strengthened relentless politicians in their attempts to use ostracism. Such must have been the already mentioned case of Themistocles in the 80s (in the face of the Persian threat) and the 70s (when the fate of the relations between Athens and Sparta was being decided), but also at the end of the 60s, due to the dispute regarding the model of the Athenian policy towards the Greeks and Sparta. Perhaps also the ostracism of Thucydides son of Melesias was connected with the times of undermining Pericles' position and political course of action in Athens.

Overall, in the light of the 'theory of cooperation', it becomes clear that refraining from using ostracism, the last resort in political struggle, was the

---

[110] Thus, e.g., Forrest (1966) 220. Alternatively, as one of my OUP referees observes, 'the controversy over the Alcmeonidai and the "shield signal" will have left them exposed after 490, which might have encouraged them to launch a "first strike"; the fate of Xanthippus would then make sense as retaliation'.

[111] Cf. above, p. 214, on the idea of ostracism by Ste. Croix (2004).

norm in Athenian politics. *Ostrakophoriai* usually happened in times of exceptional turmoil and due to decisions taken by particularly intransigent politicians, who questioned the principle of 'cooperation' when faced with the Athenian 'prisoner's dilemma' as programmed by Cleisthenes.

In this context, the last case of an Athenian *ostrakophoria*, the exile of Hyperbolus 'around 416 BC', is all the more striking. It occurred after several decades of votes resulting in a decision not to apply the procedure of ostracism in subsequent seasons of the Peloponnesian War. Therefore, this case requires a separate analysis in the last section of this book to confirm or reject my interpretation of this institution.

5.2.4 Athenian Ostracism and the 'Theory of Cooperation' II: A Theoretical Approach

I believe the analysis can be furthered if the above 'cooperative' interpretation is regarded in abstract terms.

The lawgiver inscribed into the law about ostracism several mechanisms stimulating 'cooperation'.

First, it is worth noticing that Cleisthenes gave all the 'fellow prisoners' (1) THE GUARANTEE OF A SHORT-TERM BENEFIT—by ensuring their safety from the threat of exile for the entire year to follow if they act together to achieve the negative result of the preliminary vote at the Assembly in the sixth prytany (or at the equivalent time in the earlier calendar). We should remember that immediate profit is usually prioritised in human calculations over long-term benefit. On the other hand, from the perspective of Axelrod's prescription, Cleisthenes the reformer 'enlarged the shadow of the future' by making dominating Athenian politicians include in their calculations (2) THE GUARANTEE OF PUNISHMENT FOR 'DEFECTION', through the mandatory result of *ostrakophoria* in the eighth prytany—i.e., the exile of one of the 'candidates'. The lack of a 'quorum' or a qualified majority in the vote with ostraka made the 10-year exile inevitable, and the high level of agitation of the Athenian crowd gathered on that day added to this punishment for 'defection' a decisive psychological factor—the uncertainty who from among the 'players' will be punished in this way. During the time between the preliminary vote and the moment of announcing the result of the vote with ostraka, nobody could feel secure, and everybody lived in fear of poignant 'punishment'. In the same way, the reformer guaranteed the community leaders (3) fundamental UNCERTAINTY OF LONG-TERM BENEFIT, i.e., the potential victory over the political opponent. The immediate and assured benefit must have been all the more valuable to them, namely the safety arising from the negative result of the Assembly vote.

Cleisthenes did something else as well. He ensured (4) THE INTENSIFICATION OF INTERACTION BETWEEN THE 'PLAYERS', making negotiation (or at least considering it) necessary by introducing the mandatory preliminary vote on ostracism at a specific time each year. He also guaranteed the 'players' (5) THE CERTAINTY OF THEIR FUTURE INTERACTIONS, given that, on the one hand, the exile of the defeated politician was only temporary. On the other hand, it was limited to only one leader of a given political group, who additionally retained his income from his property in Attica. In practice, this meant the prospect of the political enemy's return to Athens one day as well as the fact that his supporters, including (crucially) his closest associates and/or political heirs, remained in the city and would need to be adequately negotiated with every year (see point 4 above) before the preliminary vote at the Assembly. It should be added that the ability to retain the income in the home city must have meant in practice that the exile will be in constant, undisturbed and legally sanctioned contact with his family and his proxies in the city.

Overall, the effect of intensifying interaction and ensuring future interactions of the most important Athenian politicians was achieved through (6) INSTITUTIONALISATION OF THE PLAY between them. Such is the function I would ascribe to the annually voted procedure of ostracism. It must have fostered bonds and mutual trust (even if limited) between the 'players', as 'defection' in any previous year would naturally hinder agreement before the Assembly vote, which would put everybody at risk of a detrimental *ostrakophoria*.

The decisions of the politicians who consciously chose 'defection' instead of 'cooperation' with their 'fellow prisoners' can also be described in terms of the 'theory of cooperation'. In this case, the focus should be on the psychological factor. The conviction was that 'defection' is beneficial at the first stage of the 'game' because the popularity of the 'player' among the Athenian people remarkably diminishes the risk of 'punishment' on the day of *ostrakophoria*, and thus makes 'cooperation' unprofitable. In other words, a mighty individual in a powerful position or a relatively strong politician apt to take high risks would regard his start position in the 'game' as dominating and, confident of his own advantage, would escalate the conflict. The consciousness of this considerable advantage immunised him to all the mechanisms encouraging to 'cooperate' prepared by the reformer. The certainty of a short-term profit (1) gave way then to a strong hope for (3) a long-term profit and removed the (2) inevitability of punishment for 'defection'. Additionally, the confidence in one's dominating position in the 'game' invalidated the factor of (4) intensification of future interaction because victory in the *ostrakophoria* of a given year was supposed to increase this advantage further, making any negotiations with the opponent unnecessary in the foreseeable future. The same principle applies to the (5) certainty of future interactions with the opponent—because the 'fellow prisoner', already in a defensive position, would lose his political position entirely during the 10-year exile, and his supporters remaining in the city would become even weaker without the leader.

Briefly put, ostracism was pressed for in Athens by 'players' who, confident in their strength, consciously chose the 'ALL D strategy' ('always defect') instead of the safe, cooperation-based strategy TIT FOR TAT, which would keep them in check along the chain of annually repeated decisions on 'cooperation'.

*

These last considerations seem to indicate that the system designed by Cleisthenes could be effective only provided that the 'players' were convinced of their more or less equal political position in Athens. This is logical, as Cleisthenian ostracism was intended to solve the problem of a stalemate in which the politicians competing for dominance feel the need to violently break the rules of the game by, for instance, resorting to calling in foreign intervention. Interestingly, this system did not protect the *polis* against politicians so strong that they could pose a real threat of tyrannical rule. I have already mentioned that politicians of this sort had fewer reasons than others to fear *ostrakophoria*. It can be supposed that Cleisthenes regarded the system of new institutions in the *polis* he was constructing and the new division of the citizen body as sufficient warranty of a break with the tyrannical past. Perhaps the 'popular revolt of 508/507 BC', studied by Josiah Ober, further reinforced his conviction that the level of political consciousness of the Athenian *dēmos* and its political independence is so high that a simple manipulation by a politician with tyrannical ambition was not conceivable in the long run.

Therefore, it should be concluded that the late (fourth-century) conviction, regularly expressed in our sources, that ostracism was originally an institution intended to prevent tyranny was a complete anachronism. Nonetheless, it might have been rooted in the propaganda of some

Athenian political leaders of the 80s of the fifth century, who certainly used this argument against the opponents connectable with the Pisistratids in the eyes of the Athenians. However, this was not Cleisthenes' primary calculation. It turned out later, of course, that in critical situations, the entire democratic system could collapse, and the rule went to small groups of oligarchs (even though not individuals!). Hence the need for anti-tyrannical laws recurring in the history of Athenian democracy.

The mechanism of *ostrakophoria* integrated the citizen community and, when eliminating one of its leaders, avoided putting him at the point of no return when the only viable solution for him was to break the widely accepted rules of the political game. While introducing it to the system, Cleisthenes did not fear the destructive influence on the *polis* of self-confident politicians, determined and intransigent enough to reject 'cooperation' with partners and consistently choose 'defection'. It is unclear whether he considered this risk worth taking and the potential harm acceptable, or perhaps his imagination was insufficient, as he saw how the Athenian *dēmos* itself became an active and ultimately responsible political force. However, even if Cleisthenes erred there, we must admit that his prognoses proved correct (even in extremely difficult times for the Athenians) during the next 20 years, until the first *ostrakophoria* in 488/487 BC. It should immediately be added that in politics, a 20-year period of effective functioning of a statesman's calculations almost equals infinity. Cleisthenes proved to be an extremely far-sighted reformer, especially given that for the 70 years to follow, after the Persian Wars, the mechanism of the 'iterated prisoner's dilemma' designed by him was working well enough for the second instance of ostracism, punishing the 'defecting' players, to be employed only nine, and most probably merely seven times.

Epilogue and Conclusions
The Decline and Fall of Athenian Ostracism

In my epilogue, I need to consider two closely interconnected but in fact separate issues, often merged or even mixed up in scholarship, owing to the influence of our ancient literary sources immediately commenting on 'the Hyperbolus affair' and contemporaneous with it. On the one hand, one ought to establish what went wrong and why in 'around 416 BC', when ostracism led to the exile of Hyperbolus, who was widely regarded, as it seems, as an 'unworthy victim' of this institution. Hence the subsequent uproar echoing in our sources. On the other hand, despite the scandal of 'ca. 416 BC', one has to determine the reasons why Athenians kept ostracism 'on the books' for at least 80 years following the restoration of their democracy—and did so despite their poor experience with the ostracism of Hyperbolus. Indeed, the 'oligarchic gap' between these events and the last years of the fifth century suggests, I suppose, that we must take into account an almost entirely fresh start for ostracism in the Athenian political system after 403 BC.[1] In other words, whatever the reasons for the allegedly poor performance of ostracism in 'around 416 BC', the political, legal, and social circumstances of the revival and survival of ostracism in the fourth century BC are a different matter altogether.

From Pericles to Hyperbolus, or What Went Wrong in 'ca. 416 BC'?

One of the possible ways to verify the validity of the hypothesis presented above regarding the primary aim of the law about ostracism is considering this explanatory model in the light of the context of this law's fall, i.e., the chronologically last ostracism of Hyperbolus.

---

[1] In a similar vein, Heftner (2003) 33.

EPILOGUE AND CONCLUSIONS   241

At first sight (no matter how we solve the problem of mutual connections and reliability of the numerous sources available for this topic),[2] the political circumstances which led to the decision taken at the Assembly in 'ca. 416 BC' to carry out an *ostrakophoria*, which resulted in exiling Hyperbolus, seem to follow the pattern observed above in other ostracisms of the fifth century. In the preceding years, the two main 'candidates' for ostracism that year, Alcibiades and Nicias, had been competing in Athenian politics, representing in the eyes of the *dēmos* two extremely divergent foreign policies in the times after the armistice with Sparta in the Peloponnesian War. The picture presented by Plutarch is perfectly understandable. It suggests that in the *ostrakophoria* the Athenians would be given a chance to make the ultimate choice between these two lines of political thought. This picture corresponds very well with the view of the contemporaries, presenting Hyperbolus, who ultimately went into exile as a result of the *ostrakophoria*, in the following way: 'his lot was matching his behaviour, | but not matching his person and stigma; | for ostracism was not invented for such people' (Plato Comicus, fr. 203 K–A: [...] οὐ γὰρ τοιούτων οὕνεκ' ὄστραχ' ηὑρέθη). The scandal which broke out in consequence of this vote must have been huge.

The Athenian people, initially content about getting rid of the hated politician, were in the end outraged at the way in which Hyperbolus was selected with ostraka. They regarded as a breach of the political code of conduct (and ultimately as defiance of the very essence of this institution) the fact that two (or three)[3] prominent politicians 'set up' their supporters to vote for the fall of another demagogue, who was also less important, even though very ambitious.

From the perspective of the explanatory model proposed above, this situation includes two crucial 'anomalies'. Firstly—and this is precisely what was seen as scandalous—the 'cooperation' between the political leaders did not happen at the stage of the preliminary vote but afterwards, when (in symbolic but also in practical terms) the uncertain fate of members of the Athenian élite was supposed to rest solely in the hands of the people. This did not exclude political scheming and propaganda battles being fought

---

[2] See above, pp. 207–208 n. 23. To my knowledge, Heftner (2000a) is the most recent thorough interpretation of the relevant primary data. His scepticism regarding the tradition of the backstage deal against Hyperbolus orchestrated by Alcibiades seem unwarranted to me (Heftner (2000a) esp. 55–59). Cf. also Heftner (2000b) and (2003).

[3] Namely Alcibiades and Nicias (in Plutarch's 'mainstream' account) or Alcibiades and Phaeax (according to Theophrastus, in Plut. *Nic.* 11,10), or perhaps all three of them (Plut, *Alc.* 13,1–2).

until the last moment before the *ostrakophoria*, but such behaviour was accepted with the provision that the ultimate victim was one of the influential 'candidates' predicted by the *dēmos*. In other words, making political deals after the vote in the sixth prytany deprived the *dēmos* of its essential prerogatives.

Secondly, our sources clearly indicate that something peculiar happened even earlier, at the moment of the Assembly vote. There are two conceivable versions of the political events which took place on that day. In one of them, Hyperbolus himself was pressing for ostracism, hoping—according to the political custom—to remove one of his most powerful rivals, Alcibiades or Nicias, from the *polis* through *ostrakophoria*.[4] Another possibility is that Alcibiades (or Nicias) was the one supporting ostracism,[5] but after the vote, suddenly doubting his own popularity or listening to the voice of his 'negative electorate', he engineered a coalition with the equally endangered Nicias/Alcibiades (or perhaps also with Phaeax) to definitively get rid of Hyperbolus.

Of course, I cannot engage here in discussing the nature of the political conflict between all these politicians,[6] nor can I establish which of these versions is historically more probable.[7] In any case, both are of equal interest to us because they can explain the scandal surrounding the ultimate result of the *ostrakophoria*.

In the light of the Athenian 'prisoner's dilemma', one of two things happened then. The agreement (even if silent) between the important politicians in advance of the vote in the Assembly could have been challenged by somebody from beyond their circle, which undermined the mechanism of ostracism. (In other words, the 'cooperation' strategy of two players was derailed by a third—an outsider choosing 'defection' and thus putting all of them at risk). Alternatively, one of the important Athenian politicians decided to 'defect', but cowered and tried to change the rules of the game, aiming for 'cooperation' at the stage when he should have accepted the 'punishment'.

---

[4] Plut. *Nic.* 11,4.
[5] Such ideas are found in modern scholarship. See Heftner (2000a) 48/49 n. 52.
[6] Cf. recently Siewert (1999); Rosenbloom (2004a) and (2004b). Mann (2007) 240–241 convincingly interprets the positive vote in the Assembly as a reaction to the novelty of Alcibiades' political persona. This may be alluded to by Thucydides (VIII 73,3), where Hyperbolus is characterised as a surprising victim of ostracism, because he was not exiled for his reputation (*axiōma*), for his might (*dunamis*), nor did he incite fear (*phobos*). As Mann points out, our sources characterise Alcibiades in these terms exactly.
[7] See the overview of scholarly opinions in Rhodes (1994).

Naturally, also in normal circumstances momentary alliances could be made in the period before *ostrakophoria* to protect a given Athenian against exile. However, this time, the political 'deal' made by Alcibiades must have struck the citizens with its flagrancy. Alcibiades' political career shows that he occasionally breached the accepted norms manifestly, combining cynicism with impertinence. This is perhaps confirmed by the tradition in which the Athenian *dēmos* was initially content about Hyperbolus' exile and burst with outrage only after a while. I am inclined to interpret this sequence as evidence of a far-reaching hatred campaign, in which various groups of Athenians were captivated by the propaganda of several different political circles (Alcibiades, Nicias, perhaps Phaeax), and only after some time did many of the citizens who were in principle closer to this or that political centre realise that all of them had been misled by a momentary collusion of leaders who were officially fierce opponents.[8]

Meanwhile, if, as it is far more likely, Hyperbolus was indeed the one responsible for the positive vote of *epicheirotonia* to hold an *ostrakophoria* that year, there might have been one more reason for the Athenian *dēmos* to be appalled. As Plutarch puts it (*Nic.* 11.4), Hyperbolus believed to be himself immune to ostracism when he orchestrated the people's decision in the Assembly. In that, he broke the rules of the game as an outsider, not being himself one of the players involved in the Athenian 'prisoner's dilemma'. It would be tempting to take the words of Plato Comicus (fr. 203 Kassel–Austin) as referring not only to the ultimate result of the *ostrakophoria* but to the whole procedure of ostracism in 'around 416 BC': 'ostracism was not invented for such people'.

In either of these cases, the Athenians had the right to conclude that the mechanism of ostracism failed, and the politicians found an effective way to circumvent the 'prisoner's dilemma' designed by Cleisthenes. It is not a coincidence that some scholars link the 'extinction' of the application of ostracism in practice with the emergence of new instruments for disciplining Athenian politicians, such as the procedure of *graphē paranomōn*.[9] However, most important for my considerations is the conclusion that the case of Hyperbolus' ostracism is an exception proving the rule, an 'anomaly',

---

[8] In the eyes of the people, one additional factor to it would be the fact that, as one of my OUP referees kindly observes, this ostracism 'failed to defuse the stand-off on foreign policy'.
[9] Cf. Lehmann (1987); Hansen (1999) [1991] 205; cf. Rhodes (1994) 97 and Mann (2007) 242–243. See, however, below.

recognised as such already by the contemporaries, who acted accordingly. At least for a time.

*

The question remains what happened in Athens in the second half of the fifth century, which made the Cleisthenian 'social contract' lose its validity. How can we explain that—at least in the view of the Athenians, but perhaps also in reality—one or even two Athenian politicians chose on the day of the Assembly to vote for a model of 'defection' which fell outside the set of rules of the game, and one (or two, or three) of them additionally did not respect these rules at the second stage of the ostracism procedure, *de facto* removing the prospect of long-term 'punishment' for lack of cooperation among the Athenian élites?

Let us begin with the fact that for almost 30 years before Hyperbolus' exile, *ostrakophoria* did not happen in Athens. In the initial part of this period, this could be attributed to Pericles' dominance in political life, but after his death, during the hottest and most challenging period of the Peloponnesian War as well as soon after the armistice with Sparta, the Athenians still voted at the Assembly against *ostrakophoria* year after year. Therefore, the Cleisthenian mechanism seems to have worked very well, and Athenian politicians repeatedly chose 'cooperation'. However, it can be supposed that the disgrace of ostracism in 'ca. 416 BC' was a symptom of some more profound problem that had been weakening this institution for some time already.

First of all, it should be pointed out that all the previous *ostrakophoriai* took place at time intervals, guaranteeing the members of the Athenian élite the direct personal experience of an influential politician's exile and the experience of insecurity and fear between the sixth and the eighth prytany. Among the prominent participants in the political play around the time of the ostracism of 'ca. 416 BC', only Nicias belonged to the generation who had this experience. Hyperbolus and Alcibiades were more or less of the same age, both born around the middle of the fifth century. The key role must have been played not as much by the personal experience of this or that politician as by the generation gap of a kind within the Athenian élites. Due to that, politicians did not understand each other any longer, and the level of mutual trust necessary for surviving the Cleisthenian 'prisoner's dilemma' safely, based on the prevalence of a principally similar (even though very much rivalry-oriented) system of values among the leaders of the Athenian community, was not possible any more. This system had previously ensured some balance, but it was a wavering balance and one which was easy to upset. However, when the relations between the most influential politicians collapsed, it was always possible to return to the strategy of 'cooperation' every year, after a short period of 'defections' and revenge. The explosive mixture of community values, individual egoism, ideals of citizen equality and radical elitism which we call Athenian democracy, had, among other things, a regulating mechanism in the form of the ostracism procedure during all this time.

However, from the 60s onwards, in the times corresponding to the period of Pericles' dominance, profound changes took place in Athenian political life. The most important erosive factors of the system of values on which ostracism's mechanism was based were probably the following. First of all, Pericles' long-term dominance in Athens itself. After the exile of Thucydides son of Melesias, he lost the last rival, or a peer, with whom the unwritten agreement to 'cooperate' was possible and profitable. Although each year, as we have seen, Pericles might not have felt particularly safe around the time of the Assembly vote in the sixth prytany, he could undoubtedly rely on his popularity enough not to be forced to make alliances with other Athenian politicians in advance of this vote. Thus, even though the mechanism of ostracism still worked, this law was, to a large extent, already a dead letter. It is apparent, for instance, in the fact that Pericles' political opponents, not having enough influence to be able to bring about an open competition on the day of *ostrakophoria*, had to resort to 'guerrilla warfare' in Athenian tribunals, sometimes threatening the 'Olympian' himself but more often his associates, supporters, and friends. If Damon's exile happened around 442 BC, it would be the last chord of an ending political 'contract'.

Secondly, and connectedly, Pericles' domination, and particularly his considerable influence on the composition of the collegium of *stratēgoi*,[10] must have halted, at least to some extent, independent (or better: entirely self-sufficient) individual careers. Thus, the lack of the natural changing of the guard or generation change of individual Athenian politicians with strong authority and their own firm political position must have dramatically undermined the system of values mentioned above.

Thirdly, Pericles' long-term dominance and the style of his rule is precisely the context in which we need to consider the emergence of leaders described by W. Robert Connor as 'the new politicians of fifth-century

---

[10] Cf. Podlecki (1998) esp. 55–76 and 162–164.

Athens',[11] who ostentatiously declared 'love for the *dēmos*' and sometimes behaved in an uncompromising way in their dealings with representatives of the traditional Athenian élites.[12] Making a trustworthy alliance with somebody like Cleon must have been much more challenging than before, not least because, as Edward Harris has recently shown, Cleon's new tactics (as well as that of his successors) heavily relied on repeated attacks against his political enemies in the courts, thus changing the political atmosphere in Athens entirely.[13] However, Cleon never ventured to contend in *ostrakophoria* either, as we have seen in Aristophanes. It can be supposed that, on the one hand, the political custom which prevented people from showing excessive interest in ostracism during the preliminary vote at the Assembly was still working. On the other hand, in Athenian courts and later on in the Assembly, Cleon had at his disposal a much more effective and much safer set of political tools than ostracism.

I suspect that the final blow to the Cleisthenian political mechanism and the traditional political code of conduct which it was founded on was struck by the fourth factor, namely the emergence of an alternative system of values and an array of new means of political combat—i.e., the intellectual changes connected with the teaching of the so-called sophists.[14] These 'teachers of wisdom' offered (for money) an effective political *technē*, making contenders

---

[11] Connor (1992). I find Mann's (2007) *passim* recent criticism of this idea one-sided. Even if the 'rules of political communication' in the fifth-century Athenian democracy were relatively stable as regards the relationship between leading politicians and the sovereign *dēmos*, it is difficult to deny the appearance of new modes and tools of efficient political activity. Cf. Rhodes (2015) esp. 58–59, for an overview of 'a new kind of politics' in the last three decades of the fifth century. See also below.

[12] Of course, much can be said of the allegedly different socio-economic background of the 'old' and the 'new' leaders. I refrain from following this path of inquiry here not in the least because to deal with this problem nowadays a thorough reassessment of the notion of Greek 'aristocracy' would be required. For the time being, see Węcowski (2022), with ample bibliography as well as above, p. 13, n. 44.

[13] See Harris (2013) esp. 313–320.

[14] In his illuminating reassessment of the nature of the so-called 'sophistic movement', Wallace (1998) established that '[t]here were standard conceptions about the sophists, that they were closely linked with Athens and democracy, that they were a new intellectual and social phenomenon, and that they were a coherent philosophical movement, are thus seen to be in some measure distortions shaped by the limitations of extant evidence', and more specifically, 'that those philosophers who came [*sc.* to Athens—M.W.] after 450 should not be sharply distinguished from philosophers (and poets) who came before and that, by contrast, from 430 marked new trends appear, as a result of both political and intellectual developments. Before 430, the sophists were a positive force for Athens' democracy. Afterward, they helped to destroy it' (Wallace (1998) 222).

for a political career utterly independent of the traditional, family-based model of education, for instance, at élite *symposia*,[15] where the system of values and behaviours common to the élite was an essential element. To put it differently, in the last quarter of the fifth century BC, a void was created by the death of the long-dominating political leader Pericles. In this void, young and ambitious Athenian politicians start 'learning' politics—both its instruments (mainly rhetoric and oblique eristic, which Aristophanes memorably parodies in his comedies: *Clouds* of 423 BC and *Wasps* of 422 BC) and its opportunist system of values—from the 'second generation' of specialists,[16] who in addition were foreign outsiders in the Athenian community, without any connection whatsoever to the Cleisthenian 'social contract' and the rules of the Athenian political game in force thitherto. In consequence, in short, Alcibiades or Plato's Callicles (in *Gorgias*) and Thrasymachus (in the *Republic*) would not necessarily be able to rely on an agreement based on the word of honour of prominent politicians, nor would they be trustworthy themselves while making such (fleeting) alliances.

The fifth factor that should be considered is the significant transformation of the nature of Athenian political life after Pericles' death. It seems that after him, the Athenian politics became—which is suggested already by Thucydides (II 65,10–11)—more 'multipolar' and so more unpredictable than before, which in practice must have complicated building a reliable agreement in advance of the vote in the sixth prytany.

Sixthly, and due to all this, but also owing to the political and social changes begun in the 60s by Ephialtes and young Pericles, the *dēmos* was no longer content with the role assigned to it by Cleisthenes in the law about ostracism. The political mechanisms which gradually replaced ostracism (such as, for instance, *graphē paranomōn*) would give the voice to the people already in the 'first instance', be it at the Assembly or in the courts, without placing sufficient trust in politicians to leave to them at a certain stage of the political game the task of preventing the internal dangers lying in wait for the cohesiveness of the citizen community.

In the process of the withering of the safety mechanism designed by Cleisthenes, one thing appears as particularly striking. Namely, the level of responsibility which the people showed for a dozen years after Pericles'

---

[15] In general, see Węcowski (2014) *passim*.
[16] See Wallace (1998). After ca. 430 BC, 'various philosophical positions associated with the early sophists perhaps inevitably developed over time into more extreme and even offensive formulations, as philosophers sought fame (or notoriety) by ever bolder intellectual innovations' (Wallace (1998) 214–215).

death, in resisting the temptation of *ostrakophoria* during the Archidamian War and in the initial period of the Peace of Nicias. (Let us remember that Hyperbolus' ostracism happened during the time of the peace when the Athenians felt confident enough even to consider military expansion.) Although, as I emphasised at the beginning of this work, it is not a historian's task to draw anachronistic political or ideological conclusions, it is difficult to resist the impression that the history of ostracism testifies, quite optimistically and no doubt paradoxically, to a rational character of this at first sight most exotic institution of the Athenian democracy.

A Fourth-century Consensus?

If my interpretation of what went wrong with Athenian ostracism in 'around 416 BC' stands, the reasons for its demise become clear. And they must have been more profound and less immediate than just the political scandal of Hyperbolus' exile. On the one hand, intransigent politicians found better and less risky ways to fight against their political enemies, thus escaping the 'prisoner's dilemma' trap set up by Cleisthenes. On the other hand, the Athenian people had at their disposal much better, safer, and more direct ways to control and 'punish' their political leaders. Therefore, it is all the more striking that Athenians did keep ostracism 'on the books' throughout most of the fourth century BC. Or did they?

When carefully considering the reasons for the survival of ostracism in Athens before the time of *A.P.*, Herbert Heftner hesitantly linked this phenomenon with the fourth-century institutional conservatism and with the attachment of the Athenians to the historical memory of the times of their past greatness.[17] This idea looks plausible, but it could not have been central to the 'hard-core' constitutional decisions of the Athenians. I think we ought to start by asking ourselves about the circumstances of the revival of this law after the Peloponnesian War.

The political scandal of 'ca. 416 BC' was followed by the most disastrous years in Athens' political history. The *hermocopidae* affair and Alcibiades' accusations of parodying the Eleusinian mysteries in 415 BC triggered a witch-hunt in the ranks of the Athenian élites. The oligarchic coup in 411 BC, the radicalisation of the twilight years of democracy, the defeat of 404 BC

---

[17] Cf. Heftner (2003) 35.

and the rule of the oligarchic junta of the 'Thirty Tyrants' led to the democratic revolution and restoration. As I suggested above, all these oligarchic upheavals before 403 BC must have faded the memories of the comparatively minor scandal of Hyperbolus' ostracism. More importantly, the law about ostracism must have been a part of the new democratic order. Thus, it is fair to call it a (relatively) fresh start of ostracism in Athens after 403 BC.

I think that it would not be far-fetched to hold the very historical circumstances I have just described responsible for the revival of ostracism. As argued above (3.1), the way in which our ancient sources (all stemming from fourth-century texts and in particular from Theophrastus' *On laws*) refer to the law about ostracism and at times even quote or paraphrase it, strongly suggests that this law, alongside various earlier regulations ascribed to Solon, could be consulted in the publicly erected 'codification' prepared by the famous commission of Nicomachus. The explanation why this particular expedient found its way to this collection is, I believe, relatively straightforward. It would be awkward not to include it in these regulations after the fatal experience of the last years of the fifth century BC. Even if the 'Hyperbolus' affair' was still remembered, the tradition of a powerful tool to control Athenian élites must have played a decisive role in reinstating ostracism in the Athenian constitutional order, where it belonged with other elements of the honourable 'ancestral system' of Solon (and Cleisthenes). And however one understood this particular mechanism of control at the time, a dim recollection of the extreme adaptability of ostracism in the fifth century BC could still be there.

Once 'on the books', the vote on ostracism in the programme of the 'main Assembly session' in the sixth prytany was preserved as a purely perfunctory formula or a 'constitutional fossil'. As argued above, both the political leaders and the *dēmos* had now better, safer, and more immediate tools of political action, pressure, and control. But in considering the survival of ostracism in the fourth century BC, we need to abandon the anachronistic perspective that makes us wonder at the steadfast determination of the Athenian people to vote year after year against implementing *ostrakophoria*. Besides the apparently antiquated character of this law and, perhaps, a reasonably high level of political responsibility of the Assembly, one more factor could have been decisive here. Namely, the fact universally neglected in earlier scholarship that the usual way of implementing the law about ostracism thus far was to vote against *ostrakophoria* in the preliminary vote in the sixth prytany (or equivalent). The Assembly-goers in the fourth century could have been aware, however vaguely, of how rarely their ancestors had effectuated the vote of ostraka. In other words, the fourth-century political habit looks strange only to us. For the fourth-century Athenians, it may have seemed almost natural. This was precisely the habit of their forefathers.

General Conclusions: The Logic and Original Goals of Athenian Ostracism

Let me reiterate here the most general historical questions of previous scholarship regarding ostracism and its role in democratic Athens. Was ostracism a thoroughly democratic expedient as an instrument of the hegemony—political, symbolic, and/or ritual—of the sovereign *dēmos* over Athenian élites? Or should it rather be interpreted as a tool of the 'aristocratic politics' still operative in Athenian democracy? These are not necessarily the questions I've asked myself in this book—at least not straightforwardly. But I think my conclusions may help us answer them at this juncture.

When combining the perspectives of classics and positive social science, not unlike in the innovative study of 'mass and élite' by Josiah Ober as developed and modified by Federica Carugati and Barry R. Weingast, one can say that not only Athenian law courts but ostracism as well was a tool of 'political stability' resulting from 'negotiations among community members to lower the stakes of class and other interpersonal conflict'.[18] In very general terms, my interpretation of the original goals of ostracism seems to concur with their conclusions '[...] that to understand both Athens' stability and the *polis*' success over time, we must come to terms with a much more varied and dynamic set of compromises, whose solution was not so much a winner-takes-all model (i.e., the hegemony of a monolithic mass over competing élites) as the ability to enable genuine negotiation and cooperation among citizens, while lowering the probability that these negotiations lead to conflict'.[19]

*

---

[18] See in general Ober (1989). My quotes here are from Carugati and Weingast (2018) 180.
[19] Carugati and Weingast (2018) 180. In this context, it would be interesting to interpret the institution of ostracism in terms of an 'upside-down hegemony', as advocated for the Athenian *dēmos* by Mirko Canevaro (2021) (in general, cf. also Canevaro (2017))—exercised not through the Athenian honorific system, but through its antithesis, the ultimate punishment of *ostrakophoria*. This, however, is beyond the scope of this study.

EPILOGUE AND CONCLUSIONS 251

As regards the facts about ostracism, in this book, I maintained that, at the present state of our evidence, no similar institution in the Greek world predated the Athenian one, and I hope I have established that ancient traditions, and consequently also modern scholarly hypotheses, about the existence of pre-democratic ostracism in Athens, are untenable. I also confirmed that Cleisthenes introduced this institution alongside his other reforms in 508/507 BC, but the first time Athenians did send one of their politicians into exile did not occur until 20 years later. Next, I argued for the hypothetical existence of an early fourth-century antiquarian list of the victims of ostracism in the fifth century BC, consulted by the author of *A.P.*, and most probably compiled by the Atthidographer Cleidemus. I also insisted that the order of magnitude of the actual cases of banishing an Athenian by way of ostracism did not exceed the number of occurrences preserved in our literary sources, namely 12 securely attested cases with two more doubtful ones.

In the second half of my book, I studied the procedures of ostracism at Athens. I put forward the hypothesis that the provisions of the original law about ostracism found their way into the 'code of Nicomachus' and were on public display in Athens since the end of the fifth century BC. Meanwhile, the descriptions of the day of *ostrakophoria*, or voting using ostraka, including the manner citizens cast their potsherds and the spatial organisation of this vote in the Athenian Agora, could not have been inscribed in an official document on publicly available stelae. What we find in our ancient authorities, such as Philochorus or Plutarch, ultimately stemming from the treatise *On laws* by Theophrastus, is due to their imaginative reconstruction of such events around a century after the last *ostrakophoria* was held in 'ca. 416 BC'. In this context, I hope I have demonstrated that, on the one hand, the Agora never lost its function as the venue of *ostrakophoriai* because of its large dimensions and so of its capacity to host the huge crowds of Athenian citizens expected to show up on such occasions.

On the other hand, as regards the provisions of the law itself, two parenthetic and vague phrases in the so-called 'great scholion about ostracism', much discussed in scholarship and mentioning the 6000 'quorum' (or the 'qualified majority') of *ostrakophoria* and the reduction of the duration of exile to five years, did not belong to the original text of the law. In fact, they were Theophrastus' comments written in accordance with the Peripatetic idea of the natural 'leniency' (*praotēs*) of the Athenian *dēmos*. Conversely, one may surmise the existence of a high 'quorum', most probably conceived of in optical terms, of the initial vote of the procedure of ostracism, the *epicheirotonia*. I have proved that *epicheirotonia* was certainly in place before the Peloponnesian War, but very likely belonged to the original law about ostracism.

Accordingly, the main novelty of this book is to study the two-stage procedure of ostracism in its entirety, from the opening *epicheirotonia* vote to the final *ostrakophoria*, without ignoring the former or at least strongly prioritising the latter, as it has universally been the case in previous scholarship. This approach yielded interesting results in that it made it possible to take into account and integrate into an overall interpretation of the workings of this institution the specificity of all the three stages of its procedure: *epicheirotonia* in the Assembly, the day of *ostrakophoria* in the Agora, and the two-month intervening period between them. This all-embracing interpretation is necessary to assess the function and so the original purpose of ostracism. Notably, the most emblematic set of our historical data, often privileged in earlier studies, the ostraka, turned out to be helpful principally in interpreting the intermediary stage and much less so *ostrakophoria* itself.

The main conclusions of this study may be summarised as follows. *Ostrakophoria*—as the final, basically random, and unpredictable decision of the Athenian people regarding its leaders—cast a long shadow over the entire procedure of ostracism, hovering over the Athenian élites and substantially determining their political calculations every year. My reading of *ostrakophoria* is rather straightforward and falls in line with some of the previous interpretations. Broadly speaking, it was the final and irrevocable verdict of the *dēmos*, eagerly exercising its political and ideological hegemony over its political élites. This interpretation can be strengthened by a closer reading of the political dynamics of the preceding period, stretching from the (positive) *epicheirotonia* to the *ostrakophoria*. The broad and somewhat inconsistent range of accusations and slander we find on some Athenian ostraka points to a rather high level of political commotion and most probably to an intensive defamation campaign between the *epicheirotonia* and the *ostrakophoria* and during the latter.

Taken together, the danger of ruthless political scheming in the sixth and seventh prytany (or equivalent) and of the messy and incalculable vote in the eighth prytany by the capricious *dēmos* summarily threatening its élites on the day of *ostrakophoria*, provided the background for short-term political decisions and fleeting functional alliances among the leading Athenian politicians. They could easily avoid the certain but random danger of *ostrakophoria* by mobilising their followers to vote against it or to break the 'quorum' during the initial *epicheirotonia*. Importantly, at this time of the year, Athenian *dēmos* had little at stake to push for the positive vote and *ostrakophoria*. More often than not, political leaders must have decided to act in this manner—hence the rarity of the actual *ostrakophoriai* (despite the fact that *epicheirotonia* was held every year) and the long gap between Cleisthenes' reforms and the first *ostrakophoria*.

Such momentary compromises of, at times, sworn political enemies had a long-term effect of calming down Athenian political life or at least lowering the temperature of political infighting among the Athenian élites, thus compensating for inherent dangers of Athenian political life as laid bare in the tumultuous years after the fall of tyranny in Athens. Meanwhile, each time a self-assured and intransigent political leader was determined enough to break the rules of the intra-élite game by inciting the people to vote for *ostrakophoria*, he had to be ready to put his own political career at risk alongside those of his competitors. Although such a person could rely on his popularity and try to mobilise his followers in a smear campaign against other potential victims of ostracism, the unpredictable character of the vote of *ostrakophoria* made it a true gamble.

By way of a probabilistic approximation, I interpret the situation in which prominent Athenian politicians found themselves due to the two-stage procedure of ostracism in the light of the 'theory of cooperation' by Robert Axelrod. From this perspective, what Themistocles, Aristides, Cimon and Pericles were facing at Athens every year was a true 'iterated prisoner's dilemma'. And most of the time, they cooperated accordingly. Not unlike some other elements of the package of reforms initiated in 508/507 BC, ostracism proved to be a highly successful socio-political experiment set up by Cleisthenes and overseen henceforward by the Athenian *dēmos*.[20]

---

[20] I am confident that other theoretical models could also be helpful to better understand the workings of ostracism in Athenian democracy. Let me mention just one of them, the concept of the 'cartel', ultimately stemming from the work of Georg Simmel and advocated recently by Gunnar Seelentag: see esp. Seelentag (2020); cf. Seelentag (forthcoming). Nevertheless, I think that in this case the 'iterated prisoner's dilemma' model enables a broader scope of socio-political inquiry. See, however, Meister (2020) 341–355, where the Simmelian approach and the 'theory of cooperation' ultimately prove fully compatible.

Bibliography

Adams, J. (1851). *The Works of John Adams, Second President of the United States: with a Life of the Author, Notes and Illustrations, by his Grandson Charles Francis Adams*, vol. 4. Boston.
Alpers, K. (1981). *Die attizistische Lexikon des Oros. Untersuchung und kritische Ausgabe der Fragmente.* Berlin–New York.
Alvarez, R. M., Kiewiet, D. R., Núñez, L. (2018). 'A Taxonomy of Protest Voting', *Annual Review of Political Science* 21, 135–154.
Alwine, A. T. (2016). 'Freedom and Patronage in the Athenian Democracy', *JHS* 136, 1–17.
Ampolo, C., ed. (2012). *Agora greca e agorai di Sicilia.* Pisa.
Andrewes, A. (1977). 'Kleisthenes' Reform Bill', *CQ* 27, 241–248.
Apostolakis, K. (2006). 'The Rhetoric of an *Antidosis*: [D.] 42 *Against Phaenippus*', *Ariadne* 12, 93–112.
Avram, A. (2009). 'Héraclée du Pont et ses colonies pontiques: Antécédents milésiens (?) et empreinte mégarienne', in M. Lombardo, F. Frisone, eds, *Colonie di colonie. Le fondazioni sub-coloniali greche tra colonizzazione e colonialismo. Atti del Convegno Internazionale (Lecce, 22–24 giugno 2006).* Lecce, 209–227.
Axelrod, R. (2006) [1984]. *The Evolution of Cooperation. Revised edition, with a Foreword by Richard Dawkins.* London.
Azoulay, V., Ismard, P., eds (2011). *Clisthène et Lycurgue d'Athènes. Autour du politique dans la cité classique.* Paris.
Bacchielli, L. (1994). 'L'ostracismo a Cirene', *RFIC* 122, 257–270.
Badian, E. (1971). 'Archons and "Strategoi"', *Antichthon* 5, 1–34.
Bakewell, G. W., Sickinger, J. P., eds (2003). *Gestures. Essays in Ancient History, Literature, and Philosophy Presented to Alan L. Boegehold on the Occasion of His Retirement and His Seventy-Fifth Birthday.* Oxford.
Bakola, E. (2010). *Cratinus and the Art of Comedy.* Oxford.
Banfi, A. (1999). 'I processi contro Anassagora, Pericle, Fidia ed Aspasia e la questione del "circolo di Pericle". Note di cronologia e di storia', *Annali dell'Istituto Italiano per gli Studi Storici* 16, 3–85.
Beloch, K. J. (1914). *Griechische Geschichet (zweite neugestaltete Auflage)*, vol. II–1. Strassburg.
Beloch, K. J. (1926). *Griechische Geschichte (zweite neugestaltete Auflage)*, vol. I–2. Berlin–Leipzig.
Beloch, K. J. (1931). *Griechische Geschichte (zweite neugestaltete Auflage)*, vol. II–2. Berlin–Leipzig.
Berger, S. (1989). 'Democracy in the Greek West and the Athenian Example', *Hermes* 117, 303–314.

Bernays, J. (1869). *Die heraklitischen Briefe. Ein Beitrag zur philosophischen und religiongeschichtlichen Literatur*. Berlin.
Bertelli, L. (1997). 'Democrazia e "metabolé". Rapporti tra l'"Athenaion Politeia" e la teoria politica di Aristotele', in G. Maddoli (1997), 71–99.
Berti, M. (2001). 'L'antroponimo Megakles sugli ostraka di Atene. Cosiderazioni prosopografiche, storiche e istituzionali', *Minima epigraphica et papyrologica* 4, 8–69.
Bianchetti, S. (1979). 'L'ostracismo di Iperbolo e la seconda redazione delle "Nuvole" di Aristofane', *Studi italiani di filologia classica* 51, 221–248.
Bicknell, P. J. (1972). *Studies in Athenian Politics and Genealogy*. Historia Einzelschrift 19. Stuttgart.
Bicknell, P. J. (1974). [rev. R. Thomsen, *The Origin of Ostracism. A Synthesis* (1972)], *Gnomon* 46, 817–819.
Bicknell, P. J. (1975). 'Was Megakles Hippokratous Alopekethen Ostracised Twice?', *L'Antiquité Classique* 44, 172–175.
Blass, F. (1877). *Die attische Beredsamkeit*, vol. 1: *Von Gorgias bis zu Lysias*, 2 Aufl. Leipzig.
Bleicken, J. (1995). *Die athenische Demokratie (4, völlig überarbeitete und wesentlich erweiterte Auflage)*. Paderborn.
Bloch, H. (1940). 'Studies in Historical Literature of the Fourth Century B.C.', in *Athenian Studies presented to William Scott Fergusson*. Harvard Studies in Classical Philology suppl. 1. Cambridge, M.A.–London, 303–376.
Blok, J. (2017). *Citizenship in Classical Athens*. Cambridge.
Blundell, M. W. (1989). *Helping Friends and Harming Enemies. A Study in Sophocles and Greek Ethics*. Cambridge.
Boedeker, D., Raaflaub, K. A., eds (1998). *Democracy, Empire, and the Arts in Fifth-Century Athens*. Cambridge, M.A.–London.
Boegehold, A. E. (1963). 'Toward a Study of Athenian Voting Procedure', *Hesperia* 32, 366–374.
Boegehold, A. E. (1972). 'The Establishment of a Central Archive at Athens', *AJA* 76, 23–30.
Borlenghi, A., Chillet, C., Hollard, V., Lopez-Rabatel, L., Moretti, J.-Ch., eds (2019). *Voter en Grèce, à Rome et en Gaule*. Lyon.
Bourriot, F. (1982). 'La famille et le milieu social de Cléon', *Historia* 31, 404–435.
Bowie, A. M. (2007). *Herodotus. Histories. Book VIII*. Cambridge.
Bradeen, W. (1955). 'The Trittyes in Cleisthenes' Reforms', *TAPhA* 86, 22–30.
Bravo, B. (1997). 'Le prime reazioni (1891–1898) al racconto dell'"Athenaion politeia" su Atene arcaica e in particolare sulle riforme di Clistene', in G. Maddoli (1997), 218–239.
Bravo, B. (2000). 'Pseudo-Herodotus and Pseudo-Thucydides on Scythia, Thrace and the Regions "Beyond",' *Annali della Scuola Normale Superiore di Pisa* IV, 5.1, 21–112.
Bravo, B. (2009). *La 'Chronique' d'Apollodore et le Pseudo-Skymnos. Érudition antiquaire et littérature géographique dans la seconde moitié du IIe siècle av. J.-C.* Studia Hellenistica 46. Leuven–Paris–Walpole.
Bremmer, J. (1983). 'Scapegoat Rituals in Ancient Greece', *Harvard Studies in Classical Philology* 87, 299–320.

Bremmer, J. (1998). '"Religion", "Ritual", and the Opposition "Sacred vs. Profane". Notes towards a Terminological "Genealogy",' in F. Graf ed., *Ansichten griechischer Rituale. Geburtstags-Symposium für Walter Burkert. Castelen bei Basel 15. bis 18. März 1996.* Stuttgart–Leipzig, 9–32.

Brenne, S. (1994). 'Ostraka and the Process of Ostrakophoria', in W. D. E. Coulson et al. eds, *The Archaeology of Athens and Attica under the Democracy.* Oxford, 13–24.

Brenne, S. (2001). *Ostrakismos und Prominenz in Athen. Attische Bürger des 5. Jhs. v. Chr. auf den Ostraka.* Tyche suppl. 3. Wien.

Brock, R. (2009). 'Did the Athenian Empire Promote Democracy?', in J. Ma, N. Papazarkadas, R. Parker (2009), 149–166.

Broneer, O. (1938). 'Excavations on the North Slope of the Acropolis, 1937', *Hesperia* 7, 161–263.

Brueckner, A. (1915). 'Mitteilungen aus dem Kerameikos', *Athenischen Mitteilungen* 40, 1–26.

Bürchner, L. (1905). 'Ephesos', in *RE* 5, coll. 2773–2882.

Bull, S. (2014). *Trench: A History of Trench Warfare on the Western Front.* Oxford.

Burckhardt, L., Ungern-Sternberg, J. von, eds (2000). *Große Prozesse im antiken Athen.* München.

Burkert, W. (1985). *Greek Religion*, tr. J. Raffan. Cambridge.

Busolt, G. (1895). *Griechische Geschichte bis zur Schlacht bei Chaeroneia*, vol. 2: *Die ältere attische Geschichte und die Perserkriege (zweite vermehrte und völlig umgearbeitete Auflage).* Gotha.

Busolt, G. (1897). *Griechische Geschichte bis zur Schlacht bei Chaeroneia*, vol. 3.1: *Die Pentekontaëtie.* Gotha.

Busolt, G., Swoboda, H. (1926). *Griechische Staatskunde, von Georg Busolt*, vol. 2: *Darstellungen einzelner Staaten und der zwischenstaatlichen Beziehungen, bearbeitet von... Heinrich Swoboda.* München.

Cadoux, T. J. (1948). 'The Athenian Archons from Kreon to Hypsichides', *JHS* 68, 70–123.

Calderini, A. (1945). *L'ostracismo.* Como.

Camp, J. McK. (1992). *The Athenian Agora. Excavations in the Heart of Classical Athens.* London.

Camp, J. McK. (2015). 'Excavations in the Athenian Agora, 2008–2012', *Hesperia* 85, 467–513.

Canevaro, M. (2013). *The Documents in the Attic Orators. Laws and Decrees in the Public Speeches of the Demosthenic Corpus.* Oxford.

Canevaro, M. (2015). [rev. Carawan (2013)], *JHS* 135, 226–227.

Canevaro, M. (2017). 'The Popular Culture of the Athenian Institutions: "Authorized" Popular Culture and "Unauthorized" Elite Culture in Classical Athens', in L. Grig, ed., *Popular Culture in the Ancient World.* Cambridge, 39–65.

Canevaro, M. (2021). 'Upside-down Hegemony. Ideology and power in ancient Athens', in E. Zucchetti, A. M. Cimino, eds, *Antonio Gramsci and the Ancient World.* London–New York, 63–85.

Canevaro, M., Harris, E. M. (2012). 'The Documents in Andocides' "On the Mysteries",' *CQ* 62, 98–129.

Canevaro, M., Erskine, A., Gray, B., and Ober, J., eds (2018). *Ancient Greek History and Contemporary Social Science*, Edinburgh Leventis Studies 9. Edinburgh.
Carawan, E. (2007). *Krateros the Macedonian (342)*, in *BNJ*, http://dx.doi.org/10.1163/1873-5363_bnj2_a342 (accessed 1.08.2022).
Carawan, E. (2013). *The Athenian Amnesty and Reconstructing the Law*. Oxford.
Carcopino, J. (1935). *L'Ostracisme athénien*, 2nd ed. Paris.
Carey, C. (1989). *Lysias. Selected Speeches*. Cambridge.
Cartledge, P. (1987). *Agesilaos and the Crisis of Sparta*. Baltimore.
Cartledge, P. (2007). 'Democracy, Origins of: Contribution to a Debate', in K.A. Raaflaub, J. Ober, R.W. Wallace (2007), 155–169.
Cartledge, P. (2016). *Democracy: A Life*. Oxford.
Carugati, F., Weingast, B. R. (2018). 'Rethinking mass and elite: Decision-making in Athenian law-courts', in M. Canevaro, A. Erskine, B. Gray, and J. Ober (2018), 157–183.
Cauer, F. (1891). *Hat Aristoteles die Schrift vom Staate der Athener geschrieben? Ihr Ursprung und ihr Wert für die ältere athenische Geschichte*. Stuttgart.
Chambers, M. (1979). 'Androtion F 6: τότε πρῶτον,' *JHS* 99, 151–152.
Christ, M. R. (1992). 'Ostracism, Sycophancy, and Deception of the Demos: [Arist.] Ath. Pol. 43.5', *CQ* 42, 336–346.
Clinton, K. (1982). 'The Nature of the Fifth-Century Revision of the Athenian Law Code', in *Studies in Attic Epigraphy, History and Topography. Presented to Eugene Vanderpool*. Hesperia suppl. 19. Princeton, N.J., 27–37.
Cobetto Ghiggia P. (1995). *[Andocide,] Contro Alcibiade. Introduzione, testo critico, traduzione e commento a cura di . . . .* Pisa.
Cole, J. R. (1974). 'Cimon's Dismissal, Ephialtes' Revolution and the Peloponnesian Wars', *GRBS* 15, 369–385.
Connor, W. R. (1992). *The New Politicians of Fifth-Century Athens*, 2nd ed. Indianapolis.
Connor, W. R., Keaney, J. J. (1969). 'Theophrastus on the End of Ostracism', *AJPh* 90, 313–319.
Costa, C. D. N. (1962). 'Plots and Politics in Aeschylus', *G&R* 9, 22–34.
Cromey, R. D. (1979). 'Kleisthenes' Fate', *Historia* 28, 129–147.
Csapo, E., Slater, W. J. (1995). *The Context of Ancient Drama*. Ann Arbor.
Cuniberti, G. (2000). *Iperbolo. Ateniese infame*. Napoli.
Cuniberti, G. (2003). 'Durata e quorum dell'ostracismo ateniese: Due questioni aperte?', *Polis. Studi interdisciplinari sul mondo antico* 1, 117–123.
Davies, J. K. (1993). *Democracy and classical Greece*, 2nd edn. Cambridge, M.A.
Davies, J. K. (2003). 'Democracy without Theory', in P. Derow, R. Parker, eds, *Herodotus and his World. Essays from a Conference in Memory of George Forrest*. Oxford, 319–335.
Develin, R. (1977). 'Cleisthenes and Ostracism: Precedents and Intentions', *Antichthon* 11, 10–21.
Develin, R. (1985a). 'Bouleutic Ostracism Again', *Antichthon* 19, 7–15.
Develin, R. (1985b). 'Philochoros on Ostracism', *Civiltà Classica e Cristiana* 6, 25–31.
Develin, R. (1989). *Athenian Officials 684–321 B. C.* Cambridge.

BIBLIOGRAPHY 259

Di Cesare, R. (2020). 'Performing Athens: Urban Spaces and Polis Identity c. 530-470 BCE', in M. Meyer, G. Adornato, eds, *Innovations and Inventions in Athens c. 530 to 470 BCE - Two Crucial Generations*. Wiener Forschungen zur Archäologie 18. Wien, 189-202.

Dickey, E. (2007). *Ancient Greek Scholarship. A Guide to Finding, Reading, and Understanding Scholia, Commentaries, Lexica, and Grammatical Treatises, from Their Beginnings to the Byzantine Period*. Oxford.

Doenges, N. A. (1996). 'Ostracism and the "boulai" of Kleisthenes', *Historia* 45, 387-404.

Dover, K. J. (1957). 'The Political Aspect of Aeschylus's Eumenides', *JHS* 77, 230-237.

Dover, K. J. (1963). 'Androtion on Ostracism', *CR* 13, 256-257.

Dover, K. J. (1989) [1978]. *Greek Homosexuality. Updated with a new Postscript*. Cambridge, M.A.

Dow, S. (2004) [1939]. 'Aristotle, the Kleroteria, and the Courts', in P.J. Rhodes (2004), 62-94.

Dreher, M. (2000). 'Verbannung ohne Vergehen. Der Ostrakismos (das Scherbengericht)', in L. Burckhardt, J. von Ungern-Sternberg (2000), 66-78.

Ducat, J. (1992). 'Aristote et la réforme de Clisthène', *BCH* 116, 37-51.

Eder, W. (1998). 'Aristocrats and the Coming of Athenian Democracy', in I. Morris, K.A Raaflaub (1998), 105-140.

Edwards, M. (1995). *Andocides. Edited with a Translation and Commentary by...* Warminster.

Ehrenberg, V. (1948). 'The Foundation of Thurii', *AJPh* 69, 149-170.

Ehrenberg, V. (1950). 'Origins of Democracy', *Historia* 1, 515-548.

Ehrenberg, V. (1962). *The People of Aristophanes. A Sociology of Old Attic Comedy*, 3rd ed. New York.

Ekroth, G. (2005). 'Blood on the Altars? On the Treatment of Blood at Greek Sacrifices and the Iconographical Evidence', *Antike Kunst* 48, 9-29.

Errington, R. M. (1994). 'Ἐκκλησία κυρία in Athens', *Chiron* 24, 135-160.

Errington, R. M. (1995). 'Ἐκκλησίας κυρίας γενομένης in Athens', *Chiron* 25, 19-42.

Featherstone, M. J. (2011). 'Theodore Metochites's "Seimeioseis Gnomikai": Personal Encyclopedism', in P. van Deun, C. Macé, eds, *Encyclopedic Trends in Byzantium?* Orientalia Lovanensia Analecta 212. Leuven, 333-344.

Figueira, Th. J. (1985). 'Chronological Table', in Th. J. Figueira, G. Nagy (1985), 261-303.

Figueira, Th. J. (1987). 'Residential Restrictions on the Athenian Ostracized', *GRBS* 28, 281-305.

Figueira, Th. J., Nagy, G., eds (1985). *Theognis of Megara. Poetry and the Polis*. Baltimore.

Fisher, N. (2001). *Aeschines, 'Against Timarchos'. Introduction, Translation, and Commentary by....* Oxford.

Fisher, N. (2008). 'The Bad Boyfriend, the Flatterer and the Sycophant: Related Forms of the "Kakos" in Democratic Athens', in R. M. Rosen, I. Sluiter, eds, *Kakos: Badness and Antivalue in Classical Antiquity*. Mnemosyne suppl. 307. Leiden, 185-231.

Flensted-Jensen, P., Nielsen, Th. H., Rubinstein, L., eds (2000). *Polis and Politics. Studies in Ancient Greek History Presented to Mogens Herman Hansen on His Sixtieth Birthday, August 20, 2000.* Copenhagen.

Fontenrose, J. (1968). 'The Hero as Athlete', *CA* 1, 73-104.

Forgas, J. P., Kruglanski, A. W., Williams, K. D., eds (2011). *The Psychology of Social Conflict and Aggression.* New York-London.

Fornara, Ch. W. (1963). 'A Note on ΑΘ Π. 22', *CQ* 13, 101-104.

Forrest, W. G. (1966). *The Emergence of Greek Democracy. The character of Greek politics, 800-400 BC.* London.

Forsdyke, S. (2000). 'Exile, Ostracism and the Athenian Democracy', *CA* 19, 232-263.

Forsdyke, S. (2005). *Exile, Ostracism, and Democracy. The Politics of Expulsion in Ancient Greece.* Princeton.

Fränkel, M. (1877). *Die attischen Geschworenengerichte. Ein Beitrag zum attischen Staatsrecht.* Berlin.

Frost, F. J. (1964). 'Pericles, Thucydides, Son of Melesias, and Athenian Politics before the War', *Historia* 13, 385-399.

Garland, R. (1992). *Introducing New Gods. The Politics of Athenian Religion.* Ithaca.

Gauthier, Ph. (2011). 'Quorum et participation civique dans les démocraties grecques', in Ph. Gauthier, *Études d'histoire et d'institutions grecques. Choix d'écrits. Edité et indexé par Denis Rousset.* Genève, 421-454 [= *Du pouvoir dans l'Antiquité: mots et réalités. Cahiers du Centre Glotz* 1 (1990), 73-99].

Gazzano, F. (1999). *Pseudo-Andocide, Contro Alcibiade. Introduzione, traduzione e commento storico a cura di....* Genova.

Gehrke, H.-J. (1985). *Stasis. Untersuchungen zu den inneren Kriegen in den griechischen Staaten des 5. und 4. Jahrhunderts v. Chr.* Vestigia 35. München.

Geissler, P. (1925). *Chronologie der altattischen Komödie.* Berlin.

Giangiulio, M. (2005). 'Pericle e gli intelettuali. Damone e Anassagora in Plut. "Per." 4-8 tra costruzione biografica e tradizione', in L. Breglia, M. Lupi, eds, *Da Elea a Samo. Filosofi e politici di fronte all'impero ateniese (Atti del Convegno di studi. Santa Maria Capua Vetere, 4-5 giugno 2003).* Napoli, 151-182.

Giangiulio, M. (2015). *Democrazie greche. Atene, Sicilia, Magna Grecia.* Roma.

Giugni, E. (2004). *Problemi cronologici relative all'ostracismo alla luce dei nuovi ritrovamenti di Chersonesos Taurica.* Firenze.

Glotz, G. (1968). *La cité grecque. Le développement des institutions* (1st ed. 1928). Paris.

Gottesman, A. (2014). *Politics and the Street in Democratic Athens.* Cambridge.

Gouschin, V. (2009). 'Athenian Ostracism and Ostraka: Some Historical and Statistical Observations', in L. Mitchell, L. Rubinstein, eds, *Greek History and Epigraphy. Essays in Honour of P. J. Rhodes.* Swansea, 225-250.

Gouschin, V. (2016). 'Solon's Law on Stasis and the Rise of Pisistratus in 561/60 BC', *Acta Classica* 59, 101-113.

Graef, B., Langlotz, E. (1933). *Die antiken Vasen von der Akropolis zu Athen*, vol. 2.1: *Text*; vol. 2.2: *Tafeln*. Berlin.

Gray, B. (2015). *Stasis and Stability. Exile, the Polis, and Political Thought*, c. 404-146 BC. Oxford.
Greco, E. (2010). 'Un ostrakon da Thurii', *ZPE* 173, 97-101.
Greco, E. (2014). *Topografia di Atene. Sviluppo urbano e monumenti dalle origini al III secolo d.C. Con la collaborazione di Riccardo Di Cesare, Fausto Longo, Daniela Marchiandi*, vol. 3: *Quartieri di nord e nord-est dell'Acropoli e Agora del Ceramico*. Atene-Paestum.
Grote, G. (1907). *History of Greece. From the Earliest Period to the Close of the Generation Contemporary with Alexander the Great. A New Edition in Ten volumes*, vols. 3-4. London.
Grzesik, D. (2021). *Honorific Culture at Delphi in the Hellenistic and Roman periods*. Brill Studies in Greek and Roman Epigraphy 17. Leiden.
Guarducci, M. (1941-1943). 'Note di epigrafia attica arcaica', *Annali della Regia Scuola archeologica di Atene e delle missioni Italiane in Oriente* 3-5, 113-134.
Guarducci, M. (1995). *Epigrafia greca*, vol. 2: *Epigrafi di carattere pubblico* (1st ed. 1969). Roma.
Hall, L. G. H. (1989). 'Remarks on the Law of Ostracism', *Tyche* 4, 91-100.
Hands, A. R. (1959). 'Ostraka and the Law of Ostracism. Some Possibilities and Assumptions', *JHS* 79, 69-79.
Hansen, M. H. (1983). *The Athenian Ecclesia. A Collection of Articles, 1976-1983*. Opuscula Graecolatina 26. Copenhagen.
Hansen, M. H. (1989). *The Athenian Ecclesia II. A Collection of Articles 1983-1989*. Opuscula Graecolatina 31. Copenhagen.
Hansen, M. H. (1990). 'Solonian Democracy in Fourth-Century Athens', in W. R. Connor, M. H. Hansen, K. A. Raaflaub, B. S. Strauss, eds, *Aspects of Athenian Democracy*. Classica et Mediaevalia. Dissertationes 11. Copenhagen, 71-100.
Hansen, M. H. (1999) [1991]. *Athenian Democracy. Structure, Principles, and Ideology*. Norman.
Hansen, M. H. (2004) [1977]. 'How Did the Athenian "Ekklesia" Vote?', in P.J. Rhodes (2004), 40-61.
Hansen, M. H., Nielsen, T. H., eds (2004). *An Inventory of Archaic and Classical Poleis*. Oxford.
Harding, Ph. (1976). 'Androtion's Political Career', *Historia* 25, 186-200.
Harris, E. M. (2013). *The Rule of Law in Action in Democratic Athens*. Oxford.
Hartog, F. (2018). *Partir pour la Grèce. Edition revue et augmentée*. Paris.
Hatzfeld, J. (1951). *Alcibiade* (1st ed. 1940). Paris.
Heftner, H. (2000a). 'Der Ostrakismos des Hyperbolus: Plutarch, Pseudo-Andokides und die Ostraka', *RhM* 143, 32-59.
Heftner, H. (2000b). 'Zur Datierung der Ostrakisierung des Hyperbolos', *RSA* 30, 27-45.
Heftner, H. (2003). 'Ende und "Nachleben" des Ostrakismos in Athen', *Historia* 52, 23-38.
Heftner, H. (2005). 'Theophrast und die Vorstellung von Theseus als dem ersten Opfer des Ostrakismos in Athen', *RhM* 148, 158-160.

Heftner, H. (2012). 'Rechts- und Verfassungsinstrumente als Mittel der Konfliktbewältigung in der athenischen Demokratie: Stasisgesetze, Ostrakismos und Graphe Paranomon', *Dike* 15, 1–32.
Heftner, H. (2018). 'Das Große verfahrenstechnisch-historische Scholion über den Ostrakismos [Philochoros FGrHist 328 F 30 / Theophrast fr. 640ab Fortenbaugh]. Versuch einer Rekonstruktion', *Tyche* 33, 79–112.
Herman, G. (1987). *Ritualised Friendship and the Greek City*. Cambridge.
Herman, G. (1994). 'How Violent was Athenian Society?', in R. Osborne, S. Hornblower, eds, *Ritual, Finance, Politics. Athenian Democratic Accounts Presented to David Lewis*. Oxford, 99–117.
Herman, G. (1998). 'Reciprocity, Altruism, and the Prisoner's Dilemma: The Special Case of Classical Athens', in Ch. Gill, N. Postlethwaite, R. Seaford, eds, *Reciprocity in Ancient Greece*. Oxford, 199–225.
Herman, G. (2006). *Morality and Behaviour in Democratic Athens. A Social History*. Cambridge.
Hignett, C. (1952). *A History of the Athenian Constitution to the End of the Fifth Century B.C.* Oxford.
Hind, J. (1998). 'Megarian Colonisation in the Western Half of the Black Sea (Sister- and Daughter-Cities of Herakleia)', in G. R. Tsetskhladze, ed., *The Greek Colonisation of the Black Sea Area*. Stuttgart, 131–152.
Hobbes, T. (1651). *De cive. Philosophicall Rudiments Concerning Government and Society. Or, A Dissertation Concerning Man in his severall habitudes and respects, as the Member of a Society, first Secular, and then Sacred. Containing The Elements of Civill Politie in the Agreement which it hath both with Naturall and Divine Lawes. In which is demonstrated, Both what the Origine of Justice is, and wherein the Essence of Christian Religion doth consist. Together with The Nature, Limits and Qualifications both of Regiment and Subjection by*... London.
Hölscher, T. (1994). 'The City of Athens: Space, Symbol, Structure', in A. Molho, K. Raaflaub, J. Emlen, eds, *City States in Classical Antiquity and Medieval Italy*. Ann Arbor, 355–380.
Hommel, H. (1938). 'Petalismos', in *RE* 19, coll. 1117–1119.
Humm, M. (2019). 'Les espaces comitiaux à Rome pendant la période républicaine', in Borlenghi, Chillet, Hollard, Lopez-Rabatel, Moretti (2019), 261–276.
Humphreys, S. C. (2018). *Kinship in Ancient Athens. An Anthropological Analysis*, vol. 1–2. Oxford.
Hunter, V. (1990). 'Gossip and the Politics of Reputation in Classical Athens', *Phoenix* 44, 299–325.
Hüttl, W. (1929). *Verfassungsgeschichte von Syrakus*. Prag.
Jacoby, F. (1949). *Atthis. The Local Chronicles of Ancient Athens*. Oxford.
Jameson, M. H. (1960). 'A Decree of Themistocles from Troizen', *Hesperia* 29, 198–223.
Jones, N. F. (2015). *Androtion of Athens (324)*, in *BNJ*, http://dx.doi.org/10.1163/1873-5363_bnj_a324 (accessed 1.08.2022).
Jones, N. F. (2016). *Philochoros of Athens (328)*, in *BNJ*, http://dx.doi.org/10.1163/1873-5363_bnj_a328 (accessed 1.08.2022).

Kagan, D. (1961). 'The Origin and Purpose of Ostracism', *Hesperia* 30, 393-401.
Karavites, P. (1974). 'Cleisthenes and Ostracism Again', *Athenaeum* 62, 326-336.
Karpyuk, S. (2000). 'Crowd in Archaic and Classical Greece', *Hyperboreus* 6, 79-102.
Keaney, J. J. (1970a). 'The Text of Androtion F6 and the Origin of Ostracism', *Historia* 19, 1-11.
Keaney, J. J. (1970b). 'The Date of Aristotle's "Athenaion Politeia"', *Historia* 19, 326-336.
Keaney, J. J. (1977). 'Androtion F6 Again', *Historia* 25, 480-482.
Keaney, J. J. (1993). 'Theophrastus on Ostracism and the Character of his "NOMOI"', in Piérart (1993), 261-277.
Keaney, J. J., Raubitschek A. E. (1972). 'A Late Byzantine Account of Ostracism', *AJPh* 93, 87-91.
Kienast, D. (1953). 'Der innenpolitische Kampf in Athen von der Rückkehr des Thukydides bis zu Perikles' Tod', *Gymnasium* 60, 210-229.
Kinzl, K. H. (1991a). 'AP 22.4: The Sole Source of Harpokration on the Ostrakismos of Hipparkhos Son of Kharmos', *Klio* 73, 28-45.
Kinzl, K. H. (1991b). 'Androtion's Dating of Ostrakismos', *Ancient History Bulletin* 5, 109-111.
Kinzl, K. H. (2006). [rev. Siewert], *BMCR* 2006.07.58.
Kinzl, K. H., ed. (1995). *Demokratia. Der Weg zur Demokratie bei den Griechen.* Wege der Forschung 657. Darmstadt.
Knight, D. W. (1970). *Some Studies in Athenian Politics in the Fifth Century B.C.* Historia Einzelschriften 13. Stuttgart.
Kolb, F. (1981). *Agora und Theater, Volks- und Festversammlung.* Archäologische Forschungen 9. Berlin.
Konstan, D. (1996). 'Greek Friendship', *AJPh* 117, 71-94.
Kosmin, P. J. (2015). 'A Phenomenology of Democracy: Ostracism as Political Ritual', *CA* 34, 121-161.
Kouba, K., Lysek, J. (2019). 'What Affects Invalid Voting? A Review and Meta-Analysis', *Government & Opposition* 54, 745-775.
Kreilinger, U. (1995) [1997]. 'Neue Inschriften aus Megalopolis', *Mitteilungen des deutschen archäologischen Instituts, Athenische Abteilung* 110, 373-385.
Krentz, P. (1984). 'The Ostracism of Thoukydides, Son of Melesias', *Historia* 33, 499-504.
Kritzas, Ch. B. (1987). 'Τὸ πρῶτο μεγαρικὸ ὄστρακον', *Horos* 5, 59-73 [with Pl. 16-17].
Kyle, D. G. (1987). *Athletics in Ancient Athens.* Leiden.
Lane Fox, R. (2000). 'Theognis: An Alternative to Democracy', in R. Brock, S. Hodkinson, eds, *Alternatives to Athens. Varieties of Political Organization and Community in Ancient Greece.* Oxford, 35-51.
Lang, M. L. (1982). 'Writing and Spelling on Ostraka', in *Studies in Attic Epigraphy, History and Topography. Presented to Eugene Vanderpool.* Hesperia suppl. 19. Princeton, 75-87.
Langdon, M. K. (2015). 'Herders' Graffiti', in A.P. Matthaiou, N. Papazarkadas (2015), vol. 1, 49-58.

Leão, D. F., Rhodes, P. J. (2015). *The Laws of Solon. A New Edition with Introduction, Translation and Commentary*. London–New York.
Lehmann, G. A. (1981). 'Der Ostrakismos-Entscheid in Athen: von Kleisthenes zur Ära des Themistokles', *ZPE* 41, 85–99.
Lehmann, G. A. (1987). 'Überlegungen zur Krise der attischen Demokratie im Peloponnesischen Krieg: Vom Ostrakismos des Hyperbolos zum Thargelion 411 v.Chr.', *ZPE* 69, 33–73.
Lévêque, P., Vidal-Naquet, P. (1973). *Clisthène l'Athénien*. Paris.
Lewis, D. M. (1974). 'The Kerameikos Ostraka', *ZPE* 14, 1–4.
Lewis, D. M. (2004) [1963]. 'Cleisthenes and Attica', in Rhodes (2004), 287–309.
Lintott, A. (1992). 'Aristotle and Democracy', *CQ* 42, 114–128.
Lippolis (2019). 'Riunioni, operazioni di voto e agoni nell'Agora di Atene', in Borlenghi, Chillet, Hollard, Lopez-Rabatel, Moretti (2019), 93–120.
Longo, C. P. (1980). 'La bulé e la procedura dell'ostracismo: Considerazioni su "Vat. Gr." 1144', *Historia* 29, 257–281.
Longo, F. (2007). 'La definizione di un "nuovo" spazio pubblico: L'Agora del Ceramico dalla "nascita" all spedizione di Sicilia', in E. Greco, M. Lombardo, eds, *Atene e l'Occidente: i grandi temi. Le premesse, i protagonisti, le forme della comunicazione e dell'interazione, i modi dell'intervento ateniese in Occidente. Atti del Convegno Internazionale, Atene 25–27 maggio 2006*. Atene, 117–153.
Loomis, W. T. (2003). 'Athenian Slander: A Common Law Perspective', in G.P. Bakewell, J.P. Sickinger (2003), 287–300.
Loraux, N. (1996). 'Clistene e i nuovi caratteri della lotta politica', in S. Settis, ed., *I Greci. Storia Cultura Arte Società*, vol. 2: *Una storia greca*, 1: *Formazione*. Torino, 1083–1110.
Lugebil, K. (1861). 'Über das Wesen und die historische Bedeutung des Ostrakismos in Athen', *Jahrbücher für klassische Philologie*, Suppl. 4, 119–175.
Ma, J., Papazarkadas, N., Parker, R., eds (2009), *Interpreting the Athenian Empire*. London.
MacDowell, D. M. (1986) [1978]. *The Law in Classical Athens*. Ithaca.
Maddoli, G. ed. (1997). *L'Athenaion politeia' di Aristotele 1891–1991. Per un bilancio di cento anni di studi*. Napoli.
Maffi, A. (2007). 'L'*Onomasticon* di Polluce come fonte di diritto attico', in C. Bearzot, F. Landucci, G. Zecchini, eds, *L'Onomasticon di Giulio Polluce. Tra lessicografia e antiquaria*. Milano, 29–42.
Mann, Ch. (2007). *Die Demagogen und das Volk. Zur politischen Kommunikation im Athen des 5. Jahrhunderts v. Chr*. Klio Beihefte, N.F. 13. Berlin.
Mann, Ch. (2008). 'Politische Gleichheit und gesellschaftliche Stratifikation. Die athenische Demokratie aus der Perspektive der Systemtheorie', *Historische Zeitschrift* 208, 1–35.
Mann, Ch. (2009). 'Potere del popolo—disciplinamento dell'aristocrazia—Sulla funzione dell'ostracismo ateniese', in A. De Benedictis, G. Corni, B. Mazohl, L. Schorn-Schütte, eds, *Die Sprache des Politischen in actu: zum Verhältnis von politischem Handeln und politischer Sprache von der Antike bis ins 20. Jahrhundert*. Göttingen, 51–70.

Marr, L. J., Worswick, N. (1994). 'The Institution of Ostracism at Athens', *Ostraka* 3, 285-290.
Marshall, C. W., van Willigenburg, S. (2004). 'Judging Athenian Dramatic Competitions', *JHS* 124, 90-107.
Martin, A. (1989). *BE*: 'L'ostracisme athénien: un démi-siècle de découvertes et de recherches', *REG* 102, 124-145.
Martin, J. (1974). 'Von Kleisthenes zu Ephialtes. Zur Entstehung der athenischen Demokratie', *Chiron* 4, 5-42.
Martin, R. (1942). 'La Stoa Basileios. Portiques à ailes et lieux d'assemblée', *BCH* 66/67, 274-298.
Martin, R. (1951). *Recherches sur l'Agora grecque. Études d'histoire et d'architecture urbaines*. Paris.
Matthaiou, A. P. (2015). 'Τρία Ἀττικὰ ψηφίσματα τοῦ 5ου αἰ. π.Χ.', in A.P. Matthaiou, N. Papazarkadas (2015), vol. 2, 709-747.
Matthaiou, A. P., Papazarkadas, N., eds (2015). *ΑΞΩΝ. Studies in Honour of Ronald S. Stroud*, vols. 1-2. Athina.
Mattingly, H. B. (1991). 'The Practice of Ostracism at Athens', *Antichthon* 25, 1-26.
Matuszewski, R. (2019). *Räume der Reputation. Zur bürgerlichen Kommunikation im Athen des 4. Jahrhunderts v. Chr*. Historia Einzelschriften 257. Stuttgart.
McCargar, D. J. (1976a). 'New Evidence for the Kleisthenic Boule', *CPh* 71, 248-252.
McCargar, D. J. (1976b). 'The Relative Date of Kleisthenes' Legislation', *Historia* 25, 385-395.
McInerney, J. (1994). 'Politicizing the Past: The "Atthis" of Kleidemos', *CA* 13, 17-37.
Meier, Ch. (1980). *Die Entstehung des Politischen bei den Griechen*. Frankfurt.
Meiggs, R. (1964). 'A Note on the Population of Attica', *CR* 14, 2-3.
Meister, J. B. (2020). *'Adel' und gesellschaftliche Differenzierung im archaischen und frühklassischen Griechenland*. Historia Einzelschriften 263. Stuttgart.
Meister, J. B., Seelentag, G., eds (2020). *Konkurrenz und Institutionalisierung in der griechischen Archaik*. Stuttgart.
Meister, K. (1971). 'Zum Zeitpunkt der Einführung des Ostrakismos', *Chiron* 1, 85-88.
Meister, K. (1973). 'Damon, der politische Berater des Perikles', *RSA* 3, 29-45.
Meister, K. (1997). '"Politeiai", "Atthis" e "Athenaion Politeia"', in G. Maddoli (1997), 113-127.
Merkelbach, R. (1969). 'Das Distichon über den Ostrakismos des Xanthippos', *ZPE* 4, 201-202.
Meyer, E. (1901). *Geschichte des Alterthums*, vol. 4: *Das Perserreich und die Griechen*, fasc. 3: *Athen (Vom Frieden von 446 bis zur Capitulation Athens im Jahre 404 v. Chr.)*. Stuttgart-Berlin.
Meyer, H. D. (1967). 'Thukydides Melesiou und die oligarchische Opposition gegen Perikles', *Historia* 16, 141-154.
Mikalson, J. D. (1975). *The Sacred and Civil Calendar of the Athenian Year*. Princeton, N.J.

Millett, P. (1989). 'Patronage and its Avoidance in Classical Athens', in A. Wallace-Hadrill, ed., *Patronage in Ancient Society*. London–New York, 15–47.
Mirhady, D. (1997). 'The Ritual Background to Athenian Ostracism', *Ancient History Bulletin* 11, 13–19.
Missiou, A. (2011). *Literacy and Democracy in Fifth-Century Athens*. Cambridge.
Mitchell, L. (2009). 'The Rules of the Game: Three Studies in Friendship, Equality and Politics', in L. Mitchell, L. Rubinstein (2009), 1–32.
Mitchell, L. (2016). 'Anti-Athenian Attitudes in Fifth-Century Sicily?', in A. Powell, K. Meidani, eds, *'The Eyesore of Aigina'. Anti-Athenian Attitudes in Greek, Hellenistic, and Roman History*. Swansea, 81–93.
Mitchell, L., Rubinstein, L., eds (2009). *Greek History and Epigraphy. Essays in Honour of P. J. Rhodes*. Swansea.
Moral, M. (2016). 'The Passive-Aggressive Voter: The Calculus of Casting an Invalid Vote in European Democracies', *Political Research Quarterly* 69, 732–745.
Moretti, J.-Ch. (2019). 'La Pnyx, lieu de vote', in Borlenghi, Chillet, Hollard, Lopez-Rabatel, Moretti (2019), 93–120, 121–144.
Morison, W. S. (2016). *Klei(to)demos of Athens (323)*, in *BNJ*, http://dx.doi.org/10.1163/1873-5363_bnj2_a323 (accessed 1.08.2022).
Morison, W. S. (2014). *Theopompos of Chios (115)*, in *BNJ*, http://dx.doi.org/10.1163/1873-5363_bnj_a115 (accessed 1.08.2022).
Morris, I., Raaflaub, K., eds (1998). *Democracy 2500? Questions and Challenges*. Archaeological Institute of America. Colloquia and Conference papers 2, 1997. Dubuque, Iowa.
Mosconi, G. (2011). 'L'Odeion di Pericle, emblema di tirannide e medismo (Cratino, fr. 73 K.–A.),' *Rivista di cultura classica e medioevale* 53, 63–85.
Mossé, C., Schnapp Gourbeillon, A. (1994). 'Quelques réflexions sur l'ostracisme athénien', in E. Greco, ed., *Venticinque secoli dopo l'invenzione della Democrazia*. Paestum, 39–50.
Murray, O., Price, S., eds (1990). *The Greek City from Homer to Alexander*. Oxford.
Murray, O. (1990). 'Cities of Reason', in O. Murray, S. Price (1990), 1–25.
Musti, D. (1993). 'La chronologie du chapitre 22 de l'*Ἀθηναίων Πολιτεία* sur l'ostracisme', in Piérart (1993), 251–260.
Nawotka, K. (1999). *Boule and Demos in Miletus and its Pontic Colonies from Classical Age until Third Century A.D.* Warszawa–Wrocław–Kraków.
Ober, J. (1989). *Mass and Elite in Democratic Athens. Rhetoric, ideology, and the power of the people*. Princeton, N.J.
Ober, J. (1998). 'Revolution Matters: Democracy as Demotic Action (A Response to Kurt A. Raaflaub)', in I. Morris, K. A Raaflaub (1998), 67–85.
Ober, J. (2004) [1993]. 'The Athenian Revolution of 508/7 B.C.: Violence, Authority, and the Origins of Democracy', in P. J. Rhodes (2004), 260–286.
Ober, J. (2007). '"I Besieged That Man": Democracy's Revolutionary Start', in K.A. Raaflaub, J. Ober, R.W. Wallace (2007), 83–104.
Ogden, D. (1997). *The Crooked Kings of Ancient Greece*. London.
Okin, L. A. (1985). *Theognis and the Sources for the History of Archaic Megara*, in Th. J. Figueira, G. Nagy (1985), 9–21.

Osborne, R. (1990). 'The *Demos* and its Divisions in Classical Athens', in O. Murray, S. Price (1990), 265-293.
Osborne, R. (2006). 'When was the Athenian Democratic Revolution?', in S. Goldhill, R. Osborne, eds, *Rethinking Revolutions through Ancient Greece*. Cambridge, 10-28.
Osborne, R., Hornblower, S., eds (1994). *Ritual, Finance, Politics. Athenian Democratic Accounts Presented to David Lewis*. Oxford.
Ostwald, M. (1955). 'The Athenian Legislation against Tyranny and Subversion', *TAPhA* 86, 102-128.
Ostwald, M. (1969). *Nomos and the Beginnings of the Athenian Democracy*. Oxford.
Ostwald, M. (1986). *From Popular Sovereignty to the Sovereignty of Law. Law, Society, and Politics in Fifth-Century Athens*. Berkeley-Los Angeles-London.
Ostwald, M. (1988). 'The Reform of the Athenian State by Cleisthenes', in *CAH*, 2nd edn., vol. 4, 303-346.
Paiaro, D. (2012). 'Defendiendo la liberdad del *dêmos*. Control popular y ostracismo en la democracia ateniese', *Anales de Historia Antigua, Medieval y Moderna* 44, 33-62.
Papazarkadas, N. (2009). 'Epigraphy and the Athenian Empire: Reshuffling the Chronological Cards', in J. Ma, N. Papazarkadas, R. Parker (2009), 67-88.
Pariente, A., Piérart, M., Thalmann, J.-P., Aupert, P., Croissant, F. (1986). 'Rapports sur les travaux de l'École française en Grèce en 1985: Argos', *BCH* 110, 763-773.
Parker, R. (1983). *Miasma. Pollution and Purification in Early Greek Religion*. Oxford.
Paruta, P. (1599). *Discorsi politici di Paolo Paruta nobile vinetiano cavaliere e procurator di San Marco ne i quali si considerano diversi fatti illustri, e memorabili di principi, e di repubbliche antiche, e moderne. Divisi in due libri. Aggiontovi nel fine un suo Soliloquio, nel quale l'auttore fa un breve essame di tutto il corso della sua vita*. Venetia.
Pearson, L. (1942). *The Local Historians of Attica*. Philadelphia.
Phillips, D. J. (1982). 'Athenian Ostracism', in G. H. R. Horsley, ed., *Hellenika. Essays on Greek Politics and History*. North Ryde, 21-43.
Phillips, D. J. (1990). 'Observations on Some Ostraka from the Athenian Agora', *ZPE* 83, 123-148.
Piérart, M. (2000). 'Argos. Une autre démocratie', in P. Flensted-Jensen, Th. H. Nielsen, L. Rubinstein, eds, *Polis and Politics. Studies in Ancient Greek History Presented to Mogens Herman Hansen on His Sixtieth Birthday, August 20, 2000*. Copenhagen, 297-314.
Piérart, M., ed. (1993). *Aristote et Athènes. Aristotle and Athens. Fribourg (Suisse), 23-25 mai 1991*. Paris.
Podlecki, A. J. (1985). 'Theophrastus on History and Politics', in W. F. Fortenbaugh, P. M. Huby, A. A. Long, eds, *Theophrastus of Eresus. On His Life and Work*. Rutgers University Studies in Classical Humanities. New Bruswick-Oxford, 231-249.
Podlecki, A. J. (1998). *Perikles and His Circle*, London-New York.

Polinskaya, I. (2009). 'Fifth-Century Horoi on Aigina. A Reevaluation.' *Hesperia* 78, 231–267.

Power, T. J., Garand, J. C. (2007). 'Determinants of Invalid Voting in Latin America', *Electoral Studies* 26, 432–444.

Pownall, F. (2020). *Aristodemos (104)*, in BNJ, http://dx.doi.org/10.1163/1873-5363_bnj2_a104 (accessed 1.08.2022).

Pritchard, D. (1994). 'From Hoplite Republic to Thetic Democracy. The Social Context of the Reforms of Ephialtes', *Ancient History* 24, 111–139.

Raaflaub, K. A. (1988). 'Athenische Geschichte und mündliche Überlieferung', in J. von Ungern-Sternberg, H. Reinau, eds, *Vergangenheit in mündlicher Überlieferung*. Colloquium Rauricum. Stuttgart, 197–225.

Raaflaub, K. A. (1995). 'Einleitung und Bilanz: Kleisthenes, Ephialtes und die Begründung der Demokratie', in K.H. Kinzl (1995), 1–54.

Raaflaub, K. A. (1998a). 'Power in the Hands of the People: Foundations of Athenian Democracy', in I. Morris, K.A. Raaflaub (1998), 31–66.

Raaflaub, K. A. (1998b). 'The Thetes and Democracy (A Response to Josiah Ober)', in I. Morris, K.A. Raaflaub (1998), 87–103.

Raaflaub, K. A. (1998c). 'The Transformations of Athens in the Fifth Century', in D. Boedeker, K.A. Raaflaub (1998), 15–41.

Raaflaub, K. A. (2000). 'Den Olympier herausfordern? Prozesse im Umkreis des Perikles', in L. Burckhardt, J. von Ungern-Sternberg (2000), 96–113.

Raaflaub, K. A. (2003). 'The Alleged Ostracism of Damon', in G.W. Bakewell, J.P. Sickinger, (2003), 317–331.

Raaflaub, K. A. (2007). 'The Breakthrough of *Dēmokratia* in Mid-Fifth-Century Athens', in K.A. Raaflaub, J. Ober, R.W. Wallace (2007), 105–154.

Raaflaub, K. A., Ober, J., Wallace, R. W., eds (2007). *Origins of Democracy in Ancient Greece*. Berkeley–Los Angeles–London.

Raubitschek, A. E. (1951). 'The Origin of Ostracism', *AJA* 55, 221–229.

Raubitschek, A. E. (1955a). 'Menon, son of Menekleides', *Hesperia* 24, 286–289.

Raubitschek, A. E. (1955b). 'Philochoros Frag. 30 (Jacoby)', *Hermes* 83 119–120.

Raubitschek, A. E. (1955c). 'Theopompos on Hyperbolos', *Phoenix* 9, 122–126.

Raubitschek, A. E. (1956). 'The Gates in the Agora', *AJA* 60, 279–282.

Raubitschek, A. E. (1958). 'Theophrastos on Ostracism', *Classica et Mediaevelia* 19, 73–109.

Raubitschek, A. E. (1965). 'A Note on the Themistocles Decree', in *Studi in onore di Luisa Banti*, Roma, 285–287.

Rausch, M. (1994). 'Die athenische Demokratie', *Anzeiger zur Altertumswissenschaft* 47, 199–264.

Rausch, M. (1999). *Isonomia in Athen. Veränderungen des öffentlichen Lebens vom Sturz der Tyrannis bis zur zweiten Perserabwehr*. Frankfurt am Main.

Reggiani, N. (2016). '*Ostraka* e pietre: due aspetti della giustizia nel pensiero simbolico greco?', *Rivista di Diritto Ellenico* 6, 119–136.

Rhodes, P. J. (1972). *The Athenian Boule*. Oxford.

Rhodes, P. J. (1986). 'Political Activity in Classical Athens', *JHS* 106, 132–144.

Rhodes, P. J. (1991). 'The Athenian Code of Laws, 410–399 B.C.', *JHS* 111, 87–100.

Rhodes, P. J. (1992). 'The Athenian Revolution', in *CAH*, 2nd ed., vol. 5, 62–95.

Rhodes, P. J. (1994). 'The Ostracism of Hyperbolus', in R. Osborne, S. Hornblower (1994), 85-98.
Rhodes, P. J. (1995). 'Ekklesia Kyria and the Schedule of Assemblies in Athens', *Chiron* 25, 187-198.
Rhodes, P. J. (2003). *Ancient Democracy and Modern Ideology*. London.
Rhodes, P. J. (2008). 'After the Three-Bar *Sigma* Controversy: The History of Athenian Imperialism Reassessed', *Classical Quarterly* 58, 501-506.
Rhodes, P. J. (2015). 'Directions in the Study of Athenian Democracy', *Scripta Classica Israelica* 36, 49-68.
Rhodes, P. J., ed. (2004). *Athenian Democracy*. Oxford.
Roberts, J. T. (1994a). *Athens on Trial. The Antidemocratic Tradition in Western Thought*. Princeton.
Roberts, J. T. (1994b). 'The Creation of a Legacy: A Manufactured Crisis in Eighteenth-Century Thought', in J. P. Euben, J. R. Wallach, J. Ober, eds, *Athenian Political Thought and the Reconstruction of American Democracy*. Ithaca, 81-102.
Robertson, N. (1990). 'The Laws of Athens, 410-399 BC: The Evidence for Review and Publication', *JHS* 110, 43-75.
Robinson, E. W. (1997). *The First Democracies. Early Popular Government outside Athens*. Historia Einzelschrift 107. Stuttgart.
Robinson, E. W. (2011). *Democracy Beyond Athens. Popular Government in the Greek Classical Age*. Cambridge.
Robson, J. (2013). *Sex and Sexuality in Classical Athens*. Edinburgh.
Robu, A. (2014). *Mégare et les établissements mégariens de Sicile, de la Propontide et du Pont-Euxin. Histoire et institutions*. Berne.
Roisman, J. (2019). *Lycurgus. Against Leocrates. Introductions and Commentary by... Translation by Michael J. Edwards*. Oxford.
Roobaert, A. (1967). 'L'apport des ostraka à l'étude de l'ostracisme d'Hyperbolus', *L'Antiquité Classique* 36, 524-535.
Rosenbloom, D. (2004a). '"Ponêroi" vs. "Chrêstoi": The Ostracism of Hyperbolus and the Struggle for Hegemony in Athens after the Death of Perikles, Part I', *TAPhA* 134, 55-105.
Rosenbloom, D. (2004b). '"Ponêroi" vs. "Chrêstoi": The Ostracism of Hyperbolus and the Struggle for Hegemony in Athens after the Death of Perikles, Part II', *TAPhA* 134, 323-358.
Rosivach, V. J. (1987). 'Some Fifth and Fourth Century Views on the Purpose of Ostracism', *Tyche* 2, 161-170.
Ruschenbusch, E. (1958). '"Patrios politeia". Theseus, Drakon, Solon und Kleisthenes in Publizistik und Geschichtsschreibung des 5. und 4. Jahrhunderts v. Chr.', *Historia* 7, 398-424.
Ruzé, F. (1997). *Délibération et pouvoir dans la cité grecque de Nestor à Socrate*. Paris.
Samons, L. J. II (2004). *What's Wrong with Democracy? From Athenian Practice to American Worship*. Berkeley-Los Angeles.
Sandys, J. E. (1921). *A History of Classical Scholarship*, vol. 1: *From the Sixth Century B.C. to the End of the Middle Ages*, 3rd edn. Cambridge.

Saprykin, S. Y. (1991). 'Khersonesos Taurike: New Evidence on a Greek City-State in the Western Crimea', in J. K. Fossey, ed., *Proceedings of the First International Congress on the Hellenic Diaspora, from Antiquity to Modern Times (Montréal, 17–22 IV 1988; Athens, 26–30 IV 1988)*, vol. 1: *From Antiquity to 1453*. Amsterdam, 229–244.

Saprykin, S. Y. (1998). 'The Foundation of Tauric Chersonesus', in G. R. Tsetskhladze, ed., *The Greek Colonisation of the Black Sea Area*. Stuttgart, 227–248.

Saraga, N. (2013). 'Νέα στοιχεία από τη σωστική ανασκαφική έρευνα της Α' Εφορείας στην Αρχαία Αγορά της Αθήνας,' in S. Oikonomou, M. Doga-Tole, eds, *Αρχαιολογικές Συμβολές, Τόμος Β: Αττική. Α' και Γ' Εφορείες Προϊστορικών και Κλασικών Αρχαιοτήτων*. Museum of Cycladic Art. Athens, 129–147.

Scafuro, A. C. (2006). 'Identifying Solonian Laws', in J. Blok, A. P. M. H. Lardinois, eds, *Solon of Athens. New Historical and Philological Approaches*. Leiden, 175–196.

Schachermeyr, F. (1932). 'Zur Chronologie der kleisthenischen Reformen', *Klio* 25, 334–347.

Scheibelreiter, P. (2008). 'Der "Peri tou Ostrakismou Nomos" in einem Scholion zu Aristophanes Equites 885B? Überlegungen zum Ostrakismos-Gesetz', *Dike* 11, 111–138.

Schirripa, P., Lentini, M. C., Cordano, F. (2012). 'Nuova geografia dell'ostracismo', *Quaderni di Acme* 129, 115–150.

Schmitz, W. (2011). 'Athen – Eine wehrhafte Demokratie? Überlegungen zum Stasisgesetz Solons und zum Ostrakismos', *Klio* 93, 23–51.

Schmitz, W. (2014). 'Legitimation durch Mehrheitsentscheid? Partizipationschancen und Partizipationsgrenzen im Athen des 6. und frühen 5. Jh.', in W. Blösel, W. Schmitz, G. Seelentag, J. Timmer, *Grenzen politischer Partizipation im klassischen Griechenland*. Stuttgart, 47–70.

Schreiner, J. H. (1970). 'The Origin of Ostracism Again', *Classica et Mediaevelia* 31, 84–97.

Schuller, W. (1995). 'Zur Entstehung der griechischen Demokratie außerhalb Athen', in Kinzl (1995), 302–323.

Schwarze, J. (1971). *Die Beurteilung des Perikles durch die attische Komödie und ihre historische und historiographische Bedeutung*. Zetemata 51. München.

Schwyzer, E. (1950). *Griechische Grammatik, auf der Grundlage von Karl Brugmanns Griechischer Grammatik von...*, vol. 2: *Syntax und syntaktische Stilistik, vervollständigt und herausgegeben von Albert Debrunner*. München.

Seager, R. (1963). 'Herodotus and "Ath. Pol." on the Date of Cleisthenes' Reforms', *AJPh* 84, 287–289.

Sealey, R. (1964). 'Ephialtes', *CPh* 59, 11–22.

Seeck, O. (1904). 'Quellenstudien zu des Aristoteles Verfassungsgeschichte Athens', *Klio* 4, 164–181 and 270–326.

Seelentag, G. (2020). 'Das Kartell. Ein Modell soziopolitischer Organisation der griechischen Archaik', in J.B. Meister, G. Seelentag (2020), 61–94.

Seelentag, G. (forthcoming). 'Die Entstehung von Institutionen der Konfliktregulierung im archaischen Griechenland aus einer Kooperation der Eliten'.

Shear, T. L. (1935). 'The Excavations in the Athenian Agora', *AJA* 39, 173–181.

Sickinger, J. P. (2003). 'Archon Dates, Atthidographers, and the Sources of "Ath. Pol."' 22-26', in G.W. Bakewell, J.P. Sickinger (2003), 338-350.
Sickinger, J. P. (2004). 'The Laws of Athens: Publication, Preservation, Consultation', in E. M. Harris, L. Rubinstein, eds, *The Law and the Courts in Ancient Greece*. London, 93-109.
Sickinger, J. P. (2017a). 'New Ostraka from the Athenian Agora', *Hesperia* 86, 443-508.
Sickinger, J. P. (2017b). 'Ostraka from the Athenian Agora', [presentation at the XV *Congressus internationalis epigraphiae Graecae et Latinae*, Vienna, 28.08-1.09.2017].
Siewert, P. (1982). *Die Trittyen Attikas und die Herresreform des Kleisthenes*. Vestigia 33. München.
Siewert, P. (1991). 'Accuse contro i "candidati" all'ostracismo per la loro condotta politica e morale', in M. Sordi, ed., *L'immagine dell'uomo politico: vita pubblica et morale nell'antichità*. Milano, 3-14.
Siewert, P. (1999). 'Il ruolo di Alcibiade nell'ostracismo di Iperbolo', in E. Luppino-Manes, ed., *Aspirazione al consenso e azione politica in alcuni contesti di fine V sec. a. C.: il caso di Alcibiade (Seminario interdisciplinare, Cattedre di Storia Greca et di Epigrafia Greca, Chieti, 12-13 marzo 1997)*. Alessandria, 19-27.
Simmel, G. (1904). 'The Sociology of Conflict I', *American Journal of Sociology* 9, 490-525.
Simonton, M. (2017). *Classical Greek Oligarchy. A Political History*. Princeton-Oxford.
Solomonik, E. I. (1976). 'Некоторые группы граффити из античного Херсонеса' ['Some groups of graffiti from ancient Chersonese', in Russian], *Vestnik Drevnei Istorii* 137:3, 121-124.
Solomonik, E. I. (1987). 'Два античных письма из Крима' ['Two ancient letters from the Crimea', in Russian], *Vestnik Drevnei Istorii* 182:2, 114-131.
Sommerstein, A. H. (1981). *Knights. Edited with translation and notes by....* Warminster.
Sommerstein, A. H. (1983). *Wasps. Edited with translation and notes by....* Warminster.
Sommerstein, A. H. (2019). *Aeschylus. Suppliants. Edited by....* Cambridge.
Spivey, N. (1994). 'Psephological Heroes', in R. Osborne, S. Hornblower, eds, *Ritual, Finance, Politics. Athenian Democratic Accounts Presented to David Lewis*. Oxford, 29-51.
Stanton, G. R. (1970). 'The Introduction of Ostracism and Alcmeonid Propaganda', *JHS* 90, 180-183.
Staveley, E. S. (1972). *Greek and Roman Voting and Elections*. London-Southampton.
Ste, Croix, G. E. M. de (2004). 'Cleisthenes II: Ostracism, Archons and Strategoi', in G. E. M. de Ste. Croix, *Athenian Democratic Origins and Other Essays*, D. Harvey, R. Parker, eds. Oxford, 180-228.
Stein-Hölkeskamp, E. (1989). *Adelskultur und Polisgesellschaft. Studien zum griechischen Adel in archaischer und klassischer Zeit*. Stuttgart.
Steinbrecher, M. (1985). *Der delisch-attische Seebund und die athenisch-spartanischen Beziehungen in der kimonischen Ära (ca. 478/7-462/1)*. Palingenesia 21. Stuttgart.

Sternbach, L. (1894a). 'Appendix Vaticana I–II', *Rozprawy Akademii Umiejętności. Wydział Filologiczny* 20:5, 171–218.
Sternbach, L. (1894b). 'Excerpta Vaticana', *WS* 16, 8–37.
Stroud, R. S. (1978). 'State Documents in Archaic Athens', in *Athens Comes of Age. From Solon to Salamis. Papers of a Symposium Sponsored by the Archaeological Institute of America, Princeton Society and the Department of Art and Archaeology, Princeton University*. Princeton, N.J. 20–42.
Surikov, I. E. (2000). 'Остракизм и остраконы: в Афинах и за пределами' ['Ostracism and ostraka, in Athens and Abroad', in Russian], *Hyperboreus* 6, 103–123.
Surikov, I. E. (2006). *Остракизм в Афинах* [*Ostracism in Athens*, in Russian], Moskva.
Taylor, L. R. (1966). *Roman Voting Assemblies. From the Hannibalic War to the Dictatorship of Caesar.* Ann Arbor.
Thomas, R. (1989). *Oral Tradition and Written Record in Classical Athens.* Cambridge.
Thomsen, R. (1972). *The Origin of Ostracism. A Synthesis.* Humanitas 4. Copenhagen.
Todd, S. (1996). 'Lysias against Nikomachos: The Fate of the Expert in Athenian Law', in L. Foxhall, D. E. Lewis, eds, *Greek Law in its Political Setting. Justifications not Justice*, Oxford, 101–131.
Tokhtasyev, S. R. (2007). 'К ономастикону и датировке херсонесских остраков' ['Towards the onomastics and dating of the Chersonese ostraka', in Russian], *Vestnik Drevnei Istorii* 261:2, 110–125.
Traill, J. S. (1975). *The Political Organization of Attica. A Study of the Demes, Trittyes, and Phylai, and Their Representation in the Athenian Council.* Hesperia Suppl. 14. Princeton.
Travlos, J. (1980). *Pictorial Dictionary of Ancient Athens.* New York.
Tsetskhladze, G. R., ed. (1998). *The Greek Colonisation of the Black Sea Area.* Historia Einzelschrift 121. Stuttgart.
Valdés-Guía, M. (2019). 'War in Archaic Athens: *polis*, Elites and Military power', *Historia* 68, 126–149.
Valdés-Guía, M. (2021). 'A New Reading on Solon's Law on *Stasis*. The Sovereignty of the *Demos*', *DHA* 47, 187–219.
Valeton, I. M. J. (1887). 'Quaestiones Graecae II: De ostracismo', *Mnemosyne* 15, 129–171 and 162–238.
Valeton, I. M. J. (1888). 'Quaestiones Graecae II: De ostracismo', *Mnemosyne* 16, 1–25 and 337–426.
Van Effenterre, H. (1976). 'Clisthène et les mesures de mobilisation', *REG* 89, 1–17.
Van Straten, F. T. (1995). *Hierà kalá: Images of Animal Sacrifice in Archaic and Classical Greece.* Leiden–New York.
van 't Wout, P. E. (2010). 'Solon's Law on Stasis: Promoting Active Neutrality', *CQ* 60, 289–301.
van 't Wout, P. E. (2013). *Harbouring Discontent. The Pragmatics of 'Atimia' Discourse in the Legal Sphere of Classical Athens*, Ph.D. diss., Utrecht Universiteit.
van Wees, H. (1999). 'The Mafia of Early Greece. Violent exploitation in the seventh and sixth centuries BC', in K. Hopwood, ed., *Organised Crime in Antiquity.* Swansea, 1–51.

van Wees, H. (2007). '"Stasis, Destroyer of Men". Mass, Elite, Political Violence and Security in Archaic Greece', in Securité collective et order public dans les sociétés anciennes. Fondation Hardt. Entretiens sur l'antiquité Classique, 14. Vandoeuvres–Genève, 2–39.
Vanderpool, E. (1949). 'Some Ostraka from the Athenian Agora', in Commemorative Studies in Honor of Theodore Leslie Shear. Hesperia Suppl. 8. Princeton, 394–412 and 493–496 [plates].
Vanderpool, E. (1972). Ostracism at Athens. Louise Taft Semple Lecture, delivered 30 April and 1 May, 1969. The University of Cincinnati.
Vernant, J.-P., Vidal-Naquet, P. (1973). Mythe et tragédie en Grèce ancienne. Paris.
Vidal-Naquet, P. (1990). La démocratie grecque vue d'ailleurs. Essais d'historiographie ancienne et moderne. Paris.
Vidal-Naquet, P. (2000). Les Grecs, les historiens, la démocratie. Le grand écart. Paris.
Vinogradov, Ju. G. (1997). Pontische Studien. Kleine Schriften zur Geschichte und Epigraphik des Schwarzmeerraumes. Mainz.
Vinogradov, Ju. G. (2001). 'Ostrakismos als strenges Kampfmittel für Demokratie im Lichte der neuen Funde aus Chersonesos Taurike', in D. Papenfuß, V. M. Strocka, eds, Gab es das Griechische Wunder? Griechenland zwischen dem Ende des 6. und der Mitte des 5. Jahrhunderts v. Chr. Tagungsbeiträge des 16. Fachsymposiums der Alexander von Humboldt-Stiftung veranstaltet vom 5. bis 9. April 1999 in Freiburg im Breisgau. Mainz, 379–386.
Vinogradov, Ju. G., Zolotarev, M. I. (1990). 'La Chersonèse de la fin de l'archaïsme', in O. Lordkipanidzé, P. Lévêque, eds, Le Pont-Euxin vu par les Grecs. Sources écrites et archéologie. Symposium de Vani (Colchide), septembre–octobre 1987. Centre de Recherches d'Histoire Ancienne 100. Paris, 85–119.
Vinogradov, Ju. G., Zolotarev, M. I. (1999). 'L'ostracismo e la storia della fondazione di Chersonesos Taurica. Analisi comparata con gli "Kerameikós" di Atene', Minima epigraphica et papyrologica 2, 110–131.
Wade-Gery, H. T. (1932). 'Thucydides the Son of Melesias: A Study of Periklean Policy', JHS 52, 205–227.
Wade-Gery, H. T. (1933). 'Studies in the Structure of Attic Society: II. The Laws of Kleisthenes', CQ 27, 17–29.
Wallace, R. W. (1974). 'Ephialtes and the Areopagos', GRBS 15, 259–269.
Wallace, R. W. (1998). 'The Sophists in Athens', in D. Boedeker, K.A. Raaflaub (1998), 203–222.
Wallace, R. W. (2004). 'Damon of Oa. A Music Theorist Ostracized?', in P. Murray, P. Wilson, eds, Music and the Muses. The Culture of 'Mousikē' in the Classical Athenian City. Oxford, 249–267.
Wallace, R. W. (2015). Reconstructing Damon. Music, Wisdom Teaching, and Politics in Pericles' Athens. Oxford.
Webster, T. B. L. (1972). Potter and Patron in Classical Athens. London.
Weil, R. (1960). Aristote et l'histoire. Essai sur la 'Politique'. Paris.
Wentzel, G. (1895). 'Beiträge zur Geschichte der griechischen Lexikographen', in Sitzungsberichte der königlich Preussischen Akademie der Wissenschaften zu Berlin. Gesammtsitzung vom 16. Mai, 477–487 (= LexGrMin, pp. 1–11).
Werner, R. (1958). 'Die Quellen zur Einführung des Ostrakismos', Athenaeum 46, 48–89.

Węcowski, M. (2009). 'Demokracja ateńska w epoce klasycznej' ['Athenian democracy in the classical period', in Polish], in B. Bravo, M. Węcowski, E. Wipszycka, A. Wolicki, *Historia starożytnych Greków*, vol. 2: *Okres klasyczny*. Warszawa, 345–520.
Węcowski, M. (2014). *The Rise of the Greek Aristocratic Banquet*. Oxford.
Węcowski, M. (2016). 'Herodotus in Thucydides: A Hypothesis', in J. Priestley, V. Zali, eds, *Brill's Companion to the Reception of Herodotus in Antiquity and Beyond*. Leiden–Boston, 17–32.
Węcowski, M. (2018). 'The So-Called "Buleutic Ostracism" and the *Ekphyllophoria*: *Vaticanus Graecus* 1144 and other Late Byzantine Nonsensical Reports on the Athenian Ostracism', *Scripta Classica Israelica* 37, 7–23.
Węcowski, M. (2022). 'Aristocracy, Aristocratic Culture, and the Symposium', in L. Swift, ed., *A Companion do Greek Lyric*, Hoboken, 62–75.
Whitehead, D. (1986). *The Demes of Attica 508/7–ca. 250 B.C. A Political and Social Study*. Princeton, N.J.
Wilamowitz-Moellendorff, U. von (1879). 'ΔΑΜΩΝ ΔΑΜΩΝΙΔΟΥ ΟΑΘΕΝ', *Hermes* 14, 318–320.
Wilamowitz-Moellendorff, U. von (1893). *Aristoteles und Athen*, vols. 1–2, Berlin.
Willemsen, F. (1991). 'Ostraka einer Meisterschale', *Mitteilungen des deutschen archäologischen Instituts, Athenische Abteilung* 106, 137–145 [with pl. 17–20].
Willemsen, F., Brenne, S. (1991). 'Verzeichnis der Kerameikos-Ostraka', *Mitteilungen des deutschen archäologischen Instituts, Athenische Abteilung* 106, 147–156.
Willemsen, F., Brenne, S. (1992). 'Corrigenda', *Mitteilungen des deutschen archäologischen Instituts, Athenische Abteilung* 107, 185.
Williams, G. M. E. (1978). 'The Kerameikos Ostraka', *ZPE* 31, pp. 103–113.
Wörrle, M. (1964). *Untersuhung zur Verfassungsgeschichte von Argos im. 5. Jahrhundert von Christus*, Ph.D. diss., Friedrich-Alexander-Universität, Erlangen–Nürnberg.
Wolicki, A. (2018). *Spartan Symmachy in the sixth and fifth century BCE*. Warszawa.
Woodhead, A. G. (1949). '*IG* I² 95, and the Ostracism of Hyperbolus', *Hesperia* 18, 78–83.
Wycherley, R. E. (1955). 'Two Notes on Athenian Topography', *JHS* 75, 117–121.
Zedgenidze, R. E. (1993). 'К вопросу об удревнении даты основания Херсонеса Таврического' ['On an earlier date of the foundation of Tauric Chersonesos', in Russian], *Rossiyskaya Arheologia* 3, 50–56.
Zelnick-Abramovitz, R. (2000). 'Did Patronage exist in Classical Athens?', *L'Antiquité Classique* 69, 65–80.
Zerbinati, M. (2018). 'L'ostracismo di Santippo, figlio di Arifrone, "il più colpevole tra i pritani sacrileghi". Alcune riflessioni alla luce di recenti scoperte archeologiche', *Erga-Logoi* 6, 29–49.
Zerbinati, M. (2019). 'Clistene, Isagora e Ipparco di Carmo: qualche riflessione sull'origine dell'ostracismo ateniese', in G. Vanotti, ed., *Ostracismi e metamorfosi costituzionali nell'* Athenaion Politeia *aristotelica*. Alessandria, 1–29.

Index Locorum

A. Literary Texts

Adespota Comica, fr. 363 K–A: 6 n. 21, 116, 118
Aeneas Tacticus, *Poliorcetica* 11, 10a: 25 n. 33
Aeschines
  I [*Against Timarchus*]
    110–112: 52 n. 129
    111: 52 n. 129, 57 n. 143
  II [*On the Embassy*]
    172: 99 n. 94
    303: 92 n. 70
  III [*Against Ktesiphon*]
    3: 226 n. 88
Aeschylus
  Eum.: 20
  Pers.
    hypothesis: 103
  Supp.: 20, 20 n. 13
    517–518: 20 n. 13
    601: 20 n. 13
    604: 20 n. 13
    621–622: 20 n. 13
    698–700: 20 n. 13
    739: 20 n. 13
    942–943: 20 n. 13
Alciphron, *Epistulae*, IV 18, 11 Schepers = II 3, 11 Meineke: 137 n. 63
Andocides
  I [*On mysteries*]
    16: 107 n. 122
    77–79: 91 n. 66
    82: 124
    87: 170 n. 155, 173
    107: 6 n. 20, 92 n. 69, 117
  III [*On the peace with Sparta*]
    3: 96 n. 82, 99 n. 94
    3–4: 117

Ps.-Andocides, IV [*Against Alcibiades*]
  2: 208 n. 23
  3: 7–8, 170 n. 152
  5: 7
  4: 77 n. 24, 157, 227 n. 89
  4–5: 211
  6: 17 n. 1, 18, 18 n. 2
  32–34: 106
  32: 105
  33: 96
  35: 77 n. 24, 215 n. 52
Androtion, *FGrHist* 324 = *BNJ* 324
  F 6: 8, 70, 74 n. 18, 75 n. 20, 99 n. 95
  F 42: 94
  F 46: 74 n. 19
[Anonymus, comicus,] *FCG* IV, p. 645 Meineke, no. 161: 102
Antiphon, VI [*On the choreutes*]
  49: 52 n. 129
A.P.
  1–41: 88
  3–4: 9
  6: 9
  8.3: 123 n. 21
  11.1: 42 n. 91
  14.1: 42
  14.4: 42 n. 91
  16.5: 56 n. 139
  16.10: 74 n. 19, 213 n. 46
  21.2–6: 190
  21.5: 95 n. 78
  22–23: 88
  22.1: 9, 68, 71, 190, 191 n. 7
  22.2: 129, 196
  22.3: 69, 74, 76, 87
  22.3–4: 68, 71
  22.4: 74, 76, 88, 99 n. 95, 196 n. 24
  22.5: 87, 98, 129
  22–23: 88

A.P. (cont.)
  22.6: 9, 76 n. 22, 88, 89
  22.7: 87, 88
  22.8: 87, 89, 90, 91 n. 66, 92, 178
  23.1: 95 n. 78
  23.3–5: 88
  26.3: 56 n. 139
  27.3: 208–209
  27.4: 87, 107
  28.2: 208 n. 23
  29.3: 121 n. 10
  37.1: 178
  41.2: 72 n. 11
  43.4: 143 n. 74, 178
  43.5: 48, 49, 67, 113, 114 n. 147, 124, 127, 128, 176, 223 n. 84
  48.5: 56 n. 139
  49.2: 176
  53.1: 56 n. 139
Aristodemos, FGrHist 104 = BNJ 104
  F 1.1.4: 100 n.99
  F 1.6.1: 100 n. 100
Aristophanes
  Ach.
    22: 145 n. 81
    79: 25 n. 35
    1073–1077: 143
  Eccl.
    686: 141 n. 69
  Eq.
    137: 141 n. 68
    819: 6 n. 20, 118, 127
    850: 141–142
    855–857: 6 n. 22, 118, 127, 141–142
    1245–1247: 154 n. 102
  Vesp.
    687: 25 n. 35
    947: 6 n. 20, 106 n. 119, 118
  fr. 661 K–A: 6 n. 21, 118
  sch vet Ar. Ach. 22A: 145
  sch vet Ar. Eq.
    855B: 104, 113, 122, 129 n. 42, 132 n. 48, 133, 161, 181
    857: 142
  sch vet Ar. Vesp.
    947A: 6 n. 20, 118
    947C: 106 n. 119
Aristotle
  Politics
    1284 a 17–37: 9 n. 31
    1284 a 18: 18 n. 3
    1284 b 15–30: 9 n. 31
    1284 b 20–22: 9 n. 33
    1288 a 24–26: 9 n. 31
    1302 b 17–19: 18
    1302 b 27–31: 21 n. 19
    1304 b 31–34: 26 n. 38, 30
    1305 b 5–13: 9 n. 31, 26 n. 38
    1305 b 15–21: 9 n. 31
    1305 b 34–37: 26 n. 38
    1306 a 33–1306 b 2: 26 n. 38
    1308 b 10–19: 9 n. 31
    1319 b 15–23: 23
  Ps.-Aristotle, Constitution of the Athenians, see A.P.
Cicero, De amicitia 42: 100 n. 100
Cleidemus, FGrHist 323
  F 8: 94, 95 n. 78
  F 15: 94
  F 21: 95 n. 78
  F 22: 94–95
Cratinus
  fr. 73 K–A: 6 n. 22, 107 n. 121, 118 n. 154, 120–121, 126, 128, 165
  fr. 82 K–A: 120
Demetrius of Phaleron, FGrHist 228
  F 43: 100 n. 99
Demosthenes
  XVIII [De cor.]
    169: 145–146
  XIX [On the Embassy]
    185: 127 n. 33
    303: 92 n. 70
  XXIII [Against Aristocrates]
    86: 170 n. 155
    199: 102 n. 105
    205: 96 n. 81
  XXIV [Against Timocrates]
    45: 170 n. 155, 173
    48: 173
    51: 74 n. 19
    59: 170 n. 155, 173, 173 n. 161
    122: 56 n. 139
  XXV [Against Aristogeiton I]
    23: 137 n. 59, 144 n. 78
  XXVI [Against Aristogeiton II]
    6: 96 n. 80, 100 n. 99
  XLVI [Against Stephanos II]
    12: 170 n. 155
  Ps.-Demosthenes, LIX [Against Neaera]
    90: 145

… INDEX LOCORUM 277

Diodorus Siculus, *Bibliotheca Historica*
XI 55: 100 n. 100
XI 55, 1: 73 n. 12
XI 55, 2–3: 9 n. 32
XI 55, 2: 35 n. 75, 73 n. 12, 161, 171, 182, 183, 183 n. 189
XI 55, 3: 182 n. 187
XI 60, 1–2: 19 n. 7
XI 72, 2: 35 n. 76
XI 83, 3–4: 103 n. 107
XI 86, 4–87,6: 32
XI 86, 5: 9 n. 32, 32
XI 87, 1–2: 9 n. 32
XI 87, 1: 33, 183
XI 87, 2–3: 33
XI 87, 4: 33
XI 87, 5: 33
XI 87, 6: 33
XIII 101,6: 228 n. 91
XIV 34, 4–6: 23
XX 39: 109 n. 130

Ephorus, *FGrHist* 70 F 196: 109 n. 130

Etymologicum Magnum
s.v. *ekphyllophorēsai kai ekphyllophoriai* (325.9 Gaisdorf): 53, 52 n. 129, 77
s.v. *exostrakismos* (349.15 Gaisdorf): 54 n. 136, 139 n. 65, 161
s.v. *skēnē* (743.30 Gaisdorf): 139 n. 64

Eusebius of Caesarea, *Chronikoi kanones* II, p. 50 Schoene: 99 n. 93

Harpocration, *Lexicon*
s.v. *Alkibiades* (22.13 Dindorf): 97 n. 88, 100 n. 99, 104
s.v. *ekphyllophorēsai* (109.1 Dindorf): 52 n. 129, 53, 55
s.v. *Hipparchos* (161.2 Dindorf): 69–70

Hellanicus, *FGrHist* 323a F 23: 73 n. 12

Heracleides Lembos, fr. 4 Dilts: 99, 100 n. 98

Heraclitus of Ephesus, *FVS*[6] 22 B 121: 19

Herodotus
I 60: 42 n. 91
II 75,2: 142 n. 72
IV 161, 1–2: 40 n. 85
V 47: 209 n. 30
V 66, 1–2: 208
V 66, 2: 77 n. 25, 190 n. 6, 193–194
V 69, 1–2: 77 n. 25
V 69, 2: 190 n. 6
V 72, 2: 46

V 78: 195 n. 21
VI 131, 1: 77 n. 25
VI 131, 2: 100 n. 98
VI 136: 100 n. 98
VI 104, 2: 213 n. 46
VII 17: 209
VII 148, 2: 20 n. 12
VIII 79, 1: 6, 95, 100 n. 98
IX 70, 5: 94–95

Hesychius Alexandrinus, *Lexicon* (Latte–Hansen)
s.v. *Menonidai* (*M* 866): 102–103
s.v. *petal*[*l*]*a* (Π 2041): 32 n. 65
s.v. *pet*[*t*]*alismos* (Π 2044): 32 n. 65

Hieronymus, *Chronicon*
58 Helm: 99 n. 93
108 Helm: 100

Isocrates
VII [*Areopagitikos*] 67–69: 74 n. 19
XV [*Antidosis*] 20: 74 n. 19

Lexica Segueriana, s.v. *ekphyllophorēsai* (Bekker I, 248.7): 52 n. 129, 53, 54 n. 136

Livius, XXVI 22, 11: 154 n. 105

Lycurgus, *Against Leocrates*, 117–118: 70, 91 n. 65

Lysias, XIV [*Against Alcibiades*] 39: 97, 104

Nepos, *Themistocles* 8: 100 n. 100

Olympiodorus, *In Platonis Gorgiam commentaria*, 33.3.2, p. 171.25 Westerink: 56 n. 141

Pausanias
III 4, 10: 20 n. 12
V 9, 3: 105
VI 6, 1: 105
VI 7, 4–7: 74 n. 19

Philochorus, *FGrHist* 328 (*BNJ* 328) F 30: 48 nn. 116, 120, 56 n. 140, 73 n. 12, 124–125, 129–130, 158

Photius, *Lexicon*, s.v. *Hipparchos* (I 162): 99 n. 95

Pindar, *Pyth. VII*, 18–21: 6, 30, 99 n. 96, 106

Plato
Ap. 26D–E: 135 n. 56
Grg. 516D: 7, 117
Tht. 146A: 211

Plato Comicus
fr. 168 K–A: 118 n. 154, 210
fr. 203 K–A: 6–7, 6 n. 22, 118, 241, 243
fr. 207 K–A: 110 n. 133
Plutarch
Alc.
  13, 1–2: 208 n. 23
  13, 1–3: 241 n. 3
  13, 4: 229 n. 94
  13, 4–5: 113
  13, 4–9: 111 n. 136
Arist.
  1, 2: 100 n. 99
  1, 7: 108 n. 126
  7: 100 n. 99, 221 n. 80
  7, 1: 9 n. 30
  7, 2: 4 n. 12
  7, 3: 229 n. 94
  7, 3–4: 111 n. 136
  7, 4: 113, 139 n. 65
  7, 5–6: 9 n. 30
  7, 6: 161–162, 165
  7, 7–8: 152
Cim.
  10, 1–2: 208–209
  15: 221 n. 80
  17: 221 n. 80
  17, 2: 104 n. 111
  17, 6–7: 209 n. 32
Nic.
  6, 1–2: 109–110
  7, 1: 108 n. 126
  11: 99 n. 95
  11, 4: 242 n. 4
  11, 6: 113
  11, 1–7: 111 n. 136
  11, 4: 226 n. 87, 229 n. 94, 243
  11, 10: 207 n. 23, 241 n. 3
Per.
  4, 2–3: 108 n. 126
  4, 3: 9 n. 30
  9, 2: 107 n. 125, 108
  9, 4: 104 n. 111
  9, 5: 9 n. 30
  13, 9: 120
  10, 4: 229 n. 96
  14, 1–2: 106 n. 119
  14, 2: 233–234
  15, 1: 234
  16, 3: 107
  31–32: 109 n. 130

Them.
  22: 100 n. 100
  22, 4–5: 4 n. 12
Mor. (Quaestiones Graecae)
  295D: 21 n. 19
Mor. (Quaestiones Graecae) 295E–F:
  21 n. 19
Ps.-Plutarch, *Vit. Dec. Or.* 847A: 137 n. 63
Pollux, *Onomastikon*
  6.126: 25 n. 35
  7.123–124: 137 n. 59, 144 n. 78
  8.16–20: 170 n. 154
  8.17: 55
  8.18: 57 n. 143
  8.18–20: 55–57
  8.19: 4 n. 13, 170 n. 154
  8.19–20: 52 n. 129
  8.20: 139, 139 n. 65, 161
  8.110: 191 n. 9
  8.111–112: 211 n. 37
  9.112: 211 n. 38
Ps.-Andocides, IV [*Against Alcibiades*],
  see Andocides
Ps.-Aristotle, see *A.P.*
Ps.-Lysias, see Lysias
Ps.-Scylax, *Periplous* (*GGM* I), 68: 27 n. 42
Ps.-Scymnus, *Periegesis* (*GGM* I)
  824 (= fr. 12.9 Marcotte): 27 n. 40
  827 (= fr. 12.12 Marcotte): 27 n. 40
  828–834 with 822–827 (= fr. 12
    Marcotte): 24 n. 30
  949–950 (= fr. 27.8–9 Marcotte):
    24 n. 30
sch vet Ar., see Aristophanes
Stephanus of Byzantium, *Ethnica*, s.v. *Oa*
  (O 1 = 482.3 Meineke): 108 n. 127
Strabo, XII 3, 4 (C. 542): 27 n. 43
Suda
  s.v. *archē Skyria* (A 4101 Adler): 99 n. 93
  s.v. *eis Kynosarges* (EI 290
    Adler): 57 n. 143
  s.v. *ekphyllophorēsai kai ekphyllophoria*
    (E 721–722 Adler): 52 n. 129, 53,
    54 n. 136, 57 n. 143
  s.v. *Hipparchos* (I 523 Adler): 71,
    99 n. 95
Theodoros Metochites, *Miscellanea*,
  p. 608–609 Müller-Kiessling: 50

INDEX LOCORUM 279

Theophrastus
  Characters 26 [The Oligarch], 5: 99 n. 93
  On Laws
    fr. 18(b) Szegedy-Maszak (= 640B Fortenbaugh = sch vet Ar. Eq. 855B): 9 n. 30, 122 n. 14
    fr. 21 Szegedy-Maszak: 160
  F 638 Fortenbaugh (= 131 Wimmer): 99 n. 93
  F 640A–B, see passim, see also Philochorus, FGrHist 328 F 30
Theopompus of Chios, FGrHist 115
  F 88: 104 n. 111
  F 89: 208–209
  F 91: 106 n. 119
  F 96b: 83–184
  F 388: 27 n. 43
Thucydides
  I 102, 4: 20
  I 111, 1: 103 n. 107
  I 135, 2–3: 7 n. 23, 98
  I 135, 3: 100 n. 100
  II 65, 10–11: 247
  IV 104, 1–2: 24 n. 30
  V 43, 2: 104
  VI 62, 4: 168 n. 144
  VI 89, 2: 104
  VII 50: 23
  VIII 73, 3: 7, 98, 111, 184, 242 n. 6
  VIII 85, 3: 34 n. 70
Timaeus the Sophist, Lexicon vocum Platonicarum, s.v. exostrakismos (Ruhnken): 139 n. 65
Tzetzes, John, Chiliades
  13.441–486: 50–51
  13.448–459: 56 n. 143
  13.449–450: 51, 57 n. 143
  13.465: 56 n. 143
  13.477–482: 52
  13.481: 56 n. 143

B. Inscriptions and Papyri

Agora 25, 13 (= Siewert, T 1/24): 152 n. 91, 218 n. 53

Agora 25, 14: 152 n. 91, 218 n. 53

Agora 25, 44 (= Siewert, T 1/38): 220 n. 69

Agora 25, 56 (= Siewert, T 1/37): 220 n. 68

Agora 25, 310: 105 n. 117

Agora 25, 311: 105 n. 117

Agora 25, 312: 105 n. 117

Agora 25, 356: 219 n. 59

Agora 25, 589 (= Siewert, T 1/65): 220 n. 72

Agora 25, 647 (= Siewert, T 1/141): 219 n. 59

Agora 25, 1065 (CEG I 439 = ML 21 = Siewert, T 1/153): 100 n. 98, 220 nn. 67, 71

Agora 25, 1071 (= Siewert, T 1/155): 220 nn. 71, 74

Agora 25, 1097 (= Siewert, T 1/42): 219 n. 60

Agora 25, 1146–1336 (= Siewert, T 1/30), see Themistocles' Deposit in General Index

Agora 25, 1184 (= Siewert, T 1/143): 219 n. 59

Agora 25, 1191 B (= Siewert, T 1/144): 219 n. 59

Agora 25, 1200 B (= Siewert, T 1/146): 219 n. 59

Bacchielli (1994) nos. 1–9 (= SEG XLIV 1540.1): 23

Bacchielli (1994) no. 10 (= SEG XLIV 1540.2): 23

Bacchielli (1994) no. 11 (= SEG XLIV 1540.3): 23

Bacchielli (1994) no. 12 (= SEG XLIV 1540.4): 23

CEG I 439 (ML 21 = Siewert, T 1/153) = Agora 25, 1065: 100 n. 98, 220 nn. 67, 71

DAA 21 (= IG I² 608 + 714 = IG I³ 826): 105 n. 116

DAA 164 (= IG I² 606 = IG I³ 893): 105 n. 116

Fornara 53 (= ML 23, l. 44–47): 91–92, see also Themistocles' Decree in General Index

280　INDEX LOCORUM

Guigni (2004) no. 15 (= *SEG* XL 612.14): 25

Guigni (2004) no. 18 (= *SEG* XL 612.16): 24 n. 30

Guigni (2004) no. 19: 24 n. 30

Guigni (2004) no. 20 (= *SEG* XLIX 1031.2): 24 n. 30

Guigni (2004) no. 21: 24 n. 30

Guigni (2004) no. 30 (= *SEG* XL 612.25a): 25 n. 32

Guigni (2004) no. 31 (= *SEG* XL 612.25b): 25 n. 32

Guigni (2004) no. 32 (= *SEG* XLIX 1031.1): 25

Guigni (2004) no. 33 (= *SEG* XXXVII 661): 25, 25 n. 36

Guigni (2004) no. 34 (= *SEG* XLIX 1031.3): 25

IG I^2 95 (= *IG* I^3 85): 111, 112

IG I^2 606 (= *IG* I^3 893) = *DAA* 164: 105 n. 116

IG I^2 608 + 714 (= *IG* I^3 826) = *DAA* 21: 105 n. 116

IG I^2 913: 43 n. 97

IG I^3 85 = *IG* I^2 95: 111, 112

IG I^3 105: 173–175

IG I^3 826 (= *IG* I^2 608 + 714) = *DAA* 21: 105 n. 116

IG I^3 893 (= *IG* I^2 606) = *DAA* 164: 105 n. 116

IG XII,5 595 A: 35 n. 75, 52 n. 128

IvO 3 (= *Nomima* I.108): 174–175, 175 n. 168

IvO 7 (= *Nomima* I.109): 174–175, 175 n. 168

Kerameikos 20.2, 249 (= Siewert, T 1/41): 220 n. 70

Kerameikos 20.2, 315 (= Siewert, T 1/44): 219 n. 61

Kerameikos 20.2, 321: 220 n. 71

Kerameikos 20.2, 351 (= Siewert, T 1/48): 220 n. 71

Kerameikos 20.2, 363 (= Siewert, T 1/49): 220 n. 71

Kerameikos 20.2, 369 (= Siewert, T 1/57): 220 n. 71

Kerameikos 20.2, 373 (= Siewert, T 1/47): 220 n. 71

Kerameikos 20.2, 391 (= Siewert, T 1/54): 220 n. 71

Kerameikos 20.2, 405 (= Siewert, T 1/156): 220 n. 71

Kerameikos 20.2, 915 (= Siewert, T 1/53): 220 n. 71

Kerameikos 20.2, 1062 (= Siewert, T 1/55): 220 n. 71

Kerameikos 20.2, 1065 (= Siewert, T 1/61): 220 n. 71

Kerameikos 20.2, 1066 (= Siewert, T 1/50): 220 n. 71

Kerameikos 20.2, 1067 (= Siewert, T 1/58): 220 n. 71

Kerameikos 20.2, 1068a (= Siewert, T 1/52): 220 n. 71

Kerameikos 20.2, 1068b (= Siewert, T 1/52): 220 n. 71

Kerameikos 20.2, 1069 (= Siewert, T 1/60): 220 n. 71

Kerameikos 20.2, 1070: 220 n. 71

Kerameikos 20.2, 1071 (= Siewert, T 1/51): 220 n. 71

Kerameikos 20.2, 1072 (= Siewert, T 1/56): 220 n. 71

Kerameikos 20.2, 1073 (= Siewert, T 1/59): 220 n. 71

Kerameikos 20.2, 1110 (= Siewert, T 1/66): 220 n. 65

Kerameikos 20.2, 1336 (= Siewert, T 1/67): 97 n. 83, 219 n. 59, 221 n. 79

Kerameikos 20.2, 1624 (= Siewert, T 1/68): 220 n. 65

Kerameikos 20.2, 1741 (= Siewert, T 1/72): 220 n. 73

Kerameikos 20.2, 1745 (= Siewert, T 1/71): 220 n. 73

Kerameikos 20.2, 1781 (= Siewert, T 1/75): 219 n. 63

Kerameikos 20.2, 1782 (= Siewert, T 1/76): 219 n. 62

INDEX LOCORUM 281

Kerameikos 20.2, 1784 (= Siewert, T/81): 219 n. 62
Kerameikos 20.2, 1786 (= Siewert, T 1/79): 219 n. 62
Kerameikos 20.2, 1787 (= Siewert, T 1/80): 219 n. 62
Kerameikos 20.2, 1811 (= Siewert, T 1/86): 219 n. 64
Kerameikos 20.2, 2012–6188: 101 n. 101, see also Great Kerameikos Deposit in General Index
Kerameikos 20.2, 2019 (= Siewert, T 1/112): 219 n. 64
Kerameikos 20.2, 2028 (= Siewert, T 1/93): 220 n. 67
Kerameikos 20.2, 2044: 220 n. 66
Kerameikos 20.2, 2126 (= Siewert, T 1/92): 220 n. 67
Kerameikos 20.2, 2623 (= Siewert, T 1/158): 220 n. 66
Kerameikos 20.2, 3221 (= Siewert, T 1/101): 220 n. 66
Kerameikos 20.2, 3539 (= Siewert, T 1/107): 219 n. 64
Kerameikos 20.2, 3593 (= Siewert, T 1/108): 219 n. 64
Kerameikos 20.2, 3773 (= Siewert, T 1/106): 26, 220 n. 78
Kerameikos 20.2, 3981 (= Siewert, T 1/85): 219 n. 59
Kerameikos 20.2, 3984 (= Siewert, T 1/91): 220 n. 67
Kerameikos 20.2, 4213 (= Siewert, T 1/102): 220 n. 66
Kerameikos 20.2, 5126 (= Siewert, T 1/109): 219 n. 64
Kerameikos 20.2, 5186b (= Siewert, T 1/103): 220 n. 66
Kerameikos 20.2, 5453 (= Siewert, T 1/110): 219 n. 64
Kerameikos 20.2, 5462 (= Siewert, T 1/105): 220 n. 66
Kerameikos 20.2, 5463 (= Siewert, T 1/104): 220 n. 66

Kerameikos 20.2, 5916 (= Siewert T 1/111): 220 n. 77
Kerameikos 20.2, 6202 (= Siewert T 1/118): 220 n. 76
Kerameikos 20.2, 6247 (= Siewert, T 1/119): 219 n. 64
Kerameikos 20.2, 6259 (= Siewert, T 1/116): 103 n. 107
Kerameikos 20.2, 6262 (= Siewert T 1/117): 103
Kerameikos 20.2, 6265 (= Siewert, T 1/120): 219 n. 64
Kerameikos 20.2, 6278 (= Siewert, T 1/121): 219 n. 64
Kerameikos 20.2, 6284 (= Siewert, T 1/122): 219 n. 64
Kerameikos 20.2, 6300 (= Siewert, T 1/123): 219 n. 64
Kerameikos 20.2, 6431 (= Siewert, T 1/131): 220 n. 65
Kerameikos 20.2, 6473 (= Siewert, T 1/124): 219 n. 64
Kerameikos 20.2, 6477 (= Siewert, T 1/125): 219 n. 64
Kerameikos 20.2, 6499 (= Siewert, T 1/126): 219 n. 64
Kerameikos 20.2, 6577 (= Siewert, T 1/127): 219 n. 64
Kerameikos 20.2, 6628 (= Siewert, T 1/132): 220 n. 65
Kerameikos 20.2, 6657 (= Siewert, T 1/128): 219 n. 64
Kerameikos 20.2, 6726 (= Siewert, T 1/129): 219 n. 64
Kerameikos 20.2, 6735 (= Siewert, T 1/133): 220 n. 65
Kerameikos 20.2, 6736 (= Siewert, T 1/134): 220 n. 65
Kerameikos 20.2, 6737 (= Siewert, T 1/135): 220 n. 65
Kerameikos 20.2, 6738 (= Siewert, T 1/136): 220 n. 65
Kerameikos 20.2, 6739 (= Siewert, T 1/137): 220 n. 65

282 INDEX LOCORUM

Kerameikos 20.2, 6740 (= Siewert, T 1/138): 220 n. 65

Kerameikos 20.2, 6741 (= Siewert, T 1/139): 220 n. 65

Kerameikos 20.2, 6742 (= Siewert, T 1/140): 220 n. 65

Kerameikos 20.2, 6837 (= Siewert, T 1/130): 219 n. 64

Kerameikos 20.2, 6857 (= Siewert, T 1/115): 103 n. 107

Kerameikos 20.2, 7262 (= Siewert, T 1/150): 25

Kerameikos 20.2, 7544 (= Siewert, T 1/149): 220 n. 67

Kerameikos 20.2, 8463 (= Siewert, T 1/147): 220 n. 66

Kerameikos 20.2, 8790 (= Siewert, T 1/154): 220 n. 65

ML 21 (CEG I 439 = Siewert, T 1/153) = Agora 25, 1065: 100 n. 98, 220 nn. 67, 71

ML 23, l. 44–47 = Fornara 53, see also Themistocles' Decree in General Index

Nomima I.108 = IvO 3: 174–175, 175 n. 168

Nomima I.109 = IvO 7: 174–175, 175 n. 168

P. Berol. 5008 B: 131–132

P. Oxy. 1904: 70 n. 7

P. Oxy. 2192: 70 n. 7

SEG XII 87: 126

SEG XXXIV 751: 24 n. 31

SEG XXXVI 340: 19

SEG XXXVII 371: 22

SEG XXXVII 654: 24 n. 31

SEG XXXVII 661 = Guigni (2004) no. 33: 25, 25 n. 36

SEG XL 612: 24 n. 31

SEG XL 612.14 = Giugni (2004) no. 15: 25

SEG XL 612.16 = Giugni (2004) no. 18: 24 n. 30

SEG XL 612.25a = Giugni (2004) no. 30: 25 n. 32

SEG XL 612.25b = Guigni (2004) no. 31: 25 n. 32

SEG XLIV 1540.1 = Bacchielli (1994) no. 1–9: 23

SEG XLIV 1540.2 = Bacchielli (1994) no. 10: 23

SEG XLIV 1540.3 = Bacchielli (1994) no. 11: 23

SEG XLIV 1540.4 = Bacchielli (1994) no. 12: 23

SEG XLV 421: 29 n. 52

SEG XLIX 1031.1 = Guigni (2004) no. 32: 25

SEG XLIX 1031.2 = Guigni (2004) no. 20: 24 n. 30

SEG XLIX 1031.3 = Guigni (2004) no. 34: 25

Siewert, T 1/30 = Agora 25, 1146–1336, see Themistocles' Deposit in General Index

Siewert, T 1/37 = Agora 25, 56: 220 n. 68

Siewert, T 1/38 = Agora 25, 44: 220 n. 69

Siewert, T 1/41 = Kerameikos 20.2, 249: 220 n. 70

Siewert, T 1/42 = Agora 25, 1097: 219 n. 60

Siewert, T 1/44 = Kerameikos 20.2, 315: 219 n. 61

Siewert, T 1/47 = Kerameikos 20.2, 373: 220 n. 71

Siewert, T 1/48 = Kerameikos 20.2, 35: 220 n. 71

Siewert, T 1/49 = Kerameikos 20.2, 363

Siewert, T 1/50 = Kerameikos 20.2, 1066: 220 n. 71

Siewert, T 1/51 = Kerameikos 20.2, 1071: 220 n. 71

Siewert, T 1/52 = Kerameikos 20.2, 1068a–b: 220 n. 71

Siewert, T 1/53 = Kerameikos 20.2, 915: 220 n. 71

Siewert, T 1/54 = Kerameikos 20.2, 391: 220 n. 71

Siewert, T 1/55 = Kerameikos 20.2, 1062: 220 n. 71

INDEX LOCORUM 283

Siewert, T 1/56 = *Kerameikos 20.2*,
1072: 220 n. 71

Siewert, T 1/57 = *Kerameikos 20.2*,
369: 220 n. 71

Siewert, T 1/58 = *Kerameikos 20.2*,
1067: 220 n. 71

Siewert, T 1/59 = *Kerameikos 20.2*,
1073: 220 n. 71

Siewert, T 1/60 = *Kerameikos 20.2*,
1069: 220 n. 71

Siewert, T 1/61 = *Kerameikos 20.2*,
1065: 220 n. 71

Siewert, T 1/65 = *Agora 25*, 589: 220 n. 72

Siewert, T 1/66 = *Kerameikos 20.2*,
1110: 220 n. 65

Siewert, T 1/67 = *Kerameikos 20.2*,
1336: 97 n. 83, 219 n. 59, 221 n. 79

Siewert, T 1/68 = *Kerameikos 20.2*,
1624: 220 n. 65

Siewert, T 1/71 = *Kerameikos 20.2*,
1745: 220 n. 73

Siewert, T 1/72 = *Kerameikos 20.2*,
1741: 220 n. 73

Siewert, T 1/75 = *Kerameikos 20.2*,
1781: 219 n. 63

Siewert, T 1/76 = *Kerameikos 20.2*,
1782: 219 n. 62

Siewert, T 1/79 = *Kerameikos 20.2*,
1786: 219 n. 62

Siewert, T 1/80 = *Kerameikos 20.2*,
1787: 219 n. 62

Siewert, T/81 = *Kerameikos 20.2*,
1784: 219 n. 62

Siewert, T 1/82 (Kunsthistorisches Museum in Vienna): 220 n. 65

Siewert, T 1/85 = *Kerameikos 20.2*,
3981: 219 n. 59

Siewert, T 1/86 = *Kerameikos 20.2*,
1811: 219 n. 64

Siewert, T 1/91 = *Kerameikos 20.2*,
3984: 220 n. 67

Siewert, T 1/92 = *Kerameikos 20.2*,
2126: 220 n. 67

Siewert, T 1/93 = *Kerameikos 20.2*,
2028: 220 n. 67

Siewert, T 1/101 = *Kerameikos 20.2*,
3221: 220 n. 66

Siewert, T 1/102 = *Kerameikos 20.2*,
4213: 220 n. 66

Siewert, T 1/103 = *Kerameikos 20.2*,
5186b: 220 n. 66

Siewert, T 1/104 = *Kerameikos 20.2*,
5463: 220 n. 66

Siewert, T 1/105 = *Kerameikos 20.2*,
5462: 220 n. 66

Siewert, T 1/106 = *Kerameikos 20.2*, 3773: 26, 220 n. 78

Siewert, T 1/107 = *Kerameikos 20.2*,
3539: 219 n. 64

Siewert, T 1/108 = *Kerameikos 20.2*,
3593: 219 n. 64

Siewert, T 1/109 = *Kerameikos 20.2*,
5126: 219 n. 64

Siewert, T 1/110 = *Kerameikos 20.2*,
5453: 219 n. 64

Siewert T 1/111 = *Kerameikos 20.2*,
5916: 220 n. 77

Siewert, T 1/112 = *Kerameikos 20.2*,
2019: 219 n. 64

Siewert, T 1/115 = *Kerameikos 20.2*,
6857: 103 n. 107

Siewert, T 1/116 = *Kerameikos 20.2*,
6259: 103 n. 107

Siewert T 1/117 = *Kerameikos 20.2*,
6262: 103

Siewert T 1/118 = *Kerameikos 20.2*,
6202: 220 n. 76

Siewert, T 1/119 = *Kerameikos 20.2*,
6247: 219 n. 64

Siewert, T 1/120 = *Kerameikos 20.2*,
6265: 219 n. 64

Siewert, T 1/121 = *Kerameikos 20.2*,
6278: 219 n. 64

Siewert, T 1/122 = *Kerameikos 20.2*,
6284: 219 n. 64

Siewert, T 1/123 = *Kerameikos 20.2*,
6300: 219 n. 64
Siewert, T 1/124 = *Kerameikos 20.2*,
6473: 219 n. 64
Siewert, T 1/125 = *Kerameikos 20.2*,
6477: 219 n. 64
Siewert, T 1/126 = *Kerameikos 20.2*,
6499: 219 n. 64
Siewert, T 1/127 = *Kerameikos 20.2*,
6577: 219 n. 64
Siewert, T 1/128 = *Kerameikos 20.2*,
6657: 219 n. 64
Siewert, T 1/129 = *Kerameikos 20.2*,
6726: 219 n. 64
Siewert, T 1/130 = *Kerameikos 20.2*,
6837: 219 n. 64
Siewert, T 1/131 = *Kerameikos 20.2*,
6431: 220 n. 65
Siewert, T 1/132 = *Kerameikos 20.2*,
6628: 220 n. 65
Siewert, T 1/133 = *Kerameikos 20.2*,
6735: 220 n. 65
Siewert, T 1/134 = *Kerameikos 20.2*,
6736: 220 n. 65
Siewert, T 1/135 = *Kerameikos 20.2*,
6737: 220 n. 65

Siewert, T 1/136 = *Kerameikos 20.2*,
6738: 220 n. 65
Siewert, T 1/137 = *Kerameikos 20.2*,
6739: 220 n. 65
Siewert, T 1/138 = *Kerameikos 20.2*,
6740: 220 n. 65
Siewert, T 1/139 = *Kerameikos 20.2*,
6741: 220 n. 65
Siewert, T 1/140 = *Kerameikos 20.2*,
6742: 220 n. 65
Siewert, T 1/147 = *Kerameikos 20.2*,
8463: 220 n. 66
Siewert, T 1/149 = *Kerameikos 20.2*,
7544: 220 n. 67
Siewert, T 1/150 = *Kerameikos 20.2*,
7262: 25
Siewert, T 1/153 (*CEG* I 439 = ML 21) = *Agora*
25, 1065: 100 n. 98, 220 nn. 67, 71
Siewert, T 1/154 = *Kerameikos 20.2*,
8790: 220 n. 65
Siewert, T 1/155 = *Agora 25*,
1071: 220 nn. 71, 74
Siewert, T 1/156 = *Kerameikos 20.2*,
405: 220 n. 71
Siewert, T 1/158 = *Kerameikos 20.2*,
2623: 220 n. 66

General Index

Acropolis, Athens 36, 43, 79, 79 n. 31, 105 n. 116, 135, 150, 218, 235
Adams, J. (U.S. president) 3
adeia 170, 170 n. 155, 172
Aegina 179, 180
Aeschines 92–93
Aeschylus 20, 82 n. 43, 103
Africa 23
Agariste the Younger 100 n. 98, 107 n. 122
Agora, Athens:
  Altar of the Twelve Gods 137
  Bouleuterion, New 47, 48, 50, 54, 59 n. 145, 62 n. 155, 75, 81, 139, 145 n. 79
  Bouleuterion, Old 140
  Circle(s) (*kyklos/kykloi*) 141 n. 68
  gates of ostracism 143, 144
  gates of the Agora 135, 143, 144
  gates of the barley 141, 143
  Metroon 92
  Orchestra 135, 137, 140, 144, 154
  Panathenaic Way 137, 139
  Perischoinisma (Rope Enclosure) 135, 137, 139–140, 154
  Prytaneion (Tholos) 62 n. 155, 140, 145
  Rope Enclosure, *see* Agora, Athens, *Perischoinisma*
  Stoa *Alphitopolis* 141 n. 69
  Stoa, Royal (*Basileios*) 123, 137 n. 59
  Stoa, South I 137 n. 59
  Telia 141
  Tholos, *see* Agora, Athens, Prytaneion
Aiantis (*phylē*) 95
Alcibiades 97, 98, 104 n. 113, 111 n. 136, 163, 207–208 n. 23, 218, 229, 229 n. 94, 241, 241 n. 2, 3, 242, 242 n. 6, 243, 244, 247, 248
Alcibiades the Elder (*APF* 579) 97, 98, 104, 104 n. 113, 105, 106, 112, 117, 181, 209 n. 29, 226 n. 89, 233
Alciphron 137
Alcmaeon 191 n. 9
Alcmaeonids 98, 100 n. 98, 105 n. 116, 190 n. 3, 191 n. 9, 194, 210 n. 35

Alkandros of Argos 19
Alopeke 99, 100 n. 97, 105 n. 116
Altar of the Twelve Gods, *see* Agora, Athens
American democracy, *see* democracy, American
ancestral constitution (*patrios politeia*) 2 n. 5, 73, 77, 121 n. 10, 249
Andocides 7, 97, 99 n. 94, 111, 117, 171 n. 156, 229 n. 95
Androtion 8, 9, 48 n. 115, 67, 70–78, 91 n. 64, 93–94, 95, 96, 104 n. 113, 131, 157, 159 n. 119, 180, 181, 216
Anthesteria 63 n. 159
antidosis 232
Antiphon of Rhamnous 109–110
Apollo 24
Apollodorus 28 n. 44
Arcesilaus III 23 n. 27
archons 41, 48, 84, 87, 88, 89, 93 n. 75, 94, 98, 99 n. 95, 103, 129, 132, 134, 140, 141, 145 n. 79, 149, 162, 165, 166, 185, 191, 193, 194, 212, 212 n. 42
Areopagus 13 n. 43, 42, 43, 104, 129, 137 n. 59
Argos, Argives 11 n. 40, 18–22, 23, 28 n. 46, 30, 36, 42 n. 93, 64 n. 160, 178, 179, 181
Aristides 6, 50, 51, 82 n. 44, 84, 87, 88, 95, 96, 100, 104 n. 113, 112, 116, 117, 181, 208 n. 23, 213, 220, 233, 253
Aristiōn 42, 43, 43 n. 100
Aristōn 43 n. 100
'aristocratic politics', *see* aristocrats, aristocracy
aristocrats, aristocracy 13 n. 44, 30, 34, 39, 103, 190, 206, 207, 209 n. 32, 211–215, 228 n. 92, 229 n. 95, 246 n. 12, 250
Aristophanes 6, 18, 21, 27, 104, 109, 116, 118, 119, 121 n. 9, 122, 127–128, 130 n. 44, 141, 143, 145, 159, 160, 161, 164, 164 n. 133, 169 n. 146, 210, 246, 247

286 GENERAL INDEX

Aristotle 5 n. 14, 8–9, 18–19, 22, 26 n. 38, 30, 31, 35, 71, 73 n. 15, 108, 116, 169 n. 148, 169–170 n. 149, 181, 182, 211, 215
Artemisium 209, 226 n. 89
Assembly, see Ekklēsia
atimia 124, 184 n. 193
atthidographers, atthides 73–74, 78 n. 27, 90, 93–96, 98, 99, 108 n. 128, 116, 131, 133, 159, 180
see also Androtion
see also Cleidemus
see also Hellanicus of Mitilene
see also Philochorus
Austin, C. 120
Avram, A. 27 n. 40
Axelrod, R. 197–205, 232, 236, 253

Bacchielli, L. 23
Barringer, J. 156
Bekker, I. 53 n. 133
Beloch, K. J. 72, 233
Bendis 120
Berger, S. 35
Black Sea 11, 23, 27 n. 42
Blass, F. 97
Boeotia, Boeotians 27 n. 40, 28, 143, 179
Boulē, see Council of Five Hundred
Bouleuterion, New, see Agora, Athens
Bouleuterion, Old, see Agora, Athens
bouleutic ostracism, see ostracism, bouleutic
Bravo, B. 24 n. 30, 27 n. 42, 69 n. 5
Bremmer, J. 61
Brenne, S. 10–11, 80, 101, 147–148, 150, 205, 219, 222
Brexit 2
Brueckner, A. 42–43
Busolt, G. 120

Callias son of Didymios 97, 98, 105, 112, 117
Callias son of Hipponikos 105 n. 116, 120
Callias son of Kratios 100 n. 97, 220
Canevaro, M. 250 n. 19
Campus Martius 154
Carcopino, J. 63 n. 159, 163, 222
Caria, acropolis of Megara 22
Chaeronea 114, 126
Chambers, M. 176 n. 175, 178
Charalambidou, X. 13 n. 44

Charias 111 n. 136
Chersonesos, see Tauric Chersonesos
Cimon 19 n. 7, 82, 86, 96, 97, 99 n. 94, 100, 103–104, 105, 105 n. 116, 106, 109, 112, 117, 140, 154, 155, 179, 181, 208–209, 221, 227 n. 89, 229 n. 96, 233, 253
Circle(s), see Agora, Athens
Cleidemus 94–95, 96, 98, 99 n. 94, 104 n. 113, 251
Cleinias 209, 226 n. 89, 229
Cleisthenes, see passim
Cleomenes 190 n. 5, 191, 194
Cleon (Paphlagon) 61 n. 153, 118, 119, 127, 128, 142, 210, 246
Cleophon 110 n. 134, 111 n. 136
Clinton, K. 123 n. 21
codification in Athens, see Nicomachus, revision of the 'law-code'
Codrus 81
competition, see passim
Congress, American 201
Connor, W. R. 114, 115, 245–246
cooperation, theory of, see theory of cooperation
Cordano, F. 33 n. 67
Council of Five Hundred (Boulē) 35, 45, 48–50, 52–53, 52 n. 129, 53, 54, 55, 56, 58, 76, 84, 88, 90–91, 124, 129, 134, 146, 173–174, 180, 185, 191 n. 8, 196, 209, 212
Council of Four Hundred 43, 45, 46, 50, 191 n. 8
Craterus 93, 93 n. 73
Cratinus 6, 120–121, 128, 234
Crimea 28
Critias 165, 169 n. 148
Cuniberti, G. 163–164, 183
Cylonian miasma/curse/affair 43, 210 n. 35, 220
Cyrene 23, 28 n. 46, 30, 36, 40, 83 n. 48

Damon of Oa 87, 107–110, 112, 116, 117, 128 n. 37, 157, 224, 234, 245
Damonides 87, 107–108, 112, 116
Danielewicz, J. 52 n. 129
Darwin, Ch. 202
Davies, J. K. 14, 55, 208, 231
Decree of Miltiades and Themistocles, see Miltiades' and Themistocles' Decree

Decree of Patrokleides, see Patrokleides'
    Decree
Decree of Themistocles, see Themistocles'
    Decree
Deimeneia 44
Delion 27 n. 40
Delos, Delians 24, 24 n. 30, 27 n. 40
Delphi, Delphic oracle 175 n. 171,
    191 n. 8, 194
demagogue, demagogues 8, 30, 33, 61 n. 153,
    69, 70, 184, 206, 241
deme, demes 99, 100 n. 97, 103, 105 n. 116,
    107, 107–108 n. 125, 149, 170 n. 153,
    195 n. 22, 209 n. 32, 219, 221
democracy, American 3, 201, 215
Demosthenes 5 n. 14, 92, 96, 97, 99, 117, 118,
    130, 137, 145, 159, 160, 169 n. 148, 170,
    171 n. 156, 173 n. 161
Deposit of Kerameikos, see Kerameikos, Great
    Kerameikos Deposit
Deposit of Themistocles, see Themistocles
    deposit
Develin, R. 47, 49, 53, 58, 167, 168, 172
diacheirotonia 124 n. 24, 176
diapsēphisis 55, 56
Didymus 130, 159–160, 164 n. 133,
    169 n. 146
dikastai kata dēmous 55–56
dilemma, see prisoner's dilemma
Diodorus of Sicily 23, 32–35, 37, 161, 162,
    171, 182, 183
Dionysia 63, 128, 129 n. 41
Dionysius I 32
Dobree, P. 178
Draco 124

Eion 102 n. 105
Ekklēsia, Assembly 7, 13 n. 43, 20 n. 13,
    23 n. 25, 33, 35 n. 76, 49, 87, 90, 91 n. 65,
    113, 114, 115, 124 n. 24, 124–127, 128,
    129, 135, 135 n. 53, 143 n. 75, 145, 155,
    156, 157 n. 116, 158 n. 117, 170, 172,
    173 n. 160, 174–176, 185, 186, 191 nn. 7, 8,
    193, 196, 206, 209–210, 212, 215, 217,
    218, 221–228, 231, 233, 236–237, 241,
    242, 243, 244, 245, 246, 247, 249, 252
    ekklēsia kyria 113, 124–126, 143 n. 74,
    174, 185
    see *epicheirotonia*
    see quorum

ekphyllophoria, ekphyllophorēsis 33 n. 67, 35,
    46 n. 110, 52, 52 n. 129, 53, 54, 55–58,
    64 n. 162
Elateia 145
Ephesus 19
Ephialtes 13, 104, 129, 155 n. 107, 190 n. 2,
    206, 208 n. 23, 235, 271
Ephorus of Kyme 109 n. 130, 171, 182,
    182 n. 186, 183
epicheirotonia 114 n. 148, 124, 130, 131, 172,
    173 n. 160, 185, 223, 225–228, 243,
    252–253
    quorum of (hypothetical) 114 n. 148, 134,
    172–177, 185, 217, 225, 226, 226 n. 89,
    227, 251, 253
Erechtheus 61
Errington, R. 114, 126, 129
Eukrates, law against tyranny 126
Euripides 169 n. 148
exile, expulsion, politics of 31 n. 57,
    37–39, 60 n. 150, 61
    see also Forsdyke, S.

Figueira, T. 179, 180, 184 n. 194
Fontenrose, J. 62
Forsdyke, S. 5 n. 14, 10, 31 n. 57, 37–39, 195, 222

Gargettos 101 n. 103, 102, 103
gates of ostracism, see Agora, Athens
gates of the Agora, see Agora, Athens
gates of the barley, see Agora, Athens
generals (*stratēgoi*) 8, 34 n. 70, 70, 88, 89,
    109–110, 115, 212, 214, 228 n. 91, 245
Geraestus Promontory 92, 122, 133, 156, 161,
    169, 178, 186
Gernet, L. 59 n. 145, 62
Giangiulio, M. 34
Girard, P. 145
Giugni, E. 25
graphē paranomōn 222 n. 83, 243, 247
Great Kerameikos Deposit, Great Deposit 80,
    81, 83, 84, 84 n. 50, 86, 100 n. 97, 101, 103,
    106, 149, 152 n. 95, 157 n. 116, 163, 218
Greco, E. 31
Grote, G. 4, 214–215, 232 n. 104
Guarducci, M. 42, 44
Gylippos 23

Hall, L. G. H. 62–63
Hamilton, W. D. 202

288 GENERAL INDEX

Hansen, M. H. 156, 174, 209–210
Harding, Ph. 73–74
Harpocration 55, 55 n. 137, 68, 70–76, 104 n. 113, 216
Heftner, H. 114, 122, 123, 130, 158–159, 211–212, 248
hekatostyes ('hundreds') in Heraclea Pontica 25
Hellanicus of Mitilene 91 n. 64, 94
Heraclea Pontica 24, 25, 26, 27, 28, 30, 31
Heraclitus of Ephesus 19
Herakleitos son of Panchares 22
Herman, G. 197
hermocopidae 248
Hermodoros 19
Herodotus 6, 6 n. 17, 45, 77, 95, 98, 99, 116, 117, 168 n. 144, 190 n. 6, 193, 208
hetaireia, hetairoi 150 n. 90, 209 n. 32, 210
Hiller von Gaertringen, F. 35 n. 75
Hind, J. 27
Hipparchos son of Charmos 70, 71, 72, 75, 76, 77, 82 n. 44, 91 n. 65, 94, 99, 112, 117, 233
Hippocles 111 n. 136
Hippocrates 26, 30, 84, 97, 98, 99, 100 n. 97, 100 n. 98, 101, 112, 219, 220, 233
Hippocrates Anaxileo 100 n. 97
Hobbes, T. 3
Hyperbolus 6 n. 19, 6 n. 21, 7, 9 n. 34, 60–61, 62 n. 156, 84, 94, 98, 104 n. 113, 109, 110–111, 112, 113–115, 116, 118, 128 n. 37, 132–133, 159, 164, 171, 178, 179, 181, 183, 184, 210, 213, 217, 226 n. 87, 233, 236, 240–244, 248, 249
Hypsichides 178

Ion of Chios 165
Isagoras 190–194, 208 n. 24, 212, 230
Isocrates 73 n. 13
Italy 11
Iulianos 70 n. 7

Jacoby, F. 73–74, 75 n. 20, 77, 95 n. 79, 125, 129–131, 133, 161 n. 123, 168
Jeffery, L. H. 40, 44

Kaibel, G. 70 n. 5, 118, 124 n. 24, 176, 178
Kallixenos 84, 100 n. 97, 220
Kassel, R. 120

Keaney, J. J. 45, 114, 115
Kenyon, F. G. 69 n. 5, 178, 196 n. 23
Kerameikos 10, 36, 79. 79 n. 30, 80, 80 n. 35, 82 n. 44, 100 n. 97, 101, 104, 105, 106, 107, 108, 153 n. 98, 156
see also Great Kerameikos Deposit
kindness of the people, see *praotēs* of the *dēmos*
Kinzl, K. H. 68, 70–71, 72, 74
Knight, D. W. 212
Kolb, F. 137
Kollytos 69, 71, 99
Kostecka, K. 13 n. 44
Kreilinger, U. 23 n. 25
Krentz, P. 107
Kretines son of Mys 24 n. 30
Kritzas, Ch. 22
Kynosarges 51, 52, 56–57 n. 143

Lamachos 27 n. 40
Lang, M. 79 n. 30, 82, 111 n. 136
Latte, K. 102
law-code in Athens, *see* Nicomachus, revision of the 'law-code'
Lenaia 62, 118, 127–128, 129 n. 41
Lentini, M. C. 32
Lewis, D. 92, 193

Macedon, Macedonians 114, 126, 169 n. 148
Mann, Ch. 5 n. 14, 206–207, 242 n. 6
Matera, M. 29 n. 53
Megakles 6, 26, 30, 82 n. 44, 84, 86, 87, 97–98, 99, 100 n. 96, 101, 102, 103, 105, 106, 112, 116, 117, 164, 219, 220, 233
Megara, Megarians 11 n. 40, 18, 21, 22–23, 28, 29, 30, 42 n. 93, 180, 220 n. 65
Meiggs, R. 92
Meineke, A. 102, 103
Meister, J. 13 n. 44, 224
Menon 101 n. 103, 102–103, 112, 219 n. 64, 220
Merkelbach, R. 19
Metroon, *see* Agora, Athens
Meyer, Ed. 120
miasma (pollution), purification 24, 43, 60
mildness of the people, see *praotēs* of the *dēmos*
Miletus, Milesians 11 n.40, 18, 19, 24 n. 30, 27, 27 n. 43, 28, 28 n. 46

GENERAL INDEX 289

Miltiades 92, 93, 96, 96 n. 80, 96 n. 82, 99, 99 n. 94, 100 n. 98, 103, 106, 112, 208 n. 23, 213 n. 46
Miltiades' and Themistocles' Decree 92, 93 see also Themistocles' Decree
Mirhady, D. 59–60, 62
Mitylene 110
Mossé, Cl. 42, 44
Murray, O. 175
Mycenae 21

Naxos, Sicily 30, 32, 35, 35 n. 74
new politicians, see demagogue, demagogues see also Cleon
Nicias 110, 163, 208 n. 23, 209, 210, 229, 229 n. 94, 241–244, 248
Nicomachus, revision of the 'law-code' 78 n. 27, 123–124, 169 n. 147, 173, 177, 249, 251

Oa 107, 107–108 n. 125, 116, 117
Ober, J. 13, 191–193, 195, 238, 250
Odeon, Odeum, Odeion 120
Oie (Oia) 87, 107–108 n. 125
oligarchy 23, 124, 183, 184, 208 n. 27, 227 n. 90, 239, 240, 248
Orchestra, see Agora, Athens
ostracism, bouleutic 42 n. 95, 45–59, 59, 65, 129, 216
ostrakinda game 6 n. 22, 210–211
ostrakophoria, see *passim*
'abortive' 81, 111 n. 136, 164 n. 133
quorum of 81, 102 n. 104, 114 n. 148, 134, 158–172, 175 n. 172, 217, 221, 225, 236, 251
topography of 12, 48 n. 116, 50, 66, 134–158
turnout of 63 n. 159, 83, 154, 156–158, 157 n. 114, 157 n. 116, 163–164, 166 n. 138, 171, 172, 175, 185, 217, 219, 222, 225, 226 n. 89, 251
vote counting 36, 82, 83–85, 102, 122, 132, 134, 140, 141, 144, 145, 145 n. 79, 146, 146–150, 160, 161, 162, 165, 165, 166, 167, 169, 171, 176 n. 173, 185
ovilia in Rome 154

Paches 110
Palme, B. 127–128
Pan Painter 83, 146–150

Panathenaic Way, see Agora, Athens
Paphlagon, see Cleon
Paruta, P. 2
patrios politeia, see ancestral constitution
Patrocleides' Decree 91 n. 66
Pearson, C. 13 n. 44
Peloponnese 11, 21 n. 16, 180, 181, 184 n. 194
Peloponnesian War 6, 60, 94, 110 n. 133, 114 n. 148, 117–118, 119, 120, 121, 206, 236, 241, 244 248, 252
Pericles 6 n. 22, 82, 82 n. 43, 96, 96 n. 80, 105, 106, 107, 107 n. 121, 108, 109, 110, 120–121, 128, 165, 206, 207 n. 20, 208 n. 23, 213, 213 n. 47, 224, 229 nn. 95, 96, 234, 235, 240, 244, 245, 247, 253
Perischoinisma, see Agora, Athens
Persian Wars 60 n. 149, 76 n. 22, 88, 90, 93, 94, 95, 96, 117, 135 n. 52, 152 n. 91, 178, 179, 180, 184 n. 194, 189 n. 2, 239
petalismos 32–35, 37, 39, 52 n. 128, 170 n. 149, 183
Phaeax 111 n. 136, 163, 207–208 n. 23, 241 n. 3, 242, 243
Phaenippus 69
pharmakos, see scapegoat ritual
Pharsalus 102 n. 105, 103
Phileriphos 111 n. 136
Philinos 111 n. 136
Philippos 111 n. 136
Philippos of Croton 209 n. 30
Philochorus 81, 93 n. 74, 114, 123, 125, 130, 131, 133, 139 n. 65, 140, 141, 144 n. 76, 146, 159, 160, 162 n. 124, 162 n. 126, 165–166, 167, 168, 169, 169 n. 148, 170 n. 149, 180, 182, 182 n. 185
Philon son of Lysias 23
Piérart, M. 21
Piraeus 143, 144
Pisistratids 9, 75, 190, 194, 230, 239
Pisistratus 8, 24 n. 30, 41, 44, 69, 69 n. 5, 70, 71, 76, 194, 230
Pisistratus' ostrakon 40–42, 44
Pisistratus the Younger 41 n. 87
Pistoxenos Painter 80, 83 n. 47, 101 n.103
Plato 7, 7 n. 24, 56 n. 141, 96, 97, 99, 117, 118, 211, 247
Plato Comicus 116, 210, 210 n. 36, 211

Plutarch 4 n. 10, 9 n. 30, 22, 50, 50 n. 125, 51, 57, 98, 107, 108, 110, 111, 120, 152 n. 94, 162, 163, 163 n. 129, 164, 165, 166, 167, 207, 207 n. 23, 208 n. 23, 226 n. 87, 233–234, 241, 251
Pnyx 135, 135 n. 53, 143 n. 75, 145, 149 n. 88, 155, 155 n. 107, 156, 157, 157 n. 113, 175, 217–218, 226 n. 89
pollution, see *miasma* (pollution), purification
Polyeuktos 137
praotēs, kindness, mildness of the *dēmos* 38, 74–75, 74 n. 19, 69, 74–75, 169 n. 149, 170, 196 n. 24, 251
Praxidas son of Zenis 23
prisoner's dilemma, see *passim*
ALL D ('always defect') strategy 200, 200 n. 5, 201, 235, 238
cooperation, see theory of cooperation
defection 198, 199, 200, 201, 202, 203, 204, 205, 227, 228, 229, 233, 234, 235, 236, 237, 238, 239, 242, 244, 245
iterated prisoner's dilemma 198, 199–202, 204, 205, 227, 227 n. 90, 230, 232, 234, 239, 253, 253 n. 20
promoting cooperation, see theory of cooperation
TIT FOR TAT strategy 199–200, 200 n. 5, 204, 238
procheirotonia 124 n. 24, 176
Prytaneion, see Agora, Athens
prytaneis, prytans 145, 145 n. 80, 146, 149, 152, 153, 176 n. 173, 212
Ps.-Andocides, see Andocides in Index Locorum
Ps.-Aristotle, see *A.P.* in Index Locorum
Ps.-Plutarch, see Plutarch in Index Locorum
purification, see *miasma* (pollution), purification

quorum, see Ekklēsia
see also *epicheirotonia*, quorum of
see also *ostrakophoria*, quorum of

Rapoport, A. 199–200
Raubitschek, A. 45, 46, 103, 121, 141–144, 165, 167–168
revision of the 'law-code' in Athens, see Nicomachus, revision of the 'law-code'
revolution, Athenian 4, 189–194, 230, 249
revolution, French 192, 215
revolution, Glorious 215
revolution, Spartan 205
Rhodes, P. J. 72, 87, 90, 92, 114, 126, 129, 209
Rope Enclosure, see Agora, Athens, *Perischoinisma*
Royal Stoa, see Agora, Athens
Rubinstein, L. 19 n. 7

Salamis 88, 179
Sandys, J. E. 178
Saprykin, S. 26, 27
Saronic Gulf 89 n. 61, 179, 180, 181, 184 n. 194, 186
Sausage Seller 142, 210
scapegoat ritual (*pharmakos*) 42, 59–63, 64, 184, 216
Scheibelreiter, Ph. 121–123
Scheidel, W. 5
Schnapp Gourbeillon, A. 42, 44
Scyllaeum Promontory 92, 178, 186
Seeck, O. 87–88, 91
Ségurier, P. 53 n. 133
Sepeia 20, 21
Sicily 11, 31
Siewert, P. 143 n. 75
Simmel, G. 201 n. 6, 207 n. 21, 253 n. 20
Sinope 24 n. 30, 27 n. 40, 28 n. 43
Solon 10, 43, 123 n. 21, 124, 193 n. 18, 205, 213 n. 46, 215, 232, 249
sophists 246–247
sovereignty of the *dēmos* 38–39
Sparta, Spartans 20, 21 n. 16, 23, 104, 121 n. 7, 142, 144, 190, 191, 192, 194, 195, 205, 235, 241, 244
stasis 30, 32 n. 63, 34, 39, 124, 211–215, 222, 223, 230, 232
Ste. Croix, G. E. M. 214
Sternbach, L. 45, 47, 49
Stesimbrotos of Thasos 165
Stoa *Alphitopolis*, see Agora, Athens
Stoa, Royal (*Basileios*), see Agora, Athens
South Stoa I, see Agora, Athens
Strabo 24 n. 30, 28, 28 n. 43
stratēgoi, see generals
Sulla 195 n. 20, 212
Sybaris, Sybaritae 32 n. 63
symposion 150 n. 90, 228
Syracuse 17, 32, 33–35, 52 n. 128

GENERAL INDEX 291

Taeuber, H. 70, 77, 126 n. 29
Tauric Chersonesos 19, 24–31, 34, 36–37, 64 n. 160
Telia, see Agora, Athens
theatre in Athens, Theatre of Dionysus 13 n. 43, 119 n. 156, 135, 157 n. 113, 171 n. 158
Themistocles 25, 73, 79 n. 31, 82, 84, 86, 87, 88, 91, 92, 96, 98, 100–101, 103, 104 n. 113, 112, 116, 117, 118, 127, 150, 150 n. 90, 152–153, 155 n. 106, 165, 178, 179, 181, 182, 208 n. 23, 213, 213 n. 47, 218, 221, 233, 235, 253
see also Themistocles' Decree
see also Themistocles' Deposit
Themistocles' Decree 91–92, 93, 96, 123 n. 19, 179, 184 n. 193
Themistocles' Deposit 150–153, 155 n. 106, 218, 221
Theodoros Metochites 50, 54, 56–57, 58
Theophrastus 8, 18, 48 n. 115, 76 n. 21, 81, 99, 114, 122–123, 124 n. 21, 131, 141, 158, 159, 160, 163, 166, 169, 170, 171, 181, 182, 183, 185, 208 n. 23, 241 n. 3, 249, 251
theory of cooperation 12, 197–205, 228, 232–239, 242, 245, 253, 253 n. 20
Theramenes 73 n. 13, 228 n. 91
Theseus 99
Thessaly 169 n. 148, 184 n. 194
'Thirty' 248–249
Tholos, see Agora, Athens
Thrace, Thracians 169 n. 148
Thrasybulus 35 n. 76
Thucydides son of Melesias 6 n. 20, 87, 104 n. 113, 106–107, 109, 112, 118, 120, 181, 208 n. 24, 213, 233–234, 235, 245
Thucydides son of Oloros 7, 23, 24, 98, 104, 111, 116, 118, 168 n. 144, 169 n. 148, 184, 209–210
Thurii 30, 31, 31 n. 61, 32 n. 63, 35
Timaeus the Sophist 139 n. 65
Tiryns 21

Tokhtasyev, S. 29
topography, see Agora, Athens
see also ostrakophoria
trench war 201–202, 203
trittys, trittyes 143, 144, 149, 195 n. 22
Trump, D., Jr. (U.S. president) 2
Twelve Gods, altar of, see Agora, Athens
Tyndarides 32
tyranny 1 n. 3, 8, 9, 10, 35 n. 76, 43 n. 101, 46, 76 n. 22, 77, 124, 126, 132, 183, 190, 191 n. 9, 194, 211–213, 230, 231, 238, 253
see also Eukrates, law against tyranny
Tzetzes, John 50–52, 54, 56, 56 n. 143, 57–58

Valerius (Oualerios) Diodoros 70 n. 7
Vanderpool, E. 42, 43, 44
Vernant, J.-P. 42, 59 n. 145, 62, 62 n. 156
Vinogradov, Ju. G. 24 n. 30, 26, 27, 28, 29, 31 n. 57, 36
voting, see Ekklēsia
see also epicheirotonia
see also ostrakophoria
see also quorum

Wade-Gery, H. T. 193, 212
Wallace, R. W. 108, 246 n. 14
Webster, T. B. L. 82, 146
Wentzel, G. 70
Wilamowitz Moellendorff, U. 35 n. 75, 70 n. 5, 71, 108, 120–121, 124 n. 24, 126, 176, 176 n. 174, 178, 179
Willemsen, F. 101
Wolicki, A. 123 n. 19, 152 n. 95
World War I, see trench war

Xanthippus son of Ariphron 89, 100, 100 n. 98, 112, 220 n. 67, 208 n. 23, 233, 235 n. 110
Xerxes 6 n. 20, 87, 88, 90, 92, 95, 96, 98, 99, 108, 117, 126, 177, 178, 179, 180, 214

Żuchowicz, R. 13 n. 44